Darrell D. Hannah

Michael and Christ: Michael Traditions and Angel Christology in Early Christianity

WIPF & STOCK · Eugene, Oregon

DARRELL D. HANNAH was born 1962; Bachelor of Arts (Magna cum Laude), Grand Canyon College, 1985; Master of Divinity, Southern Baptist Theological Seminary, 1989; Master of Theology, Regent College, 1992; Doctor of Philosophy, University of Cambridge, 1996. Sir Henry Stephensen Research Fellow, University of Sheffield, 1996 – 98; New Testament Research Fellow, University of Birmingham, Westhill, from 1998.

Wipf and Stock Publishers
199 W 8th Ave, Suite 3
Eugene, OR 97401

Michael and Christ
Michael Tradition and Angel Christology in Early Christianity
By Hannah, Darrell D.
Copyright©1999 Mohr Siebeck
ISBN 13: 978-1-61097-153-9
Publication date 5/1/2011
Previously published by Mohr Siebeck, 1999

For
Perry and Charlotte,
Darla and Daniel

Acknowledgements

The present work began life as a doctoral thesis submitted to the Faculty of Divinity of the University of Cambridge in 1995. It appears here in a slightly revised form. It was a great privilege to live and work in the town of Cambridge and its historic university for the period of four years. A generous gift from Paul and Hannah Gay made this possible, as did the awards of an Overseas Research Studentship, for the period 1992-1994, and the Crosse Studentship, for 1994-95. Perry Hannah's gift of a lap top computer at the outset of my doctoral studies proved indispensable and demonstrated ἀνυπόκριτος φιλαδελφία. The Rev'd. Dr. David Hoyle, and his wife Janet, welcomed me into their home during the last months of revision before submission of the thesis. Their hospitality and understanding made this tedious task almost pleasant.

My thesis supervisor, Dr. Markus N. A. Bockmuehl, first suggested an examination of Michael traditions when I was searching for a specific approach to the general area of "angel Christology". His insights, encouragement and gently administered criticisms have contributed greatly to my own formation as a scholar and theologian. It is a pleasure to here record in print my thanks and gratitude. To Profs. Hermann Lichtenberger and William Horbury additional thanks and gratitude are due. Both of these gentlemen, in the most literal sense of that word, supervised my work for short periods, the former during a five month period when it was my privilege to study in the Universität Tübingen and the latter for shorter periods during my time in Cambridge. I have, in addition, benefited from conversations with a number of other scholars, including especially Profs. Larry W. Hurtado and Richard Bauckham, and Dr. Andrew Chester. The latter two served as my examiners during my *viva*. I have in the revisions of the thesis responded to a number of their criticisms and, consequently, the present work is stronger and more tightly argued than the thesis.

The question of "Angelmorphic Christology" has in recent years experienced phenomenal growth within the disciplines of New Testament studies and Christian Origins. I have profited from the contributions of many, including especially Larry Hurtado, Richard Bauckham, Alan Segal, Christopher Rowland, Andrew Chester, Peter Carroll, Crispin H. T. Fletcher-Louis and Loren Stuckenbruck. Even where I have disagreed with these scholars, I have learned a great deal from all of them. I have also benefited from discussions with others, among whom Charles Gieschen must be mentioned. Unfortunately, his book on the subject appeared too late to be taken into account. I, however, look forward to continuing the dialogue with him, and all of the others, in the future.

I would like to register my thanks to Prof. Martin Hengel for accepting my book for publication in the WUNT series, and to Herr Georg Siebeck for his patience during the rather long period between the work's initial acceptance and the final arrival of my manuscript. Other academic work and duties, first in the University of Sheffield and then at Westhill College kept intruding. It was my privilege to serve as the Sir Henry Stephenson Research Fellow in the Department of Biblical Studies of the former institution from 1996 to 1998. That department provided a stimulating academic environment in which to work. It was there I began the revisions, but the lion share was done at Westhill College, where I have received the warmest of welcomes. To my colleagues in both institutions I offer my thanks.

Finally, my parents, the Rev'd Harry and Grace Hannah introduced to me the art, nay life, of theological reflection. Their love and encouragement means more than I can possibly express. My four siblings, to whom this work is dedicated, have taught me again and again that theological reflection must take place in community, never in isolation. It is in the hope that it may be of some profit to the wider community of faith that this work is published.

Holy Week, 1999 Darrell D. Hannah
Birmingham

Table of Contents

Acknowledgements vii

Abbreviations xv

Part I: Introduction: Angels, Michael and Christology 1
  1. Angel Christology: A History of Research 2
     a. Pre-History 2
     b. The First Period: Angel Christology 3
     c. Interlude 5
     d. The Second Period: Angelomorphic Christology 6
     e. Summary 11
  2. Plan for this Study 12
  3. Terminology 12

Part II: Michael in Jewish Literature of the Second Temple Period 15

Chapter 1: The מלאך יהוה and Other Antecedents in the OT 15
  1. Angels in the Old Testament 15
     a. Prevalence of Angels in Ancient Near East 15
     b. Terminology 16
     c. Themes and Motifs in OT Angelology 17
  2. The מלאך יהוה (מלאך אלהים) 19
     a. The מאלך יהוה of the Patriarchal Narratives 19
     b. The Angel of the Exodus 21
     c. Later Developments 22
     d. Related Themes 23
     e. Summary 24

Chapter 2: The Archangel Michael in Jewish Apocalyptic
          and Related Literature 25
  1. Jewish Apocalyptic Literature 26

Table of Contents

- 2. The Angelology of Jewish Apocalyptic Literature 28
  - a. Messengers and Servants of God 28
  - b. Archangels and the Angelic Hierarchy 29
  - c. The Angels and Humanity 30
    - 1) Agents of Revelation 30
    - 2) Guardians of Nations 31
    - 3) Intercessors and the Heavenly Cultus 32
    - 4) Angelic Psychopomps 32
- 3. Michael in Jewish Apocalyptic Literature 33
  - a. Special Relation with Israel 33
    - 1) Angelic Guardian of Israel 33
    - 2) Leader of the Heavenly Host ('Αρχιστράτηγος) 38
    - 3) Israel's Legal Advocate and Opponent of Satan 40
  - b. Israel's Intercessor and Heavenly High Priest 42
  - c. Michael as Psychopomp 46
  - d. Michael as Angelus Interpres 47
  - e. Michael as Highest Archangel 48
  - f. Michael as the Angel of the Name 51
  - g. Summary 54

Chapter 3: The Archangel Michael in the Literature of Qumran 55
1. The Qumran Community 56
2. The Angelology of Qumran 59
   - a. Communion with the Angels 59
   - b. The Angels as a Heavenly Priesthood 60
   - c. The Four and/or Seven Archangels 61
   - d. Cosmic Dualism: The Spirits of Light and Darkness 62
3. Michael and the Prince of Light 64
4. Michael and Melchizedek 70
5. Conclusions 75

Chapter 4: Michael and Philo's Logos Doctrine 76
1. Philo's Doctrines of God, the Logos, and angels 77
   - a. Philo as Monotheist 77
   - b. The Logos of God: The relationship between God and His Logos 79
   - c. The Logos as Hypostasis 81
   - d. Philo's Doctrine of Angels 84
2. The Logos and Michael in Philo 85
   - a. The Logos as archangel 85
   - b. The Logos as High Priest 87

Table of Contents

  c. The Logos as the Exodus Angel and Angel of the Name...... 87
  d. The Logos and Israel 88
  e. The The *Prayer of Joseph*... 89
  f. Conclusions.. 90
 3. The Logos and Sophia in the Wisdom of Solomon.................. 91

Chapter 5: The Archangel Michael in Rabbinic and Hekhalot Literature 93
 1. Rabbinic Literature... 93
  a. The Angelology of the Rabbis....................................... 95
  b. Michael According to the Rabbis 97
   1) Continuity and Change... 97
    a) Highest Archangel... 97
    b) Protector of Israel and Military Commander........... 99
    c) Heavenly High Priest 100
    d) Michael's Eschatological Functions 102
    e) Summary.. 102
   2) Rabbinic Evidence for a Michael Cult...................... 104
   3) Rabbinic and Christian Exegesis of מלאך יהוה
    passages.. 111
  c. Conclusions 114
 2. Hekhalot Literature.. 115
  a. Purpose of Hekhalot Literature..................................... 115
  b. Angels in Hekhalot Literature...................................... 116
   1) Traditional elements... 116
   2) God and angels... 117
   3) Metatron 118
  c. The Michael-Metatron Identification 119
  d. Conclusions 121

Part III: Michael in Early Christian Literature............................ 122

Chapter 6: Michael and Angelic Christology in the New Testament 122
 1. The Angelology of the New Testament Authors...................... 122
  a. Michael and Gabriel 123
  b. Angelic Roles.. 123
  c. The Superiority of the Righteous over angels 124
  d. Heavenly Cultus... 124
  e. Guardian Angels.. 125
  f. Angels and Resurrection... 126
  g. Angels and the Eschaton 127

Table of Contents

- 2. Michael in the New Testament 127
  - a. Revelation 12 127
  - b. Jude 9 130
  - c. Other Passages... 132
    - 1) 2 Thessalonians 2.6-7 132
    - 2) Galatians 3.19 134
    - 3) Revelation 8.3 and 20.2 135
    - 4) The Johannine Paraclete 135
  - d. Summary 136
- 3. Angel or Angelic Christology in the New Testament 137
  - a. Christ as an Angel in the New Testament Period............... 137
    - 1) The Epistle to the Hebrews... 137
    - 2) Jude 5-6 139
  - b. Principal Angel Speculation and New Testament Christology... 142
    - 1) Christ as the Angel of the Name 142
      - a) Phil. 2.9 143
      - b) Rev. 19.11-16 144
      - c) John 17.11-12.. 145
    - 2) John 8.56, 12.41 146
  - c. Principal Angel Roles attributed to Christ......................... 148
    - 1) Christ as Leader of the Heavenly Hosts 148
    - 2) Christ as the Gate Keeper of Paradise 149
    - 3) Christ as Heavenly High Priest 150
  - d. Dissimilarities 151
    - 1) Christ never called or portrayed as an angel in the New Testament 151
      - a) Rev. 1.12-18 and 10.1... 151
      - b) Rev. 14.14-15 154
      - c) Gal. 4.14.. 155
      - d) The Son of Man 156
    - 2) Christ Superior to angels in the New Testament 158
- 4. Conclusions: Use and Transformation of Principal Angel Traditions... 161

Chapter 7: Michael and Angelic Christology in Second and Third Century Christianity.................................... 163

- 1. Michael in Second and Third Century Christianity.................. 163
  - a. Leader of the angels 164
  - b. Protector of the People of God and Opponent of Satan 165
  - c. Heavenly Priest... 166

		d. Eschatological Roles 167

- d. Eschatological Roles 167
- e. Gnostic Michael Traditions 169
- f. Summary 170
2. Angelic Christology in Second and early Third Century Christianity 171
   - a. Christ as an archangel 171
     1) "Heretical Angel Christologies" 171
        - a) Ps-Cyprian *De Centesima* 171
        - b) Epiphanius, the Ebionites and the Elchasites 173
        - c) Tertullian and Valentinian Christology 179
        - d) The *Testament of Solomon* and Magical Texts 181
     2) Other examples of angel Christologies 183
     3) Possible Jewish Precursors 184
        - a) The *Prayer of Joseph* 184
        - b) The Pre-Existent Angel of the Magharians 185
     4) Summary 186
   - b. Christ as Michael 186
     1) The *Shepherd* of Hermas 187
        - a) The Glorious angel 187
        - b) The Glorious angel: Michael 187
        - c) The Glorious angel: the Son of God 188
        - d) The Pneumatological Christology of Hermas 189
        - e) The Status of the *Shepherd* in the Early Church 191
     2) P. Oxy. 1152 192
     3) *Gospel of the Hebrews* 193
     4) Epiphanius *Pan.* xxx.16.2 and the Dualism of Qumran 193
     5) The *Pseudo-Clementines* 194
     6) Gabriel, the angel of the Holy Spirit? 195
   - c. Christ disguised as an Angel 196
     1) The annunciation 196
     2) Christ's descent 197
   - d. The tradition behind the *Ascension of Isaiah* 199
   - e. The "Theophanic" Angel Christology of the Fathers 202
     1) Justin Martyr 202
        - a) The OT Theophanies 202
        - b) The Philonic Logos 203
        - c) The Platonic Doctrine of God's Transcendence 204
        - d) The Relation of the Logos to the Father 204
        - e) The Logos as the Angel (Messenger) of God 205

  2) Theophilus 206
  3) Irenaeus 207
  4) The Angel of Great Counsel 209
   a) The Origin of the Phrase 209
   b) The Popularity of the Title 209
   c) Justin, Irenaeus, Hippolytus, and Tertullian 210
   d) Origen 210
   e) Heretical Use of the Title 211
  5) Conclusions 212
 3. Conclusions 212

Part IV: Michael and Christ 214

Conclusions: Michael and Christ 214
 1. Summary: Three Forms of Angelic Christologies 214
 2. Michael and Christ 215
  a. Theophanic Angelic Christology 216
  b. Angel Christologies 216
  c. Angelic Christology: Transformation of Michael
    Traditions 217
   1) Usefulness and fluidity of Michael Traditions 217
   2) Angelomorphic Christology as a reaction against Angel
    Christology 218
 3. A Conjectural Synthesis 219

Bibliography 221
 Primary Literature 221
 Secondary Literature 227

Index of Modern Authors 251
Index of References 256
Index of Subjects 284

Abbreviations

General abbreviations are as follows:

LXX	Septuagint
MT	Masoretic Text
MajT	Majority Text of Greek NT manuscripts
NT	New Testament
OT	Old Testament
Vg	Vulgate

All abbreviations of works from the Old Testament Pseudepigrapha and NT Apocrypha follow those used by Charlesworth, *OTP* I.xlv-xlviii, except the following:

AssMos.	*Assumption of Moses*
EpApos.	*Epistula Apostolorum*
InfGThom.	*Infancy Gospel of Thomas*
Vita Adae	*Life of Adam and Eve*

Abbreviations of Qumran manuscripts follow Vermes *Complete DSS in English*, pp. 601-619. Abbreviations of Philo's works follow those found in the Loeb Classical Library's edition of Philo, I.xxiii-xxiv. Abbreviations of Rabbinic works are according to Strack-Stemberger's *Introduction*, pp. 401-403.

Abbreviations of Periodicals, Reference works, and Serials follows the *Journal of Biblical Literature*'s "Instructions for Contributors".

Introduction: Angels, Michael, and Christology

...ὅτι ἀρχὴν πρὸ πάντων τῶν κτισμάτων ὁ θεὸς γεγέννηκε δύναμίν τινα ἐξ ἑαυτοῦ λογικήν, ἥτις καὶ δόξα κυρίου ὑπὸ τοῦ πνεύματος τοῦ ἁγίου καλεῖται, ποτὲ δὲ υἱός, ποτὲ δὲ σοφία, ποτὲ δὲ ἄγγελος, ποτὲ δὲ θεός, ποτὲ δὲ κύριος καὶ λόγος, ποτὲ δὲ ἀρχιστράτηγον ἑαυτὸν λέγει, ἐν ἀνθρώπου μορφῇ φανέντα τῷ τοῦ Ναυῆ Ἰησοῦ (Justin Martyr, *Dial.* 61.1).[1]

This passage from Justin illustrates the ease with which some early Christians identified Christ as an Angel. However, given that Justin adds θεός directly after ἄγγελος in this list of christological titles, the question arises: What did he mean in asserting that the Holy Spirit, i.e., the inspired Scriptures, called Christ an angel? Did he understand Christ to possess an angelic nature? Or did he believe that Christ shared in the divine nature? Are these categories not mutually exclusive for Justin? Justin was by no means alone in using the appellation ἄγγελος to describe the significance of Christ. It was used by very different Christians throughout the first two Christian centuries and beyond. At times, even when the word ἄγγελος is not used with reference to Christ, the influence of angelological traditions can be detected. The questions asked above of Justin can, of course, also be asked of the other theologians and authors in early Christianity who described Christ as an angel or used the title ἄγγελος for him.

In the past twenty-five years a number of NT scholars have argued that Jewish beliefs and traditions about angels, particularly the principal angel or angels, hold the key to understanding why early Christians came to make such exalted claims about Jesus of Nazareth. This conception is by no

---

[1] God begat from Himself (as a) "Beginning" before all creatures a certain rational power, who is once called by the Holy Spirit "Glory of the Lord", and (in another place) "Son", and then "Wisdom", then "Angel", then "God", then "Lord" and "Word", and once called himself "Commander-in-Chief" when he appeared in the form of a man to Joshua the son of Nun.

means new to New Testament scholarship. As long ago as 1898 Wilhelm Lueken argued that speculations which surrounded the archangel Michael in ancient Judaism greatly influenced the early development of Christology. Lueken was right to focus on Michael, for he is the most significant figure in several ancient Jewish and early Christian angelologies. The present study aims to re-examine Lueken's arguments in light of the current debate, with due attention to the mass of evidence which has come to light in the course of the last century, and with a more rigorous critical methodology than that used by Lueken, especially in regards to late sources.

1. Angel Christology: A History of Research

a. Pre-History

Before embarking, a brief historical survey of the scholarly study of angelic Christology[2] is in order. The year 1898 saw the publication of Lueken's Marburg dissertation in which he took up Bousset's suggestion that in Jewish traditions about Michael might be found "Spekulationen vorbildlich für die Entwickelung (sic) der Christologie".[3] Lueken argued that there was a direct relationship (direkte Beziehungen) between the Jewish portrait of Michael and the Christian belief in the exalted Christ, in that both are depicted as a heavenly advocate for Israel/The Church, as the heavenly high priest, and as the commander of the heavenly hosts.[4] Lueken's work is pioneering, even ground breaking, but suffers from methodological errors. First and foremost, Lueken draws evidence from heterogeneous sources to construct a unified portrait of Michael which may never have existed in ancient Judaism. In addition, Lueken uses both early and extremely late sources with little or no attention to their date. To be sure, all of the elements which Lueken believes constructive for Christology are attested in Jewish Michael traditions. However, a "direct relationship" between Michael speculations and Christology is called into question by the fact that no single pre-Christian document or tradition can be found in

---

[2] Here I use the term "angelic Christology" in the widest sense possible, including as a category within it the currently popular term "angelomorphic Christology". At the end of this chapter I will offer a number of terms and definitions for the different positions which can be subsumed under this umbrella term.

[3] Cited by Lueken, *Michael*, v.

[4] Lueken, *Michael*, 164.

which all these motifs are attributed to Michael. Finally, Lueken fails to grapple with the significant differences between early Christian confessions of Christ and beliefs about Michael in ancient Judaism. This leads him to conclude that the *only* significant difference between Jewish Michael speculation and early Christology was that the former originated because of Judaism's emphasis on the transcendence of God, while the latter testifies to the sense of the nearness of God in emerging Christianity.[5]

Between Lueken and the first extensive defence of angelic Christology in early Christianity, that of Martin Werner, there were a couple of voices which suggested that early Christology was in some way indebted to Jewish angelology. First, G. H. Dix in two articles[6] argued that some Jews expected not a human, but an angelic Messiah who was none other than the OT "Angel of Yahweh". This figure was identical with Daniel's "man clothed in linen" (10.5-12.13) and "one like to a son of man" (7.13).[7] This original conception was lost when this figure was transformed, first into Uriel and later Michael. Nonetheless, in its final "Michael" stage it had some influence on early Christology, particularly in the Fourth Gospel and the Revelation of John.[8] Five years after Dix's second article, A. Bakker appealed to an early "Testimony Book" known to Josephus,[9] Hebrews 1-2, and the *Shepherd of Hermas*, in order to show that Christ was understood by some Christians as an angel.[10]

b. The First Period: Angel Christology

With Martin Werner's *Die Entstehung des christlichen Dogmas*, published in 1941,[11] we have the first sustained argument that early Christology developed out of Jewish angelology. Werner had as his starting point the apocalyptic and eschatological nature of earliest Christianity. On the basis of the then widely accepted interpretation of the Danielic and Enochic Son of Man as a heavenly being, he argued that the earliest Christians

---

[5] Lueken, *Michael*, 166.
[6] Dix's "Babylonian Ideas" appeared in 1925, his "Seven Archangels" in 1927.
[7] Dix, "Babylonian Ideas", esp. 245-248; and "Seven Archangels", 241.
[8] Dix, "Seven Archangels", 243-244.
[9] Bakker refers here to the Slavonic version of the *Testimonium Flavianum*. For the difficulties in accepting either the Greek or Slavonic versions of the *Testimonium Flavianum* in their entireties as authentic, see Schürer/Vermes, *History*, I.60-61, 428-441.
[10] Bakker, "Christ an Angel?".
[11] A second revised edition appeared in 1954; an English translation in 1957.

understood this title as a reference to an angelic being, whom God had appointed as an eschatological judge. In Werner's words, "for Primitive Christianity, Christ was, in terms of late-Jewish apocalyptic, a being of the high celestial angel-world, who was created and chosen by God for the task of bringing in, at the end of the ages, against the daimonic-powers of the existing world, the new aeon of the Kingdom of God".[12]

According to Werner's reconstruction, the earliest stage of Christology was adoptionistic. On the basis of passages like Acts 2.32-36 and *1 Enoch* 71, Werner concludes that the man Jesus was understood to have been exalted to the heavenly position of Christ and Son of Man because of his death and resurrection.[13] At a later stage, the Apostle Paul introduced the idea of pre-existence into Christology.[14] Nonetheless, this pre-existence is not to be understood as an eternal pre-existence, but the pre-existence of an angel who was a creature of God. Werner argues from James 1.7 that for the Judaism of the period a transformation of divine nature into human was impossible. However, "the possibility of such a transformation was truly the peculiar property of the angels".[15] It is only with the "process of de-eschatologising" that the Church moved away from its conviction that the Messiah is a created and angelic being. With this process came a new Christology which took the title "Son of God" literally and thus held that the "Son" must be "in some manner...generated by the Father and like to Him in Nature and substance".[16] This new Christology coincided with, and was dependent, upon the Hellenization of the early Church.[17] Werner's angel Christology, then, can be seen as the identification of Christ with an angel. At an earlier stage Christ was held to be a human who had been exalted to angelic status. Later this developed into the view that he was an angel who had been incarnated in the man Jesus of Nazareth.

The response to Werner was swift and decisive. A year after the publication of *Entstehung*, Wilhelm Michaelis released a monograph entitled *Zur Engelchristologie im Urchristentum: Abbau der Konstruktion Martin Werners*. As the title indicates, Michaelis set out to overthrow Werner's theory. Concentrating on the NT passages appealed to by Werner, Michaelis opposes his exegesis point by point and concludes, "early Christianity had known no angel Christology".[18] Although Michaelis has

---

[12] Werner, *Formation*, 125.
[13] Werner, *Formation*, 126.
[14] Werner, *Formation*, 127-128.
[15] Werner, *Formation*, 127-128.
[16] Werner, *Formation*, 131-132.
[17] Werner, *Formation*, vii.
[18] Michaelis, *Engelchristologie*, 187.

been criticized for "over-shooting his goal" and for not always perceiving the "full weight" of his evidence,[19] his position won the day, at least in regard to the earliest christological formulations.[20]

In the same year as Werner's *Entstehung*, Joseph Barbel published a thorough examination of the "angel Christology" of the early Fathers.[21] His purpose differed from that of Werner or Michaelis. He did not examine the NT evidence and was not concerned with the earliest attempts at Christology. Rather, he sought to understand the Patristic christological usage of the term ἄγγελος. In 1964 Barbel added an appendix[22] in which he addresses the question of "Engelchristologie" in the NT. He is impressed with the evidence Werner marshals for the influence of "the conceptions and notions of late Jewish beliefs about angels on Christology",[23] but in the end Barbel concludes that no angel Christology can be detected in the NT itself.[24]

c. Interlude

Werner's argument, then, that the earliest Christians understood Christ to have been an angel by nature and that the original Christology was an angel Christology, was almost universally rejected. Twenty years after Barbel's appendix, James Dunn could dismiss Werner's thesis as a curiosity of NT scholarship.[25] For Dunn the debate is a settled issue:

> In short, the thesis that an angel christology was entertained in some parts of earliest Christianity has little or nothing to sustain it, and the suggestion that any NT author maintained an angel christology runs clearly counter to the evidence.[26]

However, Dunn oversimplifies matters. Barbel was not the only scholar who, while rejecting Werner's main thesis, also expressed admiration for

---

[19] Barbel, *Christos Angelos*, 342-343.
[20] Barbel, *Christos Angelos*, 343; Daniélou, *Theology*, 118, n.3.
[21] Barbel, *Christos Angelos*.
[22] "Die frühchristliche und patristische Engelchristologie im Licht der neueren Forschung".
[23] Barbel, *Christos Angelos*, 343.
[24] Barbel, *Christos Angelos*, 348-349.
[25] Dunn, *Christology*, 322-323, n.106.
[26] Dunn, *Christology*, 158-159.

the many parallels between Jewish angelology and early Christology that Werner put forward. Kretschmar, for example, asserts that while Werner "has made irrefutably clear" that notions and conceptions from the "late Jewish doctrine of angels" influenced Christology, "he was unable to show that (it) was the intention of the New Testament authors" to identify Christ with an angel.[27] In other words, although scholars are united in rejecting Werner's assertion that the NT authors attributed to Christ an angelic nature, a number suggested that speculations about angels may have influenced the NT authors, and other early Christians, as they sought to express their faith in the exalted Christ. In addition to Barbel and Kretschmar, Daniélou speaks of Jewish Christians borrowing "terms...from the vocabulary of (Jewish) angelology to designate the Word".[28] Daniélou, who appears to have been the first to use the term "angelomorphic Christology",[29] asserts that while this terminology often implied a "subordinationist tendency", it "in no way" suggested that Christ was understood to possess an angelic nature. On the contrary, the term "angel" was "the old-fashioned equivalent" of what later theologians meant by $\pi\rho\acute{o}\sigma\omega\pi o\nu$ and *persona*.[30]

d. The Second Period: Angelomorphic Christology

Kretschmar and Daniélou,[31] like Barbel, were chiefly concerned with post-NT evidence. From 1968 to the present there has been an increasing interest in the question of Jewish speculation about angels influencing the Christology of the NT authors. Richard Longenecker finds such influence in Gal. 4.14, as well as in the groups opposed at Col. 2.18 and Heb. 1-2.[32] Martin Hengel, in his essay *The Son of God*, points to the angelic Metatron in *3 Enoch*, Israel in the *Prayer of Joseph*, and Michael-Melchizedek in sectarian literature from Qumran as possible Jewish preparations for the early Christian understanding of the pre-existent and exalted Christ.[33] A

---

[27] See esp. Kretschmar, *Trinitätstheologie*, 221-222.
[28] Daniélou, *Theology*, 117.
[29] Daniélou, *Theology*, 146.
[30] Daniélou, *Theology*, 118-119.
[31] Kretschmar's work was published in 1956; Daniélou's in 1958 and then again, in a revised English translation, in 1964.
[32] Longenecker, "Distinctive" 528; and *Christology*, 26-32. The article was published in 1968, the book in 1970.
[33] Hengel, "Son", 44-46, 75-81. The German original dates from 1975, the English version followed a year later.

year after Hengel's work appeared in English, Alan Segal published a comprehensive study of the "Two Powers heresy" in Rabbinic Judaism. In his argument that elements within NT Christianity represent one of the earliest examples of the "Two Powers heresy", Segal concludes that early Christians identified a number of "human figures in heaven and angelic mediators" with Jesus.³⁴ In a manner approaching that of Werner, Segal places a great deal of emphasis on the use of the "Son of Man" title in both Jewish apocalypses and the Gospel tradition.³⁵ Even more Werner-like, Segal at times appears to suggest that Jesus was held to possess an angelic nature.³⁶

The same year that Segal's Yale dissertation appeared also saw the publication of Bühner's Tübingen dissertation.³⁷ An examination of the conceptions of agency and mission in Johannine Christology, Bühner finds behind the Fourth Gospel's ἐγώ εἰμι and ἦλθον-statements Ancient Near Eastern assumptions concerning the role and practice of a messenger, conceptions which also inform Jewish angelology (e.g. Raphael in Tobit). Bühner argues that Johannine Christology is indebted to Jewish notions of agency and mediation, particularly the rabbinic concept of the שליח.³⁸ In addition, Bühner finds behind the Johannine Son of Man the Danielic and apocalyptic Son of Man. Postulating a two-part development, Bühner argues that the Johannine community first, on the model of Enoch traditions, identified Jesus as a human exalted to become the angelic Son of Man. Later there evolved the complimentary conceptions of pre-existence and Jesus as a heavenly angel incarnated in a human being, on the model of the angel Israel in the *Prayer of Joseph*. This, according to Bühner, places Johannine Christianity in the same trajectory as Jewish Christianity. Clearly, at the very least, shades of Werner are to be found in Bühner's interpretation of Johannine Christology; indeed it would appear that Bühner has returned to the position of Martin Werner with the important difference that Werner's claims were made for the whole of NT Christology, while Bühner's concern is merely Johannine Christology.

---

³⁴ Segal, *Two Powers*, 208.
³⁵ Segal, *Two Powers*, 205-210.
³⁶ E.g., "Jesus is not called an angel in the New Testament because he was not believed to be *merely* an angel" (*Two Powers*, 210; emphasis is Segal's); and "...it seems safe to consider that many Christians identified the Christ with God's principal angel, who carried the divine name, because of his resurrection" (213). In a later publication ("Risen Christ", 1992), Segal is more circumspect in this regard.
³⁷ *Der Gesandte*.
³⁸ John Ashton, for one, has been greatly influenced by Bühner's reading of the Fourth Gospel. See Ashton, *Understanding*, 101, 184-189, and esp. 308-328.

In a monograph[39] and a series of articles,[40] Christopher Rowland has drawn attention to the imagery used to describe angels and other heavenly beings. He sees great significance in the similarity of the imagery used to describe the risen Christ in Rev. 1.12-18, the angelic figure of Dan. 10.5-9, the divine figure(s) of Ezek 1.26-28 and 8.2-4, the angel in *JosAsen.* 14.1-10, and Yahoel in *ApAb.* 11.1-3. This similarity of imagery, according to Rowland, demonstrates that angelological conceptions influenced the Christology of the Apocalypse. In keeping with this emphasis on imagery, Rowland, in his last and most carefully worded contribution on the subject, rejects the term "angel Christology" for "angelomorphic Christology". Contrary to Werner, he argues that the use of angelomorphic imagery "in no way implies that Christ was identified entirely with the created order".[41]

In 1985, Jarl Fossum published his monograph on the origin of Gnosticism, *The Name of God and the Angel of the Lord*. Here Fossum emphasizes the role of speculation surrounding the Name of God and the angel of the Name (Ex 23.20-21) in early Christology. He suggests that Christianity was only one of many Jewish sects which identified its "hero" with God's principal angel.[42] Fossum equates possessing the divine name with possessing the divine nature or mode of being.[43] Fossum thus sees in the angel of the Name, a figure around whom revolved no little speculation in Second Temple Judaism, an implicit binitarianism already evolving either prior to, or simultaneous with, the beginnings of Christianity.[44]

Not long after Fossum's work, Larry Hurtado produced a slender monograph in which he examined the development of early Christology in light of Jewish beliefs about "divine agents", including, in addition to angels, exalted patriarchs and personified divine attributes.[45] Hurtado believes that early Christians found in Jewish speculation on divine agents "a conceptual framework" for understanding the exalted Christ.[46] In line with Segal, Hurtado emphasizes early Christianity's borrowing from various Jewish traditions. Nowhere in pre-Christian Judaism do we find a divine agent with such an accumulation of divine honours. The subtitle of Hurtado's work, *Early Christian Devotion and Ancient Jewish Monotheism*,

---

[39] *Open Heaven* (1982).
[40] "Visions of God" (1979); "Vision of the Risen Christ" (1980); and "Man Clothed in Linen" (1985).
[41] Rowland, "Man Clothed in Linen", 100.
[42] Fossum, *Name of God*, 333.
[43] Fossum, *Name of God*, 310, 333.
[44] Cf. also Fossum's "Jewish-Christian Christology".
[45] Hurtado, *One God* (1988).
[46] Hurtado, *One God*, 21.

shows the other pole around which Hurtado's argument revolves. The "cultic devotion" which early Christians directed to the risen and exalted Christ constitutes an innovation, in Hurtado's words "a mutation", of ancient Jewish Monotheism. He contends that in the ancient world, and especially in Judaism, the difference between a heavenly being, such as an angel, and a divine being (or the Divine Being) was most clearly expressed in the realm of cultic devotion. In Judaism--Hurtado argues--God was worshipped, while divine agents were not. In early Christianity, however, Christ was an object of worship and consequently must not be understood as merely a divine agent.[47] This mutation allowed the first Christians to worship Christ as God's chief agent without compromising their monotheism.[48]

Hurtado's work has occasioned a number of responses. Paul Rainbow, for example, while accepting the main thrust of his position, criticizes Hurtado for placing the "mutation" within early Christians' post-resurrection experiences, rather than in the teachings of Jesus himself.[49] Another contribution indebted to Hurtado is a recent article by P. G. Davis.[50] He examines divine agents and mediators in Jewish literature of the Second Temple period "on the basis of whether they operate in the past, present or future with respect to the writers of the literature in question and their intended audiences".[51] Significantly for the argument of this thesis, he finds only three, other than the Christ of the NT, which function in past, present, and future: Michael in the "Book of Watchers" and the Adam literature, the Prince of Light in the sectarian works from Qumran, and Enoch in the literature associated with his name.

Hurtado's assertions of the complete absence of veneration directed toward angels in the Second Temple period has been recently challenged in a monograph and an article by Loren Stuckenbruck.[52] Stuckenbruck concludes that while Hurtado may be right in asserting that there was no "angel cult" in ancient Judaism, some texts "suggest that, to a lesser degree, angels could be made objects of veneration as beings aligned with and subordinate to God".[53] This "lesser" veneration of angels may have provided a model

---

[47] Hurtado is here building on the argument of Richard Bauckham's article "Worship of Jesus". Cf. also "Jesus".
[48] Hurtado, *One God*, 82.
[49] Rainbow, "Jewish Monotheism", 88.
[50] "Divine Agents".
[51] Davis, "Divine Agents", 502.
[52] *Angel Veneration*; and "Angelic Refusal".
[53] Stuckenbruck, *Angel Veneration*, 270.

for the worship of Christ in the Book of Revelation.⁵⁴ Following Rowland's exegesis of Rev. 1.12-18, Stuckenbruck argues that Revelation may be a subtle critique of a "shared tradition" which understood Christ in terms of an angel: although Christ appears in the opening vision in the form of an angel he is not an angel, for he is worthy of worship while angels must refuse it (19.10, 22.8-9).⁵⁵

Another recent work on angelic Christology which focuses on the Book of Revelation is Peter Carrell's monograph *Jesus and the Angels*.⁵⁶ Carrell takes as his starting point Rowland's suggestion that since the imagery surrounding the Risen Christ in Rev. 1.12-18 is dependent on the description of the principal angel found Dan. 10.5-9, the Apocalypse's Christology must be indebted to Jewish angelology. After examining in detail the Christophanies in Rev. 1.12-18, 14.14, and 19.11-16, Carrell concludes that an angelomorphic Christology is to be found in the Book of Revelation. On the basis of an interesting parallel in the *Ascension of Isaiah*, Carrell makes the intriguing suggestion that in these three visions Christ temporarily takes on the outward form of an angel.⁵⁷ Carrell, however, also emphasizes that Revelation portrays Christ as an ontologically divine figure, who "participates in the eternal being of God".⁵⁸

In addition, Andrew Chester,⁵⁹ Michael Mach,⁶⁰ Robert Gundry,⁶¹ Crispin Fletcher-Louis⁶² and John Ashton,⁶³ to name just a few of the more important other recent contributions, have all found Jewish angelic categories behind the Christologies of various NT authors. All of the above works since Barbel, Kretschmar and Daniélou, although differing in many respects, agree that traditions about angelic figures in Second Temple Judaism were useful to early Christians in their attempt to understand and elucidate the significance of Christ. With the possible exceptions of Bühner and Fossum, they all differ from Werner in that they do not find in early Christianity the belief that Christ possessed an angelic nature. Many of these scholars, then, prefer the term "angelomorphic Christology" to Werner's "angel Christology". One exception to this trend, however,

---

⁵⁴ Stuckenbruck, *Angel Veneration*, 272-273.
⁵⁵ Stuckenbruck, *Angel Veneration*, 258-261, 271-272.
⁵⁶ Published in 1997.
⁵⁷ Carrell, *Jesus*, 172-173, 192-195, 224-226.
⁵⁸ Carrell, *Jesus*, 117-118.
⁵⁹ "Messianic Expectations", esp. 75-78.
⁶⁰ *Entwicklungsstadien*, 287-291.
⁶¹ "Angelomorphic".
⁶² *Luke-Acts*.
⁶³ "Bridging Ambiguities", esp. 87-89.

should also be noted. Margaret Barker has argued that Palestinian Judaism prior to Christianity continued to believe in the ancient Israelite conception of one "High God" and many sons of God (or angels), the most important of whom was known as Yahweh. In other words, pre-Christian Judaism was already essentially ditheistic. Jesus was understood, by early Christians, to be "a manifestation of Yahweh", the second God of Judaism.[64] This is, in one respect, essentially the position of Werner. Christ is an incarnation of an angel. However, here the angel is understood as none other than Yahweh himself, with one important caveat: Yahweh, in Barker's understanding, is not the High God of the Jews, but the greatest of the sons of God, the highest of the angels.

e. Summary

Angelic Christology in modern scholarship began with Lueken's development of Bousset's suggestion of a connection between Jewish Michael traditions and early Christology. Some forty years later Werner argued that the original Christology of early Christianity understood Christ as an angelic being. Scholarship universally, or nearly universally, rejected Werner's conclusion, but many scholars took up his many parallels between Jewish angelology and early Christology to posit some influence from the former on the latter. Recent years have witnessed a virtual explosion of studies on this relationship.

There is, then, an important stream of thought in current scholarship which, while rejecting Werner's identification of Christ with an angel, places a great deal of importance on ancient Jewish conceptions and beliefs about angels in the development of the earliest Christology. In addition to rejecting Werner's position, the scholars exemplifying this stream of thought tend to avoid Werner's term "angel Christology" and prefer to speak of "angelomorphic Christology".[65]

---

[64] Barker, *Great Angel*, 3.
[65] So e.g., Longenecker, Rowland, Stuckenbruck, Gundry, Fletcher-Louis, and Carrell.

2. Plan for This Study

This study returns to the supposition of Lueken, and Bousset, that Michael traditions influenced early Christology. If angelological conceptions did indeed influence the earliest attempts at Christology there is bound to be some trace in the portrayals of Michael in ancient Jewish and Christian literature, for Michael is consistently depicted as the pre-eminent angel in many of these sources. Recent examinations of angelic Christology regularly mentioned Michael as a significant figure.[66] No study, however, has appeared which deals entirely with Michael. Given the methodological errors and the age of Lueken's work, one is certainly needed. This investigation is offered to supply this deficiency. In the interest of historical and methodological clarity it will review all the relevant data, Jewish and Christian, from the period c. 200 BC to c. AD 200. It will open with a brief overview of OT angelology, before examining, in turn, Michael traditions in Jewish apocalyptic and related literature, the sectarian works from Qumran, Philo, Rabbinic and Hekhalot literature, the NT, and the Christian literary remains of the second and third centuries. My purpose throughout is not merely to write a history of Michael traditions in ancient Judaism and early Christianity, but to examine such traditions in light of the current ferment in scholarship regarding Christology and its debt to Jewish angelological speculation. Filling this gap, I hope to make a contribution to our understanding of the origins and early development of Christology.

3. Terminology

The above brief history of this stream of thought in scholarship has indicated the importance of precise terminology. I propose to use four terms, each one indicating a distinct conception or range of conceptions. First, "angelic Christology" is an umbrella term for the whole compass of Christologies influenced, at least to some degree, by angelological ideas. This is the broadest of my four categories and is equivalent to the most common usage of "angelomorphic Christology" among scholars today. Second, "angel Christology" indicates the identification of Christ with an angel, either as an incarnation of an angel or an exaltation to angelic status and nature. It defines Christ as an angelic being. Third, the term

---

[66] So e.g., Hengel, Fossum, Rowland, Hurtado, Chester, Davis, and Carrell.

"angelomorphic Christology" is phenomenological. It refers only to visual portrayals of Christ in form of an angel. This, more precise use of the term than that found in many recent studies, confines the word to its literal meaning: Christ in the form (μορφή) of an angel. To be sure, the last two categories are not mutually exclusive--they could coincide. However, a description of Christ which uses angelic imagery need not imply that Christ possessed an angelic nature nor does the supposition that Christ was an ontological angel necessarily imply that he actually looked like an angel. Finally, "theophanic angel Christology" very specifically denotes the Patristic identification of Christ with the Old Testament מלאך יהוה.

Chapter 1

The מלאך יהוה and Other Antecedents in the Old Testament

Before examining Michael traditions as they appear in the Judaism of the Second Temple and of the early Rabbinic periods and in emerging Christianity, it will be necessary to first consider the Old Testament view of angels, particularly the מלאך יהוה. The OT documents are the authoritative sources for the various groups which we will be considering in the following chapters. Thus, many of the angelological themes which we find in Jewish apocalyptic sources, the writings of Qumran, Philo, Rabbinic and Hekhaloth documents, as well as early Christian sources, arise from interpretations of OT passages. However, any comparison of the earliest angelological conceptions of the OT and those which emerged later must also emphasize a certain discontinuity as well.

1. Angels in the Old Testament[1]

a. The Prevalence of Angels on the Ancient Near East

The idea of heavenly beings "who, in some ways, shared the nature, though not the being,"[2] of God or the gods and who functioned as servants or messengers of God or the gods was prevalent in the ancient Near East. It is, therefore, not surprising that ancient Israel shared this belief in angels. It is possible that the OT belief in angels originated from the domestication

---

[1] The angelology of the Book of Daniel will not be considered in this chapter; it must await our examination of the angelology and Michael traditions found in Jewish apocalyptic literature.

[2] Russell, *Method and Message*, 235.

of the pagan gods of Canaan, or the star-gods of Mesopotamia, or even the gods from the pre-mosaic period.³ From Ugaritic texts we learn that the Canaanite pantheon was pictured as a council of gods, organized around the Father of the gods, El;⁴ a notion not unlike what we encounter in a number of texts scattered throughout the OT.⁵ Similarly, some texts seem to imply a relation between the angelic hosts and the heavenly bodies,⁶ a link which may point to Mesopotamian influence.⁷ However, regardless of these foreign "influences", von Rad has quite rightly emphasized that in the OT, as we now have it, angels never become autonomous from Yahweh or objects of worship alongside Yahweh. They never violate "the absolute transcendence of Yahweh".⁸ Thus, while ancient Israelite religion may have borrowed from Canaanite and Mesopotamian religions, it did not do so uncritically and also contained elements which were genuinely Israelite. Pre-eminent here is that fact that the earliest material, i.e., the Patriarchal narratives, speaks of angelic beings most often in the singular: מלאך יהוה or מלאך אלהים.⁹ Finally, the OT documents do not contain a well-developed or uniform angelology. As we shall see, particularly when discussing the מלאך יהוה, speculation about the heavenly world increases and becomes more detailed in the later books of the OT.¹⁰

b. Terminology

A number of terms are used in the OT for angels. The "sons of God" of Gen. 6.2, 4 (בני האלהים) in no way implies genealogical descent and is best understood as analogous to the Hebrew term "the sons of the prophets"; the "sons of God" belong to the heavenly realm, just as the sons of the prophets belong to the sphere of the prophets.¹¹ Most other appellations are primarily functional or descriptive. These include: "holy ones" (קדשים,

---

³ See Eichrodt, *Theology*, II.195-197.
⁴ Eichrodt, *Theology*, II.196-97.
⁵ E.g., Gen. 28.12; 1 Kgs. 22.19ff; Jer. 23.18; Job 1.6-12, 15.8; Pss. 29.1, 82, and 89.6-9 (ET 5-8).
⁶ E.g., Deut. 4.19; Jos. 5.14-15; Judg. 5.20; Job 38.7; Isa. 24.21 and 40.26.
⁷ Eichrodt, *Theology*, II.196.
⁸ Von Rad, "ἄγγελος", *TDNT* I.78. So also Bietenhard, "ἄγγελος", *NIDNTT* I.101.
⁹ Although, to be sure, even the Patriarchal narratives on occasion assume a plurality of angels (e.g., Gen. 6.2, 4, 19.1, 15, 28.12, 32.2).
¹⁰ Cf. Newsom, "Angels", *ABD* I.249.
¹¹ So von Rad, *TDNT*, I.78, n.20. Cf. the *NRSV* translation of בני אלים in Ps. 89.6 as "heavenly beings".

Ps. 89.6,8); "mighty" or "valiant ones" (אבירים Ps. 78.25); "high ones" (רמים, Job 21.22); and "ministers" (משרתים, Ps. 103.21). A couple have military connotations: "hosts" or "armies" (צבאות, Ps 148.2; 1 Kgs. 22.19) and "commander" or "prince" (שר, Josh. 5.14; Dan. 10.13). The most common word used for angels in the OT is מלאך. It derives from לאך, a root which is not found in the Hebrew Bible or later Hebrew literature, but can be found in Arabic, Ethiopic and Phoenician with the meaning "to send".[12] In addition, Arabic, Ethiopic and Ugaritic all have a noun for "messenger" built on the consonants "mlk".[13] Thus מלאך means "one who is sent" or "messenger".[14] מלאך, then, is primarily functional, and can be used of men as well as of heavenly beings.[15] It follows from this that angels were thought to be divine servants sent by God to accomplish His will in the world. It seems to have been a common assumption in ancient Israel that these divine messengers were present in the world even if unseen (Gen. 28.12; Num. 22.31; 2 Sam. 5.22-25; 2 Kgs. 6.15-17).[16]

c. Themes and Motifs in OT Angelology

The OT depiction of the angels' service to God in many ways parallels the human servants of an ancient oriental potentate.[17] For example, a number of OT passages represent the heavenly court after the pattern of the royal courts of the ancient Near East, with the angelic host encircling Yahweh.[18] In 1 Kgs. 22.19-22 and Job 1.6-12, 2.1-7 the angelic host serve as counselors to Yahweh. In Ps. 82 the heavenly court is a place of judgement, in which God condemns angels for their unjust dealing with

---

[12] BDB, 521; Hirth, *Boten*, 23.

[13] Mach, *Entwicklungsstadien*, 39-40 and Freedman-Willoughby, *ThWAT* IV.888-889.

[14] Newsom, *ABD*, I.248; Heidt, *Angelology*, 8-9; and von Rad, *TDNT*, I.76. Note the Septuagint's standard translation of מלאך, ἄγγελος, which also means messenger. Indeed, the LXX translators often rendered other terms, such as אלהים and בני אלהים, with ἄγγελος when they believed angels were intended.

[15] See esp. Mach, *Entwicklungsstadien*, 37-43, 47-51.

[16] In Cherubim and Seraphim we have a special case. They are, perhaps, best described as "the animals of the heavenly world". They, at any rate, are angels only in the widest sense of the term. See Newsom, *ABD*, I. 251; and von Rad, *TDNT*, I.80; cf. also Bietenhard, *NIDNTT*, 101; Eichrodt, *Theology*, II.202-205; and Morenz, "Der Seraph".

[17] Cf. Newsom, "Angels", *ABD* I.249.

[18] E.g., Gen. 28.12; 1 Kgs. 22.19-22; Isa. 6.1-8; Jer. 23.18; Job 1.6-12, 15.8; Pss. 29.1, 82, and 89.6-9 (ET 5-8).

humanity. The heavenly council is also a place of worship (Isa. 6.1-4;[19] Pss. 29.1-2 and 148.2).

Similarly, just as kings of the ancient Orient had in their service generals and soldiers as well as counselors and courtiers, angels formed the armies of Yahweh (Deut. 33.2; Jos. 5.13-15; 2 Kgs. 6.17; 19.35 = Isa. 37.36; Ps. 68.18). This military understanding is probably reflected in the term צבאות and the frequent title for God יהוה צבאות (e.g., 1 Sam. 4.4; 1 Kgs. 18.15; Isa. 6.3, 5). As his armies, angels could be called upon to execute Yahweh's judgements (Ps. 78.49; 2 Sam. 24.15-17 = 1 Chron. 21.14-16).

While it is not a common motif in OT angelology we do on occasion encounter angelic intercessors and mediators on behalf of humanity (Job 5.1, 16.19, 33.23-28; Zech. 1.12-13). This also seems to fit the royal court pattern; angels intercede for men and women just as members of the royal court could intercede with the Monarch for those outside the court (cf. Esther 4). This theme will find a great deal of development in later, especially apocalyptic, literature.[20] On the other hand, just as an ancient court might contain those who would intercede and defend commoners, so they could also include those who would serve as public accusers. We find this reflected in the folk tale which frames the book Job (1-2 and 42.7-17). The "Accuser" or "Adversary" (השטן) here will later develop into the embodiment of evil known as Satan or the Devil, a process already under way in Zech. 3 and 1 Chron. 21.1.[21]

Finally, just as an ancient king would divide the administration of his kingdom among governors and other officals, so some OT texts appear to suggest the belief that God had appointed angels to rule various nations. Such is the case with the original text of Deuteronomy 32.8. The MT reads: "When the Most High apportioned the nations, when he divided humankind, he fixed the boundaries of the peoples *according to the number of the sons of Israel*" (למספר בני ישראל). But the LXX replaces the last phrase with: κατὰ ἀριθμὸν ἀγγέλων θεοῦ. The LXX is now supported by 4QDeutʲ which reads: ...]בני אל[22] So the original probably read either בני אל or בני אלים. Most modern commentators see the MT as a later correction of a theologically offensive text.[23] The original text appears to imply

---

[19] The LXX implies that there is a host of seraphim since it translates מִמַּעַל with κύκλῳ. The Hebrew, however, is more ambiguous and may denote either a host or merely two Seraphim.

[20] See below p. 32.

[21] Cf. Russell, *Method*, 237; and Eichrodt, *Theology*, II.205.

[22] Skehan, "Song of Moses", 12; and Ulrich et al. *DJD*, XIV.141-142.

[23] E.g., von Rad, *Deuteronomy*, 196, n.2; and Craigie, *Deuteronomy*, 378-80. Contra Driver, *Deuteronomy*, 356.

that an angel has been appointed over every nation, except Israel, who were "the Lord's own portion" (vs. 9).[24] This same idea seems to lie behind Pss. 58 and 82, where "the gods", that is, angels, are condemned for not rendering justice to the oppressed and downtrodden of humanity. As we shall see, this concept of angels set over the nations will be greatly developed in Jewish apocalyptic.[25]

2. מלאך יהוה (מלאך אלהים)

a. The מלאך יהוה of the Patriarchal Narratives

As intimated above, the patriarchal narratives only rarely speak of angels in the plural. Instead, in these stories from Genesis we encounter the enigmatic "angel of the Lord" (מלאך יהוה) or, less frequently, "angel of God" (מלאך אלהים). In nearly every case when one of these terms appears in a patriarchal narrative there is a curious oscillation between the angel and Yahweh; at times the מאלך יהוה speaks not as a messenger, but as if he is to be identified with Yahweh.[26] In some cases the identification of the angel with Yahweh seems explicit, as in Gen. 31.10-13 and 48.15-16. In the former, Jacob recounts how in a dream the angel of God had said to him: "I am the God of Bethel,...".[27] In the latter, האלהים and המלאך are

---

[24] Cf. also Deut. 4.19, where God has "allotted" to the nations to serve the "hosts of heaven".

[25] See below pp. 31 and 33-38.

[26] E.g., Gen. 16.7-16, 21.8-19; 22.9-18; 32.22-32. Cf. also Gen. 18.33. Ex. 3.1-15, and perhaps, 4.24-26 (LXX) should also be included here even though they do not strictly belong to the "patriarchal narratives". Cf. Eichrodt, *Theology*, II.25.

[27] The MT reads: אָנֹכִי הָאֵל בֵּית אֵל, which many interpreters (e.g., BDB, 42b; *NRSV*; Wenham, *Genesis*, II.263; von Rad, *Genesis*, 303) understand as a construct: "The God of Bethel". But a word in the construct state cannot take an article. Thus a marginal note in the *NRSV* indicates that the meaning of the Hebrew is uncertain and that the translation is a correction. The LXX and both the Geniza fragmentary Targum and Targum Ps.-Jon. suggest the original text may have read: אנכי האל הנראה אליך בבית־אל. This is followed by Westermann, *Genesis* II.491-492; Speiser, *Genesis*, 244; and, tentatively, Skinner, *Genesis*, 395. However, the reading of the LXX and Targums are probably corrections of a difficult text.

parallel;[28] the God before whom Abraham and Isaac walked and who shepherded Jacob his whole life *is* the "angel" called upon to bless the sons of Joseph.

This מלאך יהוה significantly differs from later Jewish angelology. Here a separate being does not appear to be in view. The variation between the מלאך יהוה and יהוה in the texts appears to have originated from the theological paradox which sought to express both Yahweh's presence and the impossibility for humans of unmediated access to God.[29] Thus, the מלאך יהוה appears to be in some sense an extension or manifestation of Yahweh.[30] It has been noted that the מלאך יהוה, at least in the patriarchal narratives and in Genesis-Judges generally, always acts to protect or guide Israel or an individual patriarch, and never acts to punish or judge.[31]

Westermann emphasizes that the מלאך יהוה belongs to the religion of the patriarchs and that after the earliest period of Israel's history, while the term continues to be used, a profound development takes place in the concept.[32] As we shall see, this development begins within the Pentateuch in narratives concerning the Exodus angel. In the narratives from the Books of Samuel and Kings, we no longer encounter the oscillation between Yahweh and His angel and references to a plurality of angels increase. By the time of post-exilic writings an interest in individual angels begins to appear.

---

[28] The Sam. Pent. reads המלך rather than המלאך, but the MT (and LXX) is surely to be preferred as the *lectio difficilior*.

[29] Newsom, "Angels" *ABD*, I.250; Freedman-Willoughby, *ThWAT*, IV.901. Cf. Hirth, *Boten*, 83-84; Westermann, *Genesis*, II.242-243.

[30] Eichrodt, *Theology*, II.27; Frost, *OT Apocalyptic*, 23-24; von Rad, *TDNT*, I.77-78; idem, *OT Theology*, I.285-287.

Röttger (*Mal'ak*, esp. 274, 282) disputes this. He argues that the מלאך יהוה was a temporary phenomenon which spent itself (erschöpft sich) in its particular mission and was always thought to be distinct from יהוה; it was only the "perplexed" who confused them. Even if Röttger's unique reading is accepted, this does not speak against my main point, i.e., the distinctiveness of the מלאך יהוה over against all later Jewish (and Christian) angelologies.

[31] Von Rad, *OT Theology*, I.286. Cf. also Freedman-Willoughby, *ThWAT* IV.897-898.

[32] Westermann, *Genesis*, II.243. Cf. also von Rad, *OT Theology*, I.286.

b. The Angel of the Exodus

I turn now to the tradition about the angel who led the people through the wilderness. This angel is mentioned in Ex. 14.19, 23.20-33, 32.34, 33.2f; Num. 20.16; Judg. 2.1-5; and perhaps Num. 22.21-35 and Jos. 5.13-15. That this was understood as the angel of Yahweh is shown first, by the designations given the angel: מלאך יהוה at Judg. 2.1-5, מלאך האלהים at Ex. 14.19 and מלאכי at Ex. 23.23 and 32.34,[33] and second, by the presence of the customary oscillation between the מלאך and יהוה.[34] Just as the מלאך יהוה expressed the presence of God in the patriarchal narratives, so in Ex. 23.20-21 the Exodus angel carries the divine Name. The Name of God was a way of affirming God's presence, especially in the Tabernacle or Temple.[35] To say that God's Name dwells in this angel affirms the divine presence in a unique way. Further, in Ex. 14.19-20 "the angel of God" is associated with the pillar of cloud, which was another way of speaking about God's presence with His people (Ex. 13.21-22, 14.24). However, the Exodus angel also becomes to some extent an expression of the divine absence in that he is a substitute for Yahweh (Ex. 33.1-3). As a replacement for the divine presence, it would appear that the angel of the Exodus is beginning to have a quasi-individual existence. Significantly, unlike מלאך יהוה in the patriarchal narratives, the Exodus angel is spoken of by God in the third person (23.20-21, 32.34 and 33.2-3). So the Exodus angel seems to betray a certain development in the מלאך יהוה concept, away from an extension or manifestation of the divine presence and toward an individual existence. However, it is only the beginning of this process and was by no means complete until much later. The oscillation between Yahweh and His angel is still encountered in the Book of Judges (6.11-24, 13.1-23).

---

[33] There was a tendency in the textual tradition to make the identification with the angel of the Lord specific in those passages where it is not. Thus, the Samaritan Pentateuch, the LXX, and the Vulgate all presuppose מלאכי at Ex. 23.20 and the LXX again at Ex. 33.2 Only Num. 20.16 has no textual witness supporting such a reading.

[34] Note Ex. 23.23, 33.2; and esp. Judg. 2.1-5. Note also the parallels between Jos. 5.13-15 and Ex. 3.1-6.

[35] Deut. 12.5, 11, 21, 14.23f, 16.2, 6, 11, 26.2; 1 Kgs. 11.36, 14.21; 2 Kgs. 21.4, 7. Cf. Eichrodt, *Theology*, II.41-43; Rose, "Names of God", IV.1003-1004; von Rad, "Deuteronomy's Name Theology". But note the important qualifications to a Deuteronomistic theology of the Divine Name in Wilson, *Divine Presence*.

c. Later Developments

It appears that the מלאך יהוה as an expression of the divine presence is limited to the period before the monarchy. After that Yahweh's presence among His people was expressed in terms of the cultus and the prophetic movement.[36] When the phrase does re-occur it is not used to indicate the presence of Yahweh. Rather, from the time of the monarchy the term is used for individual angels, though there is not yet the kind of interest in these angels which we will find later in the Jewish apocalyptic writings. None are named, they are merely called מלאך יהוה. The oscillation between Yahweh and His angel, so prominent in the pre-monarchy narratives, no longer occurs and for the first time the מלאך יהוה is described as God's agent by whom Israel is punished (2 Sam. 24 = 2 Chron. 21). This development toward an individual angel continues in the exilic and postexilic periods. The מלאך יהוה of 2 Kgs. 19.35 becomes merely an angel sent by God in 2 Chron. 32.21.

With Zechariah 1-8 and the Book of Daniel we arrive at the end of this process. In the latter, angels are even given names.[37] In the former, the מאלך יהוה clearly indicates an individual angel, not an extension of Yahweh and expression of His presence. Zechariah's "angel of the Lord" has a definite personality and shares far more with angels of Jewish apocalyptic literature than with earlier portions of the OT. He functions as an angelic interpreter and guide (1.9) answering the prophet's queries, he intercedes on behalf of Jerusalem and Judah (1.12-17), and he may be the leader of the heavenly armies in Zechariah for "the angelic patrol" reports to him (1.11) and he issues orders to it (6.7). Finally, it is possible that in the original text of Zechariah 3.1-5, the מלאך יהוה functioned as the angelic public defender, defending Joshua the High Priest before God and silencing Satan.[38] As we shall see, all these roles, *angelus interpres*, intercessor for

---

[36] Cf. Eichrodt, *Theology OT*, II.29.

[37] See the next chapter.

[38] Although the MT, followed by the LXX, in verse 2 reads יהוה, rather than מלאך יהוה as one would expect from the context, the original reading may be that of the Syriac Peshitta, which has "angel of the Lord". So also Petersen, *Haggai & Zechariah*, 187, 191; and Mitchell, *Haggai & Zechariah*, 149, 153. Contra Meyers and Meyers, *Haggai & Zechariah*, 185.

Although quite speculative, it is possible that מלאך יהוה also stood behind the text found in the Greek scroll of the Minor Prophets found at Nahal Hever. The line in question (31.21), as reconstructed by Tov, Kraft and Parsons, reads "...κ]αὶ εἶπεν [..." (*DJD* VIII.72-73). The editors would fill the lacuna of the rest of the line with only the paleo-Hebrew characters for יהוה. This, however, makes for a rather short line; a line of only 27 letters compared with 31 before it and 34 after it and an average of 32.22 letters per line in this column. If, on the other hand, ἄγγελος were added after or before the paleo-Hebrew יהוה, a line of 34 letters would result. This is, admittedly, a speculative suggestion and is

humanity, leader of the heavenly armies, judicial defender and opponent of Satan will become important themes in the angelology of Jewish apocalyptic. Indeed, in the following chapter we shall see how each of them are attributed to Michael in various apocalypses.

d. Related Themes

The OT authors had other means by which to express the divine presence other than the מאלך יהוה. These include the Glory of Yahweh and the Name of Yahweh. They are only tangential to this investigation and, therefore, they occasion only brief comments. The Glory and Name of Yahweh, to some degree, parallel the מלאך יהוה in that they also appear to be not separate beings, but extensions of Yahweh. For example, the phrase כבוד יהוה appears to have been used as a technical term expressing the "visible and mobile presence of Yahweh" which was associated in the Priestly tradition with both the tabernacle and temple, on the one hand, and with the pillar of cloud and the pillar of fire, on the other.[39] This כבוד יהוה seems to take on a near hypostatic existence in the visions of Ezekiel,[40] which had an immense influence on later apocalyptic literature.[41] Similarly, in the Deuteronomic tradition God was present in the sanctuary and the Holy City by means of His ineffable Name: יהוה.[42] As already stated, both conceptions appear to have been related to מאלך יהוה: In Ex. 23.20-21 the Exodus angel bears the divine Name, while in narrative concerning the crossing of the Red Sea (Ex. 14.19-20) the Exodus angel is in the pillar of cloud. Both conceptions also appear, with great modifications, in later Jewish traditions, particularly Rabbinic literature. The כבוד seems to have been the basis for speculations about the Shekinah,[43] while the divine Name played an important role in Jewish apocalyptic and Rabbinic theology.[44]

---

put forward only tentatively. It is a pity that this important manuscript is so fragmentary.

[39] See Newman, *Paul's Glory-Christology*, 20-24; and Weinfeld, "כָּבוֹד", *ThWAT* IV.23-40.

[40] Esp. 1.26-28, 3.23, 8.2-4, 9.3, 10.1-5, 18-19, 11.22-24, 43.1-9, and 44.4.

[41] Cf. Rowland, *Open Heaven*, 95-98.

[42] See above p. 21.

[43] Cf. Kittel, "δόξα", *TDNT*, II.245-247.

[44] For Jewish apocalyptic see below pp. 51-54. For Rabbinic theology see below pp. 110-111 and Urbach, *Sages*, 124-134.

e. Summary

The term מלאך יהוה, then, underwent a profound development during biblical history. In the earliest texts it denotes, not a separate being, but an extension of Yahweh, an expression of the divine presence. By the last books of the OT, the מלאך יהוה has become an individual angel among other angels and a member of the heavenly host, even their leader in Zechariah 1-8. This process, of course, has been sketched only in the roughest of outlines here. It indicates, however, that the movement was away from understanding the מלאך יהוה as an extension of Yahweh and toward an understanding of him as an individual member in the heavenly host. By the time of Zechariah the original conception appears to have been lost.[45]

---

[45] One very late survival or, more probably, imitation of this early concept of the מלאך יהוה as an expression of Yahweh's presence should be mentioned: The angel Uriel in 4 Ezra. In this apocalypse from the late first century AD, the angel Uriel is both addressed and speaks as if he is to be identified with God. Cf. the discussion in Stone, *Fourth Ezra*, 199. 4 Ezra, however, differs from the OT מלאך יהוה conception. The very fact that Uriel has a name, which is never true of the מלאך יהוה in the OT, implies that he is distinct from God. Indeed, that Uriel is well known from other sources (*1En.* 9-10, 20 [Grk]; *PrJos.*; *ApocMos.* 40.2; *SibOr.* II.214ff) probably means that the author of 4 Ezra was drawing on a traditional angelology of the Second Temple period in his use of the name Uriel. This is supported by the appearance of Remiel in 4.36, since both Uriel and Remiel appear in the list of seven archangels of *1En.* 20. More importantly, in 4 Ezra itself, no ontological distinction between Uriel and Remiel is ever made. It is, then, probable that the author of 4 Ezra, although indebted to the angelology of the Second Temple period, sought to imitate, without complete success, the OT מלאך יהוה.

Chapter 2

The Archangel Michael in Jewish Apocalyptic and related Literature

Jewish apocalyptic motifs had a great influence on later literature, both Jewish and Christian. Many of the apocalyptic assumptions about the heavenly world and the angelic host we will encounter again later, especially in our examination of Qumran, Rabbinic literature, the New Testament, and second century Christianity. This is due, in part, to the very long time span which Jewish apocalyptic literature covers. Apart from the Pentateuch and Prophets of the OT, the earliest documentary evidence which we will consider belongs to this genre. Portions of *1 Enoch* probably go back to the third century BC, while the books of Daniel, *Jubilees* and the Enochic *Dream Visions* date from the mid-second century BC. On the other hand, some apocalyptic works, e.g., the *Apocalypse of Abraham*, *3 Baruch*, and the Adam literature,[1] may not have attained their final form until well into the Christian period.

Ancient Jewish apocalyptic literature attributed to Michael a prominent role in the heavenly world. He was particularly important because he was related to the Jewish nation in a special way; he was their heavenly protector and champion. This special relationship with the Chosen People was often taken to imply that Michael also held a superior position in the heavenly hierarchy. Apocalyptic works also attributed to Michael a priestly or intercessory position, as well as the task of transporting the souls of the righteous to paradise at death. To be sure, the treatment of Michael and other named angels is not uniform in these documents, but there is a broad agreement among them especially on Michael's relationship with Israel and his importance in the heavenly hierarchy. I will begin with a brief discus-

---

[1] By "the Adam literature" I mean the Greek *Apocalypse of Moses*, the Latin *Vita Adae et Evae*, the Slavonic *Vita Adae et Evae*, the Armenian *Penitence of Adam*, and the Georgian *Book of Adam*. See Stone, *History*, 3, 6-41.

sion of the nature of Jewish apocalyptic, followed by a summary of the angelology of the Jewish apocalypses. Having set the stage, I will then turn to more detailed discussion of Michael in this literature. It is important to be as complete as possible, but special attention will be given to those themes which will re-appear later in other genres, so as to highlight those themes and motifs which had the widest currency in second temple Judaism.

1. Jewish Apocalyptic Literature

Recent scholarship has tended to move away from a simple identification of Jewish apocalyptic thought and eschatology, although it is still generally recognized that the two are closely related. Rowland and Collins can be taken as representative of the trend in current scholarship.[2] Both would see the revelation of divine secrets or mysteries as the primary concern of Jewish apocalyptic.[3] To be sure, there are differences between Collins' and Rowland's treatment. Collins would emphasize the importance of eschatology more than Rowland, but they both agree that earlier scholarship tended to collapse the two, apocalyptic and eschatology, into a single category.[4] This must be rejected because, while eschatology plays a significant role in many of the apocalypses, the authors and readers of the apocalypses were as concerned with the secrets of the heavenly world and of history as they were with the mysteries of the future. For our purposes, Collins' definition of the literary genre may be offered as a serviceable and succinct working definition:

> "Apocalypse" is a genre of revelatory literature with a narrative framework, in which a revelation is mediated by an otherworldly being to a human recipient, disclosing a transcendent reality which is both temporal, insofar as it envisages eschatological salvation, and spatial insofar as it involves another, supernatural world.[5]

---

[2] Collins, "Morphology" and *Apocalyptic Imagination*, esp. 1-11; and Rowland, *Open Heaven*, esp. 9-48.

[3] Rowland, *Open Heaven*, 9-11 and esp. 70-72; and Collins *Apocalyptic Imagination*, esp. 8.

[4] E.g., Rowley, *Relevance*; and Russell, *Method*.

[5] Collins, "Morphology", 9; idem, *Apocalyptic Imagination*, 4. One gets the impression that Rowland would heartily agree up to and including the words "transcendent reality", but would prefer to end the definition there. For our purposes of discussing the angelology of the apocalypses, and in particular Michael traditions, no final arbitration between these two positions is needed.

There are certain works which only partially fit the category of apocalypse. *Jubilees*, *Testaments of the Twelve Patriarchs*, and the Adam literature are examples of such borderline works which are particularly significant for the argument of this chapter. Concerning *Jubilees* there is considerable disagreement over whether or not it should be classed as an apocalypse.[6] On the other hand, most interpreters agree that while the Adam literature and the *Testaments* contain apocalyptic sections, as a whole they should not be classed as apocalypses.[7] However, since in many respects the angelology of these works parallel that of Jewish apocalyptic in general, I have included them in this chapter.

Finally, something should be said about the social milieu which produced and read this literature. N.T. Wright perhaps sums up the thinking of many when he argues that apocalyptic thought "reflects a context of social deprivation"; that is, it is "the literature of the powerless". From this Wright concludes that the appeal of the apocalypses was very limited in ancient Judaism and that they were treated as suspect by the population in general.[8] This, however, neglects the inclusion of apocalyptic sections in works which were not apocalypses (e.g., *TLevi*; *TNaph*.; Mark 13), and the immense importance of a work like Daniel in Second Temple Judaism.[9] Although other apocalypses did not share the authority of the Book of Daniel, its status testifies to the widespread acceptance of apocalyptic ideas. Further, it is now generally realized that "apocalyptic" does not necessarily mean "sectarian". The popularity of apocalyptic ideas extended to many groups within Ancient Judaism, as the inclusion of Revelation in the NT and use of *1 Enoch* at Qumran shows.[10] Finally, although the Rabbis (*mMeg*. 4.10; *mHag*. 2.1) were concerned about the dangers of esoteric literature, even they betray some interest in apocalyptic themes.[11] Indeed, a case can be made for apocalyptic literature as "a product of learned activity

---

[6] Contrast, e.g., the treatment of Rowland (*Open Heaven*, 51-52) with that of Collins ("Jewish Apocalypses," 33).

[7] Rowland, *Open Heaven*, 15-19; Collins, "Jewish Apocalypses," 40-41, 44, 46; Russell, *Method*, 37-38, 55-57.

[8] Wright, *People of God*, 287-289.

[9] Cf. Josephus, *Ant*. x.267-277, who shares little if any of the apocalyptic temperament.

[10] So Sanders, *Judaism*, 8-9; Rowland, *Open Heaven*, 245-247.

[11] Cf. Rowland, *Open Heaven*, 271-348.

rather than popular folklore".[12] The attributions of apocalypses to individuals famous for their wisdom or scribal activity and the preoccupation with exegesis which clearly stands behind many of the apocalypses supports this conclusion.[13] Thus, while many of the works discussed in this chapter may be classed as "popular" literature, in the sense that they were read by the masses, their influence was felt even among the "intelligentsia".[14]

2. The Angelology of Jewish Apocalyptic Literature

The various Jewish apocalyptic works which have survived are, to be sure, diverse; they arose out of different situations, reflect different outlooks and, not infrequently, differ in details in the areas of angelology and cosmology. However, they also shared many of the same assumptions about the heavenly world and its inhabitants. Therefore, before turning to the specific traditions about Michael it may be helpful first to sketch briefly, in rough outline, the principal motifs and themes in the angelology of this material.[15]

a. Messengers and Servants of God

In continuity with OT angelology, angels were portrayed in the Jewish apocalypses as superhuman, heavenly beings, created by and subordinate to God (e.g., *Jub* 2.2). They are eternal in that they do not die (*1En.* 15.4, 6). It is sometimes asserted that they were created out of and consisted of fire (*2En.* 29.3; *2Bar.* 21.6; cf. 59.11).

A common assumption of all the Jewish apocalypses of the Second Temple period is that the angels were agents of God who accomplish His will in the world, both in relation to humanity and with reference to the created order. Regarding the latter, it is often expressed in the apocalypses that various angels or classes of angels were set over different natural

---

[12] Collins, *Apocalyptic Imagination*, 30.
[13] Collins, *Apocalyptic Imagination*, 30; Rowland, *Open Heaven*, 215-225.
[14] Note also the knowledge and use of apocalypses by Church Fathers, e.g., Origen, *CommJo* ii.31.
[15] For this summary cf. Mach, *Entwicklungsstadien*, 114-278; and Newsom, "Angels", *ABD* I.252. Cf. also the still useful summary of apocalyptic angelology by Kuhn, "Angelology".

phenomena, such as the sun, moon, planets, rain, snow, hail, fire, earthquakes, winds, lightning, etc. (*Jub.* 2.2ff; *1En.* 60.16-21; *2En.* 14.3, 19.4-5).

b. Archangels and the Angelic Hierarchy

The authors of the apocalypses often assert that the angels are organized into a hierarchy (*2En.* 19.3; *1En.* 61.10; *2Bar.* 59.11). This often includes a belief in a small group of especially privileged archangels, or angels of the Presence, who stand before God and have responsibility over the hosts of lesser angels (Tobit 12.15; *Jub.* 2.2). The number of this, the highest rank of angels, is in some documents four and in others seven. In *1En.* 9-10 Michael, Sariel/Uriel,[16] Raphael and Gabriel function as principal angels. These same four appear again and again throughout Jewish literature of the Second Temple period,[17] with the qualification that Uriel is usually restricted to Greek texts and Sariel to Hebrew or Aramaic ones. These four archangels appear to have been the basis for an expanded list of seven archangels in *1 Enoch* 20 which consists of Uriel, Raphael, Raguel, Michael, Sariel, Gabriel, and Remiel.[18] While the tradition of seven archangels is attested more often in the subsequent apocalypses, both Jewish and Christian, the tradition of four archangels continues to be represented, most notably in the *Similitudes of Enoch*.[19]

So one literary strand behind the *Book of Watchers* (*1En.* 9-10) testifies to the belief that there were four archangels, while another strand affirms that there were seven (*1En.* 20). In the *Animal Apocalypse*, an originally independent work of the mid-second century BC which now forms chapters 85-90 of *1 Enoch*,[20] the transition from four to seven is discernible. This

---

[16] The Greek witnesses both read Οὐριήλ. 4QEn^b, however, reads שריאל. The Ethiopic MSS are divided between '*Ur'el, Sur'el*, and *Suryal wa' Uryal*. There is general agreement that Sariel is the earlier reading. So Black, *1 Enoch*, 129; and Milik, *Books*, 172-173.

[17] For example, 1QM 9.14-16; *SibOr.* II.214ff; *ApMoses* 40.2; *3Bar.* 4.7 (Slavonic version) and *GkApEzra* 6.1-2.

[18] So the Ethiopic version and the duplicate portion of the Greek Gizeh MS. The main text of the latter MS is corrupt and misses out Remiel and, consequently, lists only six archangels even though it concludes with ἀρχαγγέλων ὀνόματα ἑπτά.

[19] Albeit with an important variant: Sariel/Uriel has been replaced by "Phanuel" (cf. e.g., *1En.* 40).

[20] The *Animal Apocalypse* probably dates from c. 165-160 BC, as the career of Judas Maccabeus appears to be the last datable event referred to in it. Cf. Tiller, *Animal Apocalypse*, 62-79; Milik, *Books*, 44; Black, *1 Enoch*, 19-20; Charles, *1 Enoch*, 208; Rowland, *Open Heaven*, 252.

work's early chapters are clearly based on *1En.* 9-10.[21] Thus, while the author of the *Animal Apocalypse* inherited the tradition of four archangels from his source, he himself must have accepted the tradition of seven archangels, for he expands the four to seven. He even distinguishes the original four from the additional three: "...and behold there came forth from heaven beings who were like white men, and four went forth from that place, and three with them" (*1En.* 87.2).[22] In what follows, the first four parallel the actions of Michael, Raphael, Gabriel and Sariel/Uriel in *1En.* 9-10, while the other three archangels simply effect the ascension of Enoch. The *Animal Apocalypse*, then, bears witness to a transition from four archangels to seven.[23] However, the fact that the later *Similitudes*,[24] accepts the apparently older tradition of four archangels shows that the development from four to seven was by no means a universal one.[25]

c. Angels and Humanity

1) Agents of Revelation

In keeping with the purpose of apocalyptic literature, angels often function in the apocalypses as agents of revelation. This can take a number of

---

[21] So Charles *1 Enoch*, 189; Black, *1 Enoch*, 261-262; and Milik, *Books*, 43. Cf. Davidson (*Angels*, 102).

[22] Black's translation.

[23] Cf. also the four living creatures (4.6b-8) and the seven spirits before the throne of God (1.4, 4.5) in Revelation.

[24] The developing consensus in scholarship date the *Similitudes* to the first century AD. See Black (*1 Enoch*, 183-188); Isaac ("1 Enoch", *OTP* I.6-7); Fitzmyer ("Implications", 332-345); Knibb ("Date", 345-359). Cf. also Charles (*1 Enoch*, liv-lvi).

[25] The tradition is only *apparently* older; both traditions are already present in the *Book of Watchers*.

One other very early text which may testify to a tradition of seven archangels appears in the enochic *Astronomical Book* (*1En* 81.5). There Enoch records that seven or three "holy ones" returned him to earth after his tour of heaven. One text-type of Ethiopic MSS reads "seven" (Eth. I), while the other reads "three" (Eth. II). The larger number may very well be due to the influence of the text of the *Animal Apocalypse* (esp. *1En.* 87.2, 90.21-22) or even of *1En.* 20. On the other hand, the other reading, "three", could have been influenced by the text of the *Animal Apocalypse* as well. Since in that text it is three archangels who are responsible for Enoch's ascension into heaven, a scribe could have assumed that those three archangels also returned him to earth. Black is correct when he says that "either reading could be original" (*1 Enoch*, 253).

different forms. In some documents an *angelus interpres* serves as guide through the various heavens (*2En.* 1.3-10; *TAbr.* 10-15 A, 8-12 B; *ApAbr.* 15-18) or to the untravelled ends of the earth (*1En.* 17-36). In other works, an interpreting angel explains the significance of dreams or visions (Dan. 7.16-18, 8.15-16; 4 Ezra, *passim*).

2) Guardians of the Nations

As we have seen, the belief that angels were set over the nations was already current in OT times.[26] This concept takes two forms in the Jewish apocalypses. On the one hand, while the author of *Jubilees* assumes that angels were set over the nations, he affirms that the Lord did not turn Israel over to a guardian angel, but kept her for Himself (15.31-32; cf. Sir. 17.17). In other works (e.g., Dan. 10.13, 21, 12.1; *1En.* 89-90) Michael is Israel's guardian angel. As we shall see, this latter form predominates in the apocalypses. Indeed, even in *Jubilees* a close relation between Israel and the Angel of the Presence is presumed (1.29; 48.1-19).

There is evidence that already during the second and first centuries BC this concept of angelic guardians was beginning to expand to include guardian angels of individuals. The idea of angels assigned to individuals unambiguously appears in Ps-Philo's *LAB* (11.12, 15.5, 59.4) and *3 Baruch* (11-16), works which probably date from the first and second centuries AD respectively. A possible earlier reference to angelic guardians of individuals is found in *Jub.* 35.17. There we are told that "guardian of Jacob is greater and more powerful, glorious, and praiseworthy then Esau's guardian".[27] It is difficult to decide whether this pertains to Jacob and Esau as individuals, as fathers of nations, or both at once. From the perspective of the Second Temple period Jewish readers of *Jubilees*, the second and third options are more probable than the first. It would have been very natural for them to have understood Jacob's individual guardian as their guardian.[28] However, as we have just seen according to *Jub.* 15.31-32, Israel was not assigned to an angelic guardian, for God kept that privilege for Himself. Either the author is here making the rather obvious statement that God is greater than the angel he assigned to be over Esau/Edom or he has simply contradicted himself. The later seems the more likely option. Thus, we

---

[26] See above pp. 18-19.
[27] VanderKam's translation.
[28] Cf. Charles, *Jubilees*, 209.

have here a slip, but a slip which testifies to a belief in a guardian angel of the nation who also served as the guardian of the father of the nation.[29]

3) Intercessors and the Heavenly Cultus

In the Second Temple period there was a great deal of speculation about a heavenly temple and cult which served as the pattern for the temple and cult in Jerusalem (*2Bar.* 4.1-6; *Jub.* 31.14). The basis for this idea is very possibly to be found in the OT tradition that the altar and tabernacle were made according to heavenly models (Ex. 25.9, 40; Num. 8.4).[30] Related to this is the widespread tradition and common presupposition that angels served as intercessors for humanity. Such intercession often presupposes a cultic setting (*TLevi* 3.5-6; *3Bar.* 11-16; *ApMoses* 33.4-5), but not always (*1En.* 9.2-3; 15.2; 99.3; *Vita Adae* 9.3 = *ApMoses* 29.16).[31]

4) Angelic Psychopomps

The motif that angels actively transferred the soul of the righteous from earth to heaven or paradise at death is found in a wide variety of ancient Jewish and Christian writings.[32] It is also common to apocalyptic and related works (the lost ending of *AssMos.*; *TJob* 52; *TAbr.* A 19-20; B 14.7; *ApMos.* 37).

---

[29] Cf. also *1En.* 100.5; however, this passage, as Charles (*1 Enoch*, 249) points out, probably only refers to angelic guardians of the souls of the righteous who have died and not to living individuals.

[30] So Charles, *Testaments*, 33.

[31] The idea of a heavenly sanctuary also occurs in the literature of Qumran, in Rabbinic literature, and in Christian literature. For Qumran see below pp. 60-61; for Rabbinic literature see below pp. 100-102; for Christian literature see below pp. 124-125, 135, and 166-167.

[32] E.g., *HistRech.* 14-16; Luke 16.22; *bKet* 104b.

3. Michael in Jewish Apocalyptic Literature

I turn now to specific Michael traditions in Jewish apocalyptic and related literature. I will begin with the theme of Michael's special relationship to Israel as her protector and angelic champion. A discussion of his intercession for Israel follows naturally from this, as does the motif of his service in the heavenly sanctuary. Related to this high priestly office is the tradition that Michael was the angelic psychopomp *par excellence*. Finally, I will move on to evidence which suggests that Michael was increasingly identified as the highest archangel during the Second Temple period in apocalyptic literature, and to the related, but limited, evidence for Michael as the angel of the Name.

The earliest reference to Michael in any extant Jewish writing is found in the *Book of Watchers* (= *1En.* 1-36), followed by that in the Book of Daniel. In neither work is Michael's appearance accompanied by an explanation or introduction. Since both authors assume their readers know who Michael and the other named angels are,[33] it may be concluded that the traditions about Michael, and the other named angels, are older than the late third century B.C., the latest possible date for chapters 6-16 of the *Book of Watchers*.[34] The precise origin of Michael and other named angel traditions is a matter of much speculation, but falls outside the scope of this study.[35]

a. Special Relation with Israel

1) Angelic Guardian of Israel

The *Book of Watchers* and Daniel, while differing in many particulars, both assume a close relation between the archangel and Israel. *1 Enoch* 20, for example, gives a list of the seven archangels, their functions and

---

[33] Cf. Goldingay, *Daniel*, 292, who points out that "Michael" (מיכאל, "who is like God") refers to humans elsewhere in the OT: Num. 13.13; Ezra 8.8; 1 Chr. 5.13f, 6.40, 7.3, 8.16, 12.20, 27.18, 2 Chr. 21.2. All of these, except perhaps Num. 13.13, clearly date from the post-exilic period.

[34] Black, *1 Enoch*, 14; Milik, *Books*, 25.

[35] A Babylonian or Persian connection is often assumed. Cf. Dix, "Seven Archangels"; and Russell, *Method*, 235, 257-262. Note the rabbinic tradition, attributed to R. Simeon b. Laqish [A2] (*pRH* 1.2.54d; *GenR.* 48.9), that the Jews brought back the names of the angels from Babylon.

responsibilities. Although the Greek and Ethiopic versions of the verse about Michael (20.5) differ, and both occasion certain difficulties, the general sense is plain: Michael is the archangel or Watcher responsible for Israel. The Ethiopic version is usually translated "Michael, one of the holy angels, namely the one put in charge of the best part of mankind, in charge of the nation",[36] while the Greek text reads Μιχαήλ, ὁ εἷς τῶν ἁγίων ἀγγέλων ὁ ἐπὶ τῶν τοῦ λαοῦ ἀγαθῶν τεταγμένος καὶ ἐπὶ τῷ χαῷ (vs.5).[37] In keeping with Biblical usage, τοῦ λαοῦ refers to the People of Israel.[38] This same role is attributed to Michael in the Book of Daniel. In 10.21 Daniel is told, "There is no one with me who contends against these princes (i.e., of Persia and Greece) except Michael your Prince" and in 12.1 he is described as Israel's protector.

Another text of importance here is Daniel 7.13-14. The "one like a son of man" who received dominion and an everlasting kingdom may have been originally intended as a reference to the archangel Michael.[39] It is now generally accepted that the phrase "son of man" is an idiom for "a human being".[40] This is undoubtedly the sense in which it should be taken in

---

[36] So Knibb, *Enoch*, 107. Cf. Charles, *1 Enoch*, 43.

[37] The Greek Gizeh MS of the first 32 chapters of *1En.* contains a duplicate of 19.3-21.9. This duplicate at 20.5 reads: Μιχαήλ, ὁ εἷς τῶν ἁγίων ἀγγέλων ὃς ἐπὶ τῶν τοῦ λαοῦ ἀγαθῶν τέτακται καὶ ἐπὶ τῷ χαῷ.

[38] The final phrase, καὶ ἐπὶ τῷ χαῷ, is difficult, for it conflicts with 20.2, where Uriel is the angel over Tartarus, and a number of emendations have been proposed. The most interesting of these is that of Zimmermann (*Tobit*, 150) who suggested emending χαῷ to ναῷ. This would give the sense that Michael is over Israel and the temple. As we shall see later in this chapter (pp. 43-46), Michael was thought to serve as high priest in the heavenly temple. If Zimmermann is correct, *1En.* 20.5 would be an early expression of this tradition.

[39] Collins has revived this suggestion in a series of publications. See Collins, "Son of Man"; idem, *Apocalyptic Vision*, 123-147; idem, *Daniel*, 308-310, 318-319. For earlier commentators who argued for this position or variations of it see Collins, *Apocalyptic Vision*, 149, n.7. Those who have followed Collins include Lacocque, *Daniel*, 133-134; Rowland, *Open Heaven*, 178-182; and Hurtado, *One God, One Lord*, 77.

Traditionally, this figure was identified as the Messiah. This has been all but rejected by modern scholarship as "the product of Christian interpretation, in the light of the NT" (Collins, *Apocalyptic Vision*, 124). For a recent defense of this "traditional" position see Beasley-Murray, "Interpretation of Daniel 7", 44-58. The majority view among twentieth century critics is that which identifies the "one like a son of man" as a collective figure for the faithful Jews, i.e., the "saints of the Most High". E.g., Charles, *Daniel*, 187-188; Montgomery, *Daniel*, 319-320; Porteous, *Daniel*, 112; Hartman and DiLella, *Daniel*, 218-219; Mowinckel, *He That Cometh*, 350; Hooker, *Son of Man*, 24-30; Wright, *People of God*, 291-297.

[40] Cf. Ps. 8.4, 80.18; Job 16.21; Ezek. 2.1, *passim.* and Dan. 8.17. See Vermes, "בר נשא/נש", 310-30; Goldingay, *Daniel*, 145; Collins, *Apocalyptic Vision*, 124; idem, *Daniel*, 304-305.

Daniel 7.13. It is a common place in Jewish apocalyptic works that angels can be described as humans, and this is the practice of the Book of Daniel (8.15, 9.21, 10.5, 12.5-7). Thus the author of Daniel may very well have intended that this "one like a son of man" be understood as an angel.[41] Since the interpretation of the vision in 7.18 does not identify the human figure, but rather speaks of the kingdom being given to "the saints of the Most High" (קדישי עליונין), the interpretation of the human figure and that of the saints belong together. In the OT, "holy ones" (Hebrew קדשים; Aramaic קדישין) often refers to angelic beings.[42] If, therefore, "the saints of the Most High", stands for the angelic host, then on the basis of 7.18 the "one like a son of man" in 7.13 can only be either a symbolic figure who represents the angelic host or their leader. The latter is better, given 1) the identification of the four beasts with four kings (7.17) and 2) Michael's prominence in chapters 10-12.[43] The fact that the visions in Dan. 7 and 8, and the angelic discourse of 10-12 are parallel accounts of the same historical events supports this identification. For in 8.10-11 and 11.36 the figure which represents Antiochus Epiphanes is said to do battle with the heavenly hosts, and, in the case of 11.36, this occasions the arrival of Michael in 12.1. The "one like a son of man", then, was probably intended as a reference to Michael.[44] Moreover, since there exists a close connnection in Daniel between the angelic host and the people of Israel (12.3, cf. 12.7), it is probable that Michael is here not just the leader of the heavenly host but also Israel's guardian. The phrase, "the people of the saints of the Most High" (7.27), is to be understood in this light. Michael's reception, then, of the eternal kingdom signals Israel's redemption.[45]

---

[41] The *Animal Apocalypse* provides an important parallel here. In this work humans appear as animals and angels as humans. Similarly, the four beasts in Daniel's vision stand for four kings or kingdoms (7.17). By comparison, then, this human figure could represent an angel.

[42] Collins, *Daniel*, 313-314.

[43] But note Collins' (*Apocalyptic Vision*, 144) qualification that "the leader represents the collective unit in any case, and there is considerable fluidity between the two".

[44] Goldingay (*Daniel*, 171-172) has objected, arguing that since the "son of man" figure is not identified in the text his identity is not a matter of concern for the author. It is his role that the Seer wishes to emphasize. While this latter point is undoubtedly so, the former does not necessarily follow. Goldingay's argument that "later chapters must not be read back into this one" is odd, especially in light of the obvious relation between the dream of chapter 2 and the vision of chapter 7. Given that chapters 7 and 8-12 deal with the same crisis, they must surely be read and interpreted together.

[45] Horbury ("Messianic associations"), however, has demonstrated that the Messianic interpretation of Dan. 7 was early and widespread. Cf. also Collins, *Daniel*, 306-308; and Slater, "One Like a Son of Man". Thus the understanding of Michael as the "one like a son of man" was soon lost, either entirely or nearly so. The vision of Daniel 7 does not appear to have played a significant role in later Michael speculation, unless the close relationship between Michael and the royal Messiah at Qumran owes something to speculation

Michael's guardianship over Israel is probably also attested in the so-called *Animal Apocalypse*. In accordance with the literary strategy of this work, Michael is never named.[46] This apocalypse recounts the history of Israel as an allegory in which humans are described as animals and angels as humans. Consequently, none of the OT figures, either human or angelic, are ever named. However, the *Animal Apocalypse*, as stated above, is clearly dependent upon the *Book of Watchers*, especially *1En.* 9-10. There the story is told of the fallen Watchers who corrupted humanity and of God's intervention through the agency of Michael, Sariel/Uriel, Raphael, and Gabriel. Each of these four archangels is commissioned with different tasks, including the capture of the Watchers and their bastard children and the preparation of Noah. The *Animal Apocalypse* clearly recasts this story. The four archangels, expanded to seven, become "seven white men" (*1En.* 87-89.1). The three new archangels effect Enoch's translation, while the other four fulfill missions parallel to those described in *1En.* 9-10. Michael's mission is described in 88.3, Raphael's and Gabriel's in 88.1-2, and Sariel's in 89.1.

Later, after the *Animal Apocalypse* has left the *Book of Watchers* source, it focuses on one of the four white men. Again, as with all the characters in this apocalypse, this archangel is never identified, but in all probability represents Michael. The exile is depicted by the lord of the sheep (i.e., God) turning the sheep (i.e., Israel) over to seventy Shepherds (i.e., the seventy angels over the nations).[47] However, God also appoints "a Watcher, one of the seven white ones,"[48] to "observe and mark everything that the shepherds will do to those sheep; for they will destroy from among them more than I have commanded them" (89.61). This angel's continual activity of recording the actions of the shepherds and his intercession for the sheep is described in 89.68-76. This angelic figure appears again in 90.14-22, which corresponds to the events of the Maccabean revolt. In

---

on Daniel 7. See below pp. 65-66.

[46] See below pp. 43-44, 50 and 67-68, where I argue that the links between the author of the *Animal Apocalypse* and the Qumran sect may offer another, complementary, explanation for the absence of angel names.

[47] So Davidson, *Angels*, 98, 108-109; Black, *1 Enoch*, 270f; and Charles, *1 Enoch*, 200. *Contra* Carr, *Angels and Principalities*, 31-32.

[48] Black's (*1 Enoch*, 271) restoration of the text. The Eth. MSS all read "And He called another, and said to him...". Black thinks that 'another' may have arisen due to confusion of חור (white) with אחרן (another) and that due to homoioteleuton a clear identification of this figure dropped out. Black believes the original would then have read: ויקרא לעירא חד מן שבע חורין. In any case, 90.22 clearly identifies this "other" as one of the seven white ones.

these verses he functions as the angelic protector of Israel. Most commentators agree that 90.14 is a reference to the events recorded in 1 Macc. 4.30-35, especially as it is developed in 2 Macc. 11.6-12, where an angel clothed in white and bearing golden arms fights for Israel.[49] In 90.17 the angel shows the records of the deeds of the shepherds to God, which results in the destruction of the enemies of Israel. After this follows the final judgement. This same angel, "one of those seven white ones", delivers the seventy shepherds to God for judgement in the heavenly court (90.21-22).

Most commentators, with good reason, identify this angelic figure with Michael.[50] To begin with, it is more likely that this figure is one of the four named archangels whose missions parallel Michael's, Gabriel's, Raphael's, and Sariel's in *1En.* 9-10 than one of the three who effect Enoch's translation, for the four appear to be more important to our author than the three. If the author of the *Animal Apocalypse* knew *1En.* 20.5, which is not unlikely as he certainly knew and used other portions of the *Book of Watchers*, an identification with Michael would be certain, for this "white man" acts as Israel's guardian and champion. Finally, and most importantly, a comparison of 88.3 with 90.22-25 suggests that both passages refer to the same angel. The fallen angels bound by Michael in 88.3 are in 90.24-25 judged along with the shepherds captured by this angelic figure. The action of this figure has resulted in the judgement of both the fallen angels and the shepherds.[51]

Another example of Michael as the angelic guardian of Israel may be found in the *Assumption of Moses*. This apocryphon speaks of the angel or messenger (*nuntius*) who will arise at the time of the Kingdom of God and of Satan's demise, and will avenge Israel against her enemies (10.2). Because this parallels Daniel 12.1, many commentators assume that this is a reference to Michael.[52] Further support for such an identification may be found in the phrase "his hands will be filled" (*implebuntur manus*). In Ex. 28.41, 29.9; Lev. 21.10; and *TLevi* 8.10, this phrase (מלא יד = πληροῦν τὰς χείρας) is a circumlocution for priestly ordination and, as we shall see, at least some in Jewish apocalyptic circles held Michael to be the priest of

---

[49] So Black, *1 Enoch*, 277; Charles, *1 Enoch*, 211; Davidson, *Angels*, 100, 105-106, 109-110; and Milik, *Books*, 44.

[50] Charles, *1 Enoch*, 201, 211, 213; Hengel, *Judaism and Hellenism*, 188; Russell, *Method*, 201; Davidson, *Angels*, 109; Torrey, "Michael", 208-211; and tentatively, Black, *1 Enoch*, 271. Tiller (*Animal Apocalypse*, 326) opposes this identification. See the next note.

[51] Tiller's objection that tasks different from Michael's in 88.3 are given to this angelic figure, misses this parallel.

[52] So Charles, *Assumption*, 39; Rowley, *Relevance*, 94; and Lueken, *Michael*, 25.

the heavenly sanctuary. This identification, however, is not without difficulties. The extant text does not contain a single additional reference to an angel. Recently, Tromp has made a case for reading 10.2 as a reference to the mysterious Taxo of chapter 9.[53] In this reading, Taxo does not suddenly drop out of sight after chapter 9, and the *nuntius* of 10.2 does not appear with no connection with what has preceded. However, given that a large portion of the original text is no longer extant,[54] we cannot be sure that this is such an isolated reference. Indeed, there is evidence that Michael plays a significant role in the lost ending.[55] The question, then, cannot be decided at our current state of knowledge with any certainty, but a reference to Michael at 10.2 is not unlikely.

Finally, many commentators have suggested that the unnamed angel of *TLevi* 5.1-6 and *TDan* 6.2-7 might be Michael.[56] We will have occasion to return to these texts when we examine the traditions surrounding Michael as Israel's heavenly intercessor. For now it is sufficient to note this unnamed angel's singular relation with Israel, which parallels that of Michael in *1En.* 20.5 and the Book of Daniel.

2) *Leader of the Heavenly Hosts ('Αρχιστράτηγος)*

Clearly, then, the tradition of Michael as Israel's angelic champion and guardian was well established in the apocalypses. Given the crisis setting of much of this literature, it is not surprising that Michael's role as Israel's angelic guardian is usually expressed in military language. In Daniel 10.13, 20-21 he battles (להלחם; מתחזק) against the 'prince of the kingdom of Persia' so that the unnamed glorious angel will not be hindered in his mission to reveal the future to Daniel. In Dan. 12.1 he appears just before the final eschatological crisis as the "protector" of Israel.[57] In the *Animal*

---

[53] Tromp, "Taxo"; and idem, *Assumption*, 229-231.

[54] Priest ("Testament", *OTP* I.919) estimates that a third to half the original may be lost.

[55] See below pp. 38-39.

[56] Charles, *Testaments*, 39, 132; Hollander and de Jonge, *Testaments* 145. Cf. also Hurtado, *One God*, 29 and 140, n.44; Kee, *OTP* I.790, n.5d; and Lueken, *Michael*, 92-95.

[57] הָעֹמֵד עַל is, to be sure, ambiguous. Lacocque (*Daniel*, 240) suggests three possible meanings: 1) "to lead as chief"; 2) "to protect or defend"; and, tentatively, 3) "to judge". Porteous (*Daniel*, 149) prefers the first option, but he is the only commentator I have found who does so. Those who opt for the second include, Collins (*Daniel*, 390); Goldingay (*Daniel*, 274); Montgomery (*Daniel*, 470, 472); and Charles (*Daniel*, 325).

Apocalypse (*1En.* 90.14), Michael comes to the aid of Judas Maccabeus in battle.

Related to this tendency to cast Michael as the Protector of Israel is the tradition that he was the angelic commander of the heavenly armies. This is not explicitly stated in the Book of Daniel, but may be implied in 12.1. It seems, however, to be firmly established in the *War Scroll* from Qumran, written perhaps half a century after Daniel,[58] and appears again even later in the Christian canonical Apocalypse (Rev. 12.7). In keeping with this role of leader of the heavenly armies, the title Ἀρχιστράτηγος (Commander-in-chief) came to be applied to Michael. This is clearly a favorite title for Michael in numerous Jewish apocalypses, even in works which portray little or no interest in its military significance, e.g., *3 Baruch*,[59] *2 Enoch*,[60] and the *Testament of Abraham*.[61] Michael never functions as a military commander in either *3 Baruch* or *2 Enoch*, and this theme plays only a very minor role in the *Testament of Abraham* (2.4-5 A). The only extant use of the title for an angel other than Michael in Jewish apocalyptic literature is the *Greek Apocalypse of Ezra* (1.4), where it is used for Raphael.[62]

Since *3 Baruch*, *2 Enoch*, and the *Testament of Abraham* are usually dated to the first or second centuries A.D.,[63] their combined witness proba-

---

[58] Previous scholarship argued for the end of the first century BC as the date for the *War Scroll*. So e.g., Vermes, *DSS in English*, 124; Yadin, *Scroll*, 245-246; and Lohse, *Texte*, 178. However, more recent scholarship now places it in the late second century BC. Cf. Davidson, *Angels*, 213; Dimant, "Sectarian Literature," 516.

[59] 11.4, 6, 7, 8. Only the Greek version uses the title; it does not appear in the Slavonic. However, note that in 13.3 of the Slavonic the guardian angels of the unrighteous address Michael as "our chief".

[60] 22.6 (LR); 33.10 (LR). However, in 22.6 the short recension replaces the long recension's "the Lord's Archistratig" with "the Lord's greatest Archangel".

[61] While the title appears throughout Rec. A, in Rec. B ὁ ἀρχιστράτηγος appears only once (14.6) and even here there is significant disagreement among the MSS.

[62] *GkApEzra* is a late (second century or later) composition and is certainly Christian in its present form, but appears to have a Jewish substratum. Cf. Stone, "Greek Apocalypse of Ezra", *OTP* I.562.

[63] Dating *2 Enoch* is notoriously difficult. Charles (Morfill and Charles, *Secrets*, xxvii) dates the book to the period 1-50 A.D.; Rubinstein ("Observations", 19-20) argues for post 70 A.D., while Andersen in one publication ("2 Enoch", *OTP* I.94-97) very tentatively suggests the late first century, but in another ("Enoch, Second Book of", *ABD* II.517-522) refrains from offering a suggestion.

Concerning *3 Baruch*, Gaylord ("3 Baruch", *OTP* I.655-656) suggests the first two centuries A.D., Nickelsburg (*Jewish Literature*, 303) opts for the end of the first century or beginning of the second, as does Harlow (*Apocalypse of Baruch*, 14) and, albeit very tentatively, Argyle ("Greek Apocalypse of Baruch," *AOT*.900).

For the *Testament of Abraham*, Sanders dates the original work which underlies both recensions to "c. A.D. 100, plus or minus twenty-five years" ("Testament of Abraham",

bly indicates that the title's association with Michael dates from an earlier period. Interpreters often assume that the basis for attributing this title to Michael is the ἀρχιστράτηγος δυνάμεως κυρίου of Joshua 5.13-15 (LXX).[64] Indeed, some ancient Christian commentators identified this ἀρχιστράτηγος with Michael (Origen, *PG* 12.821 and Aphraates, *Dem.* 3.14),[65] and it is probable that they derived this exegesis from earlier Jewish commentators.[66] In addition, given Michael's importance and military role in the Book of Daniel, it is altogether possible that the Greek translators of Daniel, both LXX and Theodotion, understood the ἀρχιστράτηγος of 8.11 to refer to Michael.[67]

Michael's office, then, of Israel's angelic patron and guardian occasioned his being cast in the similar role of commander of the heavenly armies or ἀρχιστράτηγος. This is implied in Daniel, explicit in the *War Scroll*, and already traditional by time of *2 Enoch*, *3 Baruch*, and the *Testament of Abraham*.[68]

3) Israel's Legal Advocate and Opponent of Satan

Above I assumed a military nuance for the phrase העמד על־בני עמך ("the protector of your people"; Dan. 12.1). However, Collins argues for a judi-

---

OTP I.875). Delcor (*Testament*, 76) dates the book to the beginning of the first century A.D. Cf. also Turner ("Testament of Abraham", *AOT*.395), who cites Delcor approvingly.

[64] So Delcor, *Testament*, 91; Philonenko, *Joseph et Aseneth*, 178; Hurtado, *One God*, 20; and Sanders, "Testament of Abraham," *OTP* I.882, n.1c.

[65] For the Christian use of this title for both Michael and Christ, see below pp. 148-149, 165-166.

[66] Both these texts (Origen *PG* 12.821 and Aphraates *Dem.* 3.14) share themes with Rabbinic exegesis of Josh. 5.13-15 (cf. *GenR* 97.3; *ExodR* 32.2-3); see below p. 165. For Aphraates' knowledge of Jewish haggadic traditions, cf. Snaith, "Aphrahat"; and Neusner, *Aphrahat*.

[67] So also Lueken, *Michael*, 26-27.

Cf. also the angelic figure of *Joseph and Aseneth* 14.8. Many scholars assume this figure is Michael on the basis of the title ἀρχιστράτηγος. So Burchard, "Joseph and Aseneth," *OTP* Vol. 2, 225, n.14k; Delcor, *Testament*, 52; and Philonenko, *Joseph et Aseneth*, 178.

[68] Rohland's attempt (*Michael*, 9-25, 34-42) to argue that the use of the title ἀρχιστράτηγος for Michael is late and limited to Christian sources and manuscripts simply ignores the fact that Michael already *acts* as the angelic commander-in-chief in early Jewish works (1QM 17.6-8, Dan. 10.21, 12.1), even when the title itself is not used.

cial understanding, appealing to Daniel 7.13-14 with its legal context.[69] It is, perhaps, best to allow the term to remain ambiguous; Michael's protection of Israel could be understood both militarily and judicially. In any case, another example of Michael as Israel's legal advocate can found in the "white man" of the *Animal Apocalypse* pleading Israel's case against the evil shepherds before "the Lord of the Sheep" (89.70-77, 90.17).

The lost ending of the *Assumption of Moses*, as attested in Jude 9, apparently portrayed Michael contesting Satan's legal claim over the body of Moses. The *Assumption of Moses* has come down to us in only one manuscript, an incomplete Latin palimpsest. The ending is clearly missing. Origen, in *Princ.* iii.2.1, ascribes the story alluded to in Jude 9, about Michael and Satan arguing over the body of Moses, to the "*Ascensione Moysi*". Given Origen's general precision in quoting Scripture, a great deal of weight should be given this testimony. It is further supported by Gelasius Cyzicenus in his *Ecclesiastical History* (ii.21.7).[70] Gelasius' statement is sufficiently different from Origen's to insure that he is an independent witness. Later Patristic and Byzantine sources indirectly support this attribution,[71] but Origen and Gelasius are the earliest and most important. They give us sufficient reason to conclude that the now lost ending of the *Assumption* once told of a dispute between the archangel Michael and Satan over the body of Moses.[72] However, in the fragments of this lost ending two apparently conflicting presentations of the debate between the Archangel and the Accuser over the body of Moses are given. In one set of texts Satan claims that since Moses is a murderer, the body belongs to him. The other texts seemingly present Satan as a gnostic demiurge who demands Moses' body because he is the Lord of Matter. Bauckham has plausibly conjectured that these two groups of texts derive from two different versions of the same story: the former, which was also Jude's source, from the *Testament*, the latter from the *Assumption*.[73] Due to the fragmentary nature of our evidence it must be admitted that, while this is plausible, it is not demonstrable.[74] Nonetheless, as Bauckham points out,[75]

---

[69] Collins, *Daniel*, 390. So also Rohland, *Michael*, 10-14, who too quickly dismisses a military understanding.

[70] Quoted in Tromp, *Assumption*, 272.

[71] These are conveniently printed in Bauckham, *Jude*, 249-264.

[72] So also, in the main, Tromp, *Assumption*, 270-275; Charles, *Assumption*, 105-110; and Bauckham, *Jude. 2 Peter*, 73-76; idem, *Jude*, 235-280. However, to be sure, there are differences between these scholars.

[73] Bauckham, *Jude*, 238-270.

[74] Cf. J. Neyrey, *2 Peter, Jude*, 65-66.

[75] Bauckham, *Jude*, 245-246, 250-254.

Michael's response to Satan, "The Lord rebuke you", quoted from Zech. 3.2 where it appears in a judicial setting, fits well with those texts which place the legal claim to Moses' body on Satan's lips. Therefore, it is reasonable, if not demonstrable, that the dispute between Michael and Satan in the text cited by Jude reflected a legal contest between Michael and Satan.[76]

This pairing of Michael and Satan as opponents also occurs in a non-judicial setting in a legend which has been preserved in a number of sources, Jewish,[77] Christian,[78] and Muslim.[79] In this legend Michael, at God's behest, stands the newly created Adam before the heavenly hosts and orders the angels to worship him as the image of God. Many do, but Satan refuses for he asserts that he was created first and therefore Adam should worship him. Michael continues to urge him, but Satan flatly refuses. The angels under Satan also refuse to worship Adam. Satan arrogantly claims that he will set his throne above God's. Then, Satan and his angels are cast out of heaven.[80] In anger he seduces Adam and Eve to sin and thus brings about their fall just as they brought about his.

Thus, the evidence for Michael as the military protector of Israel, as well as her legal champion, is widespread and multifaceted. It appears that his role as Israel's military guardian led to the office of heavenly ἀρχιστράτηγος being attributed to him, while his judicial advocacy for Israel developed into the traditional role of Satan's opponent.

b. Israel's Intercessor and Heavenly High Priest

Related to Michael's office of advocate for Israel is the task of intercession for the nation and for individuals, a task which he shares with other angels. Numerous examples could be cited. In *1 Enoch* 9 he intercedes alongside Gabriel, Raphael, and Sariel/Uriel for humanity suffering under the Watchers. He prays for individual souls at Abraham's request in the

---

[76] Cf. also 4Q'Amram where a good and evil angel dispute over 'Amram. See below pp. 72-73, where I examine the evidence for identifying the good angel with Michael.

[77] *Vita Adae* 12-16; the Armenian *Penitence of Adam* 12-16; the Georgian *Book of Adam* 12-16; and Rabbi Mosheh ha-Darshan (according to Wells in *APOT* II.137, n.xii.1; Rabbi Mosheh ha-Darshan dates from the 11th century). Cf. *ApMos.* 39.2-3.

[78] *QuestBart.* 4.52-55; *Discourse on Abbatôn* (= Budge, *Coptic Martyrdoms*, pp. 225-249, 474-496) pp. 234-235, 483-484; *Cave of Treasures*, Budge, pp. 52-56; *ApSedr.* 5.

[79] The Qur'an, suras 7.11-22; 15.26-44; 38.71-85.

[80] Cf. Rev. 12.7.

Testament of Abraham (14.5-6, 12ff A) and, in the *Similitudes* (*1En.* 68.2-5), refuses to intercede for the Watchers.[81]

This picture of Michael as an angelic Intercessor may be reflected in two significant passages from the *Testament of the Twelve Patriarchs*, neither of which expressly mentions Michael. The first of these is *TLevi* 5.3-7. Chapters 2-5 record Levi's journey through the heavens,[82] his vision of God in the highest heaven, the bestowal of the priesthood, and his return to earth. At the end of the vision, the angel gives Levi a sword and shield and commissions him to take vengeance on Shechem. Levi then asks the angel his name, that he might petition him "in the day of tribulation" (5.5). The angel responds: "I am the angel who makes intercession for the nation Israel, that they might not be beaten".[83] Levi then awakes from his dream and blesses "the Most High [and the angel who intercedes for the nation of Israel and all the righteous]".[84]

As in *Jubilees* and the *Animal Apocalypse*, no angels are mentioned by name in the *Testaments*. Significantly, fragments of the first two works and fragments of works closely related to the Greek *Testaments* have been found at Qumran and all three works share a number of parallels with the literature of Qumran.[85] As we shall see, the sectarian writings of Qumran also reflect a certain reluctance to name angels. I will argue below[86] that the sectarian hesitancy was intentional. If this is correct, it is possible that the absence of named angels in all three documents is, as at Qumran, ideological. Therefore, the lack of the name "Michael" here should not keep us from concluding that he is in view. Indeed, a tradition recorded in *PRE* 37 and Targ. Ps.-Jon. Gen. 32.25 identifies the angel who led Levi to heaven to receive the priesthood with Michael. Admittedly, these witnesses are late, but the similarity with *TLevi* is striking.[87] However, it must be

---

[81] According to the majority of Ethiopic MSS. However, this text is not certain. Cf. Black, *1 Enoch*, 244.

[82] The α-text describes three heavens, the β-text seven.

[83] Ἐγώ εἰμι ὁ ἄγγελος ὁ παραιτούμενος τοῦ γένους Ἰσραήλ, τοῦ μὴ πατάξαι αὐτούς. So the β-text (with some witness of the α-text). The α-text, on the other hand substitutes ὁ παρεπόμενος for ὁ παραιτούμενος.

These same variants, with the same supporting witnesses, appear in *TDan* 6.2.

[84] This last phrase is omitted by the α-text.

[85] For *Jubilees*' relation with Qumran see VanderKam, *Textual and Historical*, 255-285. For the *Animal Apocalypse*, see Tiller, *Animal Apocalypse*, 102-116. For the *Testaments*, cf. Hollander and de Jonge, *Testaments*, 23-25. Note that Boccaccini (*Beyond the Essene Hypothesis*) locates all three works in Enochic/Essene Judaism, out of which the Qumran sect grew.

[86] Pp. 67-68.

[87] Cf. Hollander and de Jonge, *Testaments*, 145.

admitted that certainty is not possible; the identification of this angel with Michael in *PRE* and Targ. Ps.-Jon. could reflect a later stage in the development of the tradition. On the other hand, it could be a case of the later texts faithfully recording what was in the tradition, but was omitted in *TLevi*, especially given the fact that the Greek *Testaments of the Twelve Patriarchs* appear to purposely avoid naming angels.

In a related passage, the patriarch Dan instructs his children concerning, apparently, the same angel: "Draw near to God and to the angel who intercedes for you, because he is the mediator between God and men for the peace of Israel. He shall stand in opposition to the kingdom of the enemy" (*TDan.* 6.2). Three verses later this angel is further identified as ὁ ἄγγελος τῆς εἰρήνης. Some have thought this passage suspect. It certainly is very similar to 1 Tim. 2.5: Εἷς γάρ θεός, εἷς καὶ μεσίτης θεοῦ καὶ ἀνθρώπων, ἄνθρωπος Χριστὸς Ἰησοῦς. Hollander and de Jonge, who believe the *Testaments* is essentially a Christian work, view this passage as evidence of a primitive angel Christology.[88] Hurtado would rather describe the phrase which parallels 1 Tim. 2.5 as a Christian interpolation. While this is certainly possible, there is nothing specifically Christian about the passage. As we have seen, an angelic mediator between God and humanity could appear in Jewish as well as Christian works.[89] If the phrase "mediator between God and men" is not rejected as an interpolation, then it may reflect the tradition that Michael was a heavenly mediator for humanity in general.[90]

Parallel with this role of heavenly intercessor there developed a tradition that Michael served as High Priest in the heavenly sanctuary. This may be alluded to in *TLevi* 5 discussed above. If the angel who led Levi through the heavens to receive the priesthood is Michael, then it follows that he was chosen for this task because of his office of heavenly priest. Of course, this is, at best, only implicit in the text.

The most explicit portrayal of Michael as a heavenly priest in the apocalyptic literature is found in *3 Baruch*. In this work Michael descends to the fifth heaven to receive the prayers of men from those angels assigned

---

[88] Hollander and de Jonge, *Testaments*, 291-292.

While I doubt the *Testaments* had a Christian origin, they were unquestionably preserved by Christians. See below pp. 183-184, where I discuss the possibility that this text offers supportive evidence for angel Christology in the second century.

[89] Cf. Kee, *OTP* I.810, who does not bracket the phrase as an interpolation; and Charles, *Testaments*, who asserts that the phrase was "adopted" by St. Paul.

[90] Cf. also the longer reading of *TLevi* 5.7 mentioned above: "the angel who intercedes for the nation of Israel and all the righteous". Cf. also *2En.* 33.10 where God tells Enoch: "And I will give you Enoch, my mediator, my archistratig, Michael,...".

to individual humans (11.4). Having received their deeds as well as their prayers (11.9),[91] he places these in "a very large bowl" (φιάλην μεγάλην σφόδρα).[92] When all the angels have emptied their bowls into Michael's he re-ascends to offer these gifts to God (14.2), presumably on the altar of the heavenly temple.[93] As we shall see, the theme of Michael as the heavenly high priest appears slightly later in Rabbinic literature.[94] This picture, in *3 Baruch*, of Michael functioning as a priest in the heavenly temple is possibly the author's answer to the crisis of the destruction of the Temple in 70 A.D.: The Jerusalem Temple may be destroyed, but since the heavenly one, with its high priest, is still functioning properly the faithful may still offer their prayers confident they shall be heard.[95]

Even if this is so, it is probable that the author of *3 Baruch* was drawing on an already established tradition of Michael as heavenly high priest. As we have seen, there is reason to think that the angelic priestly figure of *AssMos.* 10.2 and, perhaps, of *TLevi* 2-5 and *TDan* 6 is to be identified with Michael. We shall see in the next chapter that there is evidence that the Qumran sectarians equated Michael with the priest Melchizedek, and it is not unlikely that the reason for such a move rested, in part, on an already traditional identification of Michael as a, or the, heavenly high priest. Finally, the fact that early Christian writings also attribute a heavenly priestly role to Michael,[96] strongly suggests that the tradition originated before the final parting of the ways between the two faiths.

---

[91] So the Greek version. The Slavonic version mentions only prayers.

[92] Φιαλην is used in the LXX for certain of the temple vessels (cf. 1 Kgs. 7.26ff) and in Rev. 5.8 for the bowls which hold the prayers of the saints. Cf. Gaylord, "3 Baruch", *OTP* I.674, n.g.

[93] Cf. Rev. 8.3. So also Gaylord, "3 Baruch", *OTP* I.674, n.11d.
Note the parallel in the β-recension of *TLevi* 3. There we read that the Great Glory (i.e., God) dwells in the highest heaven, the seventh. Below Him are the archangels in the sixth, who there fulfill their priestly duties. Below them in the fifth heaven are angels who carry the answers down from the archangels. Presumably they bear these answers from the fifth heaven to humanity on earth.

[94] See below pp. 100-102.

[95] So Gaylord, *OTP* I.656; Ego, "Diener," and Harlow, *Apocalypse of Baruch*, 155-156.

[96] See below, pp. 166-167.

c. Michael as Psychopomp

It was often presumed in literature of the Second Temple period that angels accompanied the righteous dead to heaven or paradise at the time of death. A number of apocalyptic texts portray Michael as the psychopomp of the patriarchs. For example, Michael serves as Abraham's psychopomp in the *Testament of Abraham*. Although Abraham first refuses to die, in the end Michael transports his soul to Paradise (20.10-12 A).[97]

The *Apocalypse of Moses* 37 and *Vita Adae et Eve* 47 give parallel accounts of the death of Adam and of Michael's role in transferring his soul to heaven. These accounts share many details with the *Testament of Abraham* and the *Testament of Job*. This suggests that the story of a patriarch's death and the transfer of his soul to heaven became to some degree stylized.

I have discussed above the evidence for the lost ending of the *Assumption of Moses*. This ending, as attested in Jude 9, apparently included an account in which Michael served as a pyschopomp for the soul of Moses. It seems that Michael had been sent either to bury the body or to bring the soul to heaven, or both. Concerning the former, there is a well-attested Jewish tradition that Moses was buried by angels or God,[98] which appears to be alluded to at 11.7-8 of the extant text of this apocryphon. The fact that in Jude 9 the dispute between archangel and devil was over the *body* of Moses serves to confirm the suggestion that Michael had been sent to bury Moses' body. The proposal that Michael had been sent to take Moses' soul to heaven, is admittedly more tenuous but, given the other examples of Michael transferring the soul of a righteous man to paradise at death, seems probable.[99]

In a related development, a number of apocalypses present Michael as the angel over Paradise. This may be presupposed already in *1En*. 24-25,[100] where Michael answers Enoch's questions about the tree of life and

---

[97] The MSS of recension B, however, are divided over whether Michael or "the chariot(s) of the Lord God" actually collected Abraham's soul. But even in the short recension Michael's task from the very beginning was to bring Abraham's soul to paradise.

[98] See Philo *Mos*. 2.291; Targ. Ps.-Jon. Deut. 34.6; *LAB* 19.16; Epiphanius *Pan*. ix.4.13, lxiv.69.6; and *DeutR* 10. On the midrashic evidence cf. also Loewenstamm, "The Death of Moses", 185-217.

[99] Cf. also *2 Enoch* 71-72 (LR), in which Michael takes the child Melchizedek to paradise to keep him safe until after the flood when Melchizedek will return to the world and become the source of all future priests (71.28-29). This text may be very late and it is not, strictly speaking, an example of Michael transferring the soul of the righteous dead to paradise. In the short recension Gabriel replaces Michael.

[100] Cf. Delcor, *Testament*, 54.

the mountain/throne of God. However, *1En.* 20.7, which apparently derives from another source, asserts that Gabriel is set over Paradise. In later works Michael is the gate keeper to paradise. For instance, in *3Bar.* 11.2 when Baruch asks his guide if they will be able to enter the fifth heaven, the angel replies: "We are not able to enter until Michael the holder of the keys of the kingdom of heaven (Μιχαὴλ ὁ κλειδοῦχος τῆς βασιλείας τῶν οὐρανῶν) comes". This is paralleled in Jeremiah's prayer at *4Bar.* 9.5: "And may Michael, the archangel of righteousness who opens the gates for the righteous, be (the object of) my attention until he leads the righteous in".[101]

d. Michael as *Angelus Interpres*

Often in the apocalypses an angel leads the Seer through the heavens or around the world, explaining the significance of the strange sights they encounter. On other occasions an angel interprets visions or dreams granted the Seer. This role is attributed to a number of different angels in our literature. In the Book of Daniel, Gabriel interprets a vision for Daniel (8.15ff).[102] Uriel is Ezra's *angelus interpres* throughout 4 Ezra. Phanuel guides Baruch through the heavens in *3 Baruch.*

Michael also functions as an *angelus interpres* in some Jewish apocalypses. He, Uriel, Raphael, or Raguel, guide Enoch on each of his various journeys described in *1En.* 21-37. Chapters 24-25 record his answers to Enoch's questions concerning the mountain which is both paradise

---

[101] Καὶ ἡ μελέτη μου Μιχαὴλ ὁ ἀρχάγγελος τῆς δικαιοσύνης, ὁ ἀνοίγων τὰς πύλας τοῖς δικαίοις, ἕως ἂν εἰσενέγκῃ τοὺς δικαίους.

The translation is that of Robinson, ("4 Baruch", *OTP* II.424). The sense of μελέτη is uncertain. It can mean "care, attention", but also "exercise, practice, drill (military sense), and rehearsal". Kraft and Purintun (*Paraleipomena*, 45) translate it: "And may Michael,...be my guardian (?) until he causes the righteous to enter". Their apparatus gives "choir master (?)" for the Ethiopic translation. A very plausible emendation, to my knowledge not offered before, is to see μελέτη as an error for μελέτωρ (avenger). This fits the context of Jeremiah's impending martyrdom.

[102] "The man clothed in linen", who is Daniel's interpreter for chapts. 10-12, could also be Gabriel. So Collins, "Son of Man", 55; Porteous, *Daniel*, 151-152; and, tentatively, Goldingay, *Daniel*, 291. Contrast Rowland, *Open Heaven*, 98 and Lacocque, *Daniel*, 206-207.

and the throne of God and concerning the tree of life. In the *Similitudes* (*1En.* 71), after Enoch's translation to heaven, but before his transformation into the Son of Man, Michael shows him "all the secrets of mercy and...all the secrets of righteousness". The only sustained portrayal of Michael as an *angelus interpres* appears in the latter half of the *Testament of Abraham*.[103] Of course, as I argued above, the angel who leads Levi through the heavens in *TLevi* 2-5 may be Michael. Finally, in the Adam literature Michael is an *angelus interpres* for Adam and Eve in that he teaches them various skills they need to know to survive outside of Paradise, including cultivation of plants for food (*Vita Adae* 22.2) and techniques for the burial of the dead (*Vita Adae* 48.3, 51.2 = *ApMos.* 43.2-3).

e. Michael as the Highest Archangel

From what has been said to this point there should be no doubt as to Michael's importance in Jewish apocalyptic literature of the Second Temple period. However, as we have seen, in the earliest apocalypses Michael is not *the* principal angel, but rather *a* principal angel, one among four or seven others. Nonetheless, the evidence seems to indicate that already by the beginning of the first century A.D. Michael had become *the* principal angel, if not everywhere, at least in many circles. This should not be surprising given Michael's relation to Israel; set over God's chosen people, he naturally came to be regarded as the highest of all the angels.

There is nothing in the *Book of Watchers* to suggest that Michael's authority exceeds that of the other archangels or that any of them possesses greater authority than Michael.[104] The description of Michael as "one of the chief princes" (מיכאל אחד השרים הראשנים; Dan. 10.13) could be taken to imply the same for the Book of Daniel. However, if the identification of the "one like a son of man" in Daniel 7.13 with Michael, argued for above, is sound, then it would follow that Michael was already regarded as the principal angel by the author of Daniel.

---

[103] Cf. also the *GkApEzra* 4.6-43, where "Michael and Gabriel and thirty-four other angels" guide Ezra in his tour of Tartarus.

[104] Note both *1En.* 21.5 and 24.6. In the former it is Uriel who is a leader among the angels, in the latter the same is said of Michael. It is significant that the Greek is the same in both instances: καὶ αὐτὸς αὐτῶν ἡγεῖτο. Black (*1 Enoch*, 164) captures the sense well in his assertion that the probable meaning is "that Michael or Uriel was an ἀρχάγγελος, i.e., 'a leading angel among them' rather than 'the leader of all the angels.'"

We have already seen how in the *Book of Watchers* two traditions concerning the number of archangels (four and seven) existed side by side, and that with the *Animal Apocalypse* the tradition of seven was beginning to prevail. While this development from four to seven was proceeding, Michael's role was developing from one of the archangels to their chief. It seems to be already implied in the *Animal Apocalypse*, if indeed, as I have argued, the white man singled out there is to be identified with Michael. The end of this process may be seen in such works as *3 Baruch*[105] and the *Testament of Abraham*.[106] However, neither of these works can be earlier than the late first century, and both may date from the second.[107] A probable first century work which shares this belief in Michael as first of the angels is the *Similitudes of Enoch*. In its list of the four archangels, or "angels of the presence", Michael is explicitly said to be "the first" (40.9).[108]

If the unnamed "angel of the Presence" of *Jubilees*[109] is Michael, as Charles argued,[110] then we have a clear example of Michael as the principal angel well before the first century A.D.[111] This angel, who dictates to Moses the history of the world from the creation until the renewal of the temple and the eschatological appearance of God, clearly plays a significant role in relation to Israel. He is the "Exodus angel" mentioned in the Pentateuch. The phrase, "angel of the Presence", derives from Isa. 63.9, which according to the Qere reads: "In all their distress he was distressed; the angel of his Presence (מלאך פניו) saved them". The context in Isaiah makes clear that this is an allusion to the angel who led the people out of the land of Egypt. So also for the author of *Jubilees* the angel of the Presence is he "who went before the camp of Israel" (1.29). *Jubilees'*

---

[105] See esp. 11.4-6, where Michael receives obeisance from Phanuel, who should probably be understood as one of the archangels (cf. 1.8 [2.1 in Slav.], 11.7 [Greek only], and *1En*. 40).

[106] For Rec. B, cf. esp. 4.5. For Rec. A, note the use of ἀρχιστρτάτηγος throughout and the imagery used to describe Michael in chapt. 7.

[107] See above pp. 39-40, n.63.

[108] Cf. also Michael's role in 60.4-5 and in chapts. 68 and 71.

[109] Not to be confused with "the angels of the presence". The author of *Jubilees* apparently believed in both a class of angels so named (2.2) and *the* Angel of the Presence who revealed the contents of *Jubilees* to Moses (1.27-2.1).

[110] *Jubilees*, 9.

[111] *Jubilees* can be dated with certainty to before 100 B.C. since fragments of the work from around that date have been found at Qumran. VanderKam (*Textual*, 214-285) argues for its composition c. 163-140 B.C. He is followed by Wintermute ("Jubilees", *OTP* II.43-44), but Rabin ("Jubilees", *AOT*, 5) dates it around 100 B.C.

account of the crossing of the Red Sea, based on Ex. 14.19-20, emphasizes not only this angel's relationship with Israel, but also his relationship with the God of Israel: "And I stood between the Egyptians and Israel, and *we* delivered Israel from his (i.e., Mastema's) hand and from the hand of his people. And the Lord brought them out through the midst of the sea as through dry land" (48.13, emphasis mine).

As noted above, there are good reasons to suppose that *Jubilees* was related in some way to the Qumran community. It was read there and shares many key ideas, including a reluctance to use the names of the angels.[112] It is highly significant, then, that the *Damascus Document* (CD 5.17b-19) offers a striking parallel to *Jubilees'* account of the Exodus (chapt. 48). In both texts an angelic figure (the Prince of Light in CD, the Angel of the Presence in *Jubilees*) aids Moses, and in both an evil angel (Belial in CD, Mastema in *Jubilees*) opposes them by means of the Egyptian magicians. *Jubilees'* account is much fuller but the parallels suggest a common tradition. In the next chapter, I will argue that the Qumran community identified the Prince of Light with Michael.[113] If that equation is accepted, then it seems probable that the angel of the Presence of *Jubilees* was also intended to be identified as Michael.

Finally, *Jub.* 10.1-14 tells how evil spirits, the children of the Watchers and human women, were abusing Noah's descendants after the flood. According to the Ethiopic version, at Noah's intercession for his grandchildren, God sent the angels (plural) to capture the evil spirits. A Greek fragment preserved in Syncellus (*Chronographia* 49.6-15), which corresponds to this passage in *Jubilees*, speaks not of angels in the plural, but Michael and describes him casting the evil spirits into the Abyss. However, since the citations of *Jubilees* preserved in Syncellus' *Chronographia* often show signs of editing and are not a little paraphrastic,[114] it is possible that this fragment reflects Syncellus' own identification of the angel of the Presence with Michael and, thus, cannot be regarded as more original than the reading found in the Ethiopic. Even if this is so, this text, nonetheless, indicates that at least one ancient reader equated *Jubilees'* narrator with Michael. Thus, the identification of the angel of the Presence with the archangel Michael is a natural one and should not be dismissed lightly.

---

[112] Cf. VanderKam, *Textual and Historical*, 255-285, who concludes that *Jubilees* derives from the same tradition as the Qumran texts, but dates from a period before the exile to Qumran and the sect's estrangement from the Jerusalem establishment.
[113] See below pp. 64-65.
[114] So VanderKam, *Textual and Historical*, 8.

There are good reasons, then, to conclude that by some time in the first century B.C. Michael had begun to be considered as not only an archangel of high standing, a principal angel among others, but *the* principal angel, the highest archangel. This is, incidentally, supported by his roles as psychopomp for the patriarchs and heavenly high priest. The stature of Adam, Abraham and Moses required a psychopomp of equal stature in the heavenly world. In addition, if the archangels serve as heavenly priests, as in *TLevi* 3.5, then it follows that their leader would serve as the high priest.

However, it must be noted that the belief in Michael as the prince of all angels was not universal in apocalyptic circles of the Second Temple period. In the *Prayer of Joseph*, for example, Israel was the ἀρχάγγελος δυνάμεως κυρίου καὶ ἀρχιχιλίαρός...ἐν υἱοῖς θεοῦ. Yahoel clearly holds a position higher than that of Michael in the *Apocalypse of Abraham*.[115] Eremiel has a very exalted role in *ApZeph*. 6.11-17, and 4Q529 perhaps ranks Gabriel above Michael.[116] Finally, the very early enochic *Astronomical Book* appears to suggest that Uriel is the highest angel (*1En*. 74.2, 75.3, 79.6).[117] Nonetheless, while various other angels are in isolated works put forward as the principal angel, Michael was undoubtedly the angelic figure most often so named in Jewish apocalypses by the turn of the eras.

f. Michael as the Angel of the Name

The angel in whom the Name of God dwells will be, almost by definition, the most important angel. This is certainly true of Metatron, whom we will encounter when we turn to Rabbinic and Hekhalot literature. As stated above,[118] the exegetical basis for an "angel of the Name" appears in Ex. 23.20-21, with its assertion "my Name is in him" (כי שמי בקרבו). In Jewish apocalyptic literature there is some speculation about this figure, and at least one text which seems to identify him with Michael.

I refer to *1 Enoch* 69.13-25. This passage is difficult. Verse 13 appears to be corrupt in nearly all the MSS; but one MS, Ethq, gives a meaningful text. This manuscript, as translated by Black, reads: "And it was he (refer-

---

[115] Cf. *ApAb*. 10.3, 8 with 10.17.
[116] The text of 4Q529 is conveniently printed in Eisenman and Wise, *DSS Uncovered*, 37-39.
[117] The question rests on whether or not the author of the *Astronomical Book* identified the heavenly luminaries with angelic beings.
[118] P. 21.

ring back to either Kasdeya', a satan, or Taba'et, 'the son of a serpent') who reckoned up the gematria (lit. the number) of the Chief of Days for Kasbeel, who revealed the sum of the oath to the angels when he dwelt above in glory, and its name is BIQA". Following on this, vss. 14-15, whose text is not in doubt, read:

> This (satan) told Michael to show him the hidden Name, that he might pronounce it in the oath, so that those who reveal all that was secret to the children of men might tremble before that Name and oath. And this is the power of this oath, for it is powerful and strong, and he (God) had placed this oath 'AKA' in the hand of Michael.[119]

In what follows the power of this "oath of the Name" is manifest; by means of it all things were created.[120] While it is generally accepted that "the hidden Name" can only be a reference to the divine Name,[121] the mysterious words BIQA and 'AKA' have been subject to many attempted emendations.[122] However, Black, following Dillman and Beer, suggests that BIQA and 'AKA' are gematria for יהוה האלהים and יהוה אדני respectively. BIQA is a transliteration for ביקה while 'AKA' is a transliteration of אכע. Now ביקה "equals" 117, as does יהוה האליהם. In addition, אכע "equals" 91, as does יהוה אדני.[123] If this solution is accepted, it offers strong support for following Eth^q, rather than the majority of Ethiopic manuscripts. It also confirms that the "hidden Name" refered to in vs. 14 is indeed the Name of God. Therefore it seems safe to conclude that this passage indicates that Michael was viewed by the author of the *Similitudes* as the angel of the Name, for into the "hand of Michael" the secret of the oath, that is the Divine Name, had been entrusted.

If the *Similitudes of Enoch* presents Michael as the Angel of the Name in an esoteric manner, the *Apocalypse of Abraham* makes an unambiguous case for Yahoel (or Iaoel). Ἰαωήλ is, of course, the combination of the two divine names; Ἰαώ, the Greek form of יהוה, and ελ or ηλ, transliterations of אל. Since nearly all angel names are built upon אל, Ἰαωήλ appears to be the result of speculation upon Ex. 23.20-21. God

---

[119] Black's translation. Charles, Knibb, and Isaac offer very similar translations.
[120] This idea of creation by means of an oath based on the divine Name is found also in *Jub.* 36.7 and *Sifre Deut.* 330. It became quite widespread in later Judaism. Cf. Urbach, *Sages*, 124-134 and Fossum, *Name of God*, 245-256.
[121] So E.g., Black, *1 Enoch*, 248; Segal, *Two Powers*, 196-197, esp. n.39.
[122] Cf. e.g., Knibb's suggestion in "1 Enoch", *AOT*, 253, n.19.
[123] See Black, *1 Enoch*, 247-248.

Himself is addressed with the name "Yahoel" at *ApAb.* 17.13. This is not surprising in light of the fact that Yahoel is addressed by God as "Yahoel of the same name" (10.3).[124] Furthermore, in *ApMos.* 29.4 and 33.5 God is addressed by the angels as Ἰαὴλ αἰώνιε βασιλεῦ and Ἰαὴλ ἅγιε, respectively. In addition, according to *3En.* 48D.1 (=§76), the first of Metatron's seventy names is "Yaho'el". Thus Ἰαωὴλ was considered appropriate both for God and for that angel in whom the divine Name dwelt.[125]

In the *Apocalypse of Abraham* Yahoel is sent by God to Abraham, in answer to the latter's prayer, to instruct him concerning the true God. The angel is commissioned with the following words: "Go, Yahoel of the same name, through the mediation of my ineffable name, consecrate this man for me,...". (10.3).[126] The author of this apocalypse seeks to re-enforce the close association between this angel and the divine Name in the conversation which follows between angel and patriarch. First, Yahoel tells Abraham that he has been sent to strengthen him and bless him "in the name of God" (10.6). Then, Yahoel describes himself to Abraham: "I am Yahoel,[127] and I was called by him who causes those with me on the seventh expanse, on the firmament, to shake, a power through the medium of his ineffable name in me" (10.8).

So while Michael could be identified with the angel of the Name (*1En.* 69), the *Apocalypse of Abraham* speculated on an angel whose name literally bears the name of God. Significantly, this apocalypse mentions only two angels by name: Yahoel and Michael (10.16b-17). It is possible that Michael is introduced so that there will be no doubt that the angel of the Name and Michael are two different angels, not one angel under two different names. If so, then we have here another witness to Michael as the angel of the divine Name, albeit an indirect one. Finally, we shall see

---

[124] However, this is, admittedly, an emendation of Rubinkiewicz's; it is not found in either the translation of Pennington (*AOT*) or that of Box and Landsman. However, Rubinkiewicz has done the most comprehensive study to date on the text of the *Apocalypse of Abraham.* See also n. 126.

[125] Harrington (*OTP*, II.338, n.e) suggests that *LAB* 26.12 is another possible parallel. This passage is a prediction of a future king named Jahel who will build the temple. Jahel, rather than Solomon is surprising, but there is nothing in the context to suggest that this Jahel is to be understood as an angelic or divine being.

[126] This verse is corrupt. MS S, the best extant MS of the *ApAb.*, has Naoil, rather than Iaoel and MSS KJ read "Altez". Iaoel is Rubinkiewicz's (*OTP*, 693) reconstruction, based on these and other variants and the context. This reconstruction is generally accepted, cf. Hurtado, *One God*, 158, n.42.

[127] S reads "I am Iloil"; J reads "I am Aol"; while J has "I am Jaol".

when we examine Metatron traditions there are reasons to believe that in some circles Michael and Metatron, another angel of the Name, were identified.[128] Nonetheless, it must be admitted that direct evidence for Michael as the angel of the Name is, at best, limited.[129]

g. Summary

Michael, then, held a significant position in the minds of those who wrote and read the Jewish apocalypses. The traditions about him as the protector, both in a military and judicial sense, of the holy people, and as the commander-in-chief of the heavenly armies are quite widespread. He was also popularly seen as a transporter of the souls of the righteous to heaven and, less often, as Keeper of the gates of paradise. He was regarded as high priest in the heavenly sanctuary by at least one apocalypse. Finally, by the mid-first century BC, Michael was coming to be considered as the chief of all the angels, a trend which continued and grew in strength in the following centuries. As we shall see, all of these traditions were taken up to various degrees by different circles. The Qumran sect adopted the tradition of Michael as protector of (the righteous in) Israel, highest archangel and military leader of the heavenly hosts. The Rabbis spoke of Michael as the priest in the heavenly sanctuary and the greatest of the angels. Christians adopted nearly all of the Jewish apocalyptic Michael traditions. These traditions which circulated about the archangel Michael, then, potentially provide the best test in our quest for the influence of Jewish speculations about principal angels on the development of early Christology.

---

[128] See below pp. 119-121.
[129] But see below pp. 85-88, where I discuss Philo's (*Conf.* 146) identification of the Logos as both ἀρχάγγελον and ὄνομα θεοῦ.

Chapter 3

The Archangel Michael in the Literature of Qumran

References to Michael by name in the sectarian literature[1] of Qumran are rare. His name appears four times in the *War Rule*; twice in a list of the four archangels[2] and twice in a speech of the High Priest to the troops.[3] Other than these four there is only one other certain occurrence of the name in a writing which is definitely sectarian (4Q285). There are possible citations in fragmentary material (e.g., 4Q'Amram) and at least three clear references in documents which show little or no evidence of being sectarian (viz., 4Q529 and 4Q470 [*bis*]).[4] It will be the burden of this chapter to demonstrate that Michael's importance to the Qumran sect far outweighed the meagre occurrences of his name, to offer some explanation of this dearth of actual references to him by name, and to examine the significance he held in sectarian theology. A brief sketch of certain theological beliefs of the Qumran community which are significant for my argument will open this chapter. I will then turn to an examination of the community's angelology and Michael's role in that angelology. Finally, a discussion of the proposed identification of Michael with Melchizedek will conclude the chapter.[5]

---

[1] I restrict my discussion in this chapter to those documents which are generally held to be sectarian. Those on which the argument of this chapter depends includes *The Community Rule* (1QS, 4QS), *The Damascus Document* (CD, 4QD), *The Messianic Rule* (1QSa), *The War Rule* (1QM, 4QM), *The Thanksgiving Hymns* (1QH), *Songs of the Sabbath Sacrifice* (4Q400-407, 11Q5-6), *The Blessings* (1QSb), *The Testament of Amram* (4QAmram), and *The Melchizedek Document* (11QMelch). The other writings found at Qumran which are mentioned in this chapter, owing to their fragmentary nature, may or may not be identified as sectarian. The origin of each of these will be discussed as they occur.

[2] 1QM 9.15-16.

[3] 1QM 17.6-7.

[4] Michael also appears in fragments of *1 Enoch* found at Qumran; these were considered in the previous chapter.

[5] Unless stated otherwise, the translations used in this chapter will be those of Vermes, *Complete DSS in English*. For the texts I have generally used those found in the *DJD*

1. The Qumran Community

The story of the discovery and decipherment of the Dead Sea Scrolls has been told many times,[6] and need not be repeated here. It will be impossible, because of the restrictions of space, to answer in any detail the question of the identity of the group which produced these scrolls. Rather, it will be sufficient to state briefly the consensus of scholarly opinion which developed in the fifties and sixties and some of the more important challenges to this consensus published in the last ten to fifteen years.

That consensus, which in recent years has come increasingly under attack, was formulated and polished by G. Vermes,[7] J. T. Milik,[8] F. M. Cross,[9] and others.[10] This view identifies the sect which produced the scrolls with the Essenes, known to us from descriptions in Josephus,[11] Philo,[12] and Pliny the Elder.[13] In addition, the ruins of Khirbet Qumran are recognized, according to this consensus, as the site of a monastic community which at once belonged to the wider Essene movement and was more strict than other Essenes. But these two forms of Essenes were not, according to the consensus, in opposition to each other, but were analogous to "monastic" and "secular" Christians of today. This view identifies "the Teacher of Righteousness" (hereafter TR), the founder of the movement, as a Zadokite High Priest who was deposed by Jonathan Maccabeus; "the wicked Priest" as Jonathan;[14] and the individual known as "the Spouter of Lies", "the Liar", and "the Scoffer" as a leader of a splinter movement which opposed TR.[15] It is often presumed by those who support this theory that "the Hasidim", mentioned in 1 Macc. 2.42, represent the precursors of the Essenes.[16]

---

series, although on occasion I have consulted others, such as that edited by Lohse (*Texte*).

[6] See e.g., Milik, *Ten Years*, 11-19; Vermes, *Perspective*, 9-24; and idem, *Complete DSS in English*, 3rd. ed., xiii-xvi.

[7] *Perspective* esp. 116-130; and *Complete DSS in English*, 1-66.

[8] *Ten Years*, 44-98.

[9] *Ancient Library*, 37-79.

[10] E.g., Jeremias, *Lehrer*; Stegemann, *Entstehung*; Knibb, *Qumran Community*, 1-8; and Sanders, *Judaism*, 341-379.

[11] *War* i.78-80, ii.113-161, 567, iii.11; *Ant.* xiii.171-2, xv.371-9, xviii.18-22, *Life* x-xi.

[12] *Prob.* 75-91 and *Apologia pro Iudaeis*, preserved in Eusebius, *Praep. Ev.* viii.6-7.

[13] *Nat. Hist.* v.17.4 (73).

[14] Cross (*Ancient Library*, 95-119, esp. 101-110), however, opts for Jonathan's brother and successor, Simon.

[15] Cf. Vermes, *Complete DSS in English*, 54-66; Sanders, *Judaism*, 341-349.

[16] Vermes, *Complete DSS in English*, 58-59.

The most significant challenge to this consensus comes from those who would identify the Qumran sect not with the Essenes themselves, but with a schismatic group which separated from the Essenes. Although with many differences in detail, proponents of this position include, J. Murphy-O'Connor,[17] P. R. Davies,[18] F. García Martínez[19] and, most recently, G. Boccaccini.[20] All of these would see the Essenes, following the descriptions of Josephus and Philo, as spread throughout Palestine and thus a wider movement than the sect which was isolated to a single settlement on the shores of the Dead Sea. This latter group was led into its schism from the rest of the Essenes by TR.

The jury is still out on this particular debate, but its conclusion makes very little difference to the issues I will be exploring in this chapter. Some connection between the Essenes and the Qumran sectarians are agreed upon by nearly all serious researchers into Qumran origins. I will, then, proceed under the assumption that there was some relation between the Essenes and the Qumran community, although precisely what that relationship was will be left undefined.

However the identity of the group behind the scrolls is finally decided, the scrolls themselves bear witness to a people convinced of their own special election by God and their role in His eschatological scheme. These sectarians believed that they were the final remnant of Israel and, as such, they were living "on the threshold of the eschaton".[21] This conviction determined not only the nature of their beliefs but also their religious practices and their communal life (cf. 1QS 8.13-14). Their confidence in their role as the chosen remnant was based in part on their belief that TR had been sent by God to guide them in the way of God and to reveal to them the eschatological nature of their age (CD 1.10b-12). Related to this is the apocalyptic understanding, which the sectarians evidently shared, that history had been divinely apportioned into a series of dispensations.[22] The sequence and character of these periods was one of the mysteries of God hidden even from the OT prophets who wrote about the end of the ages without understanding when their prophecies would be fulfilled. TR, however, was divinely empowered to interpret correctly the writings of the

---

[17] "Essene Missionary"; "Literary Analysis"; "Original Text"; "Translation"; "Critique"; "Essenes and Their History"; and "Damascus Document Re-visited".
[18] *Behind the Essenes.*
[19] "Qumran Origins"; and "Origins".
[20] *Beyond the Essene Hypothesis.*
[21] Dimant, "Sectarian Literature", 533.
[22] Cf. 4Q180 and Dimant, "Sectarian Literature", 536.

prophets and to discern the eschatological significance and nature of the present period.[23] The sectarians expected the approaching end to be initiated by a war between themselves and the rest of humanity, including those of Israel who opposed their sect. Convinced of their own election, the covenanters envisioned the whole of humanity divided into two camps: "the lot of light" and "the lot of darkness" (1QS 3.13-4.26). The former included themselves and the angels, while the latter included the Gentiles, the "unfaithful of Israel" and the fallen angels.

Although we cannot be certain, it seems that the sectarians believed that the eschatological age would be inaugurated by the arrival of Messiahs.[24] In harmony with certain works from the Second Temple period,[25] the covenanters, at least at one point in their history, seem to have expected two Messiahs, one Priestly, the other Royal.[26] 1QSb 5.27-28 implies that the latter will lead the sect's armies in the final battle, although, as we shall see, this role is often attributed to an angelic figure in the sectarian writings. The sect was confident of victory in this war, but only because they believed God would intervene on their behalf.[27]

All this presents an exclusive group on the fringes of society. In the words of Sanders, "[t]hey were not major players in politics and society, and no one says they were".[28] This, however, does not mean that they are unimportant for our examination of Michael in ancient Judaism. It does mean that unless parallels in other Jewish texts can be found, views about angels and Michael attested in sectarian documents should probably be treated as distinctive to the Qumran community.

---

[23] Cf. 1QpHab 2.8-10, 7.1-5.

[24] So Dimant, "Sectarian Literature", 540. For a fuller summary of the Messianism of the scrolls see Talmon, "Waiting of the Messiah"; Schiffman, "Messianic Figures"; Brown, "The Messianism of Qumran"; and idem, "The Teacher of Righteousness and the Messiah(s)", 37-44. Cf. also Chester, "Messianic Expectations", 20-27; and Collins "Maccabean Period", 104-105.

[25] Cf. *Jub.* 31.14-20; and the *Testaments of the Twelve Patriarchs*, esp. *TReub.* 6.8, 11; *TSim.* 7.1; *TIss.* 5.7-8; *TJos.* 19.11; *TNaph.* 5.1-5, 8.2; and cf. *TLevi* 18.1-9 with *TJud.* 24.1-6.

[26] Cf. e.g., 1QS 9.11; CD 7.18-21(A). It should be noted that other passages in CD (12.23, 14.19, 19.10-11[B], and 20.1[B]) speak of only one messiah, "the Messiah of Aaron and Israel"; this may be due to the medieval scribe of CD, confused by the plural, correcting his text.

[27] Cf. e.g., 1QM 11.1ff, 13.13-16, 19.2-8.

[28] Sanders, *Judaism*, 341.

2. The Angelology of Qumran

a. Communion with the Angels

Even this very brief and selective survey of sectarian theology has indicated the importance of angelology to the covenanters. The conviction that they were the elect of God led them to the conclusion that they would in the age to come experience communion with the angels and that, to some degree, this was already a reality.[29] In the *Rule of the Community* we read that God has caused His chosen ones (i.e., the Sectarians) to "inherit the lot of the Holy Ones" (בגורל קדושים), and He "has joined their assembly to the sons of heaven (ועם בני שמים) to be a Council of the Community" (1QS 11.7-8). This clearly describes this communion with angels as a present reality: The sectarians have already "inherited the lot of the Holy Ones" and their assembly has already been joined with that of "the sons of heaven".[30] In a similar passage, the poet of the *Hodayot* proclaims: "Thou hast cleansed a perverse spirit of great sin that it might stand with the host of the Holy Ones (במעמד עם צבא קודשים), and that it may enter into community with the congregation of the Sons of Heaven (ולבוא ביחד עם עדת בני שמים). Thou hast allotted to man an everlasting destiny admist the spirits of knowledge (עם רוחות דעת),..." (1QH 11.20-23 [formerly 3.20-23]). This latter passage is more ambiguous, possibly intentionally so, and thus can be taken either as an expression of present experience or of eschatological hope.[31]

Holm-Nielsen has argued that community with God, not the angels, is the primary concern of the sectarians in the *Hodayot* passage quoted above.[32] This may be so; nonetheless, the sectarians viewed this companionship with the angels as one of the outstanding characteristics which differentiated them from those outside the sect (1QM 10.8b-11a).

This fellowship with the angels meant that in the coming eschatological war against the forces of darkness, the sectarians could count on celestial help (1QM 1.9b-10, 12.4ff, 15.14b-16.1; cf. 1QH 11.29-36 [formerly

---

[29] Ringgren, *Faith*, 86.

[30] So also Davidson, *Angels*, 168-170; and the translation of Wernberg-Møller, *Manual*, 38. Wernberg-Møller, however, does not discuss this issue in his commentary. Contrast Leaney (*Rule*, 253-254).

[31] So the translations of Vermes and García Martínez. Davidson (*Angels*, 192), understands the text to describe present realities only. Cf. also 1QH 14.13-14 [formerly 6.13-14] and 19.10-14 [formerly 11.10-14].

[32] Holm-Nielsen, *Hodayot*, 68. So also Davidson, *Angels*, 312.

3.29-36]). This doctrine was appealed to by the author of the *War Scroll*, to inspire his readers with confidence in their ultimate victory.[33] Yadin[34] has noted that the sectarians could find precedent for this idea in the OT[35] and in the Books of Maccabees.[36] According to the *War Scroll*, Michael, the traditional defender of the people of Israel,[37] leads these angelic forces (1QM 17.6-8a). I will examine this in more detail when I discuss the identification of Michael with the "Prince of Lights". For now it is sufficient to point out that 1QM 9.14-16 may indicate that all four archangels will actually lead the sectarians into the battle.[38] However, the *War Scroll* affirms that, even with this angelic help the battle will be decided only by the intervention of God Himself (1QM 1.13b-15; 1QM 11.1-6).

The covenanters' belief in their fellowship with the angels had important repercussions in regard to cultic purity. A number of passages state the presence of angels in their midst as the reason for the sect's strict purity regulations (1QSa 2.3ff; 1QM 7.3b-7; 4QFlor 1.4f; 4QD^a = CD 15.15-17; cf. also 1 Cor. 11.10).[39]

b. The Angels as a Heavenly Priesthood

It is probably significant that many of the passages which speak of the sectaries' communion with angels occur in hymns, i.e, in a cultic context (1QS 11.6-8; 1QH 11.20ff [formerly 3.20ff], 14.13-14 [formerly 6.13-14], 19.10-14 [11.10-14]; 1QM 10.8b-11a). Davidson has suggested that the sectaries experienced this angelic fellowship "especially in the context of worship".[40] Implicit confirmation of this is found in a fragmentary passage from the *Sabbath Shirot* (4Q400 2 i,6-7), where the sectarian compares his worship with that of the אלים (i.e., the angels), and finds it wanting. The *Sabbath Shirot* as a whole, with its detailed description of angelic worship, implies that the communion with the angels was most keenly felt during

---

[33] Esp. 1QM 12.6-8.
[34] Yadin, *War*, 237, nn.2 and 3.
[35] Ex. 23.20-33, 33.2; 2 Kgs. 19.35; 2 Chr. 32.21; cf. also 2 Sam. 5.22-25; 2 Kgs. 6.15-17.
[36] 1 Macc. 7.41 = 2 Macc. 15.22; 2 Macc. 10.29, 11.6, 15.23.
[37] See above pp. 33-38.
[38] So Yadin, *War*, 240.
[39] Davidson (*Angels*, 278, n.4) and Knibb (*Qumran Community*, 152-153) argue that the ultimate source for this idea is Deut. 23.14.
[40] *Angels*, 192.

corporate worship.⁴¹ Finally, the solar (and cultic) calendar to which the Qumran community adhered, was, according to *Jubilees*, the calendar followed by the angels.⁴²

In concert with Jewish apocalyptic literature of this era, the sectaries envisioned an angelic priesthood and cult parallel to that on earth.⁴³ A blessing preserved in 1QSb alludes to the belief in an angelic priesthood: "May you be as an Angel of the Presence in the Abode of Holiness to the Glory of the God of [hosts]...May you attend upon the service in the Temple of the Kingdom and decree destiny in company with the Angels of the Presence, in common council [with the Holy Ones] for everlasting ages and time without end;..." (1QSb 4.24b-26).⁴⁴ 4Q400 1 i 14b-16, from the *Sabbath Shirot*, describes the sacrifices of the angelic priests: "There is [n]othing impure in their holy gifts. He engraved for them [precepts relating to ho]ly gifts; by them, all the everlastingly holy shall sanctify themselves....Their expiations shall obtain his good will for all those who repent of sin...".⁴⁵ Further, the *Sabbath Shirot* describes seven priesthoods serving in seven sanctuaries in the heavenly temple. These seven ranks of priests are led by seven chief priests (נשיאי רואש or ראשים) and by seven deputy chief priests (נשיאי משנה).⁴⁶

c. The Four and/or Seven Archangels

Following Newsom, it is possible that the seven chief priests or princes should be identified with the seven archangels.⁴⁷ However, the *War Scroll*

---

⁴¹ Cf. Newsom, *Sabbath Sacrifice*, 17-21, and 58-72.
⁴² *Jub.* 2.17-19, 6.17-18, 31-35. Cf. above pp. 43-44 and 50, where the relation of *Jubilees* to the Qumran community is noted.
⁴³ See above pp. 32, 43-46.
⁴⁴ Cf. the striking parallel in *Jub.* 31.13-14.
⁴⁵ Vermes' translation (*Complete DSS in English*, 322). "Holy gifts" is Vermes' translation of קודשיהם. Newsom translates this with "holy places". However we render קודשיהם, the reference to "expiations" clearly indicates some kind of heavenly cult. Cf. Newsom, *Sabbath Sacrifice*, 104f. Cf. *TLevi* 3.4-6.
⁴⁶ See Newsom, *Sabbath Sacrifice*, 30-37.
⁴⁷ Newsom, *Sabbath Sacrifice*, 34.

knows only four archangels: Michael, Gabriel, Sariel, and Raphael (1QM 9.14-16). As we have seen,[48] the first part of *1 Enoch* contains two traditions concerning the number of archangels. Since fragments from the *Book of Watchers* have been found at Qumran it is clear that both traditions were known to the sectarians.[49]

d. Cosmic Dualism: The Spirits of Light and Darkness

Certainly the single most distinctive component of the angelology of Qumran, over against that of the rest of Second Temple Judaism, concerns the sect's dualistic perspective on the world. As already mentioned, the covenanters envisioned all humanity divided into two camps, the "lot" or "sons of light" and the "lot" or "sons of darkness". Each of these was thought to be ruled by an angelic figure. The clearest expression of this is found in that section of the *Community Rule* known as the "Two Spirits Discourse" (1QS 3.13-4.26). Here we are told that God appointed for humanity two spirits: "the spirits of truth and falsehood". All "those born of truth" are ruled by "the Prince of Light" and all "those born of falsehood" are governed by "the Angel of Darkness". The phrase "those born of truth/falsehood" seems to indicate a deterministic orientation: God has predetermined who belongs to which camp. "It appears that people are either in one category or the other, with no middle ground".[50] Such determinism is found elsewhere in the Qumran corpus (cf. e.g., CD 2.7-11 and 1QH 12.31ff [formerly 4.31ff]).

However, a little later in this same section of the *Community Rule* we find another emphasis. At 4.15-16 it is stated that one's "work" or "deeds" are done in accordance with the share, either great or small, which one has of the two spirits. Then, in 4.23-25, it is affirmed that both these spirits struggle in human hearts. Thus humans are a combination of both good and evil, light and darkness.[51] It appears that the "Qumran theologians"

---

[48] See above pp. 29-30.
[49] So also Newsom, *Sabbath Sacrifice*, 34.
[50] Davidson, *Angels*, 160.
[51] See also 4QCryptic (= 4Q186), where individuals are a mixture of so many parts of "the house of Light" and so many of "the pit of Darkness". However, Davidson's (*Angels*, 160, n.1) caution regarding 4QCryptic should be borne in mind; we do not know to what degree this fragment, so different in thought from most of the sectarian literature, reflects the thought of the sect.

were little bothered by this apparent inconsistency.[52]

The above passage from the "Two Spirits Discourse" is strikingly paralleled in the *War Scroll* 13.9-12. In both passages two angelic figures stand opposed to each other. The advocate of the righteous is the Prince of Lights (שר אורים, 1QS 3.20) or the Prince of Light (שר מאור, 1QM 13.10) or the Angel of His (i.e., God's) Truth (מלאך אמתו, 1QS 3.24, cf. 1QM 13.10). His adversary, the champion of the unrighteous, is called the Angel of Darkness (מלאך חושך) or an Angel of Hatred (מלאך משטמה).[53] Those that follow the Prince of Lights are called sons of righteousness (בני צדק, 1QS 3.20, 22) or sons of light (בני אור, 1QS 3.24, 25). Opposed to them are the sons of perversity (בני עול, 1QS 3.21) or the sons of darkness (בני חושך, 1QS 1.10).[54]

This cosmic dualism is echoed throughout the sectarian writings and constitutes one of their major themes (CD 5.17b-19; 1QH 12.31 [formerly 4.31]; 7.13-20 [formerly 15.13-20]; 4QFlor 1.8-9; 4QCatenae^a [= 4Q177]).[55] However, although this opposition of the Prince of Light to the Angel of Darkness reflects a cosmic dualism, the sectarian authors were also at pains to stress that it was a *limited* dualism. They did this by asserting that God created both the spirit of light and the spirit of darkness (1QS 3.25; cf. 1QH 9.9ff [formerly 1.9ff], 5.8 [formerly 13.8]), by affirming

---

[52] In a change from his earlier views (*Manual*, 71), Wernberg-Møller ("Reconsideration") has argued that these two spirits denote only a psychological dualism and are not to be understood as individual and supernatural beings. Cf. also Treves, "Two Spirits". This would make the Qumran scrolls an early example of the Rabbinic doctrine of the good and evil *yetzer*. Wernberg-Møller has not persuaded many. Most scholars agree that the two conceptions are not mutually exclusive. So Davidson, *Angels*, 161; Ringgren, *Faith*, 76; and esp. Dimant, "Sectarian Literature", 535.

[53] The parallel with the Prince Mastema (שר משטמה) of *Jubilees* (10.8; 11.5, 11; 17.16; 19.28; 48.2) should be noted.

[54] For influence from Zoroastrian dualism, cf. Ringgren, *Faith*, 78ff; Leaney, *Rule*, 46-47; Shaked, "Qumran and Iran"; Dimant, "Sectarian Literature", 535, n.252; and Kobelski, *Melchizedek and Melchiresaʻ*, 84-98. Contrast Barr, "Religious Influence"; and Davidson, *Angels*, 232-234.

[55] CD 2.3-13 contrasts with such dualism. As with the dualistic passages, it emphasizes God's complete sovereignty over the elect and the damned. Nevertheless, here it is God who leads astray the wicked and who leads the righteous. He does not work through the two angels of Light and Darkness. There are many similarities between CD 2.3-13 and 1QS 3.13-4.26, which is often mentioned by commentators; e.g., Knibb, *Qumran*, 26-27; and Davidson, *Angels*, 177-178. However, both Knibb and Davidson fail to note the substantial differences, esp. the lack of a cosmic dualism in CD 2.3-13. Cf. Davies, *Damascus Covenant*, 72-73.

that in the end God would destroy the spirit of darkness (1QS 4.18-19, 23-26; 1QM 1.14f), and finally by declaring God's superiority to all angels (1QM 13.13f; 1QH 15.28ff [formerly 7.28ff], 18.8 [formerly 10.8ff]).

3. Michael and the Prince of Light

I turn now to the identity of the Prince of Light and the Angel of Darkness. I will begin with the latter. Since his identity is explicit throughout the corpus, I cite one significant passage: "But *Belial*, the Angel of Malevolence, Thou hast created for the Pit; his [rule] is in Darkness; and his purpose is to bring about wickedness and iniquity. All the spirits of his company, the angels of Destruction, walk according to the precepts of Darkness,..." (1QM 13.11-12). In Classical Hebrew בליעל means "worthlessness" or "worthless" and never represents a personal name. In the Qumran writings, however, it appears frequently as the name of the Angel of Darkness.[56] Thus its development from noun to personal name is analogous to the Hebrew שטן (Satan). While the use of Belial as a personal name, to my knowledge, occurs nowhere outside of Qumran sectarian writings, except as a variant reading at 2 Cor. 6.15, Beliar is known from a number of Jewish and Christian writings.[57]

The identification of the Prince of Light is more difficult because it rests on a single text, 1QM 17.6-8a. In the midst of the battle, the Priestly Messiah will "strengthen (the) heart" of his soldiers with the following speech, declaring that God:

> [will annihilate Belia]l in all future times of eternity. Today is His appointed time to subdue and to humble the prince of the dominion of wickedness. He will send eternal assistance to the lot to be redeemed by Him through the might of an Angel: He hath magnified the authority of Michael through eternal light to light up in joy [the house of I]srael, peace and blessing for the lot of God, so as to raise amongst the angels the authority of Michael and the dominion of Israel amongst all flesh.[58]

---

[56] Charlesworth, et al. (*Graphic Concordance*, 74-75) lists 69 occurrences!

[57] Jewish: *Jub.* 1.20, 15.33; *SibOr.* ii.167, iii.63, 73; *LivPro.* 4.6, 20; 17.2; and throughout the *T12P*. Christian: 2 Cor. 6.15; *AscenIs.* 1.8-9, *passim*; and *QuestBart.* 4.25.

[58] The Rabins' translation in Yadin, *War*, 340. See also the translations of García Martínez (*DSS Translated*, 112), van der Ploeg (*Guerre*, 52) and Lohse (*Texte*) 219.

Here Michael not only comes to the aid of the sectarian army (cf. 1QS 3.24 and 4QCatenae[a] [= 4Q177] 4.12-16), he is also directly associated with "Light". He is the agent by whom God enlightens Israel.[59] Furthermore, this portrait of the Prince of Light as leader of the heavenly hosts who comes to the aid of the Sons of Light conforms to what we know of Michael from the Jewish apocalyptic literature.[60] Further, the title "Prince" (שׂר) is attributed to Michael in the Book of Daniel (10.13, 21, 12.1). Indeed, von der Osten-Sacken cogently argues that 1QM 17.5b-8 originated from extended reflection upon Dan. 11.40-12.4.[61] This makes it difficult to resist the conclusion that "Michael" is the Prince of Light's name. Scholars in general have accepted this identification.[62] Ringgren objects that the Prince of Light "gives the impression of being more a figure in his own right".[63] This is hardly a compelling reason. The identification of the Prince of Light with a known angel would give him more of an individual personality, not less.

That God destroys Belial in the eschatological battle through the agency of Michael, raises the question of his relationship to the messianic figures in sectarian thought. As stated above, the sectaries' beliefs about the roles of the two Messiahs is not very clear. However, 1QSb 5.20-29 suggests that the role of the princely Messiah parallels that of Michael in 1QM 17; both first conquer and then rule. The community, at least according to 1QM,

---

[59] Vermes' translation (*Complete DSS in English*, 181) appears to attribute Israel's "enlightenment" to God alone: "...and He will send eternal succour to the company of His redeemed by the might of the princely Angel of the Kingdom of Michael. With everlasting light He will enlighten with joy [the children] of Israel;...". The Hebrew reads: וישלח עזר עולמים לגורל [פ]דותו בגבורת מלאך האדיר למשרת מיכאל באור עולמים להאיר בשמחה ב[נ]ית י[שראל. The Hebrew, of course, has no punctuation, and thus Vermes' rendering is grammatically plausible. However, it obscures somewhat the dualistic outlook of the *War Scroll*, in which God acts through intermediaries. Nonetheless, even Vermes (*Complete DSS in English*, 85-86) holds Michael and the Prince of Light to be identical.

[60] See above pp. 33-42.

[61] *Gott und Belial*, 95-100.

[62] So Davidson, *Angels*, 148; Yadin, *War*, 235-236; Knibb, *Qumran Community*, 97; Leaney, *Rule*, 148; Vermes, *Complete DSS in English*, 85-86; von der Osten-Sacken, *Gott und Belial*, 116-117; Collins, *Apocalypticism*, 104-105; Boccaccini, *Beyond the Essene Hypothesis*, 60-62; and Hengel, *Judaism and Hellenism*, 188, 231.

However, Wernberg-Møller (*Manual*, 71) tentatively opts for Uriel, the Angel over the Heavenly Lights in *1En.* 72.1ff and whose name means "God is Light". This suggestion is very improbable. The Qumran fragments of *1 Enoch* consistently read Sariel for Uriel, as does the list of the four archangels at 1QM 9.15-16. Indeed, Uriel appears nowhere in the Qumran corpus, not even in the extant portions of 4QEn[astr].

[63] *Faith*, 82-83.

regarded Michael as the heavenly agent of God's salvation, but, it would seem, they also awaited two earthly agents of that salvation. The *War Scroll* assumed at least some military role for the royal Messiah, for he and his shield are mentioned in 1QM 5.1-2. More importantly, 1QM 11.4-7, citing Num. 24.17-19, predicts that God will defeat "Moab" and "all the sons of Seth" through the Davidic Messiah.[64] The priestly Messiah is not mentioned in this work unless Yadin is correct in assuming that the "Chief Priest" refers to him.[65]

The very fragmentary 4Q285 (*Serekh Milhamah*) also seems to envision a messianic figure leading the Qumran forces in battle.[66] Interestingly, Michael appears in this document. According to Milik, the eighth and ninth lines of fragment six read: [...]ברחמ[י]כה] את מיכאל ג[בריא]ל [שריאל] [ורפאל...].[67] Eisenman and Wise, who reconstruct the fragments differently, place this fragment much earlier in the text and refrain from supplying the names of Gabriel, Sariel, and Raphael. Given that only the ג and ל of גבריאל and none of שריאל or רפאל are extant, Milik's reconstruction can hardly be considered certain. Furthermore, his appeal to 1QM 9.15-16 for this reconstruction works against him; for this latter text suggests that there should be a ו before the ג. Thus, it must be admitted that we know neither the order of these fragments nor whether the fragment in question refers to Michael alone or in a list of the four archangels. It is surely disappointing that so little has survived. The context indicates that the setting is the eschatological battle. Indeed, some have surmised that 4Q285, and the related 11Q14, may be from the lost ending of the *War Scroll*.[68] If so, the complete text of 4Q285 would very likely make clear the relationship between the community's beliefs about Michael and their messianic hopes.

One aspect of the eschatological nature of Michael's ministry also appears in the recently published and very fragmentary 4Q470.[69] Here Michael acts as the mediator of a covenant between Zedekiah and, presumably, God. As Larson notes, phrases such as "on [th]at day" (frag. 1.3) and "...at] that time" (frag. 1.5), as well as the imperfect tense יאמר

---

[64] So also Chester, "Messianic Expectations", 24.
[65] Yadin, "DSS and Hebrews", 51.
[66] Text and translation in Eisenman and Wise, *DSS Uncovered*, 24-29. For important criticisms of Eisenman's translation, see Bockmuehl, "Slain Messiah?"; idem. "Recent Discoveries"; and Vermes, "Oxford Forum".
[67] Milik, "Milki-sedeq", 143. Cf. also Bockmuehl, "Slain Messiah?", 162-163; and Larson, "4Q470", 224.
[68] Vermes, *Complete DSS in English*, 187-189; García Martínez, *DSS Translated*, 123-124.
[69] Larson, "4Q470".

מ[יכ]אל (frag. 1.5), "M[ich]ael shall say", are probably best explained if the text makes use of the apocalyptic technique of *vaticinium ex eventu*. In other words, it is altogether possible that this text portrays Michael's future work on behalf of the Qumran community not in terms of a military conquest as in 1QM, but in terms of the re-establishment of the covenant. To be sure, it is only the appearance of Michael and the eschatological context which suggests that this may be a sectarian text,[70] so it is also possible that 4Q470 should be classed with non-canonical, rather than sectarian, writings.

If the identification of the Prince of Light with Michael is correct, why were the sectaries so hesitant to use his name? If Michael was indeed their heavenly advocate and the commander of the angelic hosts with whom they were joined into a single community, why does his name occur so infrequently in their theological documents? This is not the problem it first appears to be. On examining the names of other angels in concordances to the Dead Sea Scrolls it becomes evident that a similar situation exists for the other named angels. Sariel occurs only in the towers passage from the *War Scroll* discussed above (1QM 9.15-16). Gabriel appears only there and in a very fragmentary text called *Book of Noah* (1QNo 2 1.4), while Raphael only appears in these two texts and in 11QapPs^a.[71] In addition, the non-sectarian 4Q529, a text to be discussed below, mentions both Gabriel and Michael. If Milik's reconstruction mentioned above is accepted it would add another reference for all four archangels. Thus, in the whole of the extant Qumran corpus there are only five references to Michael in sectarian literature (1QM 9.15-16 [*bis*], 17.6-7 [*bis*]; 4Q285) and three more in literature which may or may not be sectarian (4Q470 [*bis*], 4Q529). Gabriel appears three times in sectarian literature (1QM 9.15-16 [*bis*]; 1QNo), once more in a uncertain reconstruction (4Q285), and once in a non-sectarian text (4Q529). Raphael is certainly mentioned four times in sectarian texts (1QM 9.15-16 [*bis*]; 1QNo; 11QapPs^a) and possibly once more if Milik's reconstruction of 4Q285 is correct. Finally, only three references can be found for Sariel, two of which are certain (1QM 9.15-16

---

[70] There is evidence that Michael was regarded as mediator of the Sinai Covenant. See above pp. 49-50, where I argue that the "angel of the presence" in *Jubilees* (1.29-2.2; *passim*) may be Michael. Cf. also the preface of *ApMos.* and Hermas *Sim.* viii.3.3 and see below pp. 124 and 165-166.

[71] For the latter text, see Puech "11QPsAp^a", 387-388. Other than this last text, the above figures are based on Charlesworth, *Graphic Concordance*, and the earlier *Preliminary Concordance*, distributed by Stegemann.

[*bis*]) and one which is uncertain (4Q285). Thus there seems to be a tendency in the sectarian writings to avoid the names of the angels.[72]

Significantly, Josephus (*War* ii.142) claims that each Essene was bound by oaths "not to communicate their doctrines except as he himself received them, to abstain from robbery, and to preserve in like manner both the books of their sect, and *the names of the angels*".[73] In the most natural interpretation, this offers a natural explanation for the paucity of angelic names in the sectarian writings: The names of the angels were regarded as a part of the secret knowledge belonging to the sect. It follows from this that documents such as the *War Scroll*, which do use angelic names, were intended only for internal consumption. It is certainly not hard to imagine a work like the *War Scroll* being restricted from outsiders. However, the occasional references to Michael, Gabriel and Raphael in Daniel and Tobit, not to mention the many such references in *1 Enoch*, seem to present a fatal objection to this suggestion. Given the widespread use of Daniel, Tobit and *1 Enoch* in Second Temple Judaism, these names could hardly have been considered esoteric! However, it is possible that it was the equation of Michael with the Prince of Light, and similar identifications for the other angels, which the community considered secret.[74]

It should, however, be emphasized that the identification of the Prince of Light with Michael rests on a single passage in a document which existed in more than one form. Certainly, 1QM demonstrates that *some* of the sectarians at *one* point of time identified the two figures, but we cannot be sure how widespread this identification was. It is even possible that such knowledge was current in the community only among a certain elite.[75]

---

[72] As stated above pp. 43-44 and 50, *Jubilees*, the *Animal Apocalypse*, and the *Testament of the Twelve Patriarchs*, works sharing other affinities with the Dead Sea Scrolls, also avoid mentioning the names of angels.

[73] πρὸς τούτοις ὄμνυσιν μηδενὶ μὲν μεταδοῦναι τῶν δογμάτων ἑτέρως ἢ ὡς αὐτὸς μετέλαβεν, ἀφέξεσθαι δὲ λῃστείας καὶ συντηρήσειν ὁμοίως τά τε τῆς αἱρέσεως αὐτῶν βιβλία καὶ τὰ τῶν ἀγγέλων ὀνόματα. The emphasis is, of course, mine.

Cf. 1QS 9.16-17 where it is stated that the Master will "conceal the teaching of the law from men of injustice".

[74] If Michael was identified with Melchizedek, as I will argue below, then this also may have been part of the esoteric sectarian knowledge about Michael. On all this cf. Davidson, *Angels*, 268, n.3.

[75] There is good evidence that the priests and the 'more advanced' sectarians were privy to more esoteric knowledge than that available to the ordinary sectarian. In addition to 1QS 9.16-17 cited above, cf. 1QS 5.20ff, 6.13ff, where advancement is based on one's knowledge, and 1QS 8.1ff, where the Council of the community could be understood as a governing elite. Cf. also the existence of scrolls written in a cryptic script, which may indicate that they were restricted for a certain elite.

I now turn briefly to two texts which must be discussed for the sake of completeness. The first of these, 4Q529, is an Aramaic writing, given the title "The Words of Michael" by Eisenman and Wise.[76] It begins: "The words of the book that Michael spoke to the angels of G[od...".[77] The remainder describes Michael's account of a journey in which he saw fiery troops and nine mountains and had a discussion with Gabriel. The editors assume this to have been a heavenly journey, but there is nothing in the text which makes this necessary. A journey to the ends of the earth, such as we find in *1En.* 17-36, is just as likely. Furthermore, there is nothing in this fragmentary text which would identify it as sectarian. It has much more in common with the Enochic *Book of Watchers* and, at least in its present state, tells us nothing about the sectarian beliefs about Michael.

The second text, 4Q491 11, was once thought to be part of a recension of the *War Scroll* different from that represented by 1QM. The original editor, M. Baillet, gave this fragment the title "Cantique de Michel et cantique des justes".[78] The "song" is in the first person and the speaker claims great things for himself. He proclaims: "My glory is incomparable, and apart from me none is exalted", and a little later, "I am reckoned with the 'gods' and my dwelling-place is in the congregation of holiness". There is nothing in the text to suggest that this person is Michael, other than the supposed connection with the *War Scroll*. However, subsequent research has shown conclusively that this text has nothing to do with the *War Scroll*, but rather is related to the *Hodayot*.[79] Indeed, there is an emerging consensus that the speaker of this text is not an angel, but a human figure who has been exalted to heaven.[80] Just who this person was thought to be is very uncertain given the fragmentary nature of the text[81] and certainty is not pos-

---

[76] *DSS Uncovered*, 37-39.

[77] So Eisenman and Wise's translation, but with a correction. Their text reads: מלי כתבא די אמר מיכאל למלאכי אל [מן בתר די סלק לשמיא עליא]. The words within the brackets are pure speculation. However, it should be noted that of their last word אל, only the א is clearly visible. A portion of another letter, just before the lacuna, can also be seen and it *may* be part of the horizontal stroke of a ל, but too little survives to be sure. So Eisenman and Wise's text should read למלאכי א[ל or, at the very least, למלאכי אל. Significantly, the translations of Vermes and of Wise, Abegg and Cook end with "the angels", while García Martínez has "the angels of God".

[78] *DJD*, VII.26-30.

[79] Schuller, "Cave 4"; Collins and Dimant, "Thrice-Told"; Abegg, "Who Ascended". Cf. also Smith, "Ascent to the Heavens"; idem, "Two Ascended".

[80] So Collins and Dimant, "Thrice-Told"; Abegg, "Who Ascended"; and Smith, "Ascent to the Heavens"; idem, "Two Ascended".

[81] Actually, "texts" is more correct for there are highly significant parallels to 4Q491 11 in 4Q427 7 and 4Q471b.

sible, but I find the arguments for a human figure compelling. Thus, any connection with Michael can be dismissed.

4. Michael and Melchizedek

There is some evidence that the Prince of Light was also known as Melchizedek at Qumran. Two very fragmentary documents, 11QMelch and 4Q'Amram, may identify the Prince of Light with Melchizedek. The latter may even have originally used all three appellations, Michael, Melchizedek, and the Prince of Light, for the same angelic figure.

The first and longest of these, 11QMelchizedek, was first published in 1965.[82] This document, which gives an eschatological interpretation to a number of OT texts, presents Melchizedek as an angelic[83] figure and eschatological saviour, similar to the portrait of the Prince of Light/Michael offered above.

First, Melchizedek stands at the head of the "Sons of Light". In 2.5 "sons of heaven" (בְּנֵי הֹשָׁמַ[יִ]ם) is parallel to "the inheritance of Melchizedek" (מנחלת מלכי צדק), and both phrases seem to be identified with "the so[ns of the lot of Melchiz]edek (בְּנֵ[י] גורל מלכי צ[ד]ק).[84] Now admittedly these reconstructions are somewhat hypothetical, and may be incorrect in certain particulars,[85] but the general sense of the passage is confirmed by 2.8: "when expiation (will be made) for all the sons of [light and] for the m[e]n of the lot of Mel[chi]zedek".[86] Milik[87] opts for אל rather than אור, understanding the phrase as a reference to angels rather than men. The

---

[82] Van der Woude, "Melchisedek als himmlische Erlösergestalt". Because of this text's importance, it has been re-edited a number of times. See also de Jonge and van der Woude, "11Q Melchizedek"; Fitzmyer, "Further Light"; Milik, "Milkî-sedeq"; and Kobelski, *Melchizedek*. The "official" publication in the *DJD* series finally occurred in 1998. See García Martínez, Tigchelaar, and van der Woude, *DJD* XXIII.221-241. Cf. also Delcor, "Melchizedek from Genesis to the Qumran Texts"; Laubscher, "God's Angel of Truth"; and Horton, *Melchizedek*.

[83] That Melchizedek is an angel in this text is clear from the attribution of the title אלוהים to him (2.10). For a discussion of this line see Kobelski, *Melchizedek*, 59-62; Horton, *Melchizedek*, 75; Delcor, "Melchizedek", 133-134.

[84] These are Kobelski's (*Melchizedek*, 5) reconstructions and translations. On the whole, I will follow his text and translation, but with consultation of the others.

[85] E.g., Milik (97) reconstructs the last phrase as בְּחֹ[ל]קי מלכי צ[ד]ק, "in the lot of Melchizedek".

[86] לכגר בו על כול בני [אור ו]אנש[י] גורל מֹל[כי] צדק[....]

[87] Milik, "Milkî-sedeq", 98.

strength of this proposal is that it places both angels (בני אל) and men (אנשי גורל מלכי צדק) in one community with Melchizedek as its leader. Either way Melchizedek functions as does the Prince of Light, standing at the head of those who belong to God.

However, there is a difficulty here: We do not find in the Qumran corpus references to "the lot of the Prince of Light", rather the "lot" always belongs to God.[88] 11QMelch is the only sectarian text which speaks of a lot other than those belonging to God or Belial. However, I do not believe this should be overstressed. The Prince of Light has "all the spirits of truth under his dominion" according to 1QM 13.10, and 1QM 17.7b speaks of Michael's "authority amongst the 'gods'".[89] Furthermore, the contention of 1QS 3.20 ("All the children of righteousness are ruled by the Prince of Light and walk in the ways of light,...") does not differ greatly from saying that the children of righteousness belong to "the lot of the angel of light".[90] Certainly, there is a sense in which the men of the "lot" of light also belong to the Prince of Light.

Secondly, just as in 1QS and 1QM the Prince of Light/Michael is God's agent of retribution upon Belial, so 11QMelch 2.13 proclaims that "Melchizedek will exact the ven[geance] of E[l's] judgements [and he will protect all the sons of light from the power] of Belial and from the power of all [the spirits of] his [lot]".[91] Admittedly, a large part of this sentence must be reconstructed and therefore remains conjectural. Nonetheless the portion of text which is certain is enough to establish that Melchizedek functions as the Prince of Light/Michael by conquering Belial and his imps. The context of the final Jubilee (2.6b-7) indicates that we are dealing here with the eschatological war of the sons of light with the sons of darkness. Clearly, Melchizedek is the eschatological agent of salvation in that he conquers Belial, "proclaims liberty" to the sons of his lot (2.6), relieves "them of the burden of their iniquities" (2.6b), and makes expiation "for the all the sons of light" (2.8).

Thirdly, after conquering Belial both Michael and Melchizedek begin to reign as a monarch. According to 1QM 17.7b God will "raise amongst the gods the authority of Michael". So also in 11QMech 2.16 a herald proclaims with reference to Melchizedek: "Your God [is King]".[92] That this is a reference to Melchizedek is clear from the fact that in 2.24-25 the

---

[88] Cf. e.g., 1QS 2.12; 1QM 1.5, 4.2f, 13.5, 15.1, 17.7. Cf. Horton, *Melchizedek*, 78.
[89] Or "kingdom": להרים באלים משרת מיכאל.
[90] Cf. Davidson, *Angels*, 263.
[91] Cf. the vivid parallels in 1QS 3.24 and 4QCatenae[a] [= 4Q177] 4.12-16.
[92] Since this is an adaptation of Isa. 52.7, the reconstruction is virtually certain.

author feels the need to explain who אלוהיך refers to, which would be unnecessary if God were intended.[93]

Fourthly, Melchizedek may have been regarded as mediator of the covenant, for he is "god" of the community known as "the establishers of the covenant" (2.24). From 4Q470 we know that this was a role attributed to Michael.

All this makes a good case for an identification between Melchizedek and Michael/the Prince of Light in 11QMelch.[94] However, it must be remembered that this is a very fragmentary text and that many of the reconstructions are uncertain.[95] An explicit identification of Melchizedek with either Michael or the Prince of Light elsewhere in the Qumran corpus would confirm this reading of 11QMelch. No such identification exists, but 4Q'Amram comes close.[96] This Aramaic document has been given the title *Testament of 'Amram*,[97] for in concert with testamentary literature it is presented as the final words of 'Amram, the father of Moses. He describes a vision in which two watchers fight over him (frag. 1.9-15). They appear to be the two angelic figures of the "Two Spirits Discourse" (1QS 3.13-4.26). The angel of light describes the other to 'Amram thus: "all his way is da[r]k, and in darkness....He rules over all the dark...". (frag. 2.4-5). The same angel then describes himself: "I am ruler over all that is of God...". (frag. 2.6).[98] Clearly then we have here another example of the cosmic dualism typical of sectarian literature.

The reconstruction suggested by Milik[99] and followed by Kobelski[100] gives to each of these two watchers three names:

---

[93] So Horton, *Melchizedek*, 75. Cf. also Kobelski, *Melchizedek*, 72 and his reconstruction of 2.24-25.

[94] Kobelski (*Melchizedek*, 65), following Lueken (*Michael*, 31), points out that a number of medieval texts also identify Michael and Melchizedek. Among these *Yalqut* Had. 114/5, 3.19, which comments on Ps. 110, is especially interesting (cited from Kobelski): "Michael is called Melchizedek...the priest of El Elyon who is a priest on high" (מיכאל נקרא מלכי צדק...כהן לאל עליון שהוא כהן של מעלה). Kobelski also lists *Zohar* Had. 22.4 and 41.3.

[95] Most scholars have at least tentatively accepted this identification. Horton (*Melchizedek*, 80-82), however, thoroughly opposes it. In doing so he has to posit that 11QMelch is a very uncharacteristic sectarian writing, which as we have seen is manifestly not correct.

[96] This text was first published by Milik in his article "4Q Visions de 'Amram". Cf. also Milik, "Milkî-sedeq", 126-144.

[97] E.g., by Vermes, *Complete DSS in English*, 534-536; Kobelski, *Melchizedek*, 24.

[98] Translation, text, and line numbers come from Kobelski, *Melchizedek*, 24-36.

[99] "4Q Visions de 'Amram".

[100] *Melchizedek*, 27-28.

[And these are his three names: Belial, Prince of Darkness], and Melchiresaʻ....[and he answered and sa]id to me: "[My] three names [are Michael, Prince of Light, and Melchizedek"] (4Q ʻAmram 2.3 and 3.2).

It is to be noted that at this crucial passage only "and Melchiresaʻ" (ומלכי רשע) and "three names" (דתלתה שמה[תי) are actually preserved. The reconstruction is based on the assumption that the two figures are described according to a strict antithetical parallelism. Since one is described as a ruler over darkness (2.5) and the other is also a ruler (2.6), it makes sense to reconstruct the text so that the latter rules over light (2.5). If one has three names, so does the other. If one of the names of the first is מלכי רשע, "king of wickedness", then the other probably had the name מלכי צדק, "king of righteousness". From there the supplying of Michael and Belial, Prince of Light and Prince of Darkness is merely conjectural. This is a possible reconstruction, but rather than confirming the above reading of 11QMelch, it depends upon it.[101]

There is, however, no reason to doubt that the good angel in this text is the Angel or Prince of Light known from other sectarian works. It is, therefore, not at all surprising that he should appear in this, the testament of Moses' father, struggling with the Angel of Darkness over the life of ʻAmram; for the sectarians saw in the events of the Exodus a struggle between these two angels (CD 5.17b-19).

Milik has offered another rather bold reconstruction which would implicitly identify Michael and Melchizedek. At 1QM 13.10, just after a reference to the Prince of Light, there is a lacuna in the text which Lohse and Yadin supply as: ובג[ורלו כול בני צד[ק. Milik, on the other, suggests: וביד[כה מלכי צד[ק.[102] Such an identification of the Prince of Light with Melchizedek in the *War Scroll* would imply a Michael-Melchizedek equation.

One final text must be considered. Newsom[103] has argued that in *Sabbath Shirot* the seventh chief prince precedes the other sixth in importance

---

[101] In a recent article, García Martínez ("Eschatological Figure") has interpreted the redeemer figure of 4Q246, the so-called "Son of God" text, along similar lines. García Martínez believes that this eschatological redeemer is none other than Michael/Melchizedek/Prince of Light. This, of course, is a possibility. However, so little of this text survives that any identification remains purely speculative. Indeed, the text could simply be describing the Messiah of David, a human figure or even an "Antichrist" figure. See Flusser, "Hubris of the Antichrist".

[102] Milik, "Milkî-sedeq", 139-142.

[103] Newsom, *Sabbath Sacrifice*, 33-38.

and prestige. The seventh chief prince offers more elaborate contributions than the other chief princes in "the litany of tongues" recorded in the eighth Sabbath song (4Q403 1 ii 1-29) and in the psalms of the chief princes recorded in the sixth song (4Q403 1 i 1-9). This may suggest that he is the highest of the chief princes. Newsom further suggests that Melchizedek was the name of the principal angel in the *Sabbath Shirot*. She points to 4Q401 11 3: צדק כוהן בעד]ת אל[מלכי] and 4Q401 22:]כי צדק... .[.... While the latter reconstruction is very speculative, the former has a couple of factors in its favor. First, the singular כוהן is very unusual in this document. Second, as Newsom notes, the reconstructed phrase appears to be an allusion to Ps. 82.1, which is also cited in 11QMelch 2.10 and is there applied to Melchizedek. Newsom admits that if these reconstructions are correct, these two passages would be the only times an angel is referred to by name in the *Shabbath Shirot*. Newsom's hypothesis is possible, but conjectural.

Finally, it is not hard to imagine why the covenanters were attracted to the name Melchizedek. The popular etymology of the day understood מלכי צדק as "king of righteousness" (cf. Heb. 7.2; Philo *Leg. All*. 3.79-82; and Josephus *War* iv.438). For the angelic representative and hero of a group of religious sectarians who referred to themselves as בני צדק and to their founder as מורה צדק this is an eminently appropriate title.[104] Thus "Melchizedek" may have been understood more as a title than a name.[105]

5. Conclusions

In conclusion, I believe the evidence for Michael's identification with the Angel of Light is so strong as to be virtually certain. This makes Michael a figure of central importance for the sectarians. Since they are

---

[104] Note also the rejoicing of the heavenly צדק at Michael's triumph in 1QM 17.7-8.

[105] This, however, does not necessarily rule out a sectarian equation of Melchizedek/Michael with the OT figure by that name (Gen. 14; Ps. 110). Later documents (Heb. 7; 2*En*. 71-72; the Nag Hammadi tractate on Melchizedek [NHC IX.1]) provide evidence for ancient, widespread and varied speculation about this mysterious priest-king.

For modern speculations on these ancient ones, cf. Davila, "War in Heaven"; and Aschim, "Melchizedek the Liberator". Aschim in particular offers a fascinating suggestion about the origin of the Michael/Melchizedek identification. He proposes that there was an exegetical tradition based on Gen. 14 in which Melchizedek was understood to be an angelic figure who fought for Abraham in heaven, securing his victory, and then appeared to him on earth. He points to Josh. 5.13-15 as a possible parallel.

the "faithful of Israel", Michael functions as *their* protector (1QS 3.24-25) and as the leader of the angelic forces with whom they are in communion (1QM 13.10). His position among the angels parallels theirs among the nations, which secures for him a central role in the eschaton (1QM 17.7-8).

The evidence for the identification of Melchizedek with Michael, on the other hand, is not as firm but has much to commend it. If it is accepted, it would appear safe to conclude that the Qumran sect throughout its history affirmed a single tradition concerning its angelic prince and simply gave him different names (Michael and Melchizedek). On the other hand, it is possible that 11QMelch and 1QM testify to two divergent traditions concerning the identity of the community's angelic patron, traditions which may have been held at different times within the community's history or at the same time by different individuals. Given the complete absence of any polemic against either Michael or Melchizedek, it seems more probable that Michael and Melchizedek are to be identified.

Michael traditions at Qumran, then, are very similar to what we found in Jewish apocalyptic literature. He remains the angelic champion of Israel, although the sectarians define "Israel" much more narrowly. He is clearly the most important of the angels, as well as commander-in-chief of the heavenly armies. Finally, if the Melchizedek identification is sound and if Newsom is right that the name of the principal angel in the *Sabbath Shirot* was Melchizedek, then high priestly duties were also attributed to Michael.[106] More importantly for the thesis of this work, Michael/Melchizedek appears to have been held to be the heavenly counterpart to the earthly Messiahs. Michael's triumph in the *War Scroll* coincides with the messianic victory, and Melchizedek serves as an eschatological redemption figure. However, the sectarians do not appear to have ever taken the step of identifying Michael/Melchizedek with either of the Messiahs.

---

[106] Note also the close relation between the earthly priests and Michael in 1QM 16-17.

Chapter 4

Michael and Philo's Logos Doctrine

In the extensive extant corpus of Philo of Alexandria no reference appears to the archangel Michael, nor to any other angel with a personal name. This has led some to conclude that Philo's thought could not accommodate such beings. Goodenough, for example, can write that Philo "could not possibly have made room for a literal Gabriel or Michael in his thinking,...".[1] Other scholars have been impressed by certain passages where Philo describes the Logos as "the archangel",[2] and have concluded that Philo either identified the Logos with Michael,[3] or that traditions about him as the highest archangel influenced Philo's Logos doctrine.[4] This chapter will briefly overview Philo's teaching concerning the Logos and angels, before investigating whether there are any associations between the Logos and Jewish traditions about Michael, and other principal angels, in Philo's thought.

---

[1] Goodenough, *Light*, 79-80. In support of this, Goodenough points to Philo's allegorizing of the Cherubim so that no resemblance remained with what Goodenough terms "the Palestinian tradition".

[2] *Conf.* 146; *Her.* 205.

[3] Wolfson, *Philo*, 1.378-379; Carr, *Angels and Principalities*, 38; and Dix, "Seven Archangels", 243.

[4] Lueken, *Michael*, 59-60. Cf. also Hurtado, *One God*, 46; Nikiprowetzky, "Note", 188; and Chester, "Messianic Expectations", 48.

1. Philo's Doctrines of God, the Logos, and Angels

a. Philo as Monotheist

Recent studies have tended to portray Philo primarily as an exegete of scripture, rather than a philosopher or systematic theologian.[5] One should not, therefore, be too concerned when encountering certain inconsistencies in his thought. Indeed, earlier interpreters are now routinely criticized for attempting to force Philo's expositions into a systematic straitjacket. This criticism has above all been applied to Wolfson's magisterial effort to construe Philo as the most significant philosopher between Aristotle and Spinoza.[6] However, we should also guard against the tendency to conclude that every apparent contradiction is one. As a recent commentator has said, what often, to the modern, "looks like an inconsistency or a contradiction does so because of the intellectual and religious viewpoint of the (usually non-Jewish) reader of [Philo's] works".[7]

Philo's thought is a mixture of Hellenistic philosophy and Judaism. Three statements can be made regarding this. It is possible that Philo received a Hellenistic education, including philosophy, in the *gymnasium*.[8] It is likely that Philo was a man of means and moved in the higher circles of society in Alexandria.[9] It is certain that Philo was deeply influenced by contemporary currents in Greek philosophy, especially Middle Platonism, and to a lesser degree Stoicism and Pythagoreanism as well.[10] However, Philo was also a Jew, and thus, as a Jew he was deeply committed to the Torah and the traditions of his people. While it is probably true that the majority of Alexandrian Jews would find Philo's expositions of scripture esoteric and arcane,[11] Philo nonetheless held a prominent position in the Jewish community of his city and led a delegation from it to the Roman Emperor. It is probable that Philo's views did not have a wide currency outside intellectual circles influenced by and biased towards Hellenism.

---

[5] Sandmel, *Philo*, 4, 78; Runia, *Timaeus*, 17-20; Borgen, "Philo", 233, 259-264; idem., "Survey", 142; and above all Nikiprowetzky, *Philon*, 170-180. Contrast Winston, *Logos*, 13-14.
[6] For criticism of Wolfson's aggressive systemization, see e.g., Borgen, "Survey", 142.
[7] Williamson, *Philo*, 103.
[8] See Runia, *Timaeus*, 35-36; Sandmel, *Philo*, 12.
[9] See Runia, *Timaeus*, 34-35; Sandmel, *Philo*, 10-12.
[10] Cf. e.g., Borgen, "Philo", 256.
[11] Sandmel, *Philo*, 13-14.

However, parallels with the Wisdom of Solomon suggest that they were not entirely unique.[12]

Philo, as a Jew, was a committed monotheist. Although Philo could use very exalted language to describe the Logos, the divine powers, and even certain heroes from Israelite history (e.g., Moses), Philo remained a convinced monotheist and vigorously opposed any notion that there was a plurality of deities.[13] For example, he can state categorically that "God, being One, is alone and unique, and like God there is nothing" (*L.A.* 2.1).[14] In addition, when discussing the first commandment he writes:

> Let us, then, engrave deep in our hearts this as the first and most sacred of commandments, to acknowledge and honour one God Who is above all, and let the idea that gods are many never even reach the ears of the man whose rule of life is to seek for truth in purity and guilelessness" (*Decal.* 65).

Similarly, for Philo only God has absolute existence. This is reflected in the phrases "He that IS" (ὁ ὤν) and "the Being One" (τὸ ὄν), which Philo often uses when speaking of God. Only God has real Being and all other "beings" derive their existence from Him (*Det.* 160).

It is true that Philo can call the Logos "the divine Logos" (ὁ θεῖος λόγος; *Som.* 1.62), and "God" (θεός; *Som.* 1.227-230), and even "the second God" (ὁ δεύτερος θεός; *Q.G.* 2.62).[15] Nonetheless, he is always careful to distinguish between God and His Logos. For example, in his extended exposition of Gen. 31.13 (*Som.* 1.228-230), he carefully distinguishes between God and the Logos of God. ὁ θεὸς refers to "Him Who is truly God" (τὸν μὲν ἀληθείᾳ), while the anarthrous θεός refers to the Logos, who is "improperly" (τὸν δ' ἐν καταχρήσει) called God. Nevertheless, for Philo the author of scripture uses the title θεός for the Logos, "not from any superstitious nicety in applying names, but with one aim before him, to use words to express facts". Thus, while Philo wishes to defend the use of θεός for the Logos, he is very careful to differentiate the Logos

---

[12] See below pp. 80-81, 91-92.

[13] Cf. Wolfson, *Philo*, I.171-173; Williamson, *Philo*, 28-31; Runia, *Timaeus*, 433.

[14] Unless otherwise noted, I will be using the texts and translations of Colson, Whitaker and Marcus in the Loeb series.

[15] This phrase is very unusual even for Philo. It appears in his voluminous writings only once. Certain interpreters give the impression that it was a favorite phrase of Philo's. Cf. e.g., Segal, *Two Powers*, 159-181; and Barker, *Great Angel*, 114-133. To these, contrast the judicious statements of Runia, *Timaeus*, 449-451 and 442, n.196.

from God Himself. Not even the Logos can be called "*the* God" (ὁ θεός), since there is only one God.[16]

b. The Logos of God: The relationship between God and His Logos

How then did Philo conceive of the Logos, and what was its relation to God in his thought? Given his monotheism, why did he choose to speak of the Logos with such exalted language? The answers to these questions can only be appreciated within the complex of Philo's thought and its background in both Greek philosophy and Judaism.[17]

The Logos was for Philo a way of expressing the immanence of God, which also allowed Philo to affirm the Divine transcendence. Indeed, Williamson can assert that Philo's Logos doctrine was "a logical requirement" of his doctrine of God, "especially in regard to [Philo's] emphasis on the transcendence of God".[18] Philo's Logos can be described as "a part of God". Examples of this are those passages in which the Logos functions as the bond which holds the universe together[19] and those passages where it functions as "the divine Reason" or the Mind (Νοῦς) of God.[20] Here Philo shows dependence upon several Greek philosophical traditions. His starting point is the Platonic theory of ideas, as expressed in the *Timaeus* of Plato.[21] This "world of ideas" or "intelligible world" (ὁ κόσμος νοητὸς), as Philo calls it, served as a model (παράδειγμα) for God when he created the world. Philo uses the illustration of an architect who, in the service of his monarch, "first sketches in his own mind" a pattern of a city, and then sets about constructing it. When God wished to create the physical world, He first created the world of ideas as his pattern. This world of ideas had "no

---

[16] Cf. Williamson, *Philo*, 123-124.

[17] Admittedly, "[t]he term [Logos] is used by [Philo] very frequently and, partly because the ideas it was used to express are difficult and complex ones, and partly because Philo's own thought is also profound and complex, it is difficult to give a clear and coherent statement of Philo's thought in this area" (Williamson, *Philo*, 103). Williamson notes that for Philo the Logos can mean something (1) within God, or (2) within the natural order of the universe, or (3) within humans. As with Williamson's treatment, my discussion will focus on the first and second of these.

[18] Williamson, *Philo*, 103. Compare the slightly different position of Winston, "Logos", 49-50.

[19] *Fug.* 112; *Her.* 188; *Mos.* 2.133; *Plant.* 9.

[20] For what follows see *Op.* 16-25; and Wolfson, *Philo*, I.230-234; Winston, *Logos*, 15; Williamson, *Philo*, 104; Runia, *Timaeus*, 158-174; and Sandmel, *Philo*, 94-95.

[21] Cf. esp. Plato, *Timaeus*, 28A-29B, 30C-31A; and Runia, *Timaeus*, 158-174.

other location than the Divine Reason" (ὁ θεῖος λόγος). Philo derived the notion that ideas reside within the mind from Aristotle.[22] However, Philo went farther and affirmed that the world of ideas is identical with the divine reason or Logos (*Op.* 24-25).

Philo substitutes λόγος for Aristotle's νοῦς. By Philo's day, the term λόγος had long been used by philosophers, especially by Plato, Aristotle, and the Stoics, as a synonym for Νοῦς.[23] In addition, Platonism held to several "rough equivalent(s)" of Philo's Logos doctrine.[24] However, neither in Platonism, Stoicism nor Aristotelian thought do we find the kind of significance that the concept has for Philo, nor the range of meanings he gives to the term λόγος. Why did Philo choose to use this word, rather than Νοῦς? He appears to have been dependent upon a tradition in Alexandrian Judaism which was attributing a certain independence to God's Word. Already in Deutero-Isaiah and some of the later Psalms the דבר יהוה is beginning to be understood in a semi-hypostatic manner.[25] This process toward hypostatization will culminate in the Wisdom of Solomon (esp. 18.14-16) and the writings of Philo, but is already underway in the Greek translation of the OT. For example, Ps. 32.6 (= 33.6 MT) declares: τῷ λόγῳ τοῦ κυρίου οἱ οὐρανοὶ ἐστερεώθησαν.[26] Other passages in the Greek Psalter (147.7 [ET 147.18] and 148.8) attribute a role to God's word in the continuing administration of the natural world. In addition, it was the word of God which came to the prophets (cf. Isa. 2.1; Jer. 1.2; Ezek. 3.16), and the Law revealed at Sinai was termed τοὺς δέκα λόγους (Ex. 34.28; and Deut. 10.4). The Greek OT, therefore, could be read as affirming that the λόγος θεοῦ was an agent of both creation and revelation, roles which Philo attributes to the Logos.[27]

Significantly, in all this the Logos parallels the role of Wisdom in a number of late OT passages,[28] where Wisdom functions as agent of creation and revelation.[29] Therefore, it is not surprising that Philo explicitly

---

[22] *Metaph.* xii.7.1072b.18-22; 9.1075a.3-5; *De Anima* iii.4.429a.27-28; Williamson, *Philo*, 133; and Wolfson, *Philo*, I.229-231.

[23] See esp. Tobin, "Logos", *ABD*, I.230-231.

[24] Winston, "Logos", 49.

[25] Cf. Isa. 40.7-8, 55.10-11; Pss. 107.20; 147.15. Cf. Schmidt, "דָּבָר", 120-125.

[26] Cf. Gen. 1; and Wisdom 9.1. The Wisdom of Solomon may have been contemporary with or even later than Philo. See Winston (*Wisdom*, 59-63) on the relationship between Wisdom and Philo.

[27] Williamson, *Philo*, 104-105; Wolfson, *Philo*, I.253-261.

[28] E.g. Prov. 3.19, 8.22-31; Sir. 1.10, 24.1-34; Wis. 7.22-30, 9.1. Cf. also Job 28, Bar. 3.29; and *1En.* 42.

[29] Cf. Hengel, *Judaism and Hellenism*, 153-175.

identifies Sophia with the Logos.[30] Apparently the author of the Wisdom of Solomon shared this identification of divine Wisdom with the Logos: Θεὲ πατέρων καὶ κύριε τοῦ ἐλέους ὁ ποιήσας τὰ πάντα ἐν λόγῳ σου καὶ τῇ σοφίᾳ σου κατασκευάσας ἄνθρωπον,...(9.1).[31] It would appear, then, that Philo drew on a hellenistic Jewish tradition which asserted that by means of His Word, which was the same as His Wisdom, God created the universe and revealed Himself to the prophets.[32]

Philo then, conflating Plato with Jewish scriptures and traditions, envisions the totality of the ideas or the intelligible world as residing in the mind of God.[33] This intelligible world of ideas was for Philo the Logos (*Op.* 24-25).

c. The Logos as Hypostasis

Philo, however, also uses language which appears to imply that the Logos is a personal being with a separate identity; that is, a creature of God, and, as such, distinct from God. For example, Philo can describe the Logos as an angel or archangel,[34] as the son or firstborn of God,[35] as Israel,[36] and, as we have seen, even as θεός and ὁ δεύτερος θεός.[37] In Philo, this kind of description of the Logos as a personal, separate being perhaps predominates over the image of the Logos as part of God. This raises the principal question of Philo's conception of the Logos: "Does Philo regard the Logos as a reality, as a distinct entity having real existence, or is the Logos no more than an abstract construct, convenient to

---

[30] *L.A.* 1.65 and *Som.* 2.242-245. Cf. *Her.* 191; *Fug.* 50-51; *Q.G.* 1.57. At times the Logos and Sophia are given similar roles by Philo; cf. *Cher.* 125-127 with *Fug.* 109 and *Det.* 54. See also Tobin, "Logos", IV.350; and Wolfson, *Philo*, I.255-258.

[31] So Winston, *Wisdom*, 38; Nickelsburg, *Jewish Literature*, 180; Gilbert, "Wisdom", 311; Wolfson, *Philo*, I.255; Goodenough, *Light*, 273.

[32] Note also the correlation of Sophia and Logos in Philo's mid-second century BC precursor, Aristobulus (preserved in Eusebius, *Praep. Ev.* xiii.12.10-13). On Aristobulus, cf. Hengel, *Judaism and Hellenism*, 166-169.

[33] Cf. Dodd, *Interpretation*, 66.

[34] *L.A.* 3.177; *Deus* 182; *Conf.* 146; *Her.* 205; *Mut.* 87; *Som.* 1.239-240.

[35] *Agr.* 51; *Conf.* 63, 146. Cf. also *L.A.* 3.175; *Det.* 118; *Mig.* 6; *Her.* 205; *Som.* 1.230, in each of which the Logos is described, explicitly or implicitly, as the "eldest" of all created things.

[36] *Conf.* 146.

[37] *Som.* 1.227-230 and *Q.G.* 2.62, respectively.

Philo's philosophy, but without true existence?"[38] Since "there is no decisive clarity in Philo's presentation",[39] scholars have come down on both sides of this issue. Some argue that the Logos is nothing more than metaphorical language, a way of expressing God's action in the world,[40] while others consider Philo's Logos to be a hypostasis.[41]

Williamson's denial may serve as a serviceable definition of the term "hypostasis": "It cannot be emphasised enough that the Logos for Philo is God's Logos, the incorporeal Word or Thought of God, not a distinct and separate being having its own divine ontological status, subordinate to God".[42] A hypostasis then is a divine attribute which has attained an "ontological status, distinct and separate" from God.

With this in mind, consider the following:

> To His Word, His chief messenger, highest in age and honour, the Father of all has given the special prerogative, to stand on the border and separate the creature from the Creator. This same Word both pleads with the immortal as suppliant for afflicted mortality and acts as ambassador of the ruler to the subject. He glories in this prerogative and proudly describes it in these words 'and I stood between the Lord and you' (Deut v. 5), that is neither uncreated as God, nor created as you, but midway between the two extremes, a surety to both sides;....
> (*Her.* 205-206).

Here the Logos is explicitly said to be something other than the Creator and a creature. It occupies the position "midway between [these] two extremes". This passage certainly seems to suggest that for Philo the Logos was something more than "a way of speaking about God". Philo conceives of the Logos as something other than God and something other than a creature of God.

The principal difficulty arises from Philo's conflicting statements and images. At times he speaks of the Logos as if it were merely "a part of

---

[38] Sandmel, *Philo*, 98.

[39] Sandmel, *Philo*, 98. It should be noted that Sandmel never attempts to answer the question in this work.

[40] E.g., Williamson, *Philo*, esp. 107; Hurtado, *One God*, 44-48; and Dunn, *Christology*, 220-228.

[41] E.g., Runia, *Timaeus*, 374-375; Wolfson, *Philo*, I.231-252. Winston ("Logos", 49-50) calls the Logos a hypostasis, but his explanation shows that he really means something closer to the position of Williamson, Hurtado and Dunn; for he holds that it is "not literally a second entity by the side of God acting on his behalf".

[42] *Philo*, 107.

God" and at times as if it were a being with its own separate existence. Long ago Wolfson suggested that this implied different stages of existence in the Logos: The Logos at one stage of its existence is merely the mind of God and not separate from His essence, "later" the Logos enters a second stage as an independent entity.[43] Wolfson even posited a "third stage of existence", the Logos immanent in the world.[44]

Wolfson's position has been criticized as too systematic and artificial.[45] Nonetheless, it has the advantage of explaining the different kinds of imagery used by Philo for the Logos. Runia has returned to a modified version of Wolfson's position:

> When the Logos is regarded as the 'embodiment' of God's thought focussed on the cosmos (i.e. place of the κόσμος νοητός) or as the 'embodiment' of God's creational activity (i.e. foremost of the powers), the difference between God and his Logos appears to be kept to a minimum, perhaps to a matter of aspect rather than level. But when the immanent presence of the Logos is stressed, Philo envisages a direct contact with and permeation through the cosmos which it holds together. The Logos is πρεσβύτατος τῶν ὅσα γέγονε and πρεσβύτατος καὶ πρωτόγονος, even God's archangel. The Logos has to all appearances become a *hypostasis*, a level of God's being given real existence outside God himself.[46]

Such a position accounts for a variety of imagery used by Philo for the Logos and escapes the criticism of artificiality if we allow that Philo was primarily an exegete, not a philosopher, and thus could hold a position which was not thoroughly consistent.

Much more could be said about the Logos in Philo's thought. Hopefully this is sufficient to show the complexity of his Logos doctrine and its uniqueness within, as well as its dependence on, the Judaism of our period. I turn now to a brief summary of Philo's doctrine of angels, before examining the relation between Philo's Logos and traditions about Michael.

---

[43] Wolfson, *Philo*, I.232.
[44] Wolfson, *Philo*, I.327.
[45] Cf. Runia, *Timaeus*, 450, n.247.
[46] Runia, *Timaeus*, 450-451. The emphasis is Runia's.

d. Philo's Doctrine of Angels

In addition to the Logos, Philo conceives of God working through many powers (δυνάμεις). The chief of these powers are the creative and sovereign. Philo views the former as the merciful aspect of God and he identifies it with the divine name θεός. The latter is the punitive aspect of God and possesses the divine name κύριος.[47] At times Philo speaks as if these powers were "properties" of God, and thus a part of His essence (*Cher*. 29), and at other times as if they were created beings, separate from God (*Fug*. 94-96; *Cher*. 27-28).[48] When they are spoken of as creations of God they are equivalent to the platonic "ideas" (e.g., *Spec*. 1.45-48).[49] Philo postulates a close connection between the Logos and these powers of God. It is the Logos who unites the creative and sovereign powers (*Cher*. 28; *Q.E*. 2.68). In addition, "the Divine Logos", writes Philo, "God Himself has completely filled throughout with incorporeal potencies" (*Som*. 1.62). Thus the Logos can be said to be the sum of the divine powers. It is possible that in Philo's thought these "powers" correspond to a class of angels or the archangels. First of all, *Spec*. 1.45-48, where the powers are described as "the powers which keep guard around (God)", recalls the angels who surround God's throne (1 Kgs. 22.19-22; Pss. 82.1; 89.5-7; *1En*. 14.23; Tob. 12.15; Luke 1.19; *TAb*. A 7.11). Secondly, Philo's assertion (*Conf*. 168-175) that angels "wait upon" the heavenly powers may suggest that the powers are archangels with angels under them. Finally, it is to be remembered that δύναμεις was understood as a class of angels in the LXX (Pss. 23.9-10 [ET 24.9-10; 102.20-21 [ET 103.20-21]; 148.2) and contemporary literature (e.g. Rom. 8.38; Eph. 1.21; 1 Pet. 3.22).

Philo's discourses on the nature of angels reveal the influence of Plato, as well as that of Plato's interpreters. This is especially so in *Gig*. 6-18 and *Som*. 1.137-143, where Philo alludes to Plato's *Timaeus* 39E-40D and *Symposium* 202E and displays knowledge of the interpretation of these passages by the Middle Platonists.[50] Philo affirms that those beings which the philosophers name δαίμονες are one and the same with those Moses calls ἄγγελοι (*Gig*. 6, 16; *Som* 1.141). Following Plato and his philosophical descendants, Philo envisions angels/daemons as those souls (ψυχαί) which have not descended into flesh, but have remained wholly spiritual, and thus serve as God's ministers on behalf of humanity.[51] Thus, for Philo angels

---

[47] Cf. *Fug*. 96-100; *Cher*. 27-28; and *Q.E*. 2.68.
[48] Cf. Williamson, *Philo*, 50-51; Wolfson, *Philo*, I.220-224.
[49] See Wolfson, *Philo*, I.218-223.
[50] Dillon, "Angels", 198-199; Runia, *Timaeus*, 228-230.
[51] *Gig*. 12; *Plant*. 14; cf. *Symposium* 202E and Dillon, "Angels", 197-200.

serve as "ambassadors backwards and forwards between men and God",[52] as priests in the heavenly sanctuary,[53] as agents in the creation of matter and humans,[54] and as the punishers of evil.[55] Significantly, Philo refers to ἄγγελοι as λόγοι,[56] implying some relation between them and the Logos. Since Philo refers to the Logos as "the archangel", it appears that in some sense he understands the Logos as their leader.

2. The Logos and Michael in Philo

Having established the nature of Philo's Logos doctrine, we can now turn to the question of whether Michael and the Logos were identified in Philo's thought. It must be admitted at once that there are significant, if superficial, parallels between the traditions which surrounded Michael and Philo's Logos doctrine: Both are archangels, and the leader of the heavenly host, both perform High Priestly roles, and both are identified as the angel of the Name mentioned in Ex. 23.20-21. In addition, there are great similarities between Philo's Logos and the archangel Israel in the *Prayer of Joseph*, a Jewish apocryphon of uncertain date which provides an alternate highest archangel to the traditional Michael.

a. The Logos as archangel

As stated above, Philo refers to the Logos as an angel or the archangel on numerous occasions.[57] The two passages (*Conf.* 146-147 and *Her.* 205-206) where the Logos is termed "the Archangel" are of particular significance. The first of these declares that the Logos is "the eldest of the angels, the archangel as it were" (τὸν ἀγγέλων πρεσβύτατον, ὡς ἂν ἀρχάγγελον).[58] In other words, the Logos is the leader of the angels, a

---

[52] *Gig.* 16. Cf. *Som.* 1.141f; *Abr.* 115; Plato *Symposium* 202E.
[53] *Spec.* 1.66.
[54] *Conf.* 168-175.
[55] *Conf.* 171; *Fug.* 66.
[56] E.g., *Som.* 1.142, 147; *Post.* 91; *L.A.* 3.177.
[57] ἄγγελος: *L.A.* 3.177; *Deus* 182; *Mut.* 87; *Som.* 1.239-240. ἀρχάγγελος: *Conf.* 146; *Her.* 205.
[58] The translation is mine, but based on Colson's.

role which is usually attributed to Michael.[59] In both passages the Logos is termed "*the* archangel", implying that the Logos is the only archangel. While the presence of the article cannot be pressed, there is little evidence that Philo envisioned seven or four archangels such as we find elsewhere in Jewish literature[60] of the period.[61] Certainly, there is nothing in Philo's thought which could possibly be a rival to the Logos' chief place among the powers of God.[62]

In the second of these passages, *Her.* 205-206, the Logos is not only termed "archangel" he also intercedes for the human race. As we have seen, the idea that angels interceded for humanity has widespread attestation in the Judaism of Philo's day.[63] Furthermore, there is sufficient evidence that Michael was usually held to be the angelic intercessor *par excellence*, at least for the nation Israel.[64]

There is only one other Philonic passage extant in Greek in which the term ἀρχάγγελος appears, *Som.* 1.157. In this exposition of Jacob's dream of the ladder between heaven and earth, Philo asserts that at the top of the ladder stood "the archangel, the Lord" (τὸν ἀρχάγγελον, κύριον). Some see in this a reference to the archangel Logos.[65] However, the phrase "The One that IS" (τὸ ὄν), which immediately follows, as well as the context in general, clearly indicates that only God can be intended.[66] Philo's exegesis of Exodus 3.14 (*Det.* 160) makes it extremely unlikely that he could have used the title τὸ ὄν for any one other than God Himself.[67]

These, then, are the only occurrences of the term "archangel" in the extant writings of Philo. However, there are other instances where the Logos functions as the highest archangel. For example, in *Fug.* 111 the

---

[59] See above pp. 38-40, 64-66.
[60] See above pp. 29-30, 61-62.
[61] There is the phrase τῶν ἄρχων τις ἦν τοῦ μεγάλου βασιλέως (*Mos.* 1.166), which implies that the angel in the column of fire was only one of a number of "lieutenants". There is also a general reference to archangels in the fragment preserved in Armenian *De Deo* 3, but here archangels are grouped together with "powers and generals". See the Armenian text, German translation and reconstructed Greek text in Siegert, *Philon*, 13-37.
[62] Cf. *Fug.* 96-100; *Cher.* 27-28; and *Q.E.* 2.68.
[63] See above p. 32.
[64] See above pp. 41-46.
[65] See especially Wolfson, *Philo*, I.377-78. So also Segal, *Two Powers*, 170. Cf. Siegert (*Philon*, 64-65), who believes that the reference is to the δυνάμις κύριος, and that the other "obersten Kräfte" may also have been considered an archangel.
[66] So Drummond, *Philo*, 103-104; and Williamson, *Hebrews*, 187. This probably explains the translation of Colson-Whitaker, "the Ruler of the Angels".
[67] See above p. 78. Note also that the Logos is often called ὁ τοῦ ὄντος λόγος (the Word of the One that IS) or something similar, but never τὸ ὄν. Cf. e.g. *Fug.* 110, 112.

Logos possesses not "absolute sovereignty" (αὐτοκράτορος), for that belongs to God alone, but instead, "an admirable viceroyalty" (θαυμαστῆς ἡγεμονίας).[68] As we have seen, such a position is attributed to Michael in such diverse works as the *Testament of Abraham*, the *War Scroll*, the *Similitudes of Enoch*, and *3 Baruch*.

b. The Logos as High Priest

Related to its role as intercessor for humanity, Philo also describes the Logos as a heavenly High Priest. Philo seems to have shared not only the idea that angels interceded for humanity, but also the notion that their intercession was priestly in form and that angelic priests served in a heavenly sanctuary (*Spec.* 1.66).[69] The high priest of this heavenly temple is none other than the Logos (*Gig.* 52; *Fug.* 106-112; *Som.* 1.215). As we have seen, the Logos intercedes for humanity (*Her.* 205-206), a role which Philo elsewhere attributes to the earthly high priest (*Spec.* 1.97). So also, as we have seen, in both apocalyptic literature[70] and at Qumran[71] there is evidence that Michael served as the heavenly high priest.

c. The Logos as the Exodus Angel and Angel of the Name

Exodus 28.36 and 39.30 stipulate that the high priest wears on his turban a signet bearing the inscription "Holy to the Lord" (קדש ליהוה). There appears to have been a later tradition in which only the tetragrammaton was inscribed on the signet.[72] Philo was aware of this tradition.[73] Significantly, in one passage (*Mig.* 102-103) where he identifies the Logos as 'high priest', Philo goes on to speak of the signet worn by the high priest in terms

---

[68] Cf. also *Agr.* 51.

[69] For angelic priests and a heavenly temple in Jewish apocalyptic and at Qumran, see pp. 32 and 60-61, respectively.

[70] See above pp. 43-46.

[71] See pp. 74-75.

[72] *LetAris.* 98; Josephus *Ant.* iii.178; *War* v.235; *bShab.* 63b (R. Eliezer b. R. Yose [T3]). Cf. Wis. 18.20-25 where seemingly the Name is meant by μεγαλωσύνη σου ἐπὶ διαδήματος κεφαλῆς αὐτοῦ; and the late *PRE* 4. See also Thackeray's note in the Loeb edition of Josephus on *War* 5.235.

[73] *Mos.* 2.114-115, 132.

he uses elsewhere of the Logos: "The signet spoken of is the original principle behind all principles, after which God shaped or formed the universe, incorporeal, we know, and discerned by the intellect alone,...". It appears that Philo is identifying the Logos both with the high priest and with the signet, in which was inscribed the divine Name, worn by the high priest. Traditions which attributed to the Name an almost hypostatic existence were probably current in Philo's day.[74] Although it is doubtful that Philo knew Hebrew, it is possible that he was familiar with traditions surrounding the ineffable Name of God and transferred these to the Logos.[75] All this may suggest that Philo owed something to traditions about the angel of the Name in his conception of the Logos. Although I offer this suggestion only tentatively, there certainly was some connection between the Logos and the Name of God in Philo's thought. First, the "Name of God" (ὄνομα θεοῦ) stands among the Logos' many names listed in *Conf.* 146. In addition, Philo consistently interprets the angel of Ex. 23.20-21, in whom the divine Name resides, as the Logos (*Agr.* 51; *Mig.* 174; *Q.E.* 2.13). As I have argued above,[76] one important piece of evidence (*1 Enoch* 69.13-25) identifies Michael with this "angel of the Name". Even if this is an isolated tradition, other Angels of the Name, such as Yahoel in the *Apocalypse of Abraham* and Metatron in Hekhalot literature, are also interpreted as the angel of Exodus 23.20-21.[77]

d. The Logos and Israel

Wolfson has argued for a close connection in Philo between the Logos as "archangel" and the nation Israel. He points out that in *Conf.* 146 the Logos is called both archangel and Israel, and in *Her.* 205 the Logos is identified as the angel in the cloud who stood between Israel and the armies of Egypt.[78] In addition to these observations, one could add that when Philo equates the Logos with the Exodus angel he allegorizes the exodus as the mystical journey made by the followers of God. The end of this journey, of course, was the mystical vision of God; and the meaning of "Israel"

---

[74] See Fossum, *Name of God*, 245-256; and Urbach, *Sages*, 124-134.
[75] Cf. *L.A.* 3.207-208.
[76] See above pp. 51-53.
[77] So also Hurtado, *One God*, 49f; and Segal, *Two Powers*, 170.
[78] Wolfson, *Philo*, I.378-379. Wolfson adds the third occurrence of the term archangel (*Som.* 1.157), but I have already shown that this could not have referred to the Logos.

for Philo was "the man who sees God",[79] so once again the Logos and Israel are closely related for Philo. All this is significant because Michael was held to be the guardian angel of Israel.[80] Wolfson goes on to argue that since Philo must have been familiar with the Jewish tradition concerning the angels set over the Nations (cf. *Post.* 91-92), he also must have known the tradition concerning Michael as the angel protector for Israel. He concludes: "Thus while indeed the name of the angel Michael is not mentioned by Philo, it was the angel Michael, the guardian angel of Israel, whom he had in mind when he spoke of the archangel".[81]

e. The *Prayer of Joseph*

Finally, Philo's depiction of the Logos in *Conf.* 146 strikingly parallels the self-description of the archangel Israel in the *Prayer of Joseph*. In the only extensive passage of this apocryphon which has survived, Jacob claims to be the angel Israel: "I, Jacob, who is speaking with you, am also Israel, an angel of God and a ruling spirit.... I, Jacob, whom men call Jacob, but whose name is Israel, am the one called Israel by God, which means "a man seeing God", because I am the firstborn of every living thing to whom God gives life".[82] Here the "definition" of Israel ('Ισραήλ, ἀνὴρ ὀρῶν θεόν) is strikingly similar to Philo's: ὁ ὀρῶν, 'Ισραήλ. Furthermore, Jacob-Israel claims to be πρωτόγονος παντὸς ζῴου, just Philo calls the Logos τὸν πρωτόγονον.

In the remainder of this fragment of the *Prayer of Joseph*, Jacob/Israel relates the story of Gen. 32.24-31. However, in his version of the story the archangel Uriel opposes him and claims rank above him in the heavenly hierarchy. Jacob/Israel's response adds three more parallels to *Conf.* 146. First, both the Logos and Israel are described as an archangel. Second, some relation to the Name of God is attributed to both archangels; the Logos is identified with the Name and the angel Israel possesses the right to call upon God by means of the Name. Finally, Israel has a high priestly role (λειτουργὸς πρῶτος), which, as we have seen, corresponds to what Philo says elsewhere about the Logos.

---

[79] This etymology for Israel appears no less that 49 times in Philo, sometimes in the short form "One who sees". So Smith, *OTP*, II.703.
[80] See above pp. 33-38.
[81] Wolfson, *Philo*, I.378-379.
[82] The translation is from Smith, *OTP*, II.699-714.

We should be cautious, however, in postulating direct dependence either of Philo on *Prayer of Joseph* or vice versa. First of all, this apocryphon is of uncertain date and provenance. Since all that remains of this work are quotations in the writings of Origen and Eusebius, it must pre-date the mid-third century, but it could still be later (or earlier) than Philo. Furthermore, while the parallels between the two passages are striking, they probably only result from mutual dependence upon common traditions.[83] Nonetheless, the parallels demonstrate how important traditions surrounding the highest archangel are to *Conf.* 146, and to Philo's portrait of the Logos as a whole.

f. Conclusions

All this certainly indicates that Philo felt free to use traditions about Michael and other principal angels in Jewish literature (e.g., Israel, Yahoel, Metatron) while formulating his Logos doctrine. Nonetheless, it should not be overlooked that Philo never explicitly identifies the Logos with Michael and it would have been detrimental to his overall position had he done so. Philo's conception of the Logos differs significantly from the various traditions concerning Michael. As we have seen, Philo understood the Logos as the Mind of God and, at times, as a hypostasis. For him, the Logos was both an agent of creation and the bond which held together the universe. The Logos was the image of God and his firstborn son. No parallels to these exist in the traditions about Michael. Therefore, Michael speculations may have served Philo as models for his understanding of the Logos, but Philo does not simply take over these traditions. He transforms them by interpreting them in light of his understanding of Plato and the Stoics.

Furthermore, Philo's Logos doctrine demonstrates the fluidity of the principal angel traditions. Although Michael is generally held to be the highest of the archangels, a Jew such as Philo could and did transform the traditions for his own purposes.

---

[83] For example, the etymology "A man who sees God" for the name Israel appears to be a popular etymology which pre-dates Philo and the title "Firstborn" probably stems from Ex. 4.22. On these see Smith, "Prayer of Joseph", 265-268; and idem, *OTP* II.703-704.

3. The Logos and Sophia in the Wisdom of Solomon

Finally, a work which contains many significant parallels with Philo, the Wisdom of Solomon, may offer evidence that Michael traditions influenced Logos speculation within hellenistic Judaism outside of the writings of Philo. As we have seen, the author of Wisdom shared with Philo the identification of divine Sophia with the Logos and attributed to Sophia a role in both creation and revelation. There can be no question in light of these and other parallels that the Book of Wisdom and Philo's writings issue from the same intellectual milieu.[84] Both are concerned to interpret Judaism and the Jewish scriptures with help from Stoic and Middle Platonic philosophical traditions.[85]

Given the identification of Sophia with the Logos in the Wisdom of Solomon (9.1),[86] the portrait of the Logos in Wisdom 18.13-16 becomes very significant for the question of Michael traditions in the hellenistic Judaism of Wisdom and Philo. Here the Logos appears as a sword bearing warrior sent from the heavenly throne to administer God's vengeance upon the Egyptians.[87] Since the author of Wisdom is here interpreting Ex. 12.23, it seems probable that the phrase "into the midst of the land that was doomed" (εἰς μέσον τῆς ὀλεθρίας ἥλατο γῆς) is intended as an allusion to the "τὸν ὀλεθρεύοντα" of Ex. 12.23 LXX. The passage, therefore, presents the Logos/Sophia as the Destroying angel (τὸν ὀλεθρεύοντα) of Exodus.[88]

Given that Michael's role as the Guardian angel of Israel and the ἀρχιστράτηγος of the heavenly hosts was already well established by the time the Wisdom of Solomon was written, one wonders whether Michael traditions could have influenced this picture of the Logos as an angelic warrior. Certainly, our author has chosen not to follow another early tradition concerning the identity of "the Destroyer" of Ex. 12.23: *Jubilees* 49.2 recognized Mastema in this angel. While I know of no tradition which

---

[84] So Winston, *Wisdom*, 59-63; and Nickelsburg, *Jewish Literature*, 184.
[85] Gilbert, "Wisdom", 312.
[86] See above p. 81.
[87] As Winston (*Wisdom*, 317) points out, this passage offers us yet more reasons to conclude Sophia and the Logos are to be identified: "The description of the Logos here is strikingly similar to that of Sophia earlier in the book. Both are all-powerful (cf. 7.23); descend from the heavenly throne (cf. 9.4, 10, 17); and carry out God's commandments (cf. 7.21, 8.4)".
[88] That the "τὸν ὀλεθρεύοντα" of Ex. 12.23 was understood as an angel in the time of the composition of Wisdom is shown by Ezekiel the Tragedian's *Exagoge* 159: ὅπως παρέλθῃ σῆμα δεινὸς ἄγγελος.

identified the "τὸν ὀλεθρεύοντα" of Ex. 12.23 with Michael, Wisdom 18.13-16 definitely describes the Logos in a way that suggests Michael. For in this passage the Logos is both a warrior and a defender of Israel. This is not to say that the author of Wisdom intended to identify the two. As with Philo, Wisdom's Sophia/Logos differs significantly from the traditions concerning Michael. However, as with Philo's Logos, it is not unlikely that Michael traditions stand in the background.

Chapter 5

The Archangel Michael in Rabbinic and Hekhalot Literature

In the present chapter I turn to the evidence provided by Rabbinic and Hekhalot literature for the influence of Michael speculation and Michael traditions on the development of early Christology. To be sure, both Rabbinic and Hekhalot traditions were first committed to writing centuries after the rise of Christianity. This means, of course, that many of the traditions contained in both bodies of literature are too late to be useful for an inquiry into the origins of Christology. However, both are significant for my investigation for the following reasons: 1) it is generally agreed that Rabbinic literature contains early material, and 2) both corpora provide evidence for continued speculation about angels in Jewish contexts which both paralleled and differed radically from that which prevailed in Christian circles.

1. Rabbinic Literature

In examining Michael traditions within the writings of the Rabbis one is struck by the paucity of the material which has any bearing on the question of influence from angelology on Christology. Most references to Michael, as well as the other named angels, only appear in Amoraic sources, which is too late to shed much light on first century thought. Even in genuine Tannaitic traditions there is little evidence for contact between Rabbinic Michael traditions and early Christology. However, as we shall see, three categories of evidence may suggest a Rabbinic reaction to Christian claims for Christ. First, throughout the Rabbinic writings we encounter an enhancement of Gabriel's stature vis-à-vis Michael. Second, a complex of parallel passages provides possible evidence of a Michael-cult which the Rabbis opposed. Third, parallels exist between Rabbinic and Christian exegesis of OT מלאך יהוה passages in which the Rabbis identified the "angel of the Lord" with Michael and early Fathers identified him with the pre-incarnate Christ.

This paucity of relevant material results from the late date of Rabbinic literature, especially of the Haggadic material, and from the nature of the Rabbis' anti-Christian polemic. Those writings usually identified as Rabbinic[1] were not composed, collected and redacted until after the beginning of the third century, although it is generally agreed that these documents contain a great deal of material which is earlier and even some traditions which pre-date the destruction of the Temple.[2] Nonetheless, works which are rich in Haggadah, which by its very nature contains more information about angels than Halakhah, were for the most part collected and redacted at a comparatively late date (fifth to ninth centuries). Given the only relative reliability of dating individual traditions in Rabbinic works,[3] we can never be certain that any particular tradition from the Rabbinic material genuinely reflects our period of inquiry. In addition to this, the Rabbis attack Christian beliefs in such a way that it is very difficult to ascertain how much accurate knowledge of Christian theology they had.[4] All this means that the evidence presented below must be used very carefully and that certainty is far less possible here than in any of the material I have examined thus far.

In addition, the appearance of a tradition even in an authoritative work, such as the Babylonian Talmud, does not guarantee that it was universally accepted among the Sages, much less among contemporary Jews in general. The Rabbis frequently disagreed among themselves. More importantly, during the Rabbinic period Judaism was not a monolithic unity. Although the Rabbis increasingly succeeded in reconstituting Judaism along the lines of their ideals, this was a long process. This is reflected, in part, in the division of Jewish society into two distinct classes: The educated and cultured Rabbis and their *Haverim*, on one side, and the unlearned, coarse *'am ha'aretz*, on the other. This division, often strained, could, at times, become bitter.[5] Even within these two classes there were many social divi-

---

[1] See the definition of rabbinic literature in Safrai, *Literature*, xv-xvi.
[2] Safrai, *Literature*, xvi; and Strack-Stemberger, *Introduction*, 45, 52-54.
[3] See Strack-Stemberger, *Introduction*, 52-61. Some of the more important methods include reference to 1) the attributions, 2) the date of the final redaction of a work, and 3) parallels from non-rabbinic works. Regarding attributions I will adopt the abbreviations of Strack-Stemberger (*Introduction*, 63).
[4] So Segal, *Two Powers*, 8-9. Cf. also Bockmuehl, *Jesus*, 13-14; Bammel, "Christian Origins", 220-238.
[5] See esp. Urbach, *Sages*, 630-648.

sions and economic differences. Consequently, one must read much of the Rabbinic literature, particularly certain debates over Halakhah, as the work of academics which may have had only limited influence on the common Jew. Haggadic material, on the other hand, was more popular in nature. Indeed, much of the Haggadic material is homiletical and, therefore, directed toward those outside the academies.

a. The Angelology of the Rabbis

Schäfer has pointed out that while Rabbinic angelology stands in continuity with the angelologies of the Second Temple period (particularly apocalyptic works and the sectarian literature from Qumran), the Rabbis also seek to correct such angelologies, especially where the emphasis upon angels threatens either the principle of God's sovereignty and omnipotence or humanity's direct access to God.[6] Thus we find that one tendency in Rabbinic angelology emphasizes the uniqueness of the one God. For example, there are a number of Tannaitic texts which emphasize that God's actions of redemption and revelation on behalf of Israel were direct acts by God alone, and were not accomplished "by means of an angel and not by means of a messenger".[7] This motif may have originated in opposition to groups the Rabbis deemed heretical,[8] and certainly counters any idea that Israel's redemption was accomplished by angels. For other examples of this concern that angelology should serve monotheism, one could also point to the assertion of R. Isaac (prob. pA3) that the angels were not created on the first day so that no one would conclude that Michael or Gabriel aided God in creation,[9] or the statement that angels "are sustained only by the splendour of the *Shekhinah*".[10] Schäfer argues that another tendency of Rabbinic angelology can be seen as a response to what the Rabbis viewed as the over-emphasis on angels in apocryphal and pseudepigraphical works, i.e., the rivalry between angels and humans.[11] Passages in which this

---

[6] *Rivalität*, 41-74, esp. 74.

[7] *SifreDeut* 42; 325; *Mek* Pisha 7; Shabbeta 1; and *ARN* B 1. The first four references are unattributed (hereafter UA). Cf. Goldin's article "Not by Means".

[8] So Segal, *Two Powers*, 64.

[9] *GenR* 1.3 (parallel in 3.8); *TanB* 1.1, 1.12 (both UA); *MidrPss* 24.4 (R. Lulyani b. Tabri = Julianus b. Tiberius T2 or T3). Cf. *2En*. 29.1-3.

[10] *ExodR* 32.4 (R. Haggai; pA4); *ExodR* 47.5 (UA) *PesR* 16.2 (R. Yudan [prob. pA4] in the name of R. Isaac [prob. pA3]); and *NumR* 21.16 (R. Isaac [prob. pA3]).

[11] *Rivalität*, esp. 74 and 232-234.

rivalry occurs invariably contain a declaration of God's preference for humanity. This appears, for example, in the widespread tradition that the angels opposed the creation of humanity.[12] If humanity in general was superior to the heavenly host, then this was especially true of Israel, God's elect. Thus, *ARN* B 44 transforms R. Aqiba's statement in *mAbot* 3.14 about the pre-eminence of Israel to the rest of humanity into an affirmation of Israel's superiority to the angelic hosts. Numerous other passages could be cited,[13] but perhaps the most significant are those which favorably contrast Israel's worship of God to that of the angels.[14] This doctrine of the superiority of humans, and especially Israel, to the heavenly hosts is basic to Rabbinic angelology. As Schäfer[15] quite rightly contends, it serves to emphasize the election of Israel; because God has chosen them, they are superior even to heavenly beings.[16]

However, Rabbinic angelology also owes a great deal to the angelologies of the period preceding the Rabbinic movement. For example, the principle, well illustrated throughout the Rabbinic corpus,[17] that angels are placed over the different phenomena of nature finds close parallels in apocalyptic writings (e.g., *1En.* 60.11-24; *2En.* 19.3-4; *Jub.* 2.2). The idea that angels do not eat or drink (*GenR* 48.11; *ExodR* 47.5) is at least as old as Tobit 12.19.[18] The notion that angels are immortal and thus do not procreate appears both in the Rabbinic corpus (*bHag* 16a; *GenR* 14.3) and in *1 Enoch* 15.6-7 and Mark 12.25 pars.[19] The Rabbinic conception of angels as composed of fire and ice (*ARN* B 24; *MidrPss* 104.7) appears to owe something to the description of the heavenly world in apocalyptic works (Ezek. 1.14; Dan. 7.9-10; *1En.* 14.8-25). Finally, the four archangels (Michael,

---

[12] E.g., *bSanh* 38b (R. Yehudah [pA2] in the name of Rab [bA1]); *tSot* 6.5 (UA); *PesR* 14.9 (UA); *Tan* Wa-Yera 18; *NumR* 19.3 (R. Simeon b. Gamaliel [T3]).

Ginzberg (*Legends*, V. 69, n.12) argues that this tradition developed in opposition to Gnostic doctrine.

[13] E.g., *GenR* 78.1 (R. Meir [T3]; R. Yehudah (prob. Yehudah bar Ilai [T3]); and R. Simeon [?]); *MidrPss* 91.6 (R. Yehudah [T4?] and R. Yose [?]).

[14] E.g., *bHul* 91b; *ARN* B 27; *GenR* 65.21; *SifreDeut* 306.31; and *Tan* Kedoshim 6.

[15] *Rivalität*, 232-234.

[16] See below p. 124, where I discuss the use of this same theme by some NT authors.

[17] See esp. Schäfer, *Rivalität*, 55-59. Cf. also Lueken, *Michael*, 53-55.

[18] For a full discussion of this theme, cf. Hannah, "Docetic Christology".

[19] However, there was also an early tradition that except for the most celebrated angels, such as Michael and Gabriel, the angels have no abiding existence. They are continually being created to praise God and once they have accomplished this task they cease to be. So *bHag* 13b-14a (Rab, bA1) and *GenR* 78.1 (R. Helbo, pA4). Early parallels in 4 Ezra (8.21) and Justin Martyr (*Dial.* 128.4) demonstrate that this idea reaches back into the Tannaitic period.

Gabriel, Raphael, and Uriel) which stand about the throne in *1En.* 40 (cf. 1QM 9.14-17) have this same function in late midrashim (*NumR* 2.10; *PesR* 46.3; *PRE* 4).[20] Although both 1QM 9.14-17 and *NumR* 2.10 in varying degrees draw on Num. 2.2, *1En.* 40 is sufficiently different to counter the suggestion that the Rabbinic formulation may have resulted from an independent reflection on the same biblical text.

b. Michael According to the Rabbis

1) Continuity and Change

As with the Rabbinic angelology in general, so in the Rabbinic depiction of Michael we find a great deal of continuity with the apocalyptic and Qumranian conceptions of Michael. But some modifications appear as well. This is especially clear in the increased importance attributed to Gabriel in Rabbinic texts. In the words of Ginzberg, "at least among the Babylonian Jews Gabriel's prestige almost equals that of his rival Michael".[21] However, Gabriel never eclipses Michael. While the Rabbis may not have been uniform in their opinion as to which of the angels was the greatest, it appears that many Rabbis were content to speak of Michael *and* Gabriel as the Celestial Princes and leave the matter there.[22]

a) Michael as Highest Archangel Nonetheless, there are good reasons to surmise that when the question was asked the majority ascribed this position to Michael. First of all, Michael and Gabriel are clearly the most celebrated of the angels, as a quick glance at the appropriate concordances of Rabbinic sources shows.[23] Secondly, on the few occasions when one of

---

[20] Of course, *1En.* 40.9 reads "Phanuel" rather than "Uriel", while 1QM 9.15 has "Sariel".

[21] Ginzberg, *Legends*, V.71, n.13. Support for such a statement can be found in the many pairings of Michael and Gabriel; e.g., *GenR* 1.3 (parallel in 3.8; [R. Isaac, prob. pA3]); *TanB* 1.1, 1.12 (UA); *DeutR* 5.12 (R. Levi; prob. pA3); *CantR* 3.11 (R. Simeon b. Yohai; T3); and *NumR* 12.8 (R. Yohanan; pA2).

[22] *GenR* 78.1 (R. Helbo; pA4); *CantR* 3.7 (R. Aibo; pA4); *NumR* 11.3 (R. Yudan pA4 or pA5 in the name of R. Aibo pA4).

[23] According to a search of Rabbinic documents on CD Rom (*Davka Judaic Classical Library*), Michael is mentioned in the Babylonian Talmud 18 times and Gabriel 39 times. In the extra-canonical tractates Michael appears an additional 11 times and Gabriel another 12. Metatron, by comparison, only appears four times in the BT and not once in the extra canonical tractates. Raphael is mentioned three times in the BT and a further eight times in the the extra-canonical tractates. Uriel is never mentioned in the canonical tractates of the BT, but appears once in ARN. In the whole of the Tosefta Michael appears once (*tHul* 2.18), but appears to be the only angel mentioned by name. Michael and Gabriel (*pBer*

the Sages makes a statement about the comparative importance of these two archangels, Michael always ranks above Gabriel. For example, in *bBer* 4b, R. Eleazer b. Abina explicitly asserts: "Greater is [the achievement] ascribed to Michael than that ascribed to Gabriel".[24]

In addition, on the basis of a widespread exegesis of Gen. 18 which identifies the three men who appeared to Abraham as Michael, Gabriel, and Raphael,[25] an early tradition concludes that Michael was the most important of the three. For example, a *baraita* in *bYoma* 37a illustrates the principle, that when a teacher walks with two of his students the teacher should be in the middle, with "and thus do we find that of the three angels who came to visit Abraham, Michael went in the middle, Gabriel at his right and Raphael at his left".[26] Similarly in *GenR* 48.10, R. Hiyya (prob. pA3) maintains "on Tannaite authority" that Abraham addressed himself to Michael, "the most important of them".[27] Clearly then, at least some of the Tannaim ranked Michael above Gabriel.[28]

b) *Michael as Protector of Israel and Military Commander* Given Dan. 10.21 and 12.1 it is not unexpected that the Rabbis would consider Michael

---

ix.1.13a; *pRH* i.2.56d) are the only angels mentioned by name in the PT. In the Haggadic Midrashim, including some very late documents, there is a crescendo of named angels: Michael appears 238 times, Gabriel 186, Metatron 119, Raphael 43, and Uriel 16.

[24] *bBer* 4b also cites R. Yohanan (A2) and an unnamed Tanna as authorities, at least for the exegesis behind R. Eleazer's statement, if not for the statement itself.

[25] *bYoma* 37a; *bBM* 86b; *GenR* 50.2. *TAb*. A 6.4-6 and B 6.10-13 also affirms that Michael was one of the three men.

[26] It is not altogether clear where the *baraita* ends. Since the principle but not the illustration regarding the three archangels is also found in *bErub* 54b, it is possible that the *baraita* included only the principle and that the illustration was added by the editor of *bYoma*. However, on the basis of *GenR* 48.10, it seems that the *baraita* also included the illustration, and that *bErub* simply did not quote the whole of it.

[27] All my quotations of *Midrash Rabbah* are from the translation edited by Freedman and Simon.

[28] In his discussion of Dan. 8.16 (*CommDan.* ii), Jerome cites a Jewish tradition which identifies the unnamed angel, who directed Gabriel to explain the vision to Daniel, with Michael. Such a tradition implies Michael's superiority to Gabriel. Since Jerome conversed with Rabbis and perserved their opinions in his commentaries, it is probable that we have here another Rabbinic tradition of Michael's pre-eminence. However, since Jerome wrote his commentary on Daniel in 407 AD, this may only be a late Amorite opinion. See the discussion in Braverman, *Jerome*, 95-96.

Mention could also be made here of the few scattered references to the mysterious figure "the Prince of the World" (שר העולם) (*bYeb* 16b; *bHul* 60a [parallel in *MidrPss* 104.24]; *bSanh* 94a). This title clearly refers to an angelic figure of some importance. It is not surprising, then, that late works attempted to identify him as Michael (*PRE* 27) or Metatron (a tosafist on *bHul* 60a). See Scholem, *Jewish Gnosticism*, 44-51 and Segal, "Ruler", 247-248, 405-406, n.18.

as the angelic protector of Israel and military commander of the heavenly hosts. What is somewhat surprising is the paucity of early texts in which Michael appears in these roles. Indeed, Urbach can write that the Tannaim "assign no part to Michael in the past wars of Israel. Only in the late Midrashim does Michael take his place as the Guardian Angel of Israel, who fights their battles,...".[29] While it is correct that few, if any, texts which are certainly Tannaitic assign a military role to Michael, this may be explained as due to the genre of Tannaitic texts, which are overwhelmingly concerned with halakhah, rather than haggadah. To be sure, the Midrashim are full of stories in which Michael rescues Israel or individual Israelites from defeat or death. However, these can only rarely be dated with confidence to the Tannaitic period and very often parallel traditions can be found which attribute the same action to Gabriel, or another angel.

A good example of this is the complex of traditions concerning the identity of the angels who smote the camp of the Assyrians (2 Kgs. 19.35) and rescued the three Hebrew children (Dan. 3.25). One text identifies the first with Michael and the second with Gabriel (*ExodR* 18.5),[30] but it is not uncommon for the roles to be reversed (*bSanh* 26ab; *GenR* 44.13; *CantR* 1.12),[31] while another text attributes both tasks to Gabriel (*bSanh* 95b).[32] This complex of traditions provides an excellent example of the tendencies to equate, or nearly equate, the importance of Michael and Gabriel and to substitute them in parallel texts and related traditions.[33] Many other examples of Michael taking on a military role could be mentioned,[34] but others with Gabriel,[35] and occasionally other angels,[36] could also be enumerated.

---

[29] Urbach, *Sages*, 141.

[30] R. Nehemyah (T3). However, Urbach (*Sages*, 142-145) on the basis of parallel texts argues that this is a late harmonization and that the attribution is not to be trusted. Cf. *bSanh* 94b (R. Yehoshua b. Qarha, T3) which does not name the angel.

[31] *bSanh* 26ab is unattributed, while *GenR* 44.13 and *CantR* 1.12 both cite "our Rabbis" as authorities.

[32] R. Eliezer b. R. Yose (T3), R. Simeon b. Yohai (T3), R. Jeremiah b. Abba (bA2), R. Isaac the Blacksmith (A3), and R. Yohanan (pA2).

[33] A further example appears in the Toseftot targumic tradition. Kasher ("Targums to the Prophets", 172) notes that in the "Toseftot Targum" at 2 Kgs. 19.35 the angel who smites Sennacherib and the Assyrian army is Michael, while at Ezek. 1.1 and Isa. 10.32 this same angel is identified with Gabriel.

[34] E.g., *bBM* 86b (UA); *TanB* 9.15 (UA), 17 (R. Yohanan; pA2); *PRE* 26, 36, 38, 50; Targ. Ps.-Jon. on Gen. 38.25-26.

[35] E.g., *bShab* 55a (R. Aha b. R. Hanina, pA3); *bSot* 10b (R. Eleazer, prob. pA3); 12b (R. Yohanan, pA2); 13b (Rab, bA1); *LamR* 2.1 (Resh Laqish; pA2). Significantly Origen, who seems to have had some knowledge of rabbinic traditions, identifies Gabriel, not Michael, as the angel charged with "the supervising of wars" (*Princ.* i.8.1). Cf. also Jerome *CommDan*. ii.8.16.

[36] E.g., in *GenR* 50.2 (UA) Raphael is sent to rescue Lot, but according to *bBM* 86b (UA) it is Michael.

Clearly, the Rabbis did not consider Michael to be the only angel fulfilling military roles; nor was he the only archangel who led the heavenly hosts.

As patrons of Israel, Michael and Gabriel not only share military functions, they also intercede for Israel.[37] The rabbis viewed the angelic patrons of Israel not only as their protectors against earthly enemies in a military sense, but also as their advocates in the spiritual realm. This is especially illustrated in the many legends in which Satan or Sammael accuses Israel or individual Israelites before God and Michael acts as their defender.[38]

c) Michael as Heavenly High Priest Related to the task of heavenly intercessor is that of heavenly high priest. In common with certain apocalypses and the Qumran sect, the rabbis envisioned a heavenly cult,[39] in which Michael served as high priest. Three passages in the Babylonian Talmud, all of which cite early Amoraim (*Hag* 12b, *Men* 110a, *Zeb* 62a) allude to Michael's high priestly office.[40] The most significant of these states:

> Zebul (the fourth heaven) is that in which [the heavenly] Jerusalem and the Temple and the Altar are built, and Michael, the great Prince, stands and offers thereon an offering...(*bHag* 12b).[41]

If the attributions in these passages are correct, then we can safely date this tradition to the third century. However there are persuasive reasons for thinking that the tradition is a good deal earlier. First of all, Origen seems to be familiar with this tradition for he held that Michael was the angel over "the prayers and supplications of mortals".[42] For the tradition to have been current in Babylon, Palestine, and Alexandria in the third century, its origin must have been substantially earlier. Further, parallels[43] from apocalyptic

---

[37] *ExodR* 18.5 (R. Yehudah, T4); *RuthR* proem 1 (R. Yohanan, pA2); and *bYoma* 77a (R. Ashi, bA6). The first two references mention only Michael. The third includes two passages on this theme; the first concerns Michael and the second Gabriel. This, however, is the only such reference to Gabriel as Israel's heavenly intercessor I have found. Note also that in *LamR* Proem 24 (UA) Metatron intercedes for Israel.

[38] Esp. the saying of R. Yose [?] in *ExodR* 18.5. Cf. also *DeutR* 11.10 (R. Yohanan, pA2); *PRE* 27. For this theme in Jewish apocalyptic literature, see above pp. 41-42.

[39] *bHag* 12b (Resh Laqish [pA2]); *bTaan* 5a (R. Yohanan, pA2); *pYoma* vii.2.44b (R. Hiyya bar Abba, T5); *pBer* iv.5.8c (R. Hiyya bar Abba, T5).

[40] *bHag* 12b: Resh Laqish (pA2); *bMen* 110a (= *MidrPss* 134.1): R. Giddal (bA2) in the name of Rab (bA1); and *bZeb* 62a: R. Eleazer, probably R. Eleazer ben Pedat (pA3).

[41] All my citations of BT follow the text and translation found in Epstein's edition.

[42] *Princ.* i.8.1.

[43] *TLevi* 5.6 and *3Bar* 11-16.

literature suggest that this was already a well established tradition by the second century at the latest. Finally, the probable identification of Michael with Melchizedek at Qumran, points toward a date in the first century B.C.[44]

In an important article,[45] Ego has argued cogently that the destruction of the Temple caused a modification in the tradition concerning the heavenly sanctuary. Before AD 70 it served to legitimize the earthly cult of Jerusalem, by stressing its heavenly parallel. After the fall of Jerusalem, when there was no earthly cult, it began to be seen as a replacement for the Jerusalem temple. This is especially clear in *bMen* 110a, where Michael's service in the heavenly temple is used to solve the difficulty created after AD 70 by the statement in 2 Chr. 2.3-4 that the temple sacrifices were Israel's *eternal* duty.[46] Even if Michael's role in the tradition *originated* with this change of emphasis, this would fix his place in the tradition by the closing decades of the first century at the latest.

The earliest reference[47] to Gabriel as high priest that I have found is the statement of R. Yohanan (A2) in *LamR* 2.1[48] that Gabriel, "the man clothed in linen" of Ezek. 9.2, "served in three capacities: as scribe, executioner, and High Priest". If this attribution is correct and if the passage is authentic, then we have a high priestly reference to Gabriel nearly as early as the earliest such reference to Michael found in Rabbinic sources.[49] However, R. Yohanan's statement stands alone with only very late and tenuous support, while the tradition that Michael serves in the heavenly sanctuary is mentioned, not only by at least four early Amoraic authorities, but also in early non-Rabbinic documents as well.

Besides Gabriel, other heavenly high priests in Rabbinic literature include Metatron (*NumR* 12.12; R. Simon, pA3), Melchizedek (*Yalqut* Wa-yishlah 132),[50] Elijah-Phineas and Moses.[51] However, none of these examples are as widespread or as early as the tradition which places Michael in the heavenly sanctuary.

---

[44] See above pp. 70-74.
[45] Ego, "Diener".
[46] Ego, "Diener", esp. 370-371.
[47] Cf. also *TanB* Saw 1, and Balak 16.
[48] The text of this passage, however, is far from certain. In Buber's edition of *LamR* this text speaks of Michael, not Gabriel. The English translation of Cohen (Soncino edition), which reads "Gabriel", follows MSS cited in Buber's apparatus. See Strack-Stemberger (*Introduction*, 310-311) for the poor state of *LamR*'s text.
[49] I.e., *bMen* 110a, Rab (A1).
[50] See Lueken, *Michael*, 31.
[51] For the last two, see Ego, "Diener", 374-377.

d) Michael's Eschatological Functions In some, mostly late, Rabbinic texts Michael functions as one of the angels who guides souls of the righteous to heaven or paradise and as the angel who ushers in the Eschaton. The latter function is based upon Daniel 12.1. The former, as we have seen, has parallels in Jewish apocalyptic literature.[52]

DeutR 11.10 describes the death and burial of Moses. Its basic plot is very similar to that of the *Testament of Abraham*. God first dispatches Gabriel and then Michael to fetch Moses' soul. Both archangels object that they are not worthy. So God sends Sammael, the angel of death. However, Moses refuses to die and in the end God Himself must attend to his soul. After Moses' death Michael, Gabriel, and Zagzagel bury his body.[53] Although other versions of Moses' death, which do not mention Michael, occur in earlier sources (*SifreDeut* 305 [UA]; *ARN* A 12 [UA]; *ARN* B 25), the lost ending of *Assumption of Moses*, as cited in Jude 9, shows Michael was very early associated with the death of Moses.

On the basis of the prophecy of Daniel 12.1 some Rabbis envisioned Michael as a major player in the eschatological salvation of Israel. Most affirmations and allusions to Michael's eschatological functions among the Rabbis are late. One of the clearest, however, is attributed to R. Yehudah ha-Nasi (T4):

> And just as the Holy One, blessed be He, wrought in this world by the hand of Michael and Gabriel, so He will act through them in the time to come, for it is said (Obad. 21): 'And Saviours shall come up on Mount Zion to judge the mount of Esau'--this refers to Michael and Gabriel. But our holy master [i.e., R. Yehudah ha-Nasi] said: This refers to Michael by himself,...(*ExodR* 18.5).[54]

It is quite possible that, despite the attribution, this is a late text.[55] Significantly, this text records two interpretations: in one Michael alone ushers in the eschaton and in the other he is joined by Gabriel.

e) Summary To summarize the evidence thus far presented, Rabbinic traditions concerning Michael closely parallel earlier Jewish traditions found in writings from the Second Temple period. One very important dif-

---

[52] See above p. 46.

[53] This portion of *DeutR* may be as late as AD 800. See Strack-Stemberger, *Introduction*, 335.

[54] Note also Targ. Ps.-Jon. on Deut 34.3; *Signs of the Messiah* (אותות המשיח; *BHM* II.58-62) 8-9; and compare *ExodR* 32.9 with *ExodR* 2.5.

[55] The attribution is, at best, doubtful. *ExodR* is late and R. Yehudah was of such stature that many later sayings were attributed to him. Cf. Urbach, *Sages*, 145.

ference, however, is the increased stature of Gabriel and the implicit rivalry between the two archangels, which at times becomes explicit.[56]

How is this to be explained? Did the Rabbis attempt to counterbalance certain claims made by sectarian groups for the highest archangel by emphasizing that Michael was only one of *two* heavenly princes, both of whom were merely servants of God and Israel? Since, for at least some of the Rabbis, Michael remains superior to Gabriel,[57] I do not think we can conclude that this was so. A more likely explanation is to be found in the authority which the Rabbis accorded the Biblical text, especially Daniel, over against other apocalyptic works and the writings from Qumran. In the Book of Daniel, once the identification of the "Son of Man" was forgotten,[58] neither Michael nor Gabriel seems particularly superior to the other (10.12-11.1) and Michael is explicitly said to be only "one of the chief princes", which leaves open the possibility that Gabriel is also a chief prince. The only clue in Daniel to Michael's superiority is his responsibility for Israel, a responsibility which, as we have seen, he shares with Gabriel in the Rabbinic material. Those Rabbis who affirmed Michael's prominence probably owed this understanding, whether consciously or unconsciously, to non-canonical writings.

I turn now to two further issues of considerable importance: the possibility of a Michael-cult opposed by the Rabbis and some significant parallels between Rabbinic and Christian exegesis of מלאך יהוה passages in the OT.

---

[56] Esp. *bBB* 75a (R. Samuel b. Nahmani, pA3).

[57] See above pp. 97-98.

[58] The identification of this figure with Michael, while probably original, was clearly not held by the Rabbis. Cf. Horbury, "Messianic Associations", 45-48; and Segal, *Two Powers*, 47-49.

2) Rabbinic Evidence for a Michael Cult[59]

Along with general prohibitions against making and worshipping images of angels,[60] there is a series of warnings in Rabbinic writings which make explicit reference to Michael. This raises the question of whether there existed a cult of Michael which the Rabbis felt the need to condemn. The earliest of these warnings appears in the Tosefta:

> He who slaughters for the sake of the sun, for the sake of the moon, for the sake of the stars, for the sake of the planets, for the sake of Michael, prince of the great host, and for the sake of the small worm-- lo, this is deemed to be flesh deriving from the sacrifices of corpses (*tHul* 2.18).[61]

This is based upon *mHul* 2.8 where, however, Michael is not mentioned and only sacrifices "in honour of"[62] mountains, hills, seas, rivers, and wildernesses are prohibited. The gemara on this (*bHul* 40a) compares both the Mishnah and Tosefta readings. There Abaye (bA4) explains that the Mishnah has in view only sacrifices to inanimate objects, which strictly speaking are not idolatry. However, the *baraita*, since it includes a reference to Michael has in view the spirits or 'gods' behind these inanimate objects and thus refers to idolatry. If Abaye correctly understood the *baraita*, then clearly pagan, over against Jewish, cult practices are in view. Indeed, the accusation that the 'gods' of the Gentiles are merely

---

[59] In the following discussion I will discuss the possibility of the worship or veneration of angels. However, a definition of "worship" or "veneration" is exceedingly difficult. A phenomenological approach allows a definition based on practices rather than abstractions. Thus by "cult" or "cultic veneration" or "worship" I mean practices, either corporate or individual, which 1) express or imply the divinity of the being or beings addressed and which 2) have the sanction of a religious group or sect. Venerative actions unique to an individual are not included. I concentrate on venerative actions, rather than venerative language, not because the latter is unimportant, but because the former offers a surer criterion for worship. Hyperbole and metaphor may be misunderstood in ways liturgical actions will not be. To be sure, venerative actions and language need not be mutually exclusive; venerative language sung as a hymn or offered as a prayer often constitute an *act* of veneration. Cf. Hurtado, *One God*, 11-15; contrast Stuckenbruck, *Angel Veneration*, 13-14, 47-51.

[60] E.g., *Mek.* Bahodesh 10 (R. Ishmael, prob. T2) and Targ. Ps.-Jon. on Ex. 20.22-23.

[61] Neusner's Translation with one variation. Neusner only transliterates שלשול. However, "worm" is a probable translation. Cf. Jastrow, *Dictionary*, 1589; Stuckenbruck, *Angel Veneration*, 59-61; Epstein's edition of *bHul* 40a.

[62] Or "for the sake of" (לש[ו]ם).

angels appears to have been a regular feature of Jewish and Rabbinic polemic. For instance, in *DeutR* 2.34 when God descends to Mt. Sinai with his angels some of the nations choose Michael as their patron, others Gabriel.[63] Significantly, the above *baraita* appears once more in the Babylonian Talmud (*bAZ* 42b) where again it points to a pagan, rather than Jewish context. In response to the prohibition against using utensils with images of the sun, moon, or a dragon engraved upon them (*mAZ* 3.3), the editor of the gemara asks: "Is this to say that [the heathens] worship these objects and no others?" He then cites the *baraita* as proof that this is not so: The Gentiles worship many objects.[64] A parallel to *tHul* 2.18 in *Mek* Bahodesh 6, in which the debate is between R. Gamaliel (prob. T2) and a Gentile philosopher, is further evidence that this series of texts may have originated in disputes with pagans.[65]

However, it is to be remembered that the Rabbis were never as concerned with attacking pagan ideas as they were with preventing or correcting aberrant Jewish practices. This suggests two probabilities: either the Rabbis wished in these texts to prevent the corrupting influence of pagan religion, or that influence was already a reality which needed correcting. In the former instance, this series of passages reflects a perceived danger from the pagan environment. In case of the latter option, this complex of texts would refer either to isolated syncretistic practices or an organized sect influenced by pagan ideas.

In favor of the former option are two considerations. First, the mention of mountains, hills, rivers, and seas suggests a hypothetical situation, for there is little or no evidence that these objects were worshipped by syncretistic or sectarian Jews. Second, and more importantly, the fact that Michael is paired with "the small worm" underlines the hypothetical nature of the whole list. The worm can only be an example of hyperbole. The same therefore is probably true of Michael as well. The addition of Michael and the worm to the list of natural phenomena, then, probably serves merely to emphasize the point already present in the Mishnah: Only God may be worshipped. In the words of Schäfer, "Man darf niemandem opfern--weder dem höchsten noch dem niedrigsten Geschöpf--als Gott

---

[63] Segal (*Two Powers*, 138) would apply this passage to "groups other than Israel", presumably meaning Christians or Gnostics. But "nations of the world" (אמות העולם) seems to suggest pagans.

[64] The subject "heathens" is not actually present, but given the context of *mAZ* 3.3 it is surely intended.

[65] This parallel, however, does not mention Michael or "the little worm".

allein".⁶⁶ If an actual Michael cult were being attacked in these texts, it is unlikely that it would be merely alluded to in this way, rather than attacked outright.⁶⁷ This is especially so given the explicit manner in which the "Two Powers" heresy is attacked in Rabbinic writings.⁶⁸

On the other hand, there is plenty of evidence that some Jews, especially those within groups which practised magic, regularly invoked angels.⁶⁹ This fact, coupled with the statement in Col. 2.18 and certain accusations found in Patristic writings, has led many scholars to conclude that *tHul* 2.18 and its parallels were directed against the second option mentioned above: the worship of angels, either in the form of isolated syncretistic practices or of an organized angel cult.⁷⁰ However, this is a questionable conclusion. While Jewish invocation of angels, Col. 2.18 and the Patristic allegations of angel worship may offer *independent* evidence for a sectarian Jewish angel cult, they do not address the difficulties, just mentioned, one encounters when reading *tHul* 2.18 as anything other than hypothetical.

Furthermore, Col. 2.18 and the Patristic assertions offer doubtful evidence of a Jewish Angel cult. Beginning with the NT passage, it is often assumed or asserted that the θρησκείᾳ τῶν ἀγγέλων of Col. 2.18 should be read as an objective genitive, i.e., worship which is directed toward angels.⁷¹ However, many interpreters in recent years have argued that it is a subjective genitive and refers to the heavenly worship which angels offer and which the false teachers at Colossae have seen and participated in

---

⁶⁶ Schäfer, *Rivalität*, 69. However, despite this statement Schäfer believes *tHul* 2.18 is evidence for an angel cult. Needless to say, the fact that Michael was chosen to represent the "höchsten" of creatures is further indication of his supremacy among angels in rabbinic angelology.

⁶⁷ Cf. Hurtado, *One God*, 30-32.

⁶⁸ Cf. e.g., *Mek* Bahodesh 5; *bHag* 15a; *bSanh* 38b.

Cf. Theodoret of Cyrus' (393-466) attack on a Michael cult active in Asia Minor in his day in his commentary on Col. 2.18. He asserts that the Council of Laodicea (c. 350 AD) condemned these practices. If Theodoret is right, there may have been a Michael cult among Christians of Asia Minor in the fourth century. However, the canons of the council do not explicitly mention Michael, only the invoking of angels. In any case, the Christian Michael cult known to Theodoret is probably too far removed, both temporally and spatially, to be identified with the practices which exercised the Rabbis. The witness of the Tosefta shows the latter practices must date from the mid-third century or earlier, and suggests a Palestinian context.

⁶⁹ See esp. Arnold, *Syncretism*, 32-60.

⁷⁰ So e.g., Lueken, *Michael*, 6-7; Urbach, *Sages*, 182; Schäfer, *Rivalität*, 69-70; Mach, *Entwicklungsstadien*, 297-299; Stuckenbruck, *Angel Veneration*, 59-63.

⁷¹ Lightfoot, *Colossians*, 101-104; Schweizer, *Colossians*, 158-160; Lohse, *Colossians*, 118-119; Pokorny, *Colossians*, 113-115.

through visions.⁷² For this participation of the mystic in heavenly and angelic worship we have many significant parallels in Jewish and Jewish Christian texts from the turn of the eras (e.g., 1QSb 4.25-26; 1QH 11.20-22 [formerly 3.20-22]; *ApAb.* 17; *AscenIs.* 7.13-9.33; cf. also 1QSa 2.3ff and *Sabbath Shirot*, 4Q400 2 i 6-7). These texts demonstrate that the concept of visionary participation in angelic worship was widespread among Jews and Christians in the first two centuries of our era.⁷³ Since, as I hope to show, the evidence for Jewish cultic veneration of angels is very meagre, indeed it is restricted to the invoking of angels in the context of magical syncretism, I conclude that it is best to understand the θρησκείᾳ τῶν ἀγγέλων either as a subjective genitive and to take it as referring to visionary participation in the angelic worship of God⁷⁴ or as polemical rhetoric against magical practices and not a fully fledged Angel cult.⁷⁵

Of course, not all accept that the evidence for Jewish worship of angels is meagre, and the accusations of Aristides, Jerome, the *Kerygma of Peter*, and Celsus have been cited to support taking θρησκείᾳ τῶν ἀγγέλων as an objective genitive. But it is precisely their polemical nature which makes these accusations highly questionable evidence. Each of these explicitly accuses Jews, as a whole, of worshipping angels, even if inadvertently.

---

⁷² So Rowland, "Apocalyptic Visions"; Carr, *Angels and Principalities*, 66-72; Hurtado, *One God*, 32-33; and esp. Francis, "Humility".

⁷³ The objections raised to reading θρησκείᾳ τῶν ἀγγέλων as a subjective genitive have not been convincing. Francis' ("Humility", 181-182) response to Lohse could also be applied to Schweizer (*Colossians*, 159): The reference to "self-made worship" (ἐθελοθρησκίᾳ, vs. 23) need not imply that the actions of humans alone are in view. Arnold's (*Syncretism*, 91-93) citation of examples in which θρησκείᾳ is coupled with a subjective genitive (4 Macc. 5.7; Josephus *Ant.* xii.253, xvi.115; *J.W.* ii.198; and Chariton *De Chaerea et Callirhoe* vii.6.6) removes any force to his argument. He asserts that because of the vast majority of occurrences of θρησκεία with a genitive noun are objective, "the writer of Colossians would have intended the genitive expression τῶν ἀγγέλων as the object of the noun θρησκείᾳ; if he did not, his readers would surely have misunderstood him". The very examples Arnold offers shows that this is simply not so. If the readers of Colossians would certainly have been subject to misunderstanding, so would the readers of 4 Maccabees, Josephus and Chariton.

⁷⁴ Stuckenbruck (*Angel Veneration*, 119) argues that a subjective genitive does not rule out the possibility of a cultic worship directed to angels. He suggests that it may have been felt that visionary participation in the angels' worship could tempt the seer to worship the angels themselves. While Stuckenbruck's observation is technically correct, it does not offer any positive evidence for an angel cult.

⁷⁵ Cf. Arnold's conclusions, *Syncretism*, 101-102.

For example, Aristides in his *Apology* (Syriac recension only), written c.117-161, states: "In the methods of their actions their service is to angels and not to God, in that they observe sabbaths and new moons and the passover and the great fast, and the fast, and circumcision, and cleanness of meats".[76] The context of this passage makes it clear that Aristides realizes the Jews acknowledge only the one true God and their intention is to worship Him. However, he believes that due to their legalistic practices the Jews actually end up serving angels rather than God. Similarly, Jerome, on the basis of Acts 7.42, argues that because of their sins, especially that of rejecting the Messiah, the Jews have been given over to serve the heavenly host (*Ep.* cxxi.10). The same type of reasoning appears to be at work in a fragment from the *Kerygma of Peter* preserved both in Clement of Alexandria (*Strom.* vi.5.41) and Origen (*CommJo.* xiii.17): In their ignorance, the Jews think they serve God by their ritual feasts, but actually worship angels, as well as the month and the moon, which is shown by their inability to keep the feasts if the moon does not appear. These texts tell us more about anti-Jewish Christian polemic, than about the actual practices of Jews.[77] One wonders if they may not all three be based on a misunderstanding of Col. 2.18;[78] Jerome's comments, at any rate, are in response to a question concerning this very text.[79]

Celsus also asserts that Jews worshipped angels (*Cels.* i.26, v.6). Three things should be stated regarding Celsus' accusations. First, Origen rejects the truth of these statements. Given that 1) Origen was well informed about Judaism in his day, that 2) he had no particular reason to defend the practices of Jews, and that 3) Celsus was dependent upon pagan polemic,[80] it would appear that Origen is the more trustworthy authority in this instance.[81] Second, Celsus contradicts the assertion of *Kerygma of Peter* that Jews worship the moon, for he states that while they worship the heaven and the angels in it, they neglect the most sacred heavenly objects: Sun, moon, fixed stars, and planets (*Cels.* v.6). Thus Celsus can scarcely

---

[76] Chapt. 14. Trans. from Williams, "Cult", 426.
[77] So Williams, "Cult", 426-428; and Hurtado, *One God*, 33-34.
[78] So Longenecker, *Christology*, 31, n.22.
[79] Arnold's (*Syncretism*, 59) argument, that the consistency of the Fathers' testimony suggests that there may be something behind it, is odd. Once a polemical charge becomes fixed it will circulate with a great deal of consistency, but need not have any historical basis. Consider the common slur that Gypsies steal children or the medieval Christian polemic that Jews worshipped Satan.
[80] Cf. *Cels.* i.21-24; and Chadwick (ed.), *Contra Celsum*, xix.
[81] So Hurtado, *One God*, 33.

be used to confirm the witness of *Kerygma of Peter*.⁸² Finally, Celsus (i.26, v.9) connects Jewish angel worship with sorcery and magic. Origen's response is ambivalent here; he allows that there may be some Jews who practise sorcery, thereby contravening the Jewish Law, and have thus been led into angel worship.

This connection with sorcery is significant, for the best evidence for the Jewish veneration of angels consists of certain inscriptions and amulets in which angels are invoked. However, all or nearly all of these suggest an origin in Jewish circles influenced by magical syncretism.⁸³ These inscriptions and amulets demonstrate that in both a Jewish and a pagan setting angels could be invoked for protection, healing, success in business, vengeance on enemies, etc.⁸⁴ The connection with magic indicates that this was in all probability a syncretistic practice, and not necessarily shared by mainstream Judaism. Even Arnold, whose discussion of the issue is extensive, must admit that his evidence "does not point to an organized cult in which angels were worshipped in the same way as Yahweh--with ascriptions of praise and glory, with singing and praying, with sacrifices, etc".⁸⁵

There is, however, at least one Rabbinic text which offers evidence for Jewish prayers being addressed to angels outside of magical syncretistic circles. In *pBer.* ix.12.13a, R. Yudan (pA4) places in God's mouth "If on a man comes trouble, let him not invoke Michael and let him not invoke Gabriel, but let him invoke me, and I will immediately hear him". This rejection of prayers addressed to Michael and Gabriel is very gentle and eschews polemic. It follows, then, that rather than a fully fledged angel cult, R. Yudan is reacting to a practice of a popular nature, the uninformed activity of the *'am ha'aretz*. If this is so, then invocation of angels was practised by some common Jews at least in Amoraic times and perhaps earlier. However, it is unlikely that such a practice would have been widespread among the Rabbis themselves and we can probably limit it to the populace. Nonetheless, we must certainly distinguish between prayers being addressed to angels and the popular concept of angels interceding for humans or delivering prayers to God.⁸⁶ As we have seen, the latter is early

---

⁸² So Williams, "Cult", 427.
⁸³ See Arnold, "Mediator Figures"; idem, *Syncretism*, 32-60. Cf. also Stuckenbruck, *Angel Veneration*, 181-200.
⁸⁴ Arnold, "Mediator Figures", 26-28; idem, *Syncretism*, 11-47.
⁸⁵ *Syncretism*, 101. Note also p. 59, where he qualifies his conclusion that some Jews venerated angels: "...this is worship and veneration in a qualitatively different manner from the early Christian worship of Christ".
⁸⁶ So also Mach, *Entwicklungsstadien*, 299-300.

and widespread,[87] and apparently received the sanction of the Rabbis.[88] The former idea, while it may have been a popular practice, was rejected by the Rabbis, probably on the grounds that since it approached worship, it compromised monotheism to a unacceptable degree.

To summarize my arguments to this point, no compelling evidence has been produced for a Michael cult among Jews of the Rabbinic period. Nor is there sufficient evidence to conclude that cultic veneration of angels was practised among Jews beyond the invocation of angels. Such invocation is especially evident among certain syncretistic circles who adopted magical practices and beliefs from the surrounding pagan culture, but it also took place among the 'am ha'aretz (pBer. ix.12.13a). Since R. Yudan mentions both Michael and Gabriel, it would seem Michael was not singled out as the only angel to whom prayers were addressed. Finally, the Rabbis opposed prayer to angels, but allowed the idea that angels transported prayers from earth to heaven.

This is not to say that some "Jewish" sects did not worship heavenly beings. I turn now to a passage which clearly suggests that at least one "sectarian" group did. In *bSanh* 38b a debate between Rabbi Idith (A4?) and a *Min*, or heretic, is recorded:

> R. Nahman said: He who is skilled in refuting the *Minim* as is R. Idith, let him do so; but not otherwise. Once a *Min* said to R. Idith: It is written, "And unto Moses He said, Come up to the Lord" (Ex. 24.1). But surely it should have stated, "Come up to me!"--It was Metatron [who said that], he replied, whose name is similar to that of His Master, for it is written, "For My name is in Him" (Ex. 23.21). But if so, [he retorted] we should worship him! The same passage however,--replied R. Idith--says: "Be not rebellious against Him", i.e., exchange Me not for him. But if so, why is it stated: "He will not pardon your transgression?" (Ex. 23.21). He answered: By our troth we would not accept him even as a messenger, for it is written: "And he said unto Him, If Thy [personal] presence go not etc." (Ex. 33.15).[89]

Here the *Min* is presented as arguing from Ex. 24.1 that there are two divine figures the second of which had the divine name יהוה. R. Idith ans-

---

[87] For Jewish apocalyptic see above pp. 32, 45-46. Cf. also the evidence from Qumran for a heavenly cultus, pp. 60-61.

[88] *bSot* 33a (Rab [bA1] and R. Yohanan [pA2]); *MidrPss* 4.3 (R. Yudan [prob. pA4]) and *MidrPss* 19.7 (R. Pinhas [T4 or pA5] in the name of R. Abba [?]).

[89] There is some question on the identities of R. Nahman and R. Idith. Segal (*Two Powers*, 68) dates them mid to late third century.

wers, on the basis of Ex. 23.21, that the speaker of this verse was merely an angel, Metatron,[90] whose name is similar to the Name of God. This prompts the *Min* to suggest that this angel should be worshipped. R. Idith responds with a word play on "Be not rebellious (תמר) against Him" (Ex. 23.21), interpreting it as "exchange (תמירני) Me not for him". The *Min* then points to this figure's authority to forgive sin as further evidence that he is to be worshipped. R. Idith then appeals to Ex. 33.15.

Significantly, it is R. Idith, not the *Min*, who introduced Metatron into the debate. Apparently, Metatron was considered to be merely an angel, and thus, for the Rabbis, a safe alternative to the *Min*'s contention that of the two divine figures the second was named יהוה.[91] This suggests that the *Min* may have been a Jewish Christian, for there is evidence that some Christians interpreted Ex. 23.20-21 to refer to Christ (e.g., *Acts of Pilate* 16.6; cf. also John 17.11-12; Phil. 2.9).[92] I would suggest the *Min* was a Jewish Christian because the debate seems to be dependent upon both parties knowing Hebrew or Aramaic. Urbach,[93] Hurtado,[94] and, with some reservations, Segal[95] all accept this identification of the *Min* with a Christian. Segal also tentatively proposes the possibility that he was a Merkavah mystic. However, as we shall see below, much of current scholarship dates Merkavah mysticism too late to be a viable option.

3) *Rabbinic and Christian Exegesis of* מלאך יהוה *passages*

Although not universal, there appears to have been a tendency among some rabbis to identify the מלאך יהוה in certain OT passages with Michael. Significantly, early Church Fathers usually identified the "angel of the

---

[90] See below pp. 119-121 for the probable identification of Metatron with Michael.

[91] So also Segal, *Two Powers*, 72.

Note that according to Abba Hilfi b. Samkai (pA2) in the name of R. Yehudah (pA2), cited in *GenR* 51.2, one of the two יהוה in Gen. 19.24 stands for Gabriel! The editor of *GenR* immediately adds two explanations, by R. Eleazer (T3) and R. Isaac (prob. pA3), which render Abba Hilfi's unnecessary. So this is at best a late, minority opinion suspiciously close to Merkavah mysticism.

[92] See below pp. 143-146.

Segal (*Two Powers*, 70) also appeals to Jesus' claim to be able to forgive sins (Mark 2.7) as evidence that the *Min* is a Christian.

[93] *Sages*, 139.

[94] *One God*, 32.

[95] *Two Powers*, 70-73.

Lord" in these same passages with the pre-incarnate Christ. A full investigation of the Fathers on this issue will have to wait until a later chapter.[96] However, the corresponding Rabbinic and patristic interpretations of Gen. 18-19, Gen. 32.24-30, and Ex. 3.2 raise the possibility of some contact between Rabbinic Michael traditions and early christology.

As we have seen,[97] a Tannaitic tradition not only identifies the three angels who visited Abraham in Gen. 18 with Michael, Gabriel, and Raphael (*bYoma* 37a; *bBM* 86b; *GenR* 48.10, 50.2), but also affirms that Michael was the most important of these three (*bYoma* 37a; *GenR* 48.10). A number of early Fathers, including Justin Martyr (*Dial.* 56, 126), Irenaeus (*Dem.* 44), and Tertullian (*Prax.* xvi), saw in Abraham's visitors the pre-incarnate Christ and two angels.[98] This Christian interpretation may have begun in the first century for the Fourth Gospel records Jesus' claim that he had previously revealed himself to Abraham (John 8.56).[99] In addition, R. Yohanan (pA2) believed that Michael was the מלאך יהוה who appeared to Moses in the burning bush (*ExodR* 2.5),[100] while Justin (*Dial.* 59-60; *1 Apol.* 63), Irenaeus (*Dem.* 46; *Adv. Haer.* iv.10.1), and Tertullian (*Prax.* xvi) would see Christ here. Finally, although the Rabbinic tradition is later and much less uniform, some rabbis asserted that it was Michael who wrestled with Jacob.[101] Early Fathers again view this event as a manifestation of the pre-incarnate Christ: Justin (*Dial.* 58.10, 126.3), Clement of Alexandria (*Paed.* i.7), and Tertullian (*Prax.* xiv).

What is the significance of these parallels? Does the Christian exegesis presuppose knowledge of Rabbinic tradition, or is the Rabbinic interpretation a reaction against the Christian tendency to read Christ into the OT? Or, conversely, are the two independent of each other?

---

[96] See below pp. 202-212.

[97] See above pp. 97-98.

[98] Later Fathers would identify the three with the Trinity. See Miller, *Encounters*, 48-95.

[99] However, Miller (*Encounters*, 194, n.206) notes that Hilary of Poitiers seems to have been the first to appeal to John 8.56 in connection with Gen. 18.

[100] However, R. Hanina (pA1) disagrees and identifies the angel with Gabriel. What follows however makes it clear that it was R. Yohanan's opinion which prevailed, at least in the opinion of the editor of *Exodus Rabbah*.

[101] So *TanB* 8.7 (R. Berekhyah, pA5); Targ. Ps.-Jon. Gen. 32.25; *Midrash Abkir* (according to Ginzberg, *Legends* V.305, n.248). R. Helbo (pA4) believes that the angel was either Michael or Gabriel, but he does not commit himself to one or the other (*GenR* 78.1). R. Hama bar Hanina (pA2) identifies this angel with the guardian angel of Esau (*GenR* 77.2-3; *CantR* 3.6), while *PRE* 37 names the angel "Israel".

First of all it should be noted that Justin, through Trypho,[102] appears to have been acquainted with Rabbinic exegesis of Gen. 18 and Ex. 3.2. Both Trypho (*Dial.* 56.5) and *bBM* 86b interpret Gen. 18.1-2 to mean that Abraham received two visions: the first of the Lord, the second of three angels. In contrast, Justin would interpret Gen. 18.1-2 to mean that the Lord appeared to Abraham as one of the three "men". Justin thus sees 18.1 as a general statement about the vision, while 18.2ff describes the contents of the vision. Trypho and *bBM* 86b, on the other hand, separate the first verse from the second and assume two different visions are being related. Furthermore, Trypho relates that two of the angels were sent to destroy Sodom, the other to announce to Sarah the birth of Isaac, "and having accomplished his errand, went away". To this compare the statement in *GenR* 50.2 that "Michael announced his tidings [to Abraham] and departed"! However, it is significant that we find no indications of the angels' names in Justin's debate with Trypho. All this suggests that Trypho, and through him Justin, may have been familiar with an earlier form of the tradition contained in *bBM* 86b and *GenR* 50.2, one to which the names of Michael, Gabriel, and Raphael were not yet attached.

Similarly, Trypho seems to have been familiar with an early form of Rabbinic exegesis of Ex. 3.2 as well. For Justin quotes his argument that both God and an angel were present in the burning bush: "...there were really two persons in company with each other, an angel and God, that appeared in that vision" (*Dial.* 60.1). This recalls *ExodR* 2.5 where Michael accompanies the Shekinah in the vision to Moses at the burning bush. Clearly then, some Rabbinic traditions concerning Gen. 18 and Ex. 3.2 pre-date Justin and were known by him. Significantly, however, he does not appear to be familiar with the Rabbinic identification of the מאלך יהוה with Michael. One cannot, then, rule out the possibility that the Rabbinic and Christian interpretations of these OT מלאך יהוה passages are in some way related. Nevertheless, this seems unlikely for the following reasons. The Rabbinic texts are free of polemic, which would be expected if they were a reaction against the Christian tendency to read Christ into the OT. Further, although the Rabbinic identification of the מלאך יהוה with Michael in Gen. 18 was contemporary with Justin,[103] and although he was clearly familiar with other aspects of Rabbinic exegesis of this passage, he provides no evidence that he knew of the Michael identification. Finally,

---

[102] Assuming that Trypho was a real person. Goodenough (*Theology*, 90-93) argues that he is merely a literary creation of Justin's. But see Barnard, *Justin*, 23-24.

[103] That is, if the appeals to Tannaitic authority in *bYoma* 37a and *GenR* 48.10 are correct.

while it appears that some Christians did indeed equate Michael and Christ[104] this is not true of any of the Fathers discussed here. It seems best to conclude, then, that the two tendencies are probably independent of each other.

c. Conclusions

I return to the suggestion that Gabriel's increased significance in Rabbinic literature served to counterbalance speculation about Michael as the highest of the archangels. No firm evidence for such motivation on the part of the Rabbis exists. A Michael cult would be a clear example of heretical speculation which could very well have prompted the Sages to demote Michael. However, as I argued above, *tHul* 2.18 and its parallels (*bHul* 40a; *bAZ* 42b) are best understood as responding to a perceived, rather than a real, danger. On the other hand, if it could be shown that the Rabbis were reacting against the Patristic christological exegesis of OT מלאך יהוה passages in their tendency to read Michael into the same OT passages, this would provide an example of Michael being proposed as a safe alternative to exegesis deemed dangerous by the Sages. As we have seen, however, this does not appear to have been the case.

The corresponding Rabbinic and Christian interpretations of Gen. 18-19, Gen. 32, and Ex. 3, however, do demonstrate the usefulness of such OT passages for the early Fathers. Finally, the importance of *bSanh* 38b is not to be overlooked. Here R. Idith appeals to a principal angel tradition as a defense against a heretical, and very possibly Christian, interpretation of Ex. 23.20-21. If the *Min* in this talmudic passage was indeed a Christian, then Metatron, who as we shall see was probably, at least in some circles, equated with Michael, offered the Rabbis a safe alternative to the Christian interpretation.

---

[104] See below pp. 187-196.

2. Hekhalot Literature

I turn now to the literary remains of the Merkavah mystics: Hekhalot literature.[105] It is probably not an exaggeration to affirm that here one encounters the most exalted angels in all of Jewish literature. Indeed, the boundary between the Deity and the angels at times is quite blurred. Most often Metatron plays the role of the principal angel in Hekhalot texts, but other angels are also described in very elevated language. As intimated above, a number of scholars have argued that Michael and Metatron were originally identified. I will examine this possibility after first setting out briefly the fundamental assumptions of Hekhalot angelology and then sketching the role attributed to Metatron in the writings of the Merkavah mystics.

a. The Purpose of Hekhalot Literature

Without question, Hekhalot texts stand in some relation to Rabbinic literature. However, the exact nature of the relationship between them has been subject to some debate. Some would see the Merkavah mystics operating in secret conventicles within the Rabbinic academies, the beginnings of such conventicles reaching back into Tannaitic times.[106] However, Peter Schäfer has recently argued that these writings originated after the Rabbinic period.[107] While the issue has not been finally settled, and while it must be

---

[105] Schäfer has argued that Hekhalot "works" in the sense of self-contained texts do not exist: "we are dealing with an extremely fluctuating literature that has been crystallized in various macroforms, which are nonetheless interwoven with one another on many different levels...the redactional arrangement of the microforms into clearly defined 'works' is to be placed rather at the end of the process than at the beginning..." (*Hidden*, 6). Schäfer has not been universally followed in this. However, since his *Synopse* is the best available edition I will use his section numbers (§).

Schäfer would limit the corpus of genuine Hekhalot "macroforms" to *Hekhalot Rabbati*, *Hekhalot Zutarti*, *Ma'aseh Merkavah*, *Merkavah Rabba*, and the so-called *3 Enoch*. See Schäfer, *Hidden*, 7 and the works he cites there. "Macroforms" whose relation to merkavah mysticism are problematical include *Re'uyyot Yehezqel* and *Masekhet Hekhalot*. However, because of its content and date a discussion of *Re'uyyot Yehezqel* will be included below.

[106] So Alexander, "Historical Setting", 167-173; Scholem, *Major Trends*, 43; idem, *Jewish Gnosticism*, 9-13; and Morray-Jones, "Transformational Mysticism", 1-2.

[107] Schäfer, "Aims", 289-195; cf. also Schäfer's later and more agnostic statement in *Hidden*, 150-161.

admitted that some mystical traditions are found in Tannaitic and other early sources and that the Hekhalot texts are particularly difficult to date, most would agree they are likely to be late. Therefore, one should be very careful of attributing a Tannaitic date to the traditions found only in the Hekhalot macroforms. It is certainly perilous to assume a motif found only in a Hekhalot text could illuminate an aspect of early Christology.

Schäfer has stressed the two foci around which the thought and practice of the mystics revolved: Theurgical abjurations and the heavenly journey. The *yored merkavah*,[108] as the mystic is referred to in Hekhalot texts, sought by magical and theurgical means to ascend safely into heaven, where "direct and unobstructed contact with God or his angel" was possible and where he could obtain, again by means of magic, knowledge of the Torah.[109] The ascent could be dangerous as the angels who guarded the entrances to the various heavenly palaces would attempt to hinder the mystic. Schäfer argues for a liturgical context for the "ritual of abjuration and the heavenly journey".[110] Thus the *yored merkavah* functions as "an emissary of the earthly congregation, who not only assures Israel of the communion with God carried out in the daily liturgy, but also assures God of the communion with His people Israel".[111]

b. Angels in Hekhalot Literature

1) Traditional Elements

It is within this context that Merkavah angelology is to be understood. Given the fluid textual state of the manuscripts and their theurgical/liturgical purpose, it is hardly suprising that the Hekhalot macroforms do not contain a systematic angelology. Even *3 Enoch*, which is the most systematic, offers a number of competing angelologies.[112] However, com-

---

[108] Lit., "he who descends to the merkavah". Paradoxically, in merkavah mysticism one descends to the throne and ascends to the world. This terminology has not been sufficiently explained. See Schäfer, *Hidden*, 2, n.4.

[109] Schäfer, "Aims", 289-295. Cf. also Elior, "Mysticism", esp. 7-17. It is to be noted that one also encounters in this material adjurations which cause angels to descend to the *yored merkavah* and reveal mysteries of the heavenly world; so e.g., §§302-304; 623.

[110] Schäfer, "Aims", 294-295.

[111] Schäfer, "Aims", 288.

[112] Schäfer, *Hidden*, 141; Grözinger, "Namen Gottes", 23-24; and Alexander, *OTP* I.242.

mon themes and motifs do appear. As with Rabbinic angelology, the Merkavah portrayals of angels are at once both traditional and innovative. Traditional motifs include the rivalry between angels and humans (§§174-178,[113] 287-292, 356, 421); the worship of God as the angels' primary task (§§185-186, 582, 590-593); angels are composed of fire (§590); and the appearance of familiar angels such as Michael, Gabriel, Uriel, and Raphael (§§148; 234-236, 363, 372), Metatron (§§1-80 [= *3 Enoch*]; §§147-151; 295), and the Prince of the Countenance or Presence (§§100, 170-171; 425-426). Two further traditional elements, angels as revealers of heavenly secrets (§562, 565, 688 and 691-692)[114] and angels as guardians at the entrances to the heavens (§§207ff, 224ff, 241ff, 407ff, 413ff), take on a new significance in Hekhalot texts.

2) God and the angels

However, alongside these traditional elements there exists a very different conception of angels. The most outstanding characteristic of the angelology of these texts is the blurring of the distinction between angels and God. A clear example of this is to be found in a startling passage from *Hekhalot Zutarti*:

Uri'el [אוריאל] is his Name. ברקיאל is his Name. חניאל is his Name. משיאל is his Name. איתיאל is his Name. זהדריאל is his Name. אהניאל is his Name. ברכיאל is his Name. אנואל is his Name. קדריאל is his Name. רפיסואל is his Name. Michael [מיכאל] is his Name. אינכמול is his Name.... חזיאל is his Name. Gabriel [גבריאל] is his Name. Raphael [רפאל] is his Name. Metatron [מטטרון] is his Name. *Shaddai* [שדי] is his Name. Holy I AM [קדוש אהיה] is his Name. THAT I AM [אשר אהיה] is his Name (§363).

---

[113] See the remarks of Schäfer, *Hidden*, 46-49.
[114] Cf. esp. Elior, "Mysticism", 8-9.

Here Michael, Gabriel, Raphael, Uriel, Metatron, and many other hitherto unknown angel names stand alongside the biblical names שדי, קדוש, and אהיה אשר אהיה as names for God. On the basis of this and similar passages Grözinger has presented a good case for understanding the names of God and of angels as various hypostatic functions of the Deity.[115] In other words, in Hekhalot texts a divine or angelic name is no longer simply an appellation, but a hypostasis of a particular divine power and function.[116]

3) Metatron

This explains why the Merkavah mystics could ascribe to Metatron and other angels[117] attributes reserved only for God in other Jewish writings. For example, Metatron serves as the chief of all the angels and other heavenly beings (§13, 17 = *3En.* 10, 14). He is granted the privilege to sit on a throne similar to the divine merkavah (§13 = *3En.* 10) and wears a crown inscribed with the divine name. As "the Little YHWH",[118] Metatron shares God's Name (§15 = *3En.* 12; cf. §295). Since in Hekhalot literature God is occasionally identified with His Name,[119] it is not surprising that, on occasion, Metatron is identified with the Deity (§§277-279, 678, 310). Even omniscience is attributed to him (§14 = *3En.* 11). To be sure, an "orthodox" reaction to this Metatron speculation appears even within the Hekhalot texts themselves. The story of Aher's apostasy (§20 = *3En.* 16; cf. *bHag.* 15a), which probably only belongs to a later redaction of *3 Enoch*,[120] recounts Metatron's humiliation, punishment and dethronement.

---

[115] Grözinger, "Namen Gottes", esp. 29. Cf. also Schäfer, *Hidden*, 56-57.
[116] Grözinger, "Namen Gottes", 32-33. Grözinger (32) notes §71 (= *3En.* 48B), where Names of God receive worship.
[117] E.g., 'Anafi'el (ענפיאל, §§241-242) and Sandalphon (סנדלפון, §655) among others.
[118] יוי הקטן.
[119] "He (i.e., God) is His Name, and His Name is He, He is in Him, and His Name is in His Name" (§588) and "For His Name is His might, and His might is in His Name, it is His power, and His power is His Name" (§557). Cf. Elior, "Mysticism", 11.
[120] So Alexander, "Historical Setting", 178; idem, *OTP* 1.268, n.16a; and Schäfer, *Hidden*, 133-138, where Schäfer argues that the late redaction of *3 Enoch* reflects a more orthodox and traditional approach than the other Hekhalot texts.

c. The Michael-Metatron Identification

As stated above, there are good reasons to argue that Michael and Metatron were originally the same angel, Metatron being his secret or esoteric name. Later, the two names came to denote two separate angels. Alexander, a recent proponent of this theory, writes:

> A proper estimate of Metatron must begin with the fact that he bears a striking resemblance to the archangel Michael. Both these angels stand in a peculiar relationship to Israel as Israel's special heavenly advocate; both are High Priest of the heavenly tabernacle; both are chief of the angels; what is said in one text about Metatron is said in another about Michael, and *Metatron* appears as a manuscript variant for *Michael*.[121]

These parallels, which could be multiplied,[122] make an interesting case for such an identification, but parallel traditions in and of themselves cannot demonstrate that the two figures were indeed identified. However, we do possess a document which appears to offer מיטטרון as one of Michael's esoteric names. The "Visions of Ezekiel" (ראויות יחזקאל), two (partial) manuscripts of which survive,[123] shares many of the concerns of Merkavah mysticism, but differs in many respects from the Hekhalot macroforms.[124] It may date from as early as the fourth century AD, although this is not certain.[125] The second half of this work consists of a description of the firmament and the seven heavens; their respective distances, their contents, etc. Of the second heaven, *Zebul* (זבול) we read:

---

[121] Alexander, "Historical Setting", 162, his emphasis. The "manuscript variant" refers to *TanB* Wa-ethannen 6 (ed. Buber 7a), which reads Metatron, and *MidrProv* to 14.34 (ed. Buber 39b), which reads Michael, but includes Metatron as a variant reading.

[122] E.g., both are entrusted with the divine Name: *1En.* 69.13-25 (Michael) and *bSanh* 38b (Metatron); both are termed "angel of the Countenance" (מלאך פנים): *TanB* 1.17 (Michael) and *3En.* 3.1 and *passim* (Metatron); and both are identified with the "Prince of the World" (שר העולם): *PRE* 27 (Michael) and a tosafist on *bHul* 60a (Metatron).

[123] See Halperin, *Faces*, 263.

[124] Chief of which is the midrashic character of its opening section.

[125] Scholem (*Jewish Gnosticism*, 44-45) argues that the authorities cited all date from the fourth century Palestine. Alexander ("Historical Setting", 162) in the main follows Scholem. Halperin objects that the attributions are not trustworthy (*Faces*, 269-273), but on the basis of striking parallels with Origen's homily on Ezekiel 1.1-16 suggests that Origen was familiar with a source that lay behind the "Visions" (*Faces*, 327-331). This would place the source as early as the third century.

What is in *Zebul*? R. Levi quoted R. Hama b. 'Uqba, quoting R. Johanan: The Prince (השר) dwells only in *Zebul*. Thousands of thousands and myriads of myriads are in his presence, serving him. Daniel says of them: "While I was watching, thrones," and so forth. "A river of fire flowed" (and so forth). What is his name? *Qimos* is his name. R. Isaac says: *Me'attah* is his name. R. 'Anayni b. Sasson says: *Bizebul* is his name. R. Tanhum the elder says: *'ttyh* is his name. Eleazer of Nadwad says: Metatron (מיטטון), like the name of the Power. Those who make use of the name say: *slns* is his name, *qs bs bs qbs* is his name, similar to the name of the creator of the world.[126]

Apparently this passage is a conscious imitation of *bHag* 12b, where Michael, the Great Prince, stands in *Zebul* offering sacrifices on the heavenly altar. If so, the "Prince" must be Michael and Metatron one of his many names.[127] There is, however, one serious objection to this: According to the "Visions of Ezekiel" the heavenly Jerusalem, with its temple is in *Shehaqim* (שחקים), the fourth heaven, not *Zebul*, the second.[128] Nonetheless, שר preceded by the definite article, *with no other appellation*, would certainly have been understood by most Jewish readers in the Tannaitic and Amoraic periods to have referred to Michael, the Great Prince.[129] Further, one finds an interesting, if enigmatic, parallel to the High Priest Michael appearing in a lower heaven than that which contains the heavenly sanctuary in *3 Baruch* 11-16. There Michael receives the prayers and righteous deeds of the saints in the fifth heaven and ascends to offer them in a higher heaven, perhaps the seventh. So the presence of Michael, here in "Visions of Ezekiel", in the second heaven and the temple itself in the fourth is not necessarily a difficulty. The text says that he "dwells only" in the second, but this need not mean that he also performs his priestly ministry there.

At any rate, Alexander has argued that originally Metatron was a secret name for Michael, but that Metatron began to develop a separate identity.[130] The possible derivation of the name Metatron from the Greek

---

[126] The translation, with some modifications, is Halperin's (*Faces*, 267).
[127] So Alexander, "Historical Setting", 163; Scholem, *Jewish Gnosticism*, 44-47; Segal, *Two Powers*, 66-67; and Fossum, *Name of God*, 321.
[128] Cf. Gruenwald, *Apocalyptic*, 140, n.28; and idem, "Re'uyyot Yehezqel", 128.
[129] Interestingly, this appears to be the only such occurrence of השר in Hekhalot texts. השר is nearly always accompanied by the name of an angel in these texts, and on the few occasions when it is not the identity of the שר is clear from the context, except of course here.
[130] So Alexander, "Historical Setting", 163; cf. also Scholem, *Jewish Gnosticism*, 44-46; Fossum, *Name of God*, 321; Segal, *Two Powers*, 66-67.

title (= $\sigma\upsilon\nu\theta\rho\rho\nu\rho\varsigma/\mu\varepsilon\tau\alpha\theta\rho\rho\nu\rho\varsigma$)[131] would support such a theory. Once its initial significance was forgotten it became a name, and an esoteric one at that. The process by which Michael and Metatron became independent must have been complete by the time of the Hekhalot macroforms for here the two are clearly distinguished (e.g., §148; §21 = *3En.* 17). In these texts Metatron has completely obscured Michael as the principal angel.

d. Conclusions

To be sure, Hekhalot texts, and Merkavah mysticism as a whole, are probably too late for Metatron speculation to have influenced emerging Christology.[132] There are simply no certain Tannaitic references to Metatron in either Rabbinic or Hekhalot literature.[133] However, the Michael-Metatron identification, if true, is highly significant. The Merkavah mystics appear to have transformed Michael, by way of Metatron, into a divine hypostasis, or at least used Michael traditions in constructing the portrayal of Metatron, the most significant of their divine hypostases. This parallels what we found in Philo's use of principal angel traditions in constructing his Logos doctrine. Surely this suggests the utility Michael traditions would have had for early Christians in trying to explain the exalted Christ as divine while attempting to remain monotheists. To demonstrate this I must now turn to Christian texts.

---

[131] See esp. Lieberman, "Metatron".

[132] *Contra* Stroumsa, "Form(s) of God" and Morray-Jones, "Transformational Mysticism".

[133] Indeed, one should not dismiss out of hand the possibility that Metatron speculation developed in reaction to Christian claims made for Jesus of Nazareth.

Chapter 6

Michael and Angelic Christology in the New Testament

In this chapter I turn to the evidence of the NT documents for the earliest Christian use of Michael traditions and their influence on NT Christology. I will begin by briefly sketching the angelology of the NT authors, as best we can reconstruct it. The only two NT passages in which Michael is named (Rev. 12.7; Jude 9) will then be examined at some length, along with a few other passages which may refer to Michael. I will then turn to an investigation of those texts which may indicate that NT Christology owes something to Michael or principal angel speculation. I do not, of course, mean to imply that there was one angelology, much less a single Christology, agreed upon by all the NT authors. I hope to show, however, that despite the sociological and theological diversity of NT Christianity, 1) the angelology of all the NT authors was indebted to Jewish ideas about angels, and 2) the NT documents, with one exception, hold substantially similar views concerning the question of an angelic Christology.

1. The Angelology of the New Testament Authors

Ἄγγελος appears 175 times in the NT,[1] ἀρχάγγελος another two times. Of the NT authors, only "James" contains no reference to angels. There is, however, a marked reluctance to use the term ἄγγελος in the Pauline writings.[2] Here terms like ἀρχαί, ἐξουσίαι and δυνάμεις are much

---

[1] Of course, a few of these are references to human, rather than heavenly, messengers. Cf. Mark 1.2; Matt. 11.10; Luke 7.24; James 2.25.

[2] The epistles which are undisputedly authentic include the word ἄγγελος only nine times (Rom. 8.38; 1 Cor. 4.9, 6.3, 11.10, 13.1; 2 Cor. 11.14; Gal. 1.8; 3.19; 4.14). There are another four occurrences in the disputed epistles (Col. 2.18; 2 Thess. 1.7; 1 Tim. 3.16, 5.21).

more common. It is possible that Paul avoided the terms ἄγγελος and ἀρχάγγελος out of concern that his Hellenistic audience would find them uncultured. Philo (*Gig.* 6; *Som* 1.141) appears to betray a similar apprehension.

a. Michael and Gabriel

As with the Rabbis, the angelology of the NT lies in broad continuity with the angelology of Second Temple Judaism. For example, the only named angels to appear on the pages of the NT documents are the two most familiar and important in Jewish literature of the Second Temple period: Michael (Rev. 12.7; Jude 9) and Gabriel (Luke 1.19, 26).[3] As in *1 Enoch* 9-10, 20, 40 and 1QM 9, the NT authors assume that Michael and Gabriel hold high office in the angelic hierarchy. Jude describes Michael as ὁ ἀρχάγγελος and, in Luke 1.19, Gabriel claims to be one of the few granted continual access to the Divine presence.[4]

b. Angelic Roles

The various functions angels perform in the NT are also found in earlier texts. Gabriel serves as a heavenly herald in both the Book of Daniel and the birth narrative of Luke's Gospel. Revelation 4-5, clearly dependent upon OT (Isa. 6; Dan. 7.9-10) and Jewish apocalyptic (*1En.* 14; 39.12-40.10; *2En.* 20-22) conceptions, describes a heavenly throne room full of

---

[3] One apparent exception "Abaddon" (אבדון) or "Apollyon" (Ἀπολλύων) will be discussed below; see p. 127, n.22.

[4] Cf. similar claims by Raphael in the Book of Tobit and Michael in the *Testament of Abraham*:

ἐγὼ εἰμι Γαβριὴλ ὁ παρεστηκὼς ἐνώπιον τοῦ θεοῦ καὶ ἀπεστάλην λαλῆσαι πρὸς σὲ καὶ εὐαγγελίσασθαί σοι ταῦτα (Luke 1.19).

ἐγὼ εἰμι Μιχαὴλ ὁ ἀρχιστράτηγος ὁ παρεστηκὼς ἐνώπιον τοῦ θεοῦ, καὶ ἀπεστάλην πρὸς σὲ ὅπως ἀναγγείλω σοι τὴν τοῦ θανάτου μνήμην (*TAbr.* A 7.11).

ἐγὼ εἰμι Ραφαὴλ, εἷς τῶν ἑπτὰ ἀγγέλων, οἳ παρεστήκασιν καὶ εἰσπορεύονται ἐπώπιον τῆς δόξης κυρίου (Tobit 12.15 א).

angels whose primary purpose is to render unceasing worship to God (cf. Luke 2.13-14). The angels who appear to the women in the various evangelical accounts of the empty tomb (Mark 16.5-7; Matt. 28.2-7; Luke 24.4-7; John 20.11-13) function in a manner not unlike that of the *angeli interpretes* of the Jewish apocalypses. Other passages make it clear that angels serve as messengers to, or helpers of, humanity (e.g., Heb. 1.14; Acts 10.3; 12.6-10). The belief that angels delivered the Torah to Israel on Mt. Sinai, already alluded to in *Jubilees* 1.27-2.1, is presumed by three NT authors: Luke (Acts 7.38, 53), Paul (Gal. 3.19) and the author of Hebrews (2.2).[5]

c. The superiority of the Righteous over Angels

As we saw in the last chapter, the superiority of Israel over the angelic host was a theme of great significance to the Rabbis. Apparently Christians adopted this teaching, as did the Rabbis, from Second Temple Judaism. However, the NT authors specifically applied it to the Church (Rom. 8.38-39; 1 Cor 6.2-3; 1 Pet. 1.12; Heb. 1.14).

d. Heavenly Cultus

Evidence also exists that various NT authors subscribed to the notion, widely attested in Second Temple Judaism,[6] of a heavenly cultus parallel to the earthly one and presided over by the angelic host. Heb. 1.14 may imply that the angels serve in the heavenly cultus and liturgy on behalf of

---

[5] Silberman ("Prophets/Angels") has questioned whether there was a Jewish tradition that the law was mediated by angels. He has quite rightly pointed out that all, bar one, of the rabbinic texts cited by Strack-Billerbeck in support of angelic *mediation* of the law in fact only attest angelic *presence* at the giving of the law. The one rabbinic text which could support the existence of such a tradition, *CantR* 1.2 (R. Yohanan [pA2]), is both late and obscure. Silberman, however, ignores entirely Acts 7.38, 53 and Gal. 3.19, and proposes a reading of Heb. 2.2 which will not stand scrutiny. In the end, he has missed the cumulative effect which results from reading *Jub.* 1.27-2.1; *Apoc.Mos.* preface; Acts 7.38, 53; Gal. 3.19; Heb. 2.2; and *CantR* 1.2 together. If the existence of the tradition cannot be said to be certain, it is nonetheless likely.

[6] See above pp. 32, 43-46, 60-61, 100-102.

"those who will inherit salvation".[7] While this is not certain,[8] it is not unlikely since the Jewish tradition of angelic heavenly priests provides the most probable background for the High Priest Christology of the Epistle to the Hebrews.[9] In addition, the priestly figure of Melchizedek in Hebrews 7 is probably drawn from Jewish ideas of angelic mediation.[10] At any rate, two passages from Revelation clearly depict a heavenly cultus. First, in 8.3-5[11] an angel offers incense mixed with the prayers of the saints on the altar before the throne. Second, in 15.6 seven angels dressed as priests exit the heavenly temple as it is filled with that smoke which symbolizes the glory of God. As I argued above,[12] it is probably best to understand the θρησκείᾳ τῶν ἀγγέλων in Col. 2.18 as a subjective genitive, i.e., it refers to worship which angels offer. Apparently, some at Colossae thought they could participate in this angelic worship through visions. If this is the correct interpretation, then it is significant that the author of Colossians does not call the existence of such a heavenly cult into question, rather he merely objects to the disunity these visionaries are causing among his flock, through their arrogant boasting.

e. Guardian Angels

Related to the ideas that Israel or the Church are superior to the angels and that the angels serve humans by means of a heavenly cultus is the notion that humans, especially the faithful, are protected by guardian angels. This concept, already established in Second Temple Judaism (*LAB* 15.5; *3Bar.* 11-16; cf. *Jub.* 35.17; *1En.* 100.5), certainly lies behind Matt. 18.10 and possibly behind Acts 12.15 as well.[13] Perhaps the ἄγγελοι τῶν ἑπτὰ ἐκκλησιῶν (Rev. 1.20; 2-3) are to be understood as guardian angels of the seven congregations to which John writes. If so, it suggests a certain

---

[7] Cf. esp. *TLevi* 3.5-6.

[8] It is rejected by Attridge, *Hebrews*, 62 (but see the next note), and Montefiore, *Hebrews*, 49.

[9] So Attridge, *Hebrews*, 97-103.

[10] So Attridge, *Hebrews*, 192-195.

[11] Cf. Rev. 5.8.

[12] Pp. 106-109.

[13] So e.g., Haenchen, *Acts*, 385; Polhill, *Acts*, 282; Bruce, *Acts*, 252; Marshall, *Acts*, 210; Lake and Cadbury, *Acts*, 138; Conzelmann, *Acts*, 95; and esp. Barrett, *Acts*, 585, who points to the late parallel in *GenR* 78 (R. Hama b. Hanina [pA2]). However, see the next paragraph.

fluidity of thought concerning guardian angels. If individual believers had guardian angels (Matt. 18.10), so could groups of believers (Rev. 1.20, 2-3). Certainly, the belief attested in Jewish apocalyptic, at Qumran, and in Rabbinic literature[14] that Michael was the Patron of Israel offers an example of a guardian angel on the national or ethnic level.

f. Angels and the Resurrection

In first century Judaism it was commonly held that the righteous would at the resurrection either become angels or equal to them (*1En.* 51.4; 104.4, 6; *2Bar.* 51.1-12; Philo *Sac.* 5; cf. Dan. 12.2-3; *1En.* 89.1, 9, 36).[15] This belief is also reflected in the dominical saying recorded in Mark 12.25 and its parallels.[16] The statement of Acts 23.8 ($\Sigma\alpha\delta\delta o\nu\kappa\alpha\tilde{\iota}o\iota$ $\mu\grave{\epsilon}\nu$ $\gamma\grave{\alpha}\rho$ $\lambda\acute{\epsilon}\gamma o\nu\sigma\iota\nu$ $\mu\grave{\eta}$ $\epsilon\tilde{\iota}\nu\alpha\iota$ $\grave{\alpha}\nu\acute{\alpha}\sigma\tau\alpha\sigma\iota\nu$ $\mu\acute{\eta}\tau\epsilon$ $\check{\alpha}\gamma\gamma\epsilon\lambda o\nu$ $\mu\acute{\eta}\tau\epsilon$ $\pi\nu\epsilon\tilde{\upsilon}\mu\alpha$) can be understood along similar lines. The natural rendering, that the Sadducees deny the resurrection and the existence of both angels and spirits, occasions the difficulty of placing the Sadducees at variance with their chief source of authority; for the Pentateuch clearly assumes the existence of angels. This difficulty becomes intolerable when it is noted that Acts 23.8 is not supported in this by any other ancient source.[17] Thus, it has recently been suggested[18] that a better translation of Acts 23.8 would run something like: "For the Sadducees say that there is no resurrection, either as an angel or as a spirit". Daube has cogently argued[19] that in this context both "angel" and "spirit" refer to the intermediate state prior to resurrection. Either way the author of Acts would not be suggesting that Sadducees do not believe in angels, but rather would be offering further evidence that some Jews believed that after death the righteous become angels or become like angels. It is, thus, possible that Acts 12.15 refers to Peter himself in an intermediate state, and not to his guardian angel.[20]

---

[14] See pp. 33-38, 64-66, 99-100.

[15] Cf. *bBer* 17a (Rab [bA1]).

[16] Matt. 22.30 closely follows Mark, but Luke 20.35-36 is different enough that some have suggested that Luke cites another version. So Taylor, *Mark*, 483.

[17] Cf. Daube's ("Acts 23", 493) assertion that it is inconceivable "that so flagrant an excision of a major element of biblical theology would never be criticized in the sources".

[18] So Viviano and Taylor, "Sadducees", 496-498.

[19] Daube, "Acts 23".

[20] So Daube, "Acts 23", 495-496.

g. Angels and the Eschaton

Finally, angels play an important role in the eschaton in the NT documents. A host of angels accompany the returning, triumphant Christ (Matt. 13.41; Mark 13.26f pars.; 2 Thess. 1.7; Jude 14-15; Rev. 19.11-16), an archangel heralds Christ's return (1 Thess. 4.16; cf. 1 Cor. 15.52; Matt. 24.30f; Rev. 8.1-5), and an angel captures Satan at the eschaton (Rev. 20.1-3). All this suggests the influence of Jewish apocalyptic (e.g., Dan. 12.1-3; *1En.* 9-10; 90.20-27; cf. Zech. 14.5; Joel 3.11).

These examples make it clear that the NT writers viewed angels much as their Jewish contemporaries did. The same is true of the specific references to Michael in the NT.

2. Michael in the New Testament

a. Revelation 12

Many commentators believe that behind this chapter stands a Jewish source, either oral or written.[21] My primary concern is the meaning of this passage within the present context. Nonetheless, one piece of evidence for John's use of sources is significant: Rev. 12.7 is the only time he mentions an angel by name.[22] John does not seem to be interested in the names of angels. He generally refers to angels with phrases like "another angel" or "a mighty angel" or "the four angels who had been given power to damage earth and sea", or something similar. For all the angels which appear in his book, John does not seem that interested in their names and their individual characteristics, not even with one as important as Michael. After introducing him in 12.7 he drops him and never mentions him again, even when it might have been appropriate to do so--as at 20.1-3. This makes Michael's appearance here somewhat surprising and could be explained as arising

---

[21] So. e.g., Gunkel *Schöpfung und Chaos*, 200ff; Charles, *Revelation*, I.299-314; Beasley-Murray, *Revelation*, 191-197; Yarbro Collins, *Combat Myth*, 101-155.

[22] The only apparent exceptions to this are two fallen angels. First, in 9.11 the locust demons from the Abyss have as King over them τὸν ἄγγελον τῆς ἀβύσσου, whose name in Hebrew is אבדון and in Greek 'Απολλύων, both of which mean destroyer. אבדון as the name of a fallen angel also appears in *bShab* 55a and 89a. The other possible exception is Σατανᾶς/Διάβολος. It is never stated that Satan is a fallen angel, but may be implied in 12.4.

from John's source. However, even if he found Michael in his source, John was too accomplished an artist to retain the name simply for that reason alone. It appears that he must have had some reason for introducing Michael at this point.[23] Moreover, given the central importance of Christ in his apocalypse, one would expect that John would view Christ rather than Michael as the vanquisher of Satan.[24]

So we are confronted with two closely related questions. First, why does John introduce (or retain) Michael here, especially as he has no use for him anywhere else in his apocalypse? Second, why is Michael, rather than Christ, portrayed as casting the dragon out of heaven?

There is, of course, no question of a rivalry between Christ and Michael in John's thought.[25] This is clear when one contrasts 12.7-12 with 19.11-17. Michael's victory over Satan depicted in chapter 12 is only partial in nature; his victory, although real, is only an anticipation of one that is yet to come. Satan is cast out of heaven, but is still free to work his poison on earth (12.12). The final and conclusive defeat of Satan is not recorded until 19.11-20.10, where significantly it is Christ, not Michael, who leads the heavenly hosts. The victory which Michael achieves only expels Satan from heaven, the victory of the Logos will end Satan's threat forever. Since it is John's purpose to assert that Satan, although still very much at work on earth, is now barred from heaven, it would hardly have been appropriate to attribute to Christ an incomplete victory.[26] Thus Michael, the traditional ἀρχιστράτηγος, offers a convenient alternative leader of the heavenly armies.

John apparently intended that these two passages, chapter 12 and 19.11-20.10, be linked. Military imagery is common to both. More importantly, both contain an allusion to Ps. 2.9 (LXX): ποιμανεῖς αὐτοὺς ἐν ῥάβδῳ σιδηρᾷ. The only other citation of or allusion to this verse in Revelation occurs in the epistle to the church at Thyatira (2.26-27), where it is a promise to those in the church who overcome. In both 12.5 and 19.15, on the other hand, it is used to describe Christ. In other words, the reference to Ps. 2.9 in both passages serves to identify the one who rides a white horse and leads the armies of heaven (19.11ff) with the child of the heavenly woman who is caught up to God's throne (12.5).

Of even greater significance is the hymn of 12.10-12, which interprets Michael's victory as dependent upon Christ's victory accomplished by the

---

[23] For John's artistry, see Bauckham, "Structure and Composition".
[24] This difficulty is noted by a number of commentators; see esp. Caird, *Revelation*, 153-154. Cf. also Beasley-Murray, *Revelation*, 201, 203; and Sweet, *Revelation*, 198.
[25] Still less of an identification of the two.
[26] Cf. Roloff, *Revelation*, 148.

Cross. Throughout the Book of Revelation, Christ is presented as a conqueror or victor (3.21, 5.5, 17.14, 19.14-15), but paradoxically his victory was accomplished through his death (5.6, 12.11).[27] Bauckham is surely correct when he asserts that "the continuing and ultimate victory of God over evil which the rest of Revelation describes is no more than the working-out of the decisive victory of the Lamb on the Cross".[28] For John, this "working-out" of the Lamb's victory consists primarily in the participation in his death which Christians realize in their martyrdom (6.9, 7.14, and esp. 12.11). A comparison of 6.9, where the martyrs were killed διὰ τὸν λόγον τοῦ θεοῦ καὶ [διὰ][29] τὴν μαρτυρίαν ἣν εἶχον, with 12.11, where the martyrs have overcome the dragon διὰ τὸ αἷμα τοῦ ἀρνίου καὶ διὰ τὸν λόγον τῆς μαρτυρίας αὐτῶν, indicates that the martyrs' death and their victory over Satan are one and the same. Further, their conquering of Satan is accomplished through the blood of the Lamb; their victory depends upon his.[30] This explains John's paramount concern that his readers are victorious (2.7, 11, 17, 28; 3.5, 12, 21; 15.2; 21.7).

All of this establishes that Michael's victory is not decisive in its own right, but dependent upon Christ's. It also suggests that Michael's traditional role of ἀρχιστράτηγος makes him the logical choice for the angelic leader of the heavenly forces. It does not, however, explain why an angelic leader is needed. If John's chief concern is the victory that Christ achieved and which Christians participate in through martyrdom, why introduce an angel? Caird is, I believe, fundamentally correct when he places Christ's sacrificial victory on earth in conjunction with Michael's victory in heaven as its heavenly counterpart.[31] Caird argues that Christ's entire earthly career is encapsulated in vss. 4b-5: The birth and the snatching away of the man-child to God's throne refers to the crucifixion, resurrection and ascension. The war in heaven of vss. 7-9, then, is "not to be regarded as a sequel to the birth and enthronement of the Messiah, but rather as a second view of the same events in light of a different myth".[32] And this explains why it is Michael, rather than Christ, who leads the heavenly army. John shares the apocalyptic conviction that earthly events are mirrored by

---

[27] See Bauckham, "Christian War Scroll"; and *Theology*, 66-108.

[28] Bauckham, *Theology*, 75.

[29] Perhaps the second διὰ should be omitted with A 1854 it Vg^mss; Cyprian and Primasius. The first διὰ would then serve both phrases and indicate that τὸν λόγον τοῦ θεοῦ and τὴν μαρτυρίαν ἣν εἶχον are two ways of expressing the same reality.

[30] Bauckham, *Theology*, 75-76. Cf. Swete, *Apocalypse*, 156; and Caird, *Revelation*, 157.

[31] Caird, *Revelation*, 153-157; and "Deciphering" 13-14.

[32] Caird, *Revelation*, 156.

heavenly ones. Just as the angelic princes of Persia and Greece opposed by Michael (Dan. 10.13-21) correspond to earthly empires, and just as the epistles to the seven churches of Asia are addressed to the seven (heavenly) angels responsible for them, so while Michael leads the heavenly host in battle against the dragon, Christ fights the real battle, as it were, from the cross. "Because he is part of the earthly reality, he cannot at the same time be part of the heavenly symbolism".[33] As a number of commentators have noted, the idea of the Cross as the moment of Satan's defeat is well illustrated by a statement of Jesus in the Fourth Gospel: νῦν κρίσις ἐστὶν τοῦ κόσμου τούτου, νῦν ὁ ἄρχων τοῦ κόσμου τούτου ἐκβληθήσεται ἔξω· κἀγὼ ἐὰν ὑψωθῶ ἐκ τῆς γῆς, πάντας ἑλκύσω πρὸς ἐμαυτόν (12.31-32).[34]

In summary, in common with Jewish tradition, John views Michael as the angel who leads the heavenly hosts in a military sense and as the angel who stands for the people of God against their Accuser in a judicial sense (cf. vs. 10), but as a Christian he views the work of Michael as subordinated to and dependent upon that of Christ. Indeed, he mentions Michael only once and even then he carefully interprets his victory, by adding the hymn of vss. 10-12, as participating in and dependent upon Christ's.

b. Jude 9

I have already discussed the source for the debate between Michael and Satan in Jude 9 in the chapter on Jewish apocalyptic literature,[35] and need only state here that it is generally considered an assured result of scholarship that Jude refers in vs. 9 to the lost ending of an apocryphon which was known in antiquity either as the *Assumption of Moses* or the *Testament of Moses*.[36]

---

[33] Caird, *Revelation*, 153-154. Cf. idem, "Deciphering", 13; and Bauckham, *Theology*, 74. Cf. also the insightful statement of Lohmeyer (*Offenbarung*, 101): "Im Zusammenhang der Apc hat die Nennung Michaels dadurch besonderen Sinn erhalten, daß sein Kampf und Sieg durch eine Tat Gottes, die Entrückung, eingeleitet und durch den größeren Kampf und Sieg des Logos (19.11ff) beendet wird".

[34] So Caird, *Revelation*, 155; and Kraft, *Offenbarung*, 168. Cf. also Swete, *Apocalypse*, 154; Lohmeyer, *Offenbarung*, 102; Sweet, *Revelation*, 201; Roloff, *Revelation* 149. Note also Luke 10.18, where Satan's downfall is apparently due to the ministry of Jesus.

[35] See above pp. 41-42.

[36] So e.g., Charles, *Assumption*, 107; Tromp, *Assumption*, 271-273; Bauckham, *Jude*, 235-280.

Jude uses this story of the archangel's reluctance to issue a sentence of blasphemy against the Devil to illustrate the arrogance of his opponents. Even Michael, the angelic advocate of the righteous, did not dare pronounce a verdict against Satan, for that right belongs to the Lord alone as the only true Judge. For Michael to have done so would have been an infringement upon divine prerogative. Not even Michael, the greatest of the angels, had the authority to set aside the moral law with regard to a murder committed by Moses, on the basis of which the Devil was claiming Moses' body. Michael could only appeal to the Lord, who alone can set aside the due penalty of the Law.[37] He does so with the words, "The Lord rebuke you"![38] This interpretation harmonizes well with the tradition of Michael as the judicial advocate of the righteous.[39]

Opposed to this interpretation, many commentators take κρίσιν...βλασ-φημίας as a genitive of quality. According to this view, Jude uses the example of Michael, who did not dare to revile or blaspheme the Devil, to criticize his opponents who "blaspheming what they do not understand", "blaspheme glorious ones", i.e, angels (vss. 8, 10).[40] In other words, Michael by not insulting the Devil serves as an example of the kind of humility Jude's opponents should have. This results in the implication that even the Devil should be treated with a certain respect, and not be insulted. Although this is how 2 Peter 2.11 understood κρίσιν...βλασφημίας, it is surely odd that any NT author would be concerned that the Devil be accorded a proper amount of respect.[41] It is to be noted that the author of 2 Peter drops all mention of Satan and ends up directing the βλάσφημον κρίσιν against fallen angels. It seems best, therefore, to understand Jude as commending Michael, not for his politeness toward Satan, but for recognizing that judgement belongs to God alone.[42]

Everything here points to Jude alluding to a story which his readers knew well. This explains his brevity. That all reference to the legend is

---

[37] κύριος is ambiguous. It could refer to either God or Christ and some scribes sought to clarify the issue by replacing κύριος with ὁ κύριος or ὁ θεός. However, κύριος nearly always refers to Christ in this Epistle, and he may very well be in view here.

[38] So Bauckham, *Jude* 273-274; idem, *Jude, 2 Peter*, 43-44, 59-62; Paulsen, *Judasbrief*, 68; Bigg, *Epistles*, 331.

[39] See above pp. 41-42.

[40] So Kelly, *Epistles*, 263-265; Green, *2 Peter, Jude*, 169-170; Moule, *Idiom-Book*, 175; RSV ("a reviling judgement") and NIV ("a slanderous accusation").

[41] So Bauckham, *Jude*, 273-274.

[42] Kelly (*Epistles*, 263-265) approaches this understanding, although he takes κρίσιν...βλασφημίας as a genitive of quality, arguing that "a reviling judgement" fits the context better than "a judgement on his reviling".

dropped by the author of 2 Peter probably indicates that the story was either unknown to him or to his readers, or that he did not approve of the source from which Jude derived this story. So we cannot conclude that the legend was widespread throughout the early Church, still less that it was widely believed. However, Jude's allusion to it indicates that at least Jude and his readers had adopted Michael's traditional roles of archangel,[43] advocate of the righteous, and opponent of Satan. Although no mention of his transferring Moses' soul to heaven or paradise is made, it may have been assumed. If so, Michael's role of psychopomp has also been accepted by Jude and his readers. Nonetheless, even as archangel, Michael does not presume to usurp a prerogative which belongs to the Lord.

c. Other Passages

Before leaving the NT evidence for Michael traditions, a few passages should be discussed which, while not expressly mentioning Michael by name, may be construed as referring to him, for they speak of angelic roles with which he has been traditionally associated.

1) 2 Thessalonians 2.6-7

I begin with ὁ κατέχων of 2 Thess. 2.7.[44] That "the Restrainer"[45] of the anti-God figure of 2 Thess. 2.3-12 denotes an angel has been suggested by a number of commentators and probably remains the most popular solution

---

[43] One should not conclude from the use of the article in ὁ ἀρχάγγελος, that Jude identified Michael as the only archangel. Although we cannot be certain, it is probable that he assumed the existence of either four or seven archangels, especially since he cites (Jude 14-15) a work, *The Book of Watchers*, in which both traditions appear (*1En.* 9-10; 20).

[44] For a fuller statement of the argument presented here, see Hannah, "Angelic Restrainer".

[45] I take "to restrain, to hold back, to check" as the most likely meaning of κατέχω in 2 Thess. 2.7. Not only is this the most common meaning for the verb (see LSJ and BAGD), it also makes the most sense in the context. On this see Menken, *2 Thess.*, 109. Note also the use of κατέχω with reference to the antichrist in *GkApEzra* 4.25; and with reference to the messianic woes in the Greek fragment of *2Bar* 12.4 (Denis, *Fragmenta*, 118).

at the present time.[46] This interpretation fits the author's[47] apocalyptic world view. It emphasizes that God is in control of history, even in the dark days of the messianic woes leading up to the parousia of Christ. The image of an angel restraining an evil personage, either Satan or one of his underlings, is comparatively common in apocalyptic literature: In Rev. 20.2 an unnamed angel binds (ἔδησεν) Satan for a thousand years, while in *1En.* 10.4, 11-12 Raphael and Michael are commanded to bind (δῆσον) Azâzêl and Semjâzâ (cf. also Tob. 8.3; *1En.* 18.12-19.2; 21.1-6; 54.4-6; *Jub.* 48.15; *TLevi* 18.12). Admittedly "restraining" (κατέχων) and "binding" (δῶν) are different words, but they express similar concepts and κατέχειν can denote "imprisonment" (Gen. 39.20 LXX; *GkApEzra* 4.25; and *QuestBart.* 4.12). Furthermore, the suggestion that ὁ κατέχων refers to God[48] runs into grief at vs. 7b, where it is said that "the Restrainer" is "taken away" or "disappears". This, of course, is not a problem if one of God's agents is in view; God orders his angels and archangels as He sees fit. Finally, the neuter form τὸ κατέχον of vs. 6 can be explained as God's plan which finds expression in the work of the angel or Restrainer in vs. 7.[49]

To my knowledge no one, until now, has attempted to identify this angel with Michael, or any other named angel. My case for Michael rests above all on the use of the Book of Daniel in 2 Thessalonians. That our author's portrait of the Man of Lawlessness is based upon the depiction of Antiochus Epiphanes in Daniel 11.36-37 is generally accepted by scholars.[50] We can, then, safely conclude that the Book of Daniel or, at the very least, a tradition derived from Daniel was known to him. Now according to Dan. 10.13, Michael *restrains* the Prince of Persia so that the "man clothed in linen" can get away and deliver his revelation to Daniel. In addition, while the verb κατέχειν does not appear in either the LXX's or Theodotion's translation of Daniel, in 10.21 (θ´) a similar word, ἀντεχόμενος, is used for Michael's action vis-à-vis the princes of Persia and Greece. Finally, Dan. 12.1 predicts that the coming of Michael will coincide with the career of "the antichrist" (11.36-12.3). All this suggests that ὁ κατέχων can be

---

[46] So Menken, *2 Thess.*, 112-113; Holland, *Tradition*, 110-113; Müller, *Anfänge*, 50-51; Dibelius, *Thessalonicher I-II*, 46-51; and Bockmuehl, *Revelation*, 195-196.

[47] The question of whether or not 2 Thessalonians is a genuine work of the Apostle Paul does not directly affect the interpretation I am here proposing.

[48] So e.g., Aus, "God's Plan".

[49] So Menken, *2Thess.*, 112.

[50] E.g., Menken, *2 Thess.*, 104-105; Aus, "God's Plan", 541; Best, *Thessalonians*, 288; Frame, *Thessalonians*, 255.

seen as deriving from our author's reading of Daniel 10-12[51] or his understanding of a Danielic tradition. The cryptic ὁ κατέχων may be related to the Pauline tendency to avoid explicit references to angels in favour of terms like ἀρχαί, ἐξουσίαι and δυνάμεις.[52] It hardly needs to be said that the view of Michael as an opponent of a diabolic eschatological figure easily coalesces with Jude 9 and Rev. 12.7. Another important piece of evidence is an incantation from a magical papyrus copied in the first half of the fourth century (*PGM* 4, 2770) which reads: Μιχαὴλ...κατέχων, ὃν καλέουσι δράκοντα μέγαν. This demonstrates that Michael was known to some individuals in antiquity, who were at least acquainted with Jewish or Christian angelology, as (ὁ) κατέχων.

To be sure, this chapter of 2 Thessalonians remains one of the most difficult texts in the NT. By no means are all its difficulties solved by this suggestion, and I offer it merely as a plausible explanation of an otherwise obscure passage. The proposal takes seriously the author's apocalyptic thought and has the strength of locating the origin of the otherwise opaque ὁ κατέχων in a text or tradition known to have been authoritative for the author.

2) Galatians 3.19

Another extremely difficult passage which may include an oblique reference to our archangel is Gal. 3.19b. While the majority of interpreters understand ἐν χειρὶ μεσίτου as a reference to Moses,[53] Vanhoye has argued that two mediators are alluded to here, the "angel of the presence" (cf. *Jub.* 1.27-2.2) who represented the angelic host and Moses who represented the children of Israel.[54] Paul was not the only NT author who held that the Torah was mediated by angels (Acts 7.38, 53; Heb. 2.2). Significantly, as I have argued earlier,[55] the "angel of the presence" in *Jubilees* is probably to be identified with Michael. That Michael was the mediator of the Law is also alluded to in the preface of the *ApMos.* and *Hermas* viii.3.3, while in

---

[51] Note vs. 5. If 2 Thessalonians was written by Paul, then it is possible that he had previously taught this exegesis of Daniel while in Thessalonica.

[52] See above pp. 122-123.

[53] E.g., Burton, *Galatians*, 189; Betz, *Galatians*, 170; Dunn, *Galatians*, 190; Callan, "Pauline Midrash", 555.

[54] Vanhoye, "Un médiateur", esp. 408-411. He is followed by Bruce, *Galatians*, 178-179.

[55] See above pp. 49-51.

4Q470 he appears as the mediator of a future covenant.[56] Furthermore, an interesting, but weakly attested, variant reading seems to support Vanhoye's proposal.[57] All this could suggest that "the angel" was Michael and "the mediator" Moses.

Even if Vanhoye is correct, Paul may still have been unaware or uninterested that the "angel of the presence" and Michael are one and the same. If he did mean to allude to Michael here, then he subordinates Michael, the mediator of the Law, to Christ, the Seed to whom the promise was given (vs. 19a). Vanhoye's suggestion is ingenious, perhaps too ingenious. It is, at the very least, just as likely that Paul was referring to Moses alone as to Moses and Michael.

3) Revelation 8.3 and 20.2

Other possible references to Michael in the NT include Rev. 8.3 and 20.2. Charles[58] suggested that the priestly angel of Rev. 8.3 may have been indentified with Michael in an earlier form of Revelation. Further, the identification of Michael with the angel who captures the dragon in 20.2 would be consonant with Rev. 12.7, Jude 9 and the proposed interpretation of 2 Thess. 2.6-7. However, as stated above, John shows no interest in angels as individuals and only introduces Michael in chapter 12 for specific reasons. While it is not possible to demonstrate that Michael did not appear in an earlier version of 8.3, Charles' source theories have not found wide acceptance among commentators.

4) The Johannine Paraclete

Finally, O. Betz, appealing to parallels from Qumran, has made a case for identifying the Johannine Paraclete with Michael.[59] Betz argues that the

---

[56] See above pp. 66-67.

[57] C* 3 209* it^{dcorr} Theodoret^{pt} all read δι' ἀγγέλου rather than δι' ἀγγέλων. Cf. a similar phenomenon at Heb. 2.2, where codex L reads δι' ἀγγέλου rather than δι' ἀγγέλων.

[58] *Revelation*, I.225-226.

[59] Betz, *Paraklet*, 149-158. Contrast the opposite thesis of Johnston (*Spirit-Paraclete*, esp. 119-122), who argues that John opposed a Michael-Paraclete identification which was current in certain quarters.

sectarian figure variously known as "the Spirit of Truth" and "the Angel (or Prince) of Light" served as background for John's Paraclete, who also has the title "Spirit of Truth" (14.17, 15.26). Although he believes that the sectarians originally distinguished Michael and the Angel of Light/Spirit of Truth, they were well on the way to being identified as a single figure in the principal texts 1QS and 1QM. The Fourth Evangelist combined this figure with the Michael myth found in Revelation 12 to produce his Paraclete. Betz marshals a wealth of interesting parallels from Qumran and elsewhere in support of his thesis, but in the end he has convinced few. First of all, it should be noted that direct influence from the Qumran sect on the Johannine circle cannot be demonstrated; at best they share some common assumptions and beliefs.[60] Second, the differences between the sectarian Michael/Prince of Light and the Johannine Paraclete must not be passed over. The Paraclete is not said to be an angel and nothing in the text indicates that he should be identified as one.[61] Furthermore, the two figures do not function in the same way: the Paraclete does not have the military role attributed to Michael/Prince of Light, while neither the Johannine Paraclete nor the Qumranian Michael/Prince of Light appear as a heavenly Advocate, which is for Betz the central function of the Paraclete concept.[62] Finally, Betz's dependence upon the Apocalypse of John is a fatal weakness, for there is little or no evidence that the author of the Fourth Gospel was familiar with this work.[63]

d. Summary

In summary, the picture which the NT documents afford us of the archangel Michael stands in broad continuity with that found elsewhere in the Second Temple period. He leads the heavenly armies (Rev. 12.7), and defends the righteous against the accusations of Satan (Jude 9; cf. Rev. 12.10). His office as psychopomp may stand in the background of Jude 9, and 2 Thess. 2.6-7 may attribute an eschatological role to him. Significantly, in all these texts he is clearly subordinated to Christ. His victory over the dragon in Revelation is limited and dependent upon the victory

---

[60] Brown, "Paraclete", 125-126; Johnston, *Spirit-Paraclete*, 106; Burge, *Anointed Community*, 19.
[61] Brown, "Paraclete", 126.
[62] Burge, *Anointed Community*, 20; Johnston, *Spirit-Paraclete*, 107.
[63] Burge, *Anointed Community*, 20; Johnston, *Spirit-Paraclete*, 116-118.

Christ achieved on the Cross. In Jude 9 he does not condemn the Devil, but defers to the Lord's judgement. Finally, assuming that my proposal identifying him with "the Restrainer" of 2 Thess. 2.6-7 is sound, he himself does not destroy the eschatological anti-God figure; that also belongs to Christ. Michael merely restrains him so that his appearance is in accordance with the divine plan.

3. Angel or Angelic Christology

It remains to examine those passages which might suggest that Christ was identified with an angel in the NT period (i.e., an angel Christology) or that NT Christology may owe something to current Michael or principal angel speculations (i.e., an angelic Christology). I will argue that the former is found, albeit indirectly, in the opening chapters of the Epistle to the Hebrews and, perhaps, in Jude. The latter, I would suggest, is found in a number of NT texts. I will argue that the influence Michael and principal angel speculations had on Christology took two forms. There are those passages in which tasks that traditionally belong to the principal angel are transferred to Christ and, in addition, there is evidence that Christ was at times viewed in ways reminiscent of the מלאך יהוה of the OT. I will begin with the evidence for an angel Christology, and then turn to both kinds of evidence for an angelic Christology. Then, having discussed both angel and angelic Christology in the NT, I will turn to the dissimilarities which exist between portrayals of the principal angel in Second Temple period Judaism and the NT portraits of Christ.

a. Christ as an Angel in the New Testament Period

1) The Epistle to the Hebrews

The opening chapters of the Epistle to the Hebrews have occasionally been cited as evidence for an angel Christology. That the author here explicitly affirms the pre-eminence of Christ over the angels has led some interpreters to suggest that he was attacking a view, shared by his readers, that Christ was an angel.[64] Montefiore, for example, argues that such an

---

[64] So Michel, *Hebräer*, 131-132; Lueken, *Michael*, 139-148; Montefiore, *Hebrews*, 39-42; Rowland, *Open Heaven*, 112-113; and tentatively, Bruce, *Hebrews*, 9.

angel Christology was a compromise position which the readers of the epistle, attracted by Judaism, were in danger of adopting. If they reverted to Judaism they would be forced to deny the divinity of Christ, but given their experience as Christians, they would still wish to confess him as more than a man, and so they began to confess him as an angel. The lack of polemical language in Heb. 1-2, however, makes this unlikely. Our author at this early stage of his exhortation appears to be adhering to common ground with his readers; he is, in the words of Barnabas Lindars, "recalling agreed positions" from the primitive kerygma.[65] That the superiority of Christ to angels was part of the primitive kerygma is shown by explicit mention of it throughout the NT (Phil. 2.9-10; Rom. 8.38-39; Col. 1.15-18; Eph. 1.21; 1 Pet. 3.22).[66] Lindars argues that the rhetorical structure of the Epistle shows that our author begins gently, aiming to "establish rapport with the readers before winding up to the main issue".[67] Lindars supports this with two observations. First, our author does not directly address the readers in chapter 1. Second, after 2.9 the issue of Christ's superiority to angels is not brought up again in the whole of the letter.[68] Indeed, the rhetoric of the opening chapter about Christ's surpassing superiority to the angels culminates, rather anti-climactically, in a seemingly unrelated paraenesis (2.1-4).[69] Surely, if he opposed an angel Christology on the part of his readers, the author would have been compelled to dwell on it more than he does. Furthermore, it is difficult to account for the appeal to Melchizedek in chapter 7 if our author was worried that his readers were confusing Christ with an angelic figure. An argument based on Melchizedek would only encourage them to understand Christ in terms of a heavenly, if not angelic, high priest.[70]

Nonetheless, it must be admitted the author of Hebrews does "go on a bit" in stressing Christ's superiority to angels. Why does he list a chapter and a half of proof texts if no one in his day was in danger of blurring the distinction between Christ and angels? The answer may be that while this was not an error which appealed to his readers, it *was* in the air. Indeed, one could argue that he emphasized his agreement with them, building rapport with his addressees by stressing his "orthodoxy" over an issue which

---

[65] Lindars, *Theology*, 27-28, 37-38. Cf. Isaacs, *Sacred Space*, 176; Attridge, *Hebrews*, 51-52; and Stuckenbruck, *Angel Veneration*, 123-139.
[66] So Attridge, *Hebrews*, 53.
[67] Lindars, *Theology*, 27.
[68] Lindars, *Theology*, 27-28, 37-38.
[69] Cf. Stuckenbruck, *Angel Veneration*, 126; and Lindars, *Theology*, 27.
[70] So Isaacs, *Sacred Space*, 176.

was of no little concern to them. The appeal to Melchizedek does not tell against this theory; having established his opposition to angel Christology early on, he was then free to make use of the idea of a heavenly or angelic high priesthood without any danger of being misunderstood.[71] If this interpretation is correct, then the Epistle to the Hebrews offers indirect evidence of an angel Christology in the first century. We shall see that this is supported by evidence of a more direct character in Jude's epistle.

A number of commentators object that the purpose of affirming Christ's superiority to angels serves merely to support the contention (2.2-3) that the salvation offered in Christ transcends the Law delivered by angels. In this view, the primary contrast is not Christ and angels, but Christ and the Law. Therefore, no angel Christology is in view.[72] However, the two concepts are by no means mutually exclusive. The author may very well have been combining the two arguments: Christ supersedes the Law *and* He is superior to all angels. The latter point proves the author's "orthodoxy", while the former addresses an issue on which he feels his readers are in some danger of lapsing. He first concentrates on the issue in which he and they are in agreement; and only after establishing his doctrinal correctness does he turn to the issue for which he is afraid for their "orthodoxy".[73]

2) Jude 5-6

While the identification of Christ with an angel appears to have been opposed in Hebrews 1-2, such an equation may have been embraced and utilized in Jude 5-6. Here it is the pre-existent Christ who is said to have "saved the people from Egypt, but afterwards destroyed those who did not believe". This interpretation is explicit if, in vs. 5, the original reading is Ἰησοῦς. It may still be present, but only implicit, if the text originally read

---

[71] Cf. Attridge (*Hebrews*, 52): "[b]y clearly stating at the outset Christ's superior status, he perhaps forestalls any possible objection to his christology that might arise among those familiar with the sources of his imagery of the heavenly High Priest".

[72] So Lane, *Hebrews*, I.17; Manson, *Hebrews*, 50. Cf. Westcott, *Hebrews*, 16.

[73] So Lindars, *Theology*, 38.

Cf. the similar interpretation of Stuckenbruck, *Angel Veneration*, 123-139. However, Stuckenbruck 1) argues from a pre-history of the text which, while plausible, is hardly demonstrable; and 2) cannot decide whether an angel Christology or angel veneration is being attacked. The former is the better alternative since the nature and function of Christ and of angels are clearly contrasted (1.7-9), while an angel veneration is, at best, merely hinted at (1.6-7).

κύριος. While the problems surrounding the textual variants of this verse may never be completely resolved, there are good reasons to hold that Jude's autograph read "Jesus". Its attestation is early and widespread, supported by both Alexandrian and Western authorities.[74] It is the most difficult reading and it best explains the others. This last point has been disputed.[75] Some would hold that κύριος best explains the others; not knowing which "Lord" was meant, later scribes substituted either θεός or Ἰησοῦς.[76] However, if this were so surely Χριστός would have been substituted rather than Ἰησοῦς. The uniqueness of the pre-existent Christ being called "Jesus" in the NT makes this the most difficult reading. It further accounts for the origin of κύριος: faced with the difficulty of the reading Ἰησοῦς, scribes harmonized Jude 5 with Num 14 and 16 LXX, where κύριος appears many times and to which Jude is alluding in the latter half of this verse.[77]

However, even if κύριος were original, the pre-existent Christ may still have been intended since κύριος always, or nearly always, refers to Christ, rather than God, in this epistle.[78] So Jude in all likelihood views the pre-existent Christ as actively leading the children of Israel out of Egypt. As 1 Cor. 10.4, 9 shows, Christians had already come to conceive of Christ as active in the central event of the OT. Here Paul identifies Christ with the supernatural rock which provided the Israelites with water and followed them in their wilderness wanderings.[79] But in what capacity does Jude envision the pre-existent Christ as active in the Exodus? I would suggest that it is as the Exodus angel, for Jude seems to be consciously echoing OT language about this angel. Just as in Num. 20.16 the "Lord sending [his] angel brought us out of Egypt" (κύριος... ἀποστείλας ἄγγελον ἐξήγαγεν ἡμᾶς ἐξ Αἰγύπτου) and the Hebrew text of Isa. 63.9 can be read as "the angel of His presence saved them", so here, Jude writes, "Jesus saved the people from the land of Egypt" (ὅτι Ἰησοῦς λαὸν ἐκ γῆς Αἰγύπτου σώσας).[80]

There was undoubtedly a great deal of speculation around this angel in Judaism of the Second Temple period. From Ex. 23.20-21 it can be seen that the two duties of the Exodus angel were to 1) guard and lead the chil-

---

[74] Alexandrian: A B 33 81 1241 1739 1881 Origen Didymus. Western: it Vg Jerome.
[75] Bauckham, *Jude*, 309; Kelly, *Epistles*, 255.
[76] It should be remembered that in the earliest uncial MSS θεός, κύριος, and Ἰησοῦς appear as ΘC, KC, and IC.
[77] Cf. Osburn, "Jude 5", 111-115; and Metzger and Wikgren's minority opinion in Metzger, *Textual Commentary*, 726.
[78] So vss. 4, 17, 21, 25, and probably 14. Only vs. 9 is a possible exception.
[79] See Ellis, "Χριστός", 168-171; and Hanson, *Jesus in OT*, 11-16.
[80] So Fossum, "Jude 5-7", 234. Cf. Justin Martyr *Dial*. 75.1-2.

dren of Israel in the wilderness and 2) to punish their disobedience. And these are precisely the two activities attributed to Christ in Jude 5. Furthermore, the allusion in the latter half of vs. 5 is to the plague recorded in Num. 16.41-50. In this text no angel is mentioned; it merely states that "wrath went out from the Lord" (Num. 16.46). However, there is abundant evidence that in the first century this "divine wrath" was understood as a destroying angel (See Wis. 18.20-25, ὁ ὀλεθρεύων; 4 Macc. 7.11, ἄγγελον; and 1 Cor. 10.10, τοῦ ὀλοθρευτοῦ). The latter half of vs. 5, then, seems to confirm the suggestion that Jesus saved the people from Egypt as the angel of the Exodus.[81]

Some[82] would object that the following verse, Jude 6, tells against this interpretation. Jude's syntax is difficult here, but it is simplest to take the subject of vs. 5 as serving vs. 6 as well. Therefore, if my interpretation of vs. 5 is correct, vs. 6 would read as follows: "and the angels who did not keep their appointed place, but left their habitation, *he* (i.e., the pre-existent Christ) has kept in eternal bonds under gloom for the judgement of the great day". However, since no tradition is known in which Christ, or indeed the Exodus angel, imprisoned fallen angels, it is argued that this reading of vs. 6 cannot be correct. This is not a real difficulty since Jude, as in the previous verse, is taking a known tradition and adapting it to Christ. His source for this tradition is, in all likelihood, the *Book of Watchers*, since he quotes the opening chapter of this work (vss. 14-15). *1 Enoch* 10 records God charging Michael and Raphael with the binding of the two leaders of the Fallen angels. Jude appears to be taking this tradition about the two archangels and adapts it, applying it to the pre-existent Christ.[83] The re-interpretation of *1En.* 10 by the author of the *Similitudes of Enoch* is instructive here. In *1En.* 69,[84] the story of the binding of the fallen angels is re-told, but here the roles of Michael and Raphael are coalesced and attributed to a single figure: the Son of Man. Jude seems to be doing something similar.[85]

Thus, I conclude that in vss. 5-6 Jude intended to identify the pre-existent Christ with an angel, the angel that "saved the people from Egypt".

---

[81] So Fossum, "Jude 5-7", 233.

[82] E.g., Kelly, *Epistles*, 255.

[83] Fossum, "Jude 5-7", 231-233.

[84] Cf. esp. vss. 1-12 and 26-28.

[85] Cf. Osburn, "Jude 5", 112-113. Fossum ("Jude 5-7", 228-231) also sees Jude attributing the destruction of Sodom and Gomorrah to Christ in vs. 7. The text itself cannot sustain this. Sodom and Gomorrah are simply said to "serve as an example" (NRSV), and the context does not necessarily imply the activity of the pre-incarnate Christ here.

Nonetheless, we cannot simply conclude that Jude was here espousing an angel Christology. As we shall see, later authors, such as Justin Martyr, could identify Christ with the OT Angel of the Lord without implying that he shared an angelic nature.[86] Such may have been Jude's view. Vss. 5-6 of his epistle are simply too brief to be sure of all the ramifications of Jude's Christology. Furthermore, it should be noted that Jude is alone among NT writers in making this identification. The Exodus angel is also mentioned in Stephen's speech in Acts 7, but there is no indication that Luke saw Jesus in this angel.[87]

It would seem, then, that the NT affords us some limited evidence for Christologies which understood Christ as an angel. Such a view was opposed by the author of the Hebrews, and, if my interpretation is correct, by his readers as well. On the other hand, Jude, who alone of NT authors explicitly identified the pre-incarnate Christ with an angel, may or may not have intended to imply that Christ shared an angelic nature.

b. Principal Angel Speculation and NT Christology

I turn now to those passages which, while not identifying Christ with an angel, seem to owe something to Michael or principal angel speculations. I begin with those which seem to draw on the tradition about the angel in whom the divine Name dwelt (Ex. 23.20-21) and then turn to those passages which attribute to Christ a role or function which traditionally belonged to Michael or other principal angels.

1) Christ as the Angel of the Name

While Jude identifies the pre-incarnate Christ with the Exodus angel, other NT authors may have drawn on the single most distinctive element of

---

[86] See below pp. 202-212.

[87] Werner's (*Formation*, 124) suggestion that in Luke's account of the burning bush (Acts 7.30-34), the angel which appeared to Moses in the bush is identified with ὁ κύριος, and thus with the pre-existent Christ, has nothing to commend it. For ὁ κύριος is equated with ὁ θεός in vss. 31-32, but ὁ θεός is clearly distinguished from the angel in vs. 35. Furthermore, Werner ignores the possibility that the tradition that both an angel and God appeared to Moses in the bush (*ExodR* 2.5; Justin Martyr *Dial.* 60.1) was known to Luke.

the Exodus angel tradition: his relationship to the divine Name. The Israelites were told to obey him, "for he will not pardon your transgression; for my name is in him" (Ex. 23.21). While speculations about the divine Name did not always proceed from an angelological base (cf. e.g., *GosTruth* 38.6-41.14; *GosThom.* 13), Ex. 23.21 did inspire speculations about Michael (*1En.* 69.13-25), Yahoel (*ApAb.*), and Metatron (*bSanh* 38b; *3En.* 12 = §15).[88] Even Philo's Logos could be described both as an archangel and as the divine Name (*Conf.* 146). There are a number of NT texts which seem to imply that Christ also had some relationship to the divine Name.

a) Phil. 2.9 The earliest text which implies Jesus possessed the divine Name is Phil. 2.6-11. After recalling Jesus' death on the cross followed by his exaltation, the hymn continues, God καὶ ἐχαρίσατο αὐτῷ τὸ ὄνομα τὸ ὑπὲρ πᾶν ὄνομα, ἵνα ἐν τῷ ὀνόματι Ἰησοῦ πᾶν γόνυ κάμψῃ...".[89] Many commentators agree that "the name above every name" can only be κύριος, which in the LXX renders יהוה, and which is explicitly attributed to Jesus in vs. 11.[90] The phrase ἐν τῷ ὀνόματι Ἰησοῦ must then be translated "at the name *of* Jesus", i.e., the name which belongs to Jesus, rather than "at the name Jesus".[91] In other words, the Lordship of God, and His Name which guarantees that Lordship, now belong to Christ. Significantly, the hymn culminates in transferring to Christ an OT text (Isa. 45.21-23) which declares the universal worship of the one God, but does it in a way which does not set up Christ as a rival to that one God (vs. 11). In many ways this text parallels 1 Cor. 8.6, where Paul seemingly modifies the *Shema* to include a confession of Christ as κύριος.[92] The deutero-Pauline Eph. 1.20-

---

[88] See above pp. 51-54, 110-111, 117-118.

[89] The article before the first ὄνομα is omitted by Western (D F G), Byzantine (MajT) and late Alexandrian witnesses (Ψ 075 0278 1881), but is strongly supported by early Alexandrian witnesses (P46 ℵ A B C 33 1175 1739 Or), and should be retained. Lightfoot (*Philippians*, 114) notes the tendency on the part of scribes to alter the text when τὸ ὄνομα occurs absolutely.

[90] So Hawthorne, *Philippians*, 92-94; Martin, *Philippians*, 101; idem, *Carmen*, 236-237; Lightfoot, *Philippians*, 113. Cf. Hurtado, *One God*, 96-97; and Fossum, *Name of God*, 95, 293-297. Note the discussion by Fitzmyer ("*Kyrios*-Title", 120-123) on the possibility that pre-Christian copies of the LXX did not use κύριος for יהוה. Fitzmyer is too cautious. He does not take into account the evidence of Philo, whose text of the LXX clearly renders יהוה with κύριος. Nor can Fitzmyer account for the overwhelming substitution of κύριος for the tetragrammaton in Christian MSS if it were not the traditional rendering.

[91] So Hawthorne, *Philippians*, 92; Lightfoot, *Philippians*, 114.

[92] See, among others, Hurtado, *One God*, 97-98; Dunn, *Christology*, 179-183; de Lacey, "One Lord", 199-202.

21 and the author of Hebrews (1.4) provide later but important parallels to Phil. 2.6-11. The three texts taken together imply a conjunction between Christ's exaltation and his possession of a new name.[93]

This bestowal of the divine Name upon Christ at his exaltation and in consequence of his obedience, it must be admitted, differs significantly from the Exodus angel who possesses God's Name so that he can take God's place in leading the Israelites (Ex. 23.20-21, 32.31-33.6), and from Michael's being given knowledge of the Name as the secret oath by which the world was created (*1En.* 69.13-25), and even from Yahoel's (*ApAb.*) possession of the Name as the key to his status as the principal angel. However, there is a significant similarity with Metatron's reception of the Name on the occasion of his exaltation to heaven and his elevation over the heavenly hosts in *3 Enoch* 4-12 (= §§5-15). Two other NT passages, Rev. 19.11-16 and John 17.11-12, offer parallels to the Exodus angel's, Michael's and Yahoel's possession of the Name.

b) Rev. 19.11-16 I have already discussed this passage briefly above in connection with Rev. 12.[94] There I suggested that the allusions to Ps. 2.9 serve to identify the Leader of the heavenly host in 19.11-16 with the man-child of chapter 12. In addition, allusions to the vision of the resurrected Christ (1.12-20), which opens the book, in 19.12, 15 make it clear that it is the same resurrected Christ who will lead the heavenly armies at the climax of history. Significantly, Christ wears many diadems on which is "inscribed a name which no one knows but he himself" (12c). It is just possible that the longer reading supported by mostly late witnesses,[95] ἔχων ὀνόματα γεγραμμένα καὶ ὄνομα γεγραμμένον, is original and that ὀνόματα γεγραμμένα καὶ fell out due to haplography--the eye skipping from ὄνομα to ὀνόματα.[96] If so, then, the secret name cannot be explained as one of the names mentioned in this passage: πιστὸς καὶ ἀληθινός, ὁ λόγος τοῦ θεοῦ, or βασιλεὺς βασιλέων καὶ κύριος κυρίων. For they are merely examples of the "many names". The secret name must be another, unidentified name. Most commentators believe that this "name which no one knows but (Christ) himself" is unknowable.[97] However, the fact that the name is inscribed upon his diadems suggests that it is the tetragram-

---

[93] Cf. Stuckenbruck, *Angel Veneration*, 128-134.

[94] See above pp. 128-129.

[95] 1006 1841 1854 2030 MajT^k Syr^h.

[96] The argument which follows is not dependent upon this textual variant, but certainly harmonizes with it.

[97] So Swete, *Apocalypse*, 251-252; Kiddle, *Revelation*, 385; Caird, *Revelation*, 242; Beasley-Murray, *Revelation*, 279-280; apparently Mounce, *Revelation*, 344-345.

maton. It was widely held in the first century that the divine name was inscribed upon the High Priest's diadem,[98] and more than one interpreter, both ancient and modern, has concluded that the description of Christ's clothing in the opening vision is drawn from priestly models.[99] Furthermore, elsewhere in Revelation (3.12, 14.1, 22.3-4) it is the name of God and the Lamb's new name which is placed upon the forehead of the martyrs. Thus it seems the secret name inscribed upon Christ's diadem is none other than the ineffable Name of God.[100] If this is accepted, then the picture of Christ here is not far from that of the Exodus angel, who had military functions in that by him God drove out the peoples of Canaan (Ex. 23.20-28, 33.2). It also provides a further link with Michael: Christ has not only taken over Michael's role as leader of the heavenly hosts--he also possesses the divine Name as Michael does in *1En.* 69.13-25.

c) *John 17.11-12* In John 17.11-12 Christ's possession of the Name is, in some respects, similar to the portraits of Yahoel in the *Apocalypse of Abraham* and Metatron in *3 Enoch*. In this prayer Jesus affirms that he has completed the work God had given him to do (vs. 4) and that this was nothing other than revealing the divine Name (vs. 6). Jesus can reveal the Name because it had been given to him (vss. 11b-12). Further, the Name shared between the Father and the Son signifies their unity, for keeping the disciples in that Name will bring about their unity with both the Father and the Son (vs. 11b). Furthermore, making known the Name to the disciples secures for them a share in that love which exists between the Father and the Son (vs. 26).[101] In other words, Jesus' possession of the divine Name expresses his unique relationship with God. This is not unlike Yahoel's possession of the Name in *ApAb.* 10.3, 8-17 or Metatron's in *3En.* 12 (= §15). In all three cases possession of the Name implies a special relation to God different from and higher than every other being. However, in the case of the two principal angels the purpose is undoubtedly to signify their role as God's vice-gerent, whereas in the Fourth Gospel Jesus' possession of the Name expresses his unity with the Father.[102] Further, in contrast to

---

[98] See my discussion above pp. 87-88 and n.72, and the texts cited there.

[99] So Irenaeus, *Adv.Her.* iv.20.11; Victorinus and Arethas (acc. to Swete); cautiously Swete himself, *Apocalypse*, 15-16; Farrer, *Revelation*, 65-66; Caird, *Revelation*, 25; Holtz, *Christologie*, 118-121; Mounce, *Revelation*, 77-78; Sweet, *Revelation*, 71.

[100] So Farrer, *Revelation*, 198.

[101] Note also vs. 22, where the δόξα of the Father, which is given to the Son, is another expression of their unity.

[102] See Ashton, *Understanding*, 141-147 and Brown, *John*, II.754-756, for similar interpretations. However, Ashton too easily adopts the suggestion of Barker that the fourth evangelist was not "a die-hard monotheist". He misses the significance of John 10.30.

Metatron and Phil. 2.6-11, but similar to Yahoel in the *Apocalypse of Abraham* and the Exodus angel of Ex. 23.20-21, Jesus is not given the Name only upon his exaltation but already possesses it during his earthly mission. The Fourth Gospel, then, seems to use the tradition about the angel of the Name, but transforms it to present Jesus as both the revealer of God and the Revelation of God--as well as expressing the Son's unity with the Father.

2) *John 8.56, 12.41*

All this shows that NT authors could and did make use of current speculation about the Name of God, and that the authors of Revelation and the Fourth Gospel may have made use of the Exodus angel tradition. However, it is probably significant that no NT author ever cites Ex. 23.20-21 or explicitly identifies Jesus as the angel of the Name. A similar situation prevails in another passage which appears to make use of an OT מלאך יהוה text unrelated to the Exodus narrative. Jesus' statement in John 8.56 that Abraham had seen his "day", may imply that Jesus was one of the "men" who appeared to Abraham in Gen. 18. This interpretation was common at least from Justin Martyr (*Dial.* 56.1, 57.2) onwards and, as we shall see, John could view the pre-existent Christ as active in OT events. However, most commentators prefer to see here a reference to a Rabbinic tradition in which God showed Abraham the future of the world (*GenR* 44.22 [R. Yohanan b. Zakkai (T1) and R. Aqiba (T2)]; but already alluded to in 4 Ezra 3.14) or an allusion to Abraham's joy at the promise of a son in Gen. 17.17.[103] Because of the enigmatic nature of the saying it is impossible to say for certain to which event in the life of Abraham the Evangelist was alluding. However, if he does intend to recall the three men of Gen. 18, the absolute ἐγώ εἰμί saying placed on the lips of Jesus in 8.58 demonstrates that the Fourth Evangelist does not see Jesus merely as an angel.[104]

---

[103] So Brown (*John*, I.360); Schnackenburg (*John*, II.221-223); Barrett (*John*, 351-352) and Dodd (*Interpretation*, 260-262). However, Hanson (*Jesus in the OT*, 123-126) argues that Gen. 18 is one of three OT passages the Fourth Evangelist has in mind.

[104] Contrast the Rabbinic interpretation of Gen. 18 which identifies the three angels as Michael, Gabriel and Raphael (*bYoma* 37a; *bBM* 86b; *GenR* 48.10, 50.2). For the absolute ἐγώ εἰμί saying and its affirmation of Christ's divinity, see esp. Brown (*John*, I.366-367) and Dodd (*Interpretation*, 261-262); cf. also Bultmann (*John*, 327-328).

Mention should probably also be made of John 12.41. Here we have a clear affirmation of the pre-existent Christ's activity during OT times. The Evangelist writes: "Isaiah said these things because he saw his [Jesus'] glory, and spoke concerning him". As most commentators agree,[105] this is an allusion to the vision of the Lord in Isa. 6.1-5.[106] Because of his insistence that no one other than the Son had ever seen the Father (1.18, 5.37, 6.46, cf. 14.9), the Evangelist could not have interpreted Isa. 6.1-5 as a vision of the Father. However, he can quite happily see this as a vision of the pre-incarnate Christ.[107] This is not far from Paul's assertion that the Rock which followed the Israelites in the wilderness was Christ or Justin's identification of the מלאך יהוה as the pre-incarnate Christ.

All of this indicates that there was a reluctance on the part of the NT authors to identify Christ explicitly as the Exodus angel, the angel of the Name, or the מלאך יהוה. Only Jude 5-6 does so explicitly, and even there the text is in question. The NT authors are not shy to state that Christ was active in the events of the OT (1 Cor. 10.4; John 12.41) or that he possesses the Name of God (Phil. 2.9; John 17.11-12). In other words, the NT authors happily allude to traditions about the מלאך יהוה in their portrayal of Christ, but only once is an explicit identification made. How is this reluctance to be explained? It seems that we are left with two options. Either the identification was assumed and simply never stated or it was never made because the NT writers felt it to be inadequate. When we turn to the dissimilarities between the Christ of the NT documents and traditions about the principal angel in Second Temple Judaism it will become increasingly clear that only the second option adequately accounts for all the differences.

---

[105] Brown, *John*, I.486-487; Barrett, *John*, 432; Dodd, *Interpretation*, 207; Hanson, *Jesus in the OT*, 104-108; Bultmann, *John*, 452, n.4.

[106] Note that Isa. 6.10 is cited in vs. 40.

[107] So Brown, *John*, I.487; Hanson, *Jesus in the OT*, 106-108; Schnackenburg, *John*, 416; Rowland, "John 1.51", 499. For a summary of the interpretation of Isa. 6 in the early Church, see Hannah, "Isaiah's Vision".

c. Principal Angel Roles attributed to Christ

1) Christ as the Leader of the Heavenly Hosts

The NT authors not only spoke of Christ in ways reminiscent of the OT מַלְאַךְ יהוה, they also attributed to him roles which had been traditionally associated with Michael or other principal angels. I have already discussed above how Christ appears in Rev. 19.11-16 as the heavenly ἀρχιστράτηγος, leading the heavenly armies.[108] John's clear distinction between Michael's subsidiary victory and Christ's, on which the former depends, must not be allowed to obscure that Christ is here portrayed in an office which usually belongs to Michael in Jewish apocalyptic literature.[109] Indeed, in terms of their literary strategies, the arrival of Christ in Rev. 19.11-20.3 does for the Apocalypse of John what the advent of Michael (Dan. 12.1) does for the Book of Daniel. Given John's knowledge and use of Daniel, it is not unlikely that Daniel 12.1 served as a model for Rev. 19.11-20.3.[110] The crucial fact to note here is that the Seer knew the role was traditionally Michael's (12.7) and yet readily transfers it to Christ and feels no need to defend this novel move.[111] Of perhaps even greater significance is the complete absence of Michael in Rev. 19.11-20.3. He isn't even mentioned as one of Christ's Lieutenants. Christ has not just taken over Michael's traditional role, he has completely eclipsed him. When John relates Michael's victory over Satan he carefully indicates that that victory is subsidiary to Christ's. When he describes Christ's conquest of Satan, he feels no need whatever to re-introduce Michael. His concern lies not with his readers' perception of Michael, but with their recognition of the reality of Christ's victory.

Carrell[112] has quite rightly pointed out that Christ is here portrayed not merely in an office frequently attributed to Michael. He also assumes a

---

[108] It is probable that both angels and saints make up the heavenly hosts which follow Christ. So Charles, *Revelation*, II.135-136; Mounce, *Revelation*, 346. *AscenIs*. 4.14 provides a precise parallel of an army of angels and saints. Carrell (*Jesus*, 206-207) discusses this question and concludes: "...it does not, in fact, seem crucial to attempt to decide the composition of the armies one way or the other. What is important is that they are *heavenly* armies" (Emphasis original).

[109] See above pp. 38-40. In Christian literature the title ἀρχιστράτηγος belongs to both Christ and Michael. Christ: Justin Martyr, *Dial*. 34.2, 61.1, 62.4-5 and apparently the Nag Hammadi tractate *Melchizedek* (IX,1.18.5-6). Michael: *EpApos*. 13 (Copt); Origen, *PG* 12.821. See below pp. 165-166, for a discussion of the Michael texts.

[110] Cf. Carrell, *Jesus*, 209.

[111] Cf. Collins, "Son of Man", 65-66.

[112] *Jesus*, 207-208.

role which in the OT often belongs to Yahweh. In many OT passages it is Yahweh himself who, as the divine Warrior, fights for Israel and leads the heavenly host on behalf of his people (e.g., Ex. 15.3; Deut. 7.1-2, 17-24; Isa. 24.21-23, 27.1; Pss. 18.6-19, 68.1-35). Indeed, Rev. 19.13-15 alludes to one such OT passage in which Yahweh appears as the divine Warrior (Isa. 63.1-3). This allusion serves to identify Christ with Yahweh. Just as in Isa. 63 it is the Lord who tramples the wine press *alone* and has stained his garments, so in Rev. 19.13 the rider wears garments "dipped in blood" and in 19.15 it is stated that he "treads the wine press of the fury of the wrath of God the Almighty". As often in his apocalypse, in 19.11-20.3 John combines a number of symbols and images from the OT and apocalyptic tradition. Christ is portrayed in a role which usually belongs to Michael. He treads the wine press of God's wrath as Yahweh does in Isa. 63. He is also presented as the messiah, for allusions to two classic OT messianic passages (Ps. 2.9 and Isa. 11.4) are included, both of which attribute messianic and militaristic roles to the returning Christ. This mixing of images is significant. Christ takes over Michael's traditional role of ἀρχιστράτηγος, but in no way can Christ be explicated merely in terms of his fulfilling of an angelic office. He also functions as Yahweh and Yahweh's messiah.

Finally, it is possible that this conception of Christ as leader of the heavenly hosts is not limited to the Book of Revelation. A number of other passages (e.g., Mark 13.26 pars.; Matt. 13.41; 2 Thess. 1.7) appear to portray the parousia in terms of Christ leading armies of angels. However, in these the military imagery is far less explicit. At any rate, Christ is certainly portrayed as the heavenly ἀρχιστράτηγος in later Christian writings (cf. Justin Martyr *Dial.* 61.1, 62.4-5).

2) *Christ as the Gate Keeper of Paradise*

Another example of an office traditionally belonging to Michael, but appropriated to Christ by NT authors, is perhaps found in the claim of the risen Christ to hold the keys of death and Hades in Rev. 1.18 and in the promise of Paradise to the penitent thief recorded in Luke's Gospel (23.43; cf. also *QuestBart.* 1.29). For Michael is often portrayed as the angelic gate-keeper of Paradise in Jewish apocalyptic literature.[113]

---

[113] E.g., *4Bar.* 9.5; *3Bar.* 11.2; *ApMos.* 37.4-5. See above p. 47.

3) Christ as the Heavenly High Priest

Similarly the author of Hebrews envisions Christ in Michael's office of heavenly high priest. To be sure there is no direct evidence that the tradition of Michael serving in the heavenly sanctuary was known to this author. However, it is not impossible. For in developing his high priestly Christology the author of Hebrews exploited the notion of a heavenly sanctuary (e.g., 8.1-6), which in Jewish sources was officiated by angels and presided over by Michael (*TLevi* 3.4-7; *3Bar* 11-16; *bHag* 12b; *bMen* 110a; *bZeb* 62a). Furthermore, he appeals to the priesthood of Melchizedek to buttress his argument that Christ's priesthood is eternal and supersedes the Aaronic priesthood. In light of the evidence from Qumran, it is possible that some contemporaries of the author of this epistle accepted an identification of Melchizedek with Michael.[114] However that may be, it is clear from 7.3 that the author of Hebrews understood Melchizedek not only as a priest, but also as some kind of heavenly being, although whether he is merely an exalted patriarch or a patriarch transformed into an angel (cf. *1En.* 71; *2En.* 22) is unclear.[115] 11QMelch, *2En.* 71-72 and *Melchizedek* (NHC IX,1) demonstrate that speculation about a heavenly Melchizedek was not uncommon in the first two centuries of the Christian era. It is possible, then, that our author knew of these or similar conceptions about Melchizedek.[116] If so, then, in writing of Christ's high priestly office the author of Hebrews may have been consciously transferring to Christ what had previously been Melchizedek's/Michael's. To be sure, the author does not assert that Melchizedek's, or Michael's, priesthood has come to an end. But the point of his argument is that now only Christ's priesthood has any continuing validity for Christians.

Significantly, for the author of Hebrews, Christ's high priesthood implies a role of heavenly advocate and intercessor (Heb. 7.25, 9.24). Other NT authors also assume that the exalted Christ intercedes for Christians (Rom. 8.34; 1 John 2.1). Here again is a role which belongs to Michael, and other principal angels, in Jewish literature (*1En.* 89.70-77, 90.17; *3Bar.* 11-16;[117] *ExodR* 18.5; *RuthR* proem 1; and *bYoma* 77a).[118] However, while NT authors may have been dependent upon Michael or

---

[114] See pp. 70-74 for my discussion of 11QMelch and 4Q'Amram.

[115] Contra Isaacs, *Sacred Space*, 163-164.

[116] Attridge, *Hebrews*, 194; Lindars, *Theology*, 74-77; Hengel, "Son", 81. Cf. also Longenecker, "Melchizedek Argument", 171-179; and Yadin, "DSS and Hebrews", 48-53.

[117] See above pp. 43-46.

[118] See above pp. 100-102.

angelological traditions for this, at least Paul did not apply it exclusively to Christ. He assumes that the Holy Spirit, as well as the exalted Christ, intercedes for Christians (Rom. 8.26-27).

To be sure, in attributing these principal angel roles to Christ the NT writers avoid specifically recognizing Christ as an angel. He leads the heavenly armies, but he is not Michael. Melchizedek is likened to him (7.3), but the two are clearly distinguished. The NT authors found these roles helpful in illustrating the present and future significance of Christ, but they go no further in the direction of an explicit angel Christology.

d. Dissimilarities

Heretofore I have examined the positive evidence for angelic Christology in the NT. In what follows I will be concerned with the negative evidence or the dissimilarities between NT Christology and principal angel traditions.

1) *Christ Never Called or Portrayed as an Angel in the NT*

a) Rev. 1.12-18 and 10.1 Although the NT 1) describes Christ's activity in OT events in ways reminiscent of the מלאך יהוה and the Exodus angel and 2) contains significant and striking parallels between Christ and Michael or other principal angels of Second Temple Judaism, the fact remains that, except for Jude, the NT authors never identify Christ with an angel or describe him as an angel. Some would question these assertions. Rowland, to cite one of the most important examples, has argued that the description of Christ in Rev. 1.12-18 draws upon the description of the glorious angel in Dan. 10.5-6.[119] He quite rightly points to the very similar language used to describe the appearance of the Glory of God in Ezekiel 1, the "man clothed with linen" in Dan. 10.5-6, Yahoel in *ApAb.* 10, the angel (possibly Michael) who appears to Aseneth in *JosAsen.* 14, and the risen Christ in Rev. 1.12-18. Rowland has, I believe, demonstrated that John used the angelophany of Dan. 10.5-6 as a "quarry for imagery to des-

---

[119] Rowland, "Vision of the Risen Christ"; idem, "Man Clothed in Linen"; and idem, *Open Heaven*, 94-113. Rowland is followed in the main by Stuckenbruck, *Angel Veneration*, 209-221.

cribe" Christ.[120] However, it is very doubtful that John intended to identify Christ with the angel of Dan. 10--or any other angel. First of all, nothing is taken over from Dan. 10 and left untouched. In concert with his use of the OT generally, John here transforms everything he borrows. For example, Daniel's καὶ τὸ πρόσωπον αὐτοῦ ὡσεὶ ὅρασις ἀστραπῆς,[121] becomes καὶ ἡ ὄψις αὐτοῦ ὡς ὁ ἥλιος φαίνει ἐν τῇ δυνάμει αὐτοῦ. Significantly, the risen Christ of John's vision also wears the white hair of the Ancient of Days of Dan. 7.9 and *1En*. 46.1, and so could be construed as having divine characteristics.[122]

More important is a methodological concern: similar and even parallel imagery often indicates only very general comparisons. As Rowland himself points out, in his description of "the One Seated" upon the throne (Rev. 4.3), John draws on the imagery of the *Urmensch* of Ez. 28.13.[123] But surely no one will suggest that the divine Occupant of the throne of John's vision is modelled on, even less is to be identified with, Ezekiel's *Urmensch*! In the words of Dunn, Rowland fails to ask

> how much of the similarity of language of these visions is due to the fact that descriptions of glorious heavenly figures in visions could draw on only a limited pool of metaphors and images? Hence the prevalence of the impression of fire and brightness.[124]

One has only to recall the descriptions of God in *1En* 14.20 and *2En* 22.1 (LR), 39.5 (LR); of Michael in *TAb*. A 7.2-7; and of the Woman clothed with the sun in Rev. 12.1 to see the truth of this. This "limited pool of metaphors and images" means that by necessity many of these descriptions will begin to sound familiar.[125] Indeed, to the angel of Rev. 10.1 belong paraphernalia elsewhere associated with divinity;[126] however, for John he remains simply one of the many anonymous angels (ἄλλον ἄγγελον

---

[120] *Open Heaven*, 100.

[121] Here the LXX and Theodotion have the same text, except that for Theodotion codices A Q and a few minuscules replace ὡσεὶ with ὡς.

[122] So, e.g., Holtz, *Christologie*, 121-122.

[123] Rowland, "Visions of God", 146.

[124] Dunn, *Partings*, 218.

[125] One must also keep in mind the fluidity of apocalyptic images. For example, in Rev. 5.5 and 4 Ezra 11-12 a lion is used as a symbol for the Messiah. In 1 Pet. 5.8 it is a simile for the Devil. Too much weight must not be placed on imagery alone.

[126] He is clothed with a cloud, which traditionally belongs to theophanies. Further, the rainbow upon his head recalls the rainbow around the divine throne (Rev. 4.3).

ἰσχυρὸν) which make up the heavenly hosts.[127] Contrary to Rowland (and Gundry),[128] the similarities between this angel and the risen Christ of chapter 1 are not so great as to make them almost indistinguishable.[129] The only real parallel is the comparison of his face to the sun: τὸ πρόσωπον αὐτοῦ ὡς ὁ ἥλιος (10.1). Compare 1.16: καὶ ἡ ὄψις αὐτοῦ ὡς ὁ ἥλιος φαίνει ἐν τῇ δυνάμει αὐτοῦ. Later when John intends to identify the Leader of the heavenly armies (19.11-16) with the Son of Man from the vision of the opening chapter, he lifts whole phrases with very little variation (cf. 1.14 with 19.12 and 1.16 with 19.15).

In other words, one cannot decide on the basis of such imagery alone whether a heavenly being is divine or an angel or an exalted patriarch or an exalted saint. The imagery of Rev. 1.12-18 certainly identifies the Son of Man figure as a heavenly being, but what kind of heavenly being can only be answered by close attention to the text of Revelation itself. There we find clues which suggest a distinction between angels and Christ. First, in 5.8-14 Christ receives the same worship that is offered God (cf. also 4.11), while John's angelic guide rejects any attempt to be worshipped by him (19.10, 22.8-9). Second, Christ is associated with God's throne (3.21, 7.17, 22.3) in ways which infer he is classed on the divine side of the chasm between Creator and creatures.[130] This conclusion is further supported by Christ's claim to the divine titles "Alpha and Omega, the First and the Last, the Beginning and the End" (22.13, cf. 1.8, 21.6).

To be sure, Rowland carefully avoids implying that John understands Christ as an angel.[131] Nevertheless, he assumes the glorious imagery of Rev. 1.12-18 suggests that John was drawing on angelomorphic categories, when John's imagery probably only points to the heavenly character of the risen Christ.[132] What kind of heavenly being he is only becomes clear as John proceeds.

Recently, Gundry has like Rowland appealed to similarity of imagery, as well as similarity of function, for the identification of the "mighty angel" of 10.1, and a number of other angels in the Book of Revelation (e.g., 18.1-3, 18.21, 7.2-3, 20.1-3), with Christ.[133] He does not explain, however, why

---

[127] For a cogent presentation of this "mighty angel" as the "angel of Jesus" mentioned in 1.1 and 22.16, see Bauckham, "Conversion", 243-257; and idem, *Theology*, 80-84.

[128] Rowland, *Open Heaven*, 102; Gundry, "Angelomorphic", 663-668.

[129] So also Stuckenbruck, *Angel Veneration*, 231-232.

[130] See Hall, "Living Creatures".

[131] See esp. "Man clothed in Linen", 100.

[132] This same criticism applies to Stuckenbruck's (*Angel Veneration*, 209-221) exegesis as well.

[133] Gundry, "Angelomorphic".

John, who elsewhere freely uses the names or titles "Jesus", "Christ", and "Lamb", should in these passages hesitate to identify explicitly these angels with Christ. Gundry's reading of the text results in a certain incoherence. For example, in 7.2-3 the angel who ascends with the rising sun is in reality the ascending Christ.[134] Once in heaven he is no longer termed ἄγγελος, but "the Lamb" (7.9), but the text of chapter 7 itself offers no clue that these two figures are one and the same. To the contrary, the context suggests that they be treated as distinct personages. Chapters 6 and 8 depict the Lamb in the heavenly throne room opening the seven seals. Chapter 7 also places him in the throne room (7.9-10, 17). Gundry's identification of the angel of 7.2 with the Lamb must presuppose that the Lamb has left heaven after opening the sixth seal in 6.12, that he re-ascends into heaven in 7.2-3 and resumes opening the seals in 8.1. The text itself offers no support for such a complicated reading.

For Gundry's thesis to be sustainable he must produce a passage in Revelation which unequivocally applies the term ἄγγελος to Christ. He believes he has found this in the opening verse. Gundry understands this verse to affirm that God both gave a revelation to Jesus to pass on to God's servants and sent Jesus as His angel to John. To arrive at this, he must take ὁ θεός as the subject of the sentence even though it appears in a subordinate clause. The majority of commentators take Jesus as the subject of ἐσήμανεν ἀποστείλας διὰ τοῦ ἀγγέλου αὐτοῦ τῷ δούλῳ αὐτοῦ Ἰωάννῃ.[135] In other words, διὰ τοῦ ἀγγέλου αὐτοῦ refers to an angel sent by Jesus himself, a reading which is confirmed by 22.16.[136] Thus, διὰ τοῦ ἀγγέλου αὐτοῦ in 1.1 refers, not to Jesus, but to his angel, and cannot be used to support Gundry's need for unequivocal application of ἄγγελος to Christ in the Apocalypse of John.[137]

b) Rev. 14.14-15 Nor can one appeal to Rev. 14.14-15 as if the ἄλλος ἄγγελος implied that the ὅμοιον υἱὸν ἀνθρώπου was also an angel. Most commentators recognize that ἄλλος ἄγγελος is John's usual mode of referring to angels (7.2, 8.3, 18.1, cf. 10.1). In this chapter alone the phrase occurs six times (vss. 6, 8, 9, 15, 17, 18).[138] But how is it that an angel

---

[134] Gundry, "Angelomorphic", 672-673.

[135] Swete, *Apocalypse*, 2; Charles, *Revelation*, I.1; Sweet, *Revelation*, 57-58; Bauckham, *Theology*, 81-82; idem, "Conversion", 254-255. Cf. also Farrer, *Revelation*, 59; Beasley-Murray, *Revelation*, 50-51.

[136] Gundry ("Angelomorphic", 675, n.39) mentions this verse, but does not give sufficient attention to it.

[137] So Bauckham, "Conversion", 243-257; and idem, *Theology*, 80-84.

[138] See, e.g., Swete, *Apocalypse*, 188-189; Beckwith, *Apocalypse*, 662; Sweet, *Revelation*, 231; Dunn, *Christology*, 323, n.110. Contrast Charles, *Revelation*, II.21.

here gives the command to Christ to begin the harvest? Does not this imply that the man-like figure, clearly a reference to Christ,[139] is to be ranged with the angels rather than with God? Beasley-Murray is probably correct to emphasize that this angel has come from the heavenly temple, that is from the presence of God, and is understood as conveying His command.[140] Stuckenbruck objects 1) that such an explanation does not alleviate the difficulty which rises from the fact that an angel mediates between God and Christ and 2) that Christ performs a task (14.16: harvest of grain) parallel to that of an angel (14.19-20: harvest of vintage and treading of a winepress).[141] The first objection has weight only so long as this passage is examined in isolation from the rest of the Apocalypse. Given the angelic worship of Christ (5.11-13) and other assertions of Christ's superiority to angels in the book (1.16, 20; 22.16) it seems unlikely in the extreme that Christ is here being depicted as dependent upon an angel for communication with God. The purpose of the angel issuing from the temple and relaying the command to Christ is probably only intended to emphasize the divine origin of the edict. Further, we must allow for the fact that Revelation is a narrative and an apocalypse, not a theological treatise. Thus, we cannot make too much of certain inconsistencies which result from the limitations inherent to narratives.[142] Stuckenbruck's second objection neglects the parallel in 19.15, where Christ treads the wine press. Reading 14.20, where the subject is not named, in light of 19.15 it appears that the man-like figure, not an angel, is intended as the unnamed subject of vs. 20.[143]

c) *Gal. 4.14* Some have argued that Paul's statement in Gal. 4.14 that the Galatians had accepted Paul ὡς ἄγγελον θεοῦ...ὡς Χριστὸν Ἰησοῦν should be read as if the two ὡς phrases were in apposition.[144] This would make Paul assert that Christ Jesus was the angel of God, or at least imply that this was the Galatians understanding which he was seeking to correct. The grammar certainly permits this, but it is hardly compelling. As Paul's own view, it finds no support elsewhere in the Pauline corpus, and con-

---

[139] Cf. Carrell, *Jesus*, 192-195.
[140] Beasley-Murray, *Revelation*, 229. Cf. Sweet's (*Revelation*, 231) appeal to Mk. 13.32.
[141] Stuckenbruck, *Angel Veneration*, 243-244.
[142] Cf. Carrell's (*Jesus*, 191) explanation that "Jesus' ignorance can be understood as a result of his being separated from God at the point at which God concludes that the harvest should be cut".
[143] So Bauckham, "Conversion", 294-295; idem, *Theology*, 96-97.
[144] So Longenecker, "Distinctive", 532; idem, *Christology*, 31; and Gieschen, "Apostle".

tradicts Gal. 3.19 where Paul contrasts the Law given by angels with the promise which was fulfilled in Christ.[145] On the other hand, if this were a view of the Galatians, which Paul is correcting, we would not expect Paul to be so allusive, and positive, in his only reference to this Galatian error. It seems best, therefore, to take the second ὡς phrase as a progressive, rather than a synonymous, parallel.[146]

d) *The Son of Man* As long ago as 1941 Werner appealed to the Son of Man tradition as evidence of an angel Christology. On the basis of Daniel 7.13-14 and the *Similitudes of Enoch*, he argued that the earliest Christians understood the title "Son of Man" as a reference to an angelic being, whom God had appointed as an eschatological judge. Werner, assuming that in Jewish apocalyptic generally the Son of Man was understood as an angel, argued that the Synoptics took over this understanding when they described the Son of Man as the prince of angels (Mark. 1.13, 8.38, 13.26-27; Matt. 13.41-42; Luke 22.43; cf. 1 Thess. 4.16).[147] Werner goes a step further arguing that just as Enoch was transformed into the heavenly Son of Man in *1En.* 71, so in Acts 2.32-36 Jesus is said to have been raised by God, and, in fulfilment of Psalm 110, exalted to the right hand of God.[148]

Leaving to one side the complex question of the original meaning of the phrase ὁ υἱὸς τοῦ ἀνθρώπου on the lips of Jesus, to say nothing of the debate regarding the sayings' authenticity, there is little or no evidence that the Evangelists, who identified the "Son of Man" with Jesus, understood the term as referring to an angel. In predictions of the parousia, angels are said to accompany the Son of Man and fulfill his directions, but no equation with an angelic being is ever made. Werner, at this point, depends not upon evidence from the NT, but upon a scholarly construction which assumed a widespread expectation in apocalyptic circles of an angelic Son of Man. This scholarly construction was, and is, dependent upon the *Similitudes of Enoch* and 4 Ezra 13, works which are contemporary with, or a little later than, the Gospels. More recent interpreters have argued cogently that these and other works probably reflect a *messianic*, not angelic, interpretation of Dan. 7.13 which was current in the first century.[149] More to the point, while many of the Synoptic Son of Man sayings are also based upon Dan 7.13 (e.g., Mk. 8.38, 13.24-27, 14.62), there is nothing in the Synoptic Gospels to suggest that their authors

---

[145] Dunn, *Christology*, 155.
[146] Burton, *Galatians*, 242; Dunn, *Christology*, 156.
[147] Werner, *Entstehung*, 302-304 (= *Formation*, 120-121).
[148] Werner, *Formation*, 126.
[149] E.g., Horbury, "Messianic Associations"; and Collins, "First-Century Judaism".

understood the Son of Man of Daniel 7 to be an angel. While a pre-existent, heavenly messiah, such as we find in the *Similitudes* or 4 Ezra, may not in our view differ much from an angelic figure, we must be careful before assuming that those who accepted such a messianic interpretation of Daniel 7 would have happily identified the Messiah with an angel. As we have seen, the evidence from Qumran suggests that at least some in Second Temple Judaism distinguished the expected messiahs from angelic redeemers.[150] More importantly, the Son of Man figure is never identified with an angel in either the *Similitudes* or 4 Ezra. Indeed, especially in the former the precise nature of the Son of Man figure is unclear. While he is listed alongside the various angelic orders (*1En.* 61.10), he is also termed "that child of woman" (*1En.* 62.5).[151] We must, then, concluded that while the Son of Man of the *Similitudes of Enoch* and 4 Ezra may be angel-like he is never explicitly identified as such and, even if he were, it would be too much of a jump, without further evidence, to conclude that the Synoptic Evangelists thereby intended to imply that Jesus as the Son of Man was an angelic being.

Recently, Yarbro Collins has returned to a position similar to, but more nuanced than, Werner's. She follows Rowland in postulating the dependence of John's vision of Christ in Rev. 1 on Daniel's vision of the angel in Dan. 10, but also emphasizes the role that the vision of the Son of Man in Dan. 7 had on the author of Revelation. She further argues that for Daniel the Son of Man represented the archangel Michael, but since John seemingly identified the angel of Dan. 10 with the Son of Man he probably understood the Son of Man to be Gabriel. Yarbro Collins appeals to the LXX text of Dan. 7.13 which states that "the one like a son of man came, and as (the) Ancient of Days (ὡς παλαιὸς ἡμερῶν) he arrived". She assumes the LXX text identifies the Son of Man and the Ancient of Days.[152] She proposes that this text was known to the author of Revelation and that he followed a tradition which identified both figures with hypostatic manifestations of God. She concludes that John identified both Danielic figures with Christ/Gabriel.[153]

The LXX text *may* have been known to John and it *may* have inspired him to attribute to the risen Christ the white hair of the Ancient of Days in

---

[150] See above pp. 58, 65-66.
[151] This reading is supported by one text-type (Eth. II). The other (Eth. I) reads: "Son of Man". For "that child of woman" as the more difficult, and thus the preferred, reading see Black, *1 Enoch*, 235-236.
[152] So also Lust, "Daniel 7,13", 67-68; and Stuckenbruck, *Angel Veneration*, 217-218.
[153] Yarbro Collins, "Son of Man", 548-558.

Daniel 7. Nonetheless, it should be recognized that we are uncertain of the LXX reading's origin and we cannot rule out the possibility that the LXX reading was introduced by Christian scribes influenced by Rev. 1.12-20. More to the point, even if we assume the priority of the LXX version of Daniel over against John's apocalypse, it is highly questionable that the LXX text implies that "the one like a son of man" and the Ancient of Days are one and the same figure.[154] The LXX text, taken in its entirety, presupposes not one, but two figures. First, more than one throne is mentioned in vs. 9. Further, the myriads of angels surrounding the Ancient of Days (vs. 10) approach[155] "the one like a son of man" (vs. 13) after his arrival, which would be a nonsense statement if the two were to be understood as a single figure. Furthermore, vs. 14 states that authority was given to "the one like a son of man", implying that the Ancient of Days confers this authority. In other words, the LXX envisions not the identity of these two figures, but rather expresses the similarity of the Son of Man to the Ancient of Days.[156] Thus it is more natural to conclude that John identified the "one like a son of man" with the risen Christ and "the Ancient of Days" with God. This means that John need not have seen either figure as angelic, but rather understood the LXX text as emphasizing the Son of Man's affinity with the Ancient of Days.

2) *Christ Superior to Angels in the NT*

Finally, there can be no question but that the NT authors held Christ to be superior to angels. In the Synoptics, for example, at the parousia the angels do Christ's bidding in gathering the elect and separating the righteous from the unrighteous (Mark 13.26 pars.; Matt. 13.41; cf. Matt. 25.31). Indeed, the angels are often termed either "the angels *of* the Son of Man" or "*of* Christ" (Matt. 16.27; 2 Thess. 1.7). Similarly, various authors affirm that Christ at his resurrection or exaltation was elevated above all the heavenly beings (Eph. 1.20-22; 1 Pet. 3.22; Heb. 1.1-4;

---

[154] To sustain this, Yarbro Collins asserts that Greek-speaking Jews of the LXX version of Daniel 7 "would probably have taken vss. 9-12 and vss. 13-14 as parallel accounts of the same event" ("Son of Man", 557). This seems to me to be extremely unlikely. Yarbro Collins offers no positive evidence that Dan. 7 LXX was ever so understood.

[155] προσήγαγον αὐτῷ in Pap. 967 and the marginal reading of the Syro-Hexapla; παρῆσαν in Cod. 88 and the Syro-Hexapla.

[156] So also Kim, *Son of Man*, 22-24.

Matt. 28.18; cf. 1 Cor. 15.23-28). Other passages imply that Christ's superiority to the angels was a fact prior to his incarnation (Col. 1.15-20; Heb. 1.5-14). In the Revelation, the Risen Christ holds in his hand the seven stars which signify the seven angels who correspond to the seven churches. Finally, while John's angelic guide twice refuses worship, angels venerate the Lamb with the very same language they use to worship God (Rev. 4-5, 19.10, 22.8-9).

All this, in and of itself, does not disprove the existence of an angel Christology, for by definition the highest archangel would have been considered superior to all other angels. The issue is whether this superiority is one of degree or of kind. Some passages can be understood either way. First, those predictions of the parousia in which the Son of Man is accompanied by angels (e.g., Mark 13.26-27 par. Matt. 24.30-31; Matt. 13.41, 16.27, 25.31; 2 Thess. 1.7) could be construed as a superiority of degree; the angels are "his" in the same way that each angelic host was thought to be under the command of an archangel (Rev. 12.7; *2En.* 19.1-3; *Vita Adae* 15.1, 16.1). These passages could also be understood as implying a superiority analogous to God's sovereignty over the angels, in which case it would be a superiority of kind, rather than of degree. The descriptions of the parousia, then, are ambiguous and can be understood either way.

Many of the passages which affirm that Christ at his resurrection or exaltation was elevated above all the heavenly beings (e.g., Eph. 1.20-22; 1 Pet. 3.22; Heb. 1.1-4; Matt. 28.18; cf. Phil. 2.10-11) are similarly ambiguous. Even a text, Phil. 2.6-11, which implies that Christ was superior to all angels before his incarnation offers little help. All of these are silent on the nature of Christ vis-á-vis the angels; they can all be construed as declaring a superiority of degree *or* of kind. However, this is not the case with Heb. 1.5-14. Here the contrast of angels with the Son imply that the Son differs not just in degree but also in kind. The author asks, "To which of the angels has he ever said...?" (vs. 13, cf. also vs. 5).[157] In vss. 7-8 he utilizes a $\mu\grave{e}\nu...\delta\grave{e}$ clause to contrast angels with the Son. Furthermore, in vs. 6 the author declares that God commanded all the angels to worship the Son. Clearly the author of Hebrews did not classify Christ as an angel, not even the highest of the angels, but rather held him to be of another order entirely. Indeed, he affirms the Son's eternality (1.11-12) and twice calls him $\theta \varepsilon \delta \varsigma$ (1.8-9). In a similar vein, the author of Colos-

---

[157] Cf. 1QM 13.13-14 and 1QH 15.28ff (formerly 7.28ff) where this same rhetorical device is used to contrast God with the angels.

sians asserts that Christ was the agent of creation "through whom and for whom" the angelic orders of thrones, dominions, authorities and powers were created (Col. 1.16). Their creation not only depended upon him, so does their continued existence, for τὰ πάντα ἐν αὐτῷ συνέστηκεν (1.17). Here again, Christ's superiority to the angelic hosts is a superiority of kind, rather than just degree.

Likewise, the saying of Jesus in John 1.51 that Nathaniel would see "heaven opened and the angels of God ascending and descending on the Son of Man", implies that the latter belongs to a different order from that of the angels. John is here alluding to Jacob's dream of the ladder between earth and heaven (Gen. 28.12). Many commentators would understand John to be interpreting the ladder of Jacob's dream with the Son of Man: Jesus is the "bridge" between the heaven and earth.[158] However, Rowland has recently made a convincing case for understanding this passage in light of Jewish exegesis of Gen. 28.12, where the angels descend to look upon Jacob whose face is identical to an image engraved upon the divine throne. Rowland renders the final phrase "descending *to* the Son of Man", taking the phrase ἐπὶ τὸν υἱὸν τοῦ ἀνθρώπου only with καταβαίνοντας. In this interpretation, the Fourth Evangelist replaces Jacob in the Jewish exegesis of Genesis, with Jesus, the Son of Man, in his own. He thus presents Jesus as the "embodiment of the revelation of the divine *Kabod*".[159] Both of these interpretations suggest that Jesus' superiority to the angels is more than just one of degree. In the first, the angels belong to the heavenly world and need the mediation of the Son of Man to descend to earth and re-ascend to heaven. In the second, they descend for the purpose of beholding the embodiment of the divine glory, who is none other than Jesus, the Son of Man.

I argued above that in the Book of Revelation Christ fundamentally differs from the angels; for he shares the divine throne (3.21, 7.17, 22.3) and, unlike the angels (19.10, 22.8-9), he receives the same worship as God (5.8-14; cf. John 5.23). Other evidence for the worship of Jesus in the NT suggests that the practice was widespread in early Christianity.[160] For example, Acts 13.2 pictures the leaders of the church at Antioch "worshipping the Lord". Furthermore, Eph. 5.19 speaks of hymns which were sung to the Lord, i.e., to Christ. Phil. 2.6-11, Col. 1.15-20, and John 1.1-18 may very well be first century examples of these hymns to Christ. That

---

[158] So Barrett, *John*, 187; Ashton, *Understanding*, 347-348; cf. Brown, *John*, I.91.

[159] Rowland, "John 1.51", esp. 503-506.

[160] Cf. Bauckham, "Worship of Jesus", 118-149; idem, "Jesus, Worship of", *ABD* III.812-819; and Hurtado, *One God*, 99-114.

they are not explicitly addressed to Christ, but rather recite his origin and deeds, does not tell against this just as ancient psalms (cf. e.g., Pss. 106, 107, 121) and modern hymns often do the same and yet were and are considered acts of worship. Indeed, Phil. 2.6-11 ends with a prediction that every creature in heaven and earth will eventually kneel before and confess Jesus Christ as Lord; two liturgical actions which at the very least imply the eschatological worship of Jesus. Confession of Jesus as Lord was an early practice of central importance in the first century Church (Rom. 10.9-13) and one which seems to have had a cultic context (1 Cor. 12.1-3). Doxologies addressed to Christ (2 Tim. 4.18; 2 Pet. 3.18; Rev. 1.5b-6; 5.13) and a benediction which include him alongside God (2 Cor. 13.13) are also found in the NT. Petitions were directed to Christ (2 Cor. 12.8; 1 Thess. 3.11-13; 2 Thess. 2.16-17, 3.5; 1 Cor. 16.22; Rev. 22.20; cf. *Did.* 10.6). Finally, the Lord's Supper, at least in Pauline circles, probably included the idea of communing with the Risen Christ (1 Cor. 10.14-17).

This evidence for the worship of Jesus is varied; some of it early, much of it late. Some of the evidence carries more weight than others. However, taken as a whole the passages listed above offer the startling and exceptional phenomenon of cultic actions being rendered to a man who just decades earlier had been executed by crucifixion. And the authors of the writings in question all make claims of monotheism. The NT authors go to great lengths to ascribe honour to Christ, while none give evidence for the honouring of angels in a cultic setting. Indeed, it was widely assumed that the angels worshipped Christ (Phil. 2.10; Heb. 1.6; Rev. 5.8-13)! This cultic veneration of Christ indicates that Christ's superiority to angels was understood by many NT authors as one of kind, and not just of degree.

4. Conclusions: Use and Transformation of Principal Angel Traditions

The evidence reviewed in this chapter is, to be sure, somewhat ambiguous. The NT authors used Michael and other principal angel traditions in their portrayals of Christ. Christ appears in Revelation as the Leader of the heavenly armies, in Hebrews he is the heavenly High Priest, in both Luke and Revelation he is the Keeper of Paradise. He has been entrusted with the divine Name. All of these roles belong to Michael in Jewish traditions. However, Christ is never called an angel and never portrayed as an angel, except in Jude 5-6, where he is identified with the OT מלאך יהוה. Further, Christ was held to be superior to the angels. At least in Colossians (1.16-17), Hebrews (1.7-8, 13), Revelation (5.8-13), and the Gospel of John (1.51), this is a superiority of kind and not just of degree. When principal angel motifs are used to elucidate Christ or his work, they are used cautiously and, with the exception of Jude, an explicit identification with Michael or the מלאך יהוה is meticulously avoided. However, the fact that they are used means that angelology did have some effect on NT Christology. The NT authors found traditions about principal angels convenient for asserting the activity of Christ in OT events and in clarifying the heavenly and exalted nature of Christ. Thus we are justified in speaking of NT angelic Christology. In the following chapter we shall see that this ambiguity resulted in different Christologies among Christians in the following centuries. Some understood the pre-incarnate Christ as an angel. Some even identified this angel with Michael. While "orthodox" Christians found this unacceptable, they could and often did call Christ an angel and identified him with the OT מלאך יהוה.

Chapter 7

Michael and Angelic Christology in the Second and Third Century

There is evidence that during the second century a Christology which identified Christ with the highest of the archangels gained ascendancy in certain circles. Not surprisingly such an angel Christology, on at least one occasion, equated Christ with Michael. The various forms this angel Christology took, especially its Michael-Christ form, will be the subject of the bulk of this chapter, but I begin by briefly summarizing Michael traditions as they appear in both Christian apocalyptic, and related, literature and Patristic works. Discussions of two ancillary phenomena will conclude the chapter: First, the theme of Christ disguised as an angel, and second, a discussion of the "theophanic" angel Christology of Justin and Irenaeus.

1. Michael in Second and Third Century Christianity

As we found to be the case with the NT documents, the Michael traditions which appear in Christian writings of the second and early third centuries owe a great deal to Jewish angelological traditions of the Second Temple period. Indeed, it would seem that Christians adopted many Jewish beliefs about Michael. Significantly, many of the traditions taken over by Christians are found in writings outside the Jewish Scriptures. This is true both of the treatises of intellectuals, like Tertullian and Origen, and of "popular" literature, like Hermas' *Shepherd* and the *Epistula Apostolorum*.

a. Leader of the Heavenly Angels

Michael remains the leader of the angels in many of these texts. For example, in the *Ascension of Isaiah* (3.16) Michael is the ἄρχων τῶν ἀγγέλων τῶν ἁγίων. There is an emerging consensus which would place the origin of this early apocalypse in the opening decades of the second century or earlier.[1] Another second century Christian work, the *Epistula Apostolorum*, in a list of the four archangels (Michael, Gabriel, Raphael, and Uriel) refers to Michael as "the archistrategos of the angels" (Chapt. 13).[2] In the *Questions of Bartholomew*,[3] Satan claims to be the first created angel and that "Michael, the captain of the hosts above", was the second (4.28-29). This implies that Michael should now be reckoned as the prince of those angels who did not fall.[4] Finally, on the basis of Hermas *Sim.* viii.3.3-6, Origen[5] argued that individual Christians when they first believe are placed under the guardianship of Michael, but when they fall into sin they are transferred to lesser (ὑποδεέστερον) angels. This probably indicates that Origen held Michael to be superior to all angels.[6]

---

[1] So Hall, "Community, Situation, Date", 300-6; Acerbi, *L'Ascensione*, 277-82; Pesce, *Isaia*, 299-300; Knight, *Disciples of the Beloved One*, 33-39; and Bauckham, "Gospel Traditions", 9-14. Most of these scholars would also stress the unity of the *Ascension of Isaiah*. Earlier scholarship tended to divide the *Ascension* into three sources. So e.g., Charles (*Ascension*, xliv-xlv) who placed each of the three sources in the late first century, but dated the final redaction to the second or early third centuries; Barton (*AOT*, 779-781) who basically follows Charles; and Müller (*NTA*, 604-605) who doesn't appear to have taken the most recent research into consideration. Knibb (*OTP* II.149-150), one of the few recent scholars who still finds three distinct sources behind our text, places all the constitutive parts in the first or second centuries, but the final version in the third or fourth centuries.

[2] Coptic version. The Ethiopic ("...the archangels Michael and Gabriel, Uriel and Raphael followed me...") smoothes the rough grammar of the Coptic and should probably be considered secondary. Cf. Schmidt, *Gespräche Jesu*, 47.

[3] Scholarly opinion on the origin of *QuestBart.* is divided. Elliott (*ANT*, 652) reports that others have suggested dates from between the second and sixth centuries. Scheidweiler (*NTApoc.* I.540) asserts that there is no reason not to assign the original recension to the third century.

[4] Cf. Rohland, *Michael*, 40-41.

[5] *CommMatt.* xiv.21. According to Eusebius (*HE* vi.36.1-3), the commentary on Matthew is one of Origen's latest works, and thus dates from the middle of the third century.

[6] Cf. also *ApPaul* 14, 43-44, 48. However, this apocalypse in its present form cannot be earlier than the fourth century.

b. Protector of the People of God and Opponent of Satan

The passage in Hermas appealed to by Origen portrays Michael as the guardian angel of the people of God, the Church (ὁ δὲ ἄγγελος ὁ μέγας καὶ ἔνδοξος Μιχαὴλ ὁ ἔχων τὴν ἐξουσίαν τούτου τοῦ λαοῦ καὶ διακυβερνῶν [αὐτούς] Hermas *Sim.* viii.3.3).[7] This is an example of how the traditional belief of Michael as the protector of the Jewish people was taken over by early Christian writers and applied to the Church. While Origen (*CommMatt.* xiv) used it to support the idea that Michael was the guardian of individual Christians, he elsewhere retains the notion of Michael as the patron of the Jews. In a catena fragment on Jos. 5.14 (*PG* 12.821), Origen affirms that after the death of Moses the people were turned over to Michael, the ἀρχιστράτηγος who appeared to Joshua. Origen's interpretation here is very similar to one found in Rabbinic sources (*ExodR* 32.2-3; *GenR* 97.3): God himself led the children of Israel until the death of Moses when he handed them over to an angel. The Rabbis interpreted Jos. 5.13-15 as the story of this angel taking up his role as patron of Israel.[8] Similarly, Hippolytus identifies Michael with the angel who led the children of Israel in the wilderness and opposed Moses at the inn (*CommDan.* iv.36-40). In these various texts Michael's role as protector of the people of God, both of the Jews in the OT period and of Christians in the present, is affirmed. Significantly, none of our extant sources argue that Michael is no longer patron of the Jews. Rather it would seem that his guardianship of Christians derives from the assumed continuity of the Church with the saints and prophets of the OT.[9]

The adoption of this tradition takes an interesting form in the passage from Hermas cited above (*Sim.* viii.3.3-6). Here Michael delivers the Law to believers. This recalls the role attributed to him by the Jewish apocalyptic tradition of mediating the Law to Israel on Mt. Sinai.[10] However,

---

[7] The final form of the *Shepherd* of Hermas is generally dated to the middle of the second century. So Quasten, *Patrology*, I.92-93; Dibelius, *Hirt*, 421-422; Brox, *Hirt*, 22-25; Lake, *Apostolic Fathers*, II.3; and tentatively Lightfoot, *Apostolic Fathers*, 293-294. The αὐτούς is omitted by the Greek MSS A and M, but was apparently present in the Greek text(s) which stood behind the two Latin versions and the Ethiopic.

[8] Origen elsewhere (*HomJos.* vi.2; cf. *HomJud.* ix.1 and *HomEz.* i.7) interprets this passage as a reference to Christ rather than Michael. On balance it is probably best to see this as an example of an inconsistency in Origen's thought, but it is not impossible that this catena fragment has been incorrectly attributed to Origen.

[9] One exception in Christian literature of the second century may be found in *AscenIs.* 3.14-16 where "the angel of the Church" appears to be distinguished from Michael.

[10] *Jub.* 1.27-2.1; *ApMos.* Preface; 4Q470; cf. Gal. 3.19; Heb. 2.2; Acts 7.53; and above pp. 49-51, 66-67, 124. Cf. also *ApPaul* 14, 44 where Michael is called "the (arch)angel of the covenant".

Hermas interprets the Law neither as the written Torah nor as oral traditions, but rather as the proclamation of the Son of God (ὁ δὲ νόμος οὗτος ὁ υἱὸς τοῦ θεοῦ ἐστιν κηρυχθεὶς εἰς τὰ πέρατα τῆς γῆς; *Sim.* viii.3.2). Indeed, as the context makes clear, for Hermas "the Law" is the Christian way of life.[11] Hermas, then, while probably indebted to Jewish apocalyptic thought for this conception, has adapted it to his own purposes. In due course, I will return to this passage for a far more significant adaptation of Michael traditions by Hermas.

In Jewish apocalyptic, the literature of Qumran, and in Rabbinic thought Michael's guardianship of Israel often implied a military role.[12] Such a role is probably also assumed by those early Christian texts which give him the title ἀρχιστράτηγος (*EpApos.* 13 [Coptic]; *QuestBart.* 4.29 v.l.;[13] Origen, *PG* 12.821).[14] However, just as in Rabbinic literature, in early Christian documents military functions could be attributed to other angels. For example, Origen (*Princ.* i.8.1-3) held that the supervising of wars was Gabriel's responsibility.

Related to this military office is the theme of Michael as the opponent of Satan on behalf of humanity.[15] This theme appears in *QuestBart.* 4.52-55. Here Beliar recounts the story of his fall: Michael orders Beliar to worship Adam, the image of God. In his pride Beliar refuses, Michael insists and when Beliar continues to refuse, he is cast out of heaven.[16]

c. Heavenly Priest

Turning to the tradition of Michael as a heavenly priest, a passage from Origen's *De Principiis* (i.8.1-3) is very significant. In it Origen attributes to Raphael "the work of curing and healing", to Gabriel "the supervising of

---

[11] Cf. e.g., *Sim.* viii.3.5-8. So Lake, *Apostolic Fathers*, II.199, n.1.

[12] See above pp. 33-42, 64-66, 99-100.

[13] One Grk MS, Cod. G, reads: Μιχαήλ, τὸν ἀρχιστράτηγον τῶν ἄνω δυναμέων, but the other, Cod. H, omits everything after Μιχαήλ. H is usually the more reliable, but in this instance, Scheidweiler (*NTApoc*, I.547) prefers G.

[14] Cf. also the angel of *QuestBart.* 1.23-26 who has military functions and whom Scheidweiler (*NTApoc*, I.551, n.8) identifies with Michael. This unnamed angel's superiority to the other angels certainly fits the depiction of Michael later in this document (4.28-29, 52-55), but it seems odd that the author would choose not to identify him here as Michael when earlier in the same vision he mentions Michael by name (1.9).

[15] See above pp. 41-42, 64-66, 127-130.

[16] This story is based on the legend found in *Vita Adae* 12-16 and various other sources. See above, p. 42.

wars", and to Michael "the task of attending to the prayers and supplications of mortals".[17] Although the whole passage is typical of Origen's thought, the roles attributed to the three archangels are probably traditional. This association with human prayers recalls Michael's priestly office in Rabbinic and apocalyptic literature.[18] Although its date is uncertain, one recension of the *Ascension of Isaiah*[19] also presents Michael in an intercessory office which may be priestly. In the seventh heaven Isaiah asks his guide about an angel who appears more glorious than the others. His guide tells him that this is "the great angel Michael ever praying on behalf of humanity and the poor" (*magnus angelus Michael deprecans semper pro humanitate et humilitate*).[20] A priestly office is certainly in view in *Sim.* viii.2.5, where Michael charges the Shepherd, or angel of repentance, with the careful examination of those committed to his charge. Michael is concerned that none who are unworthy get past the Shepherd. "But," he says, "if anyone does bypass you, I shall test them at the altar". Similarly, *EpApos.* 13 records how Christ, during his descent to earth, conferred upon Michael, Gabriel, Raphael and Uriel the ability to serve at the heavenly altar. Here, however, the priestly office is shared by the four archangels and seemingly amounts to a substitution for Christ during the time of his incarnation.

d. Eschatological Roles

Finally, Michael fulfills various eschatological roles in early Christian thought. As in Jewish apocalyptic and Rabbinic literature,[21] Michael often appears in early Christian literature as the escort of the souls of the righteous to Paradise or, alternatively, as the Gatekeeper of Paradise. For

---

[17] Cf. *Cels.* i.25 and Jerome *CommDan.* ii.8.16. According to Eusebius, *De Principiis* dates from Origen's Alexandrian period (*HE* vi.24.4), which ended with his removal to Caesarea in 231 or 233, while *Contra Celsum* dates from late in his Caesarean period (*HE* vi.36.2). Jerome, of course, dates from the late fourth to early fifth century.

[18] See above pp. 43-46, 100-102.

[19] Charles' G^2. The witnesses of this recension are the so-called second Latin (L^2) and the Slavonic (S) versions.

[20] 9.23 acc. to L^2; S differs slightly. C. Leonardi, who edited the Latin text for the Corpus Christianorum series, believes that the words *et humilitate* are a later addition; see Norelli, *Ascensio*, 227. Cf. also 9.29, 42 (L^2 S). *ApPaul* 43 also asserts that Michael continually prays for humanity.

[21] See above pp. 46-47, 102.

example, we have descriptions of Michael transferring to Paradise the souls of Isaac and Jacob in a Testament under the name of each,[22] the soul of the Virgin Mary in a complex of narratives and traditions preserved in texts of various languages,[23] and the soul of Jesus' human father in the *History of Joseph the Carpenter*.[24] Admittedly much of this literature is late, dating from the fourth century and beyond. However, the common theme of Michael as psychopomp certainly derives from an earlier tradition since it is attested in the *Testament of Abraham*[25] and the *Apocalypse of Moses*,[26] works which, although Jewish in origin, were preserved by Christians. Examples of Michael as the Majordomo of Paradise in works of Christian origin, such as the *Apocalypse of Paul*[27] and the *Gospel of Nicodemus*,[28] are also late. Nonetheless, here again earlier works of Jewish origin which were adopted and re-written by Christians demonstrate that this concept was accepted in Christian circles as early as the second or third centuries.[29] However, given such scriptural passages as Rev. 1.18 and Luke 23.43, it is not surprising that some Christians concluded that Majordomo of Paradise was a task more suited to Christ than to an angel. Thus, in *QuestBart*. 1.29 Jesus says "and unless I am present there they (i.e., the souls of the righteous) cannot enter into paradise". One could also point to *Passio Perpetuae* 1.3, where Christ greets Perpetua in a heavenly garden.[30]

Mention should probably be made of *QuestBart*. 4.12, where Michael's trumpet calls up Beliar bound with fiery chains and restrained by 660 angels. Although this is not an eschatological event, it contains eschatological imagery. It is just possible that this text is based upon a tradition which held that Michael will be the angel who blows the trumpet heralding the Eschaton. That the final judgement will be preceded by a trumpet blast was apparently well established in Biblical and apocalyptic tradition.[31]

---

[22] Note esp. *TIsaac* 2.1ff, 6.24-28; *TJac*. 1.5-6.

[23] *The Assumption of the Virgin* (Lat. B), or *The Narrative of Pseudo-Melito*, 9.2, 17.1 (*ANT*, 711, 714); and the Syriac *Obsequies of the Holy Virgin* 1 (*ANT*, 721-722).

[24] Chapts. 22-23 (*ANF* VIII.392).

[25] *TAb*. B 14.7. In rec. A (20.10-12), Michael shares this duty with all the angels.

[26] *ApMos*. 37.4-6. Cf. *Vita Adae* 47.2-3.

[27] *ApPaul* 22, 25-27, 49.

[28] *GNic*. 25.1, 26.1.

[29] See esp. *4Bar*. 9.5; and *3Bar* 11.2.

[30] In the *Apocalypse of Peter* (early second century) Uriel is the angel "appointed over the resurrection of the dead on the day of judgement" (4). However, in the two examples given (chapts. 6 and 12) Uriel delivers up not the souls of the righteous, but of the damned.

[31] Cf. Isa. 27.13; Joel 2.1; Zeph. 1.14-16; 1 Thess. 4.16; 1 Cor. 15.52; Matt. 24.30-31; and 4 Ezra 6.23. Cf. Bockmuehl, "The Trumpet Shall Sound".

And, in at least one Jewish work, Michael is responsible for a trumpet call prior to a scene of divine judgement, although not the final judgement. In *ApMos.* 22.1-3, Michael summons the angels for the judgement of Adam by means of a trumpet blast. Michael's connection with the final trumpet reappears in much later works of both Jewish and Christian provenance.[32]

e. Gnostic Michael Traditions

The Gnostics also preserved Michael traditions, although they seem to have been less interested in him. Probably his traditional association with the Jews made him suspect to those who disparaged the God of the Jews as the ignorant Demiurge. At any rate, Michael appears only once in all of the Nag Hammadi documents (*Ap. John* [NHC II.1] 17.30). Gabriel, on the other hand, is referred to six times in the Nag Hammadi Corpus (*Gos. Eg.* [NHC III.2] 52.23, 53.6, 57.7, 64.26; and *Zost.* [VIII.1] 57.9, 58.22). In addition, Michael and Gabriel play an important role in the rescue of Pistis Sophia from Chaos in *Pistis Sophia* 64-67.[33] Gabriel also appears, without Michael, in *Pistis Sophia* 7, a Gnostic re-telling of Luke's annunciation story.[34] Thus, Michael seems to have been eclipsed somewhat by Gabriel in the Gnostic works, at least in those which have survived. Finally, a diagram belonging to a Gnostic sect called the Ophites and described by both Origen and Celsus,[35] lists Michael, Gabriel, Raphael, Suriel among "the seven archontic daemons" ($\tau\hat{\omega}\nu$ $\dot{\epsilon}\pi\tau\dot{\alpha}$ $\dot{\alpha}\rho\chi\dot{o}\nu\tau\omega\nu$ $\delta\alpha\iota\mu\dot{o}\nu\omega\nu$) who attempt to impede the Soul in its ascent through the heavens after death. Here Michael is not merely eclipsed by another archangel, but transformed, with all the archangels, into an evil demon. No doubt this resulted from the Gnostic programme of re-interpreting the OT God and his agents as the evil or ignorant Demiurge and his archons.

---

[32] *Apocalypse of St. John the Theologian* (*ANF* VIII.583) 9 [Fifth to Ninth century]; and *Signs of the Messiah* (אותות המשיה; *BHM* II.58-63) 8-9 [Early Medieval].
[33] *Pistis Sophia* is generally dated to the third century. So Rudolph, *Gnosis*, 27; and Pétrement, *Separate God*, 73.
[34] See below pp. 196-197.
[35] *Cels.* vi.24-38.

f. Summary

In summary, Michael traditions in Christian writings of the second and third centuries look similar to what we have found elsewhere. In these texts Michael is the Leader of the angels. He stands in a special relationship to the People of God as their protector and defender. This implies a military office, as well as a special role in opposing Satan. He serves as a heavenly priest and as an intercessor on behalf of humanity. He is the angelic guide for the souls of the righteous at their death and presides over the gates of Paradise. To be sure, not one of the works cited in this chapter attributes all these traditional roles to Michael. The second and third-century Christian portrait of Michael which I have summarized here is a composite one, dependent upon very different sources. However, it is significant that most, if not all, of these various elements are derived from either Jewish sources, both canonical and apocryphal, or the NT. This underlines the degree to which early Christians were dependent upon Judaism for its conceptions about angels in general and Michael in particular.

Furthermore, as with the NT documents, most of the writings examined to this point clearly picture Michael as subordinate to Christ. For example, in the *Ascension of Isaiah* the Risen Christ emerges from the tomb on the shoulders of Michael and of the angel of the Holy Spirit (3.16-17). In the *Epistula Apostolorum* the four archangels are only able to serve at the heavenly altar because of the gift of a wondrous voice bestowed on them by Christ (13).[36] Christ commands or beckons (ἔνευσεν) Michael to blow his trumpet at *QuestBart.* 4.12, while in 1.9 Christ descends to Hades because of Michael's request (κατ[ὰ] τὴν παράκλησιν τοῦ ἀρχαγγέλου Μειχαήλ). As we shall see, Tertullian (*Carn.* xiv) argued that Christ is not to be understood as an angel "by nature,...in the sense of a sort of Gabriel or Michael", but rather as their superior.[37] However, in what follows, it will become clear that Hermas, in his *Shepherd*, assumed the identity of Christ with Michael. While this conception always remained a minority opinion in early Christianity, it may not have been unique to Hermas.

---

[36] Following the Coptic. The Ethiopic and Latin has Christ distracting the archangels by means of this voice. Schmidt (*Gespräche Jesu*, 49) prefers the Coptic.

[37] Cf. also Origen, *Cels.* viii.13.

2. Angelic Christology in Second and early Third Century Christianity

I turn now to the evidence for angelic Christology or, more correctly, angelic Christologies in the second and early third centuries. The evidence suggests that various Christian groups found the principal angel category useful for elucidating the work and person of Christ, but they found it useful in different ways. A number identified Christ with the highest of the archangels. At least one went further and identified that archangel with Michael. Still others found the concept of archangel useful in other ways. I will begin with the less specific examples of Christ as the highest archangel and then move to the evidence for a Michael-Christ equation.

a. Christ as an archangel

1) "Heretical Angel Christologies"

In this section I am concerned with only the clearest evidence that some in the early Church identified Christ with an archangel. They easily fall into four groups, which I will discuss in the following order: Ps.-Cyprian's *De Centesima*, Epiphanius' description of the Ebionites and the sect of the Elchasaites, Tertullian's attack on Valentinian Christology, and certain magical texts, especially the *Testament of Solomon*.

a) Ps.-Cyprian Sometime near the end of the second century an unknown, North African Christian ascetic with encratite tendencies composed a sermon, subsequently ascribed to Cyprian, on the rewards awaiting martyrs, virgins, and "the righteous" (i.e., those who remain continent within marriage).[38] Sexual ethics and continence, not Christology, are the primary concerns of this preacher. Nonetheless, in two very significant

---

[38] *De Centesima, Sexagesima, Tricesima*. First published in 1914 by Reitzenstein ("Eine frühchristliche Schrift"). I follow the line numbers of Reitzenstein's text.

Many earlier scholars dated this document later than the second century. E.g., both Koch ("Die ps-cyprianische Schrift", 270) and Wohlenberg ("Eine pseudocyprianische Schrift", 219) place it in the fourth century. Daniélou (*Latin Christianity*, 63-92), on the other hand, has demonstrated that this writing was known and used by Cyprian. Thus, it cannot be later than the mid-third century. Daniélou opts for the late second century, as did Reitzenstein ("Eine frühchristliche Schrift", 73). Beatrice (*EEC* I.223) places it in the period "late 2nd to mid 3rd c(entury)".

passages he appeals to the example of Christ and, in so doing, reveals an unequivocal example of angel Christology. First, in *ll*. 50-54 he speaks of Christ's creation by divine fiat.

> If Christ, he who is Son of God and who was created by the divine mouth, resolved not to do his own will, but the will of the Father, for he is His Word and Will, how much more must we who name God Father, also do His will (and) not that of the world, because we ourselves are also His will.[39]

Here Christ is created by God's speech, just as the angels are in Rabbinic and early Christian literature.[40] Later, the preacher returns to this theme in *ll*. 216-220:

> When the Lord created the seven principal angels from fire, he determined to make one of them his Son [he says that the Son is a creature, against the Catholic faith]. He it is whom Isaiah declares to be the Lord Sabaoth. We see that there remained then six angels who had been created with the Son, whom the ascetics imitate.[41]

The words in brackets are, of course, a scribal gloss. Christ is again said to have been created, but in this passage he is created from fire, a motif common to early Jewish and Christian angelology.[42] Furthermore, Christ is here explicitly numbered among the seven archangels and is identified with the divine figure who appeared to Isaiah in the Temple (Isa. 6). Interestingly, in Hermas *Sim*. ix.12.8, the Son of God is surrounded by the six, not the expected seven, first created angels.[43] Another example, this time from the fourth century, of Christ numbered amongst the seven archangels

---

[39] *si Christus, cum sit dei filius atque diuino ore creatus, uoluntatem suam non disposuit facere, sed patris, cuius ipse uerbum et uoluntas est, quanto magis nos, qui deum patrem uocamus, et uoluntatem eius, non quae sunt saeculi, facere debemus, quia et ipsi uoluntas eius sumus.*

[40] Rabbinic: *bHag* 14a (R. Samuel b. Nahmani [A3] in the name of R. Yohanan [A2]); cf. *3En*. 40.4 (§58). Christian: *Ps.-Clem. Hom*. iii.33.2.

[41] *angelos enim dominus cum ex igne principum numero vii [creaturam filium dei dicit contra catholicam fidem] crearet, ex his unum in filium sibi constituere, quem Isaias dominum Sabaot [ut] praeconaret, disposuit. remansisse ergo repperimus sex quidem angelos cum filio creatos, quos agonista imitatur.*

[42] Jewish: *2En*. 29.1-3; *ExodR* 15.6 (UA); *ANR* B 24 (UA); *MidrPss* 104.7 (R. Yohanan [A2]). Christian: *QuestBart*. 4.54; Clement Alex. *Ex. Theod*. 12.2; Hipp. *Ref*. x.29; Tertullian *Marc*. iii.9.

[43] For these six as "the first created" see *Vis*. iii.4.1-2 and *Sim*. v.5.3.

is found in an inscription on an amethyst. The gem bears an image of Christ with the Chi-Rho symbol behind his head. On his left ἐν ἀρχῇ ἦν ὁ λόγος is inscribed, while on his right stands:

ΡΑΦΑΗΛ
ΡΕΝΕΛ
ΟΥΡΙΗΛ
ΙΧΘΥC
ΜΙΧΑΗΛ
ΓΑΒΡΙΗΛ
ΑΖΑΗΛ.[44]

Here ΙΧΘΥC, as the Chi-Rho makes abundantly clear, stands for Christ. The central position of ΙΧΘΥC, flanked on either side by three archangels, recalls Hermas *Sim.* ix.12.8. In these three texts Christ is numbered among the seven archangels; in *De Centesima*, he is unambiguously said to have been created as an archangel and promoted to the status of the "Son of God".

b) Epiphanius, the Ebionites and the Elchasaites Significantly, Epiphanius attributes to the Ebionites an angel Christology identical to that found in *De Centesima*:

> But they say he is not begotten of God the Father, but was created as one of the archangels [and is even greater than they], and that he is the ruler both of angels and of all creatures of the Almighty...(*Pan.* xxx.16.4; cf. also xxx.3.4).[45]

However, Epiphanius' description of the Ebionites bristles with difficulties. First of all, Epiphanius himself admits that the Ebionites held a number of conflicting Christologies (*Pan.* xxx.3.1-6). In this he is joined by other heresiologists of the early Church. Tertullian (*Carn.* xiv), Origen

---

[44] See Daniélou, *Theology*, 122; Barbel, *Christos Angelos*, 208; and Leclerq, "Anges", *DACL* I.2088-2089.

[45] οὐ φάσκουσι δὲ ἐκ θεοῦ πατρὸς αὐτὸν γεγεννῆσθαι ἀλλὰ κεκτίσθαι ὡς ἕνα τῶν ἀρχαγγέλων [καὶ ἔτι περισσοτέρως], αὐτὸν δὲ κυριεύειν καὶ ἀγγέλων καὶ πάντων [τῶν] ὑπὸ τοῦ παντοκράτορος πεποιημένων...

The phrase in brackets is supplied by the editor (Holl, 354). The MSS are corrupt or lacunose at this point. The corrector of one MS supplies in the margin: μείζονα δὲ αὐτῶν ὄντα.

(*Cels.* v.61), Epiphanius (*Pan.* xxx.2.2, xxx.34.6), and Eusebius (*HE* iii.27) all state that at least some Ebionites held that Christ was a mere man, born through natural generation by Mary and Joseph. On the other hand, Origen (*Cels.* v.61), Eusebius (*HE* iii.27), and Jerome (*Ep.* cxii.13.1-2) know of some Ebionites who believed that Christ was born of the Virgin Mary. Significantly for this study, Irenaeus (*Adv. Haer.* i.26.2), Hippolytus (*Ref.* vii.34), Epiphanius (*Pan.* xxx.3.6, xxx.18.5-6), and the so-called *Gospel of the Ebionites* (Epiph. *Pan.* xxx.13.7-8) all attribute to this Jewish-Christian sect a doctrine which depicts Christ as a pre-existing heavenly power or spirit which descended on and entered into the man Jesus at the latter's baptism.[46]. Similar expressions of "adoptionistic Christology" are well attested both in heresiological and heretical texts. It appears to have been especially popular among Gnostics.[47] Finally, Epiphanius claims that some Ebionites identified Christ with the first man, Adam (*Pan.* xxx.34.6; cf. also xxx.3.3-5).

All this raises the question of just how much first hand knowledge the Fathers had of the Ebionites and similar movements. Clearly, some of the heresiologists were guilty of shifting the evidence to fit their presupposed systems of the origin and growth of early heresy.[48] Another difficulty with the Patristic reports of the heretical movements lies in the fact that later Fathers invariably depended upon the findings of earlier Fathers. This, of course, means that unless independence can be demonstrated, the witness of several late Fathers carries no more weight than that of one early Father.[49]

---

[46] Irenaeus in *Adv. Haer* i.26.2 does not attribute this "adoptionistic angel Christology" to the Ebionites per se. Rather he describes the adoptionistic angel Christology of Cerinthus (i.26.1) and Carpocrates (i.25.1), and then states that the Ebionites held a Christology "similar" to that of Cerinthus and Carpocrates. There is, however, a very important textual variant here. The Latin MSS read *non similiter*, asserting that the Ebionites' Christology was *not* similar to that of Cerinthus and Carpocrates. This cannot be right; if the Ebionite Christology differed, one would expect a discussion of it, not a single sentence denying its similarity. Furthermore, Hippolytus' *Refutatio* follows Irenaeus so closely here that it can be used to supply Irenaeus' original Greek and it omits the negative particle (*Ref.* vii.34). Theodoret of Cyrus (*Adv. Haer.*ii.3), who also used Irenaeus' work, further supports this conclusion. Cf. Simon, *Verus Israel*, 476, n.14. Contrast Klijn and Reinink, *Patristic Evidence*, 20.

[47] See e.g., Irenaeus *Adv. Haer.* i.7.2; iii.16.1; *Gos. Eg.* (*NHC* III.2) 64.1-4; *Trim. Prot.* (*NHC* XIII.1) 50.12-13. Cf. Rudolph, *Gnosis*, 162-163.

[48] A classic example of this fact is the creation of "Ebion" (referred to by Tertullian, Hippolytus, Hilary, Epiphanius, among others), the supposed "father" of the Ebionites. Ebion was seemingly introduced to fit the Patristic assumption that all heresies originated with an individual heretic. See Simon, *Verus Israel*, 240-247; Schoeps, *Jewish Christianity*, 10-11; idem, *Theologie*, 8-9.

[49] This is especially the case with Irenaeus, whose *Adversus Haereses* was immensely influential on all subsequent Patristic attempts to discuss and classify heretical movements.

Thus, one simply cannot assume accurate knowledge of the Ebionites on the part of the Fathers. One cannot even be certain that a given Father did not subsume a number of different Jewish-Christian groups under the title "Ebionite".[50]

To return to Epiphanius, it is clear that while he was dependent on the writings of earlier heresiologists, especially Irenaeus and Eusebius, he also used sources which he believed to be Ebionite in origin. These include the Περίοδοι Πέτρου (*Pan.* xxx.15.1-4), Πράξεις δὲ ἄλλας...ἀποστόλων (*Pan.* xxx.16.6), the Ἀναβαθμοὶ Ἰακώβου; (*Pan.* xxx.16.7), and a gospel called by the Ebionites "according to the Hebrews" (*Pan.* xxx.3.7), but which scholarship has named the *Gospel of the Ebionites*. Of the Gospel nothing has survived apart from Epiphanius' citations of it. However, the situation is very different with the other three works. Many scholars would see these as sources which lay behind the pseudo-Clementine *Homilies* and *Recognitions*. The Περίοδοι Πέτρου appears to be either the *Grundschrift*, used by both the Homilist and the author of the *Recognitions*, or a work closely related to it.[51] The Ἀναβαθμοὶ Ἰακώβου appears to have been extensively used in *Rec.* i.33-71.[52]

While it is, therefore, probably safe to conclude that Epiphanius knew certain sources which lay behind the pseudo-Clementine literature, we cannot simply assume that Epiphanius was correct in attributing these works to the Ebionites. Indeed, Epiphanius' accuracy on this point has been questioned by a number of scholars.[53] If they were used by the Ebionites, then the information Epiphanius derived from them would have to be accorded a high level of trustworthiness. As it is, when Epiphanius appeals to one of these documents we cannot be sure that the source in question is truly Ebionite. Nonetheless, there is no *prima facie* reason to doubt the existence of such writings or to suggest that Epiphanius cites them inaccurately. In other words, even though Epiphanius may have been incorrect in attributing these sources to the Ebionites, they did belong to some group within early Christianity. We are probably not far wrong in ascribing them to Christian circles of a Jewish-Gnostic bent.[54]

---

[50] However, Klijn and Reinink (*Patristic Evidence*, 67) go too far in asserting that "Patristic observations on Jewish Christianity have no great historical value".

[51] E.g., Schoeps, *Theologie*, 461; Strecker, *Judenchristentum*, 265; and Luttikhuizen, *Elchasai*, 130-131. See Jones, "Pseudo-Clementines", for a history of research on the Pesudo-Clementines.

[52] Strecker, *Judenchristentum*, 251-253; Klijn and Reinink, *Patristic Evidence*, 31.

[53] E.g., Strecker, *Judenchristentum*, 256-266, n.1; and Klijn and Reinink, *Patristic Evidence*, 38.

[54] Cf. Simon, *Verus Israel*, 245.

Epiphanius' statements about Ebionite Christology fall into four categories: 1) Jesus was a mere man, born though natural generation (*Pan.* xxx.2.2, xxx.3.1, xxx.14.4); 2) Christ was the greatest of the archangels (*Pan.* xxx.16.2, 4, cf. xxx.3.4); 3) the spirit called "Christ" descended upon and entered into the man Jesus at his baptism (*Pan.* xxx.3.6, xxx.14.4, xxx.16.3); and 4) Christ and Adam are identified; that is, Christ clothed himself in the body of Adam (*Pan.* xxx.3.3, 5; xxx.34.6). Two of these conceptions are paralleled in the *Pseudo-Clementines*; Christ is identified with Adam (*Hom.* iii.17-28), and Christ is described as the highest of the archangels (*Rec.* ii.42.3-8; *Hom.* xviii.4). In addition, the passage in Epiphanius which speaks most clearly of Christ as an archangel, *Pan.* xxx.16.2-5, appears to be a quotation from or allusion to the "Ebionite Gospel".[55] Another category, the "adoptionistic angel Christology", is attributed by Epiphanius to this Gospel (*Pan.* xxx.13.7-8). All this indicates that each of the categories listed above, except the first, can be found in written sources known to Epiphanius.

Thus, Epiphanius testifies to two different angel Christologies which he found in sources known to him. On the one hand, Epiphanius was familiar with the claim that Christ had been created as the highest of the archangels, a position paralleled in *De Centesima* and on the amethyst described above. On the other hand, Epiphanius knew of an "adoptionistic angel Christology", in which the power or spirit "Christ" descended upon and entered the man Jesus at his baptism. As we have seen, this conception is supported by parallel accounts of the Ebionites and other heresies in Irenaeus and Hippolytus. These two approaches appear side by side in Epiphanius (*Pan.* xxx.16.2-5), and may have been harmonized by him into a single, complex but, it must be admitted, coherent picture in which the pre-existent power "Christ", who entered Jesus at his baptism was, prior to this incarnation, the highest archangel. However, if *Pan.* xxx.16.2-5 does derive from the "Ebionite Gospel" then Epiphanius found this complex harmonization already in his source. I suspect that the two conceptions were originally independent and only later combined, since the first appears alone in *De Centesima*. Whether they were first combined by the author of the *Gospel according to the Ebionites* or by Epiphanius we cannot be certain given the fragmentary nature of our sources.

In attempting to account for the contradictory christological systems within the one sect of the Ebionites, Epiphanius supposed that, after the death of their founder, a group of Ebionites had come under the influence of another sect known as the Elchasaites (*Pan.* xxx.3.2, xxx.17.4-8). In

---

[55] Cf. Vielhauer and Strecker, *NTApoc*, I.170.

the scant remains of the *Revelations of Elchasai*,[56] we indeed find an angel Christology, but one very different from that which emerges from Epiphanius' depiction of the Ebionites. This *Revelations of Elchasai* probably originated in Mesopotamia, sometime near the end of the reign Trajan.[57] Not enough of this work has survived to be sure of its character. It certainly contains Jewish, as well as pagan, ideas. Scholars are divided over whether it was originally Jewish or Jewish-Christian or pagan.[58] What is clear, however, is that it found its way into Christian circles, by the early third century at the latest, and its teachings were opposed by the Church's theologians.

According to Hippolytus the book claims to be a revelation communicated to Elchasai by a huge male angel, 96 miles in height, who was accompanied by a female angel of equal proportions. According to Hippolytus the male angel is called the Son of God, while Epiphanius records that he is identified with Christ. The female angel is named the Holy Spirit (Hipp. *Ref.* ix.13.2-3; Epiph. *Pan.* xxx.17.7). Hippolytus (*Ref.* ix.13.1) states that Elchasai was the name of the man who received the revelation from the angel. This is accepted at face value by most scholars.[59] However, Luttikhuizen has recently argued that Elchasai was the name of the male angel who revealed the book. In his view, the identification of this angel with Christ would have been a later development which took place after the sect had come into contact with Christians.[60] The name doubtlessly goes back to the Aramaic חיל כסי which means "Hidden Power", as Epiphanius already recognized (*Pan.* xix.2.2). The similar sobriquet for Simon Magus, ἡ δύναμις τοῦ θεοῦ ἡ καλουμένη μεγάλη (Acts 8.10), suggests that "Hidden Power" could have been adopted by a human leader of a sect. At the same time, however, it must be admitted that within an apocalyptic or gnostic sect the "Hidden Power" would have been

---

[56] Most of which are preserved in Hippolytus' *Refutatio* and Epiphanius' *Panarion*.
[57] Luttikhuizen, *Elchasai*, 190-192; and Irmscher, "Elchasai", *NTApoc.* II.686. Cf. Strecker, "Elkesai", *RAC* IV.1172-1173.
[58] Luttikhuizen (*Elchasai*, 88, 128-129, 190) and Klijn and Reinink (*Patristic Evidence*, 66-67) understand the book as essentially Jewish. For Irmscher ("Elchasai", *NTApoc.* II.686) the work "is Jewish, but it is a syncretistic and not a pure Judaism". Strecker ("Elkesai", *RAC* IV.1185) characterizes it as a product of "synkretistisch-gnostisches Judenchristentum". For Schoeps (*Theologie*, 330) it is essentially a pagan work, with Jewish and Jewish-Christian elements artificially grafted on.
[59] So e.g., Irmscher ("Elchasai", *NTApoc.* II.685) and Strecker ("Elkesai", *RAC* IV.1171-1172).
[60] Luttikhuizen, *Elchasai*, 186-188. Cf. Klijn and Reinink, *Patristic Evidence*, 55. n.3.

an eminently appropriate title for an angel of revelation. At our present state of knowledge, with so little of the work surviving, it is not possible to decide between these two options.[61]

However, once the book had passed into Christian or Jewish-Christian circles, the "Son of God" in the book would have been identified with Christ. This explains why Hippolytus and Epiphanius were so exercised by the book and its teachings. In the above passages, the angelic Son of God functions as an angel of revelation. The immense size of both angelic figures recalls a common motif in Jewish and early Christian apocalyptic.[62] For our purposes, the most important parallels appear in Hermas *Sim.* ix.6.1-2 and ix.12.8, where the Son of God is described as "a man so tall, that he overtopped the tower", and in *Sim.* viii.1.2 and viii.3.3, where Michael is described as "an angel of the Lord, glorious and very tall". As I will argue below, the *Shepherd of Hermas* implicitly identifies Christ with Michael.

Further indication of the work's Jewish or Jewish-Christian origin lies in a cryptic prayer, preserved by Epiphanius (*Pan.* xix.4.3), which Elchasai taught his followers to repeat: ἀβὰρ ἀνὶδ μωῒβ νωχιλὲ δαασὶμ ἀνὴ δαασὶμ νωχιλὲ μωῒβ ἀνὶδ ἀβὰρ σελάμ. This transliterates into Aramaic as:

שלם רבא דינא ביום עליכון מסהד אנא מסהד עליכון ביום דינא רבא

Reading outward from אנא this is seen to be a single phrase repeated twice, with the Aramaic word for peace appended to the whole. This phrase can be translated as "I am witness over you (plu.) on the day of the great judgement".[63] This, along with other considerations, has led some scholars to posit an Aramaic original behind the Greek version known to Hippolytus and Epiphanius.[64] In the Greek version, the phrase has become an esoteric

---

[61] Fossum (*Name of God*, 65-68) assumes that "Elchasai" or "the Hidden Power" was the name which the *writer* of the book appropriated to himself in conjunction with his claim to be "the final manifestation of Christ". This assumption falters on the recognition that in the fragments which have survived the angelic "Son of God" is the source of the revelation and is distinguished from the writer. It is extremely unlikely that the writer would claim to have received the revelation from the angelic Christ *and* at the same time to be his final manifestation.

[62] Cf. CD 2.19; *TReub.* 5.7; *2En.* 1.4; *3En.* 9.2 (§12), 48C.5 (§73); *GosPet.* 40; *Passio Perpetuae* 10; 4 Ezra 2.43. This motif may ultimately go back to 1 Chr. 21.16.

For a similar concept in Hekhalot texts regarding the great stature of the appearance of God, see Cohen's *The Shi'ur Qomah: Texts and Recensions* and *The Shi'ur Qomah: Liturgy and Theurgy*.

[63] So Irmscher, "Elchasai", *NTApoc.* II.689.

[64] Luttikhuizen, *Elchasai*, 124-125, 193-194; Irmscher, "Elchasai", *NTApoc.* II.685. Contra Strecker ("Elkesai", *RAC* IV.182-183).

incantation whose meaning is not to be investigated (*Pan.* xix.4.3). In its original form, however, the statement appears to be a promise to intercede for the believers. Luttikhuizen has argued that in the original Aramaic version this promise was given by the huge male angel, חיל כסי.⁶⁵ If he is right, then in the original Aramaic version this angel, later identified with Christ, served as a heavenly intercessor.

All this indicates that the *Revelations of Elchasai*, at least as it was read in certain Christian or Jewish-Christian circles, understood Christ as an angel of revelation, and perhaps as a heavenly intercessor. This may be related in some way to the conception of Christ as one of the seven archangels and their chief. It certainly does not contradict it. On the other hand, it appears to have little in common with the other type of angel Christology we have been investigating: the "adoptionistic angel Christology" with its strong emphasis on the historical Jesus as the one in whom the heavenly Christ dwelt. However, both Hippolytus (*Ref.* ix.14.1) and Epiphanius (*Pan.* liii.1.8) attribute to the Elchasaites, but not explicitly to the *Revelations of Elchasai*, a Christology related to the Adam-Christ doctrine of the *Pseudo-Clementines* (*Hom.* iii.17-28), which Epiphanius also attributed to the Ebionites (*Pan.* xxx.3.3, 5; xxx.34.6). In all these sources Christ appeared in Adam and then again in Jesus. Epiphanius (*Pan.* liii.1.8) appears to accept that both notions, the Adam-Christ doctrine and Christ as the highest of the first created archangels, were held by some of the Elchasaites. Again, however, we may be dealing with nothing more than Epiphanius' desire to systematize and find links between the various sects.

c) Tertullian and Valentinian Christology In the fourteenth chapter of his treatise *De carne Christi*, Tertullian takes issue with yet another type of angel Christology. Tertullian disputes with those who say "Christ was clothed upon by an angel" (lit. "wore an angel"; *et angelum...gestavit Christus* [*ll.*1, 5, 10, cf. 27]) and that "there was an angel in the Son" (*l.*25).⁶⁶

Some have supposed that Tertullian is here attacking the Ebionites, for he mentions "Ebion" (xiv.32ff).⁶⁷ However, Tertullian's language leaves little doubt that he does not have "Ebion" principally in mind. Rather, he merely introduces him as an example of someone who would have found the Christology here opposed convenient: "This view of the matter could have suited Ebion,..." (*poterit haec opinio Hebioni convenire...*; *l.*32).

---

⁶⁵ Luttikhuizen, *Elchasai*, 196.

⁶⁶ The line numbers are from Evans' edition of *De carne Christi*.

⁶⁷ So Werner, *Entstehung*, 331; Schoeps, *Theologie*, 463.

Indeed, when Tertullian goes on to describe "Ebion's" Christology, he asserts that "Ebion" held Jesus to be merely a man and a prophet (*ll*.32-33). Apparently, the Ebionites known to Tertullian held Christ to be a man who was more glorious than the other prophets only in that he had an angel within him. Applying Zech. 1.14[68] to Christ, they argued that Zechariah and Christ were inspired by angels who dwelt "within" them. Tertullian counters that neither Zechariah's saying, nor anything like it, can be found on the lips of Christ (*ll*. 32-39). However, given the overall context, it is clear that in Tertullian's reference to "Ebion" we have a short digression consisting of an attack on a second group, the Ebionites, who could have found the view he was primarily attacking convenient, for it suited their assertion that Christ was merely a human prophet.[69]

Whom, then, is Tertullian attacking? The context[70] would suggest that unnamed Valentinian gnostics are in view.[71] According to Tertullian, these unnamed Valentinians held that Christ was "clothed upon with an angel" for the same reason that orthodox Christians held that he was "clothed" with a man. In other words, according to Valentinians, he was "clothed" by an angel for the salvation of angels (*ll*.1-4).[72] This appears to fit one element of Valentinus' system. According to Clement of Alexandria's *Excerpta ex Theodoto*, the Valentinians taught that the salvation of the superior seed among humans, that is the Valentinians themselves, and of angels is inextricably tied together (22.5, 35.1-4). In this conception, the unity of the Pleroma rested on the principle of Syzygy. The fall within the Pleroma, and the flawed creation by the Demiurge which took place because of it, resulted in the separation of what previously had been united. Thus salvation consisted in the reuniting of the angels, conceived of as male, with the superior seed or the "spiritual" among humans, conceived of as female (21.1-3; cf. Irenaeus *Adv. Haer* i.7.1). Christ, as "the angel of the Pleroma" (ἄγγελος ἦν τοῦ πληρώματος; *Ex. Theod.* 35.1), accomplished this re-union.[73] Tertullian's objection that God in Christ was concerned only with the "restitution of humanity" (*l*.19, cf. *ll*.2-10) seems to have this Valentinian doctrine in view.

---

[68] "And the angel that spoke in me said unto to me...". Apparently, the Old Latin text available to Tertullian read: *Et ait mihi angelus qui in me loquebatur*, rendering בִּי with *in me*, just as the LXX translates it as ἐν ἐμοί.

[69] Cf. Klijn and Reinink (*Patristic Evidence*, 21-22).

[70] Cf. chapters x-xiii and xv-xvii.

[71] So Barbel, *Christos Angelos*, 71, 204-205.

[72] This appears similar in some respects to a doctrine found in Origen. See below pp. 211-212.

[73] Note Irenaeus *Adv. Haer.* i.2.6 and i.4.5, where the second Christ of Valentinus' system is conceived of as an angelic being.

This angel Christology appears to play a much more significant role in the system of Theodotus, who belonged to the Oriental branch of the Valentinian gnostics,[74] than it does in the system of Valentinus, as described by Irenaeus. Tertullian himself only discusses it as one among many errors held by Valentinians regarding Christ. For our purposes, this Valentinian conception, and that of the Ebionites known to Tertullian discussed above, demonstrate the diversity of forms which angel Christology could take.[75]

d) The Testament of Solomon and other Magical Texts Another source of evidence for heretical angel Christologies lies in magical texts. A prime example of a magical text which interprets Christ as an angel is the *Testament of Solomon*, a document often dated to the early third century or earlier,[76] but, in view of the document's fluid textual tradition, any proposed date for this text must be treated with extreme caution.[77] This entertaining story recounts how King Solomon with the aid of a magic ring delivered by the archangel Michael captures various demons, compels them to divulge the names of their "thwarting angel", and then conscripts their help in the building of the temple. Among the various angels who thwart ($\kappa\alpha\tau\alpha\rho\gamma\acute{\epsilon}\omega$) demons we find the familiar Uriel (2.4, 18.7), Raphael (5.9, 13.6, 18.8), Gabriel (18.6), and Michael (18.5, cf. also 1.6-7). Many of the other names of thwarting angels are unattested elsewhere in Jewish or Christian angelological literature, especially those in chapter 18. Some are known from other contexts. Azael ($\mathrm{'A\zeta\alpha\acute{\eta}\lambda}$), for example, elsewhere appears as a

---

[74] Rudolph, *Gnosis*, 324.

[75] In *Carn.* vi Tertullian challenges the position of Apelles, that Christ assumed a human body but was never born. Apelles, and others who held this position, appealed to OT angelophanies to prove that a heavenly being could take a human body without being born. This is not necessarily an example of an angel Christology. Apelles does not assert that Christ was an angel. He merely appeals to angelophanies as analogous to his docetic Christology.

[76] Duling, "Testament of Solomon", *OTP* I.941-942; McCown, *Testament*, 106-108. However, Preisendanz ("Papyrusfragment", 161-162) has opted for the first or second century.

[77] Since writing the first form of this chapter I have, for a period of two years, participated in a seminar on the *Testament of Solomon*, under the direction of Dr. Loveday Alexander of the University of Sheffield. During that time, having worked closely with McCown's text, I have become convinced that we are here dealing with a textual tradition in which pericopes were freely added and deleted over the centuries in the various recensions and manuscripts. The situation is not unlike that encountered in the Hekhalot texts. One must be very careful, then, when analyzing the evidence of the *Testament of Solomon*. We simply cannot be certain what the *Grundschrift* contained and what was added later.

fallen angel,[78] but in the *Testament of Solomon* is mentioned as an angel who thwarts the demon "Lix Tetrax" (7.7).

However, it is the frequent mention of Christ, most often referred to by the name "Emmanuel", as a thwarting angel (6.8, 11.6, 12.3, 15.10-12, 17.4, 22.20, cf. 4.11) which demands our attention.[79] The *Testament* does not contain a consistent Christology. Some texts speak of Christ or Emmanuel as if he were an angel among others. In 12.3 a demon tells Solomon that he is thwarted "by (the site) which is marked 'Place of the Skull', for there the Angel of Great Counsel foresaw that I would suffer, and he shall dwell publicly on the cross. He is the one who will thwart me, being the one among (the angels) to whom I am subject".[80] In 11.6 Emmanuel can be "conjured" (κατάγεται; lit. "brought down") by magicians who know the right three letters. On the other hand, the prophecy attributed to the demoness Enepsigos in 15.8-12 explicitly affirms the superiority of Emmanuel to all other thwarting angels. This author's confession that in Christ all the demons have been overcome (15.10-11), stands in an uncomfortable tension with the continuing need to use the names of thwarting angels and other magical acts to overcome the power of demons. This inconsistency is perhaps best explained by the *Testament*'s very chequered textual history. However, the fact that the *Testament of Solomon* is a document which is above all concerned with magical practices, and not theological doctrine,[81] has doubtless contributed to this inconsistency. Nevertheless, this is not to conclude that such a work had no influence upon the thought of some Christians. Judging by the repeated remonstrances of Church Fathers[82] and the legislation of Church councils,[83]

---

[78] E.g., *1En.* 8.1, 9.6, 10.4-8, 13.1ff, 54.5, 55.4, 69.2; *ApAb.* 13.1-14, 20.1-7, 23.11, 31.5; *3En.* 4.5, 5.9; Targ. Ps.-Jon. Gen. 6.4; and *bYoma* 67b (attributed to the School of Ishmael [T2-T3]).

[79] All of these passages appear in at least one MS of both McCown's recensions A and B, with the possible exception of 15.10-12, which, although it appears in a MS of B, may or may not have been present in Rec. A; the question cannot be finally settled because of lacunae in all three MSS of Rec. A. None of the passages, except 4.11, appear in MSS of Rec. C. However, 6.8 may have appeared in an ancestor of two MSS of Rec. C.

[80] ὑπὸ τοῦ σημειομένου τόπου ἐγκεφάλου, ἐκεῖ γὰρ προώρισεν ἄγγελος τῆς μεγάλης βουλῆς με παθεῖν, καὶ νῦν φανερῶς ἐπὶ ξύλου οἰκήσει. ἐκεῖνός με καταργήσει ἐν οἷς καὶ ὢν ὑποτέταγμαι.

The reading, ἐν οἷς καὶ ὤν, of MS L, and followed by McCown and Duling, is difficult and probably best explains the others which are simplifications of it. H reads ἐν εἷς ὃν καί; while P reads ἐν ᾧ.

[81] See esp. McCown, *Testament*, 89-90. Cf. Duling, "Testament", *OTP* I.944.

[82] Irenaeus *Adv. Haer.* i.13.2; Origen *Cels.* viii.60-61; Augustine *De doc. Christ.* ii.29.45; Chrysostom *Adv. Judaeos* viii.5.

[83] E.g., the 36th decree of the Council of Laodicea (c. AD 350) declares: "It is not right for priests or clergy to be magicians or enchanters or mathematicians or astrologers,

it would appear that many Christians in the early Church held magical beliefs similar to those found in the *Testament of Solomon*.

Furthermore, it is probable that the inscribed amethyst, described above,[84] was made and used as a magical amulet. First, Azael's appearance as one of the seven archangels supports this. As noted above, Azael is generally considered a fallen angel, but in the *Testament of Solomon*, which is clearly magical, he is an archangel. In at least one other magical text, an apotropaic charm printed in *Papyri Graecae Magicae* (XXXVI.168-78), Azael appears alongside of Michael, Raphael, Suriel and a number of other angelic names. To my knowledge, only magical texts present Azael as a good angel. Second, according to Metzger, while passages of Scripture appear often in magical amulets, the Gospel of John, especially its opening chapter, is used most often.[85] This amulet, then, is probably another magical text which understands Christ as an angel. We shall, in due course, encounter another magical charm, one which seemingly identifies Christ with Michael.

2) Other Examples of Angel Christologies

Other, for our purposes less significant, texts from the second and third centuries could be adduced to show the extent to which Christ was identified with an angel. These include: The Coptic *Gospel of Thomas*; the *Gospel of Nicodemus*; the *Testament of Dan*; and the *Epistle to Diognetus*. The *Gospel of Thomas* (13) explicitly gives the title ἄγγελος to Jesus,[86] while the *Gospel of Nicodemus* (15-16) implies that such a title is appropriate for him. While in neither case is it absolutely certain that ἄγγελος means anything other than "messenger", it is probable that in both cases a heavenly messenger is intended. The *Testament of Dan*, originally a Jewish apocryphon but preserved by Christians and used by them during

---

or to make amulets (φυλακτήρια) as they are called, for such things are prisons of their souls: and we have enjoined that they which wear them be cast out of the Church". Quoted from Lightfoot, *Colossians*, 69.

[84] See above p. 173.

[85] Metzger, "Magical Amulet", 106-107, n.4.

[86] Peter's identification of Jesus as "a righteous angel", while not equal to the insight of Thomas that Jesus' true identity transcends human language, is not explicitly rejected. Although the Coptic *Gospel of Thomas* in its present form dates from the mid-second century, it certainly contains earlier material. See Blatz, *NTApoc*. I.113.

our period,[87] presents an angel who intercedes for humans, serves as "the mediator between God and men" (cf. 1 Tim. 2.5), and is superior to all other angels (6.1-8). If this text was known to groups who advocated an angel Christology, it could readily have been understood as a reference to Christ.[88] Finally, the assertion in the *Epistle to Diognetus* 7.2 that God sent neither a servant, nor an angel, nor an archon, nor "one who directs earthly elements", nor "one entrusted with heavenly administration", but instead He sent the divine Logos, the very creator of the universe, is probably best understood as a reaction against some form of angel Christology.[89]

3) Possible Jewish Precursors

Before summarizing the evidence thus far, mention should be made of two pieces of evidence, which possibly come from pre-Christian Jewish sources, and which may go a little way in explaining why some, in a Jewish-Christian environment, could have come to understand the man Jesus in angelic terms.

a) The Prayer of Joseph The *Prayer of Joseph* testifies to the belief that a high angel could appear both as an angel and as a man. Indeed, it is even possible that this text presents the man Jacob as the incarnation of the angel Israel. Although, to be sure, J. Z. Smith is quite right when he admits that

> whether the earthly Jacob-Israel is to be understood as a thoroughly docetic figure, the incarnation of a heavenly power, or a heavenly messenger is not clear.[90]

Not enough of this important text has survived to be sure which conception is in view. Nonetheless, one can see how this text could have easily suggested an angelic incarnation, even if this was not the author's original intention. According to Origen this text was known and used by Jews in his day (*CommJo.* ii.31), but his and Eusebius' (*Praep. Ev.* vi.11.64) cita-

---

[87] Cf. Origen *HomJos.* xv.6; and de Jonge, "Transmission", 15-22.
[88] See above p. 44.
[89] Cf. also Hippolytus, *Ref.* x.29.
One could also add that Celsus frequently calls Jesus ἄγγελος (Origen *Cels.* ii.44, 70, v.52-55). While Celsus may be dependent on Jewish Christian circles for this, it is more likely that he understands ἄγγελος only in a pagan sense. See Barbel, *Christos Angelos*, 7-8.
[90] Smith, "Prayer of Joseph", *OTP* II.704.

tions from it demonstrate that it was also known among some Christians. The fact that neither Origen nor Eusebius applied this text to Christology is no reason to suppose that other Christians were as judicious. In fact, Justin Martyr (*Dial.* 75.1-2) appeals to a tradition which is similar to that found in the *Prayer of Joseph*, and may have been dependent upon it. In both, the *Prayer of Joseph* and Justin, the name "Israel" belongs to a high heavenly being: an archangel and the Logos, respectively. Justin, however, differs from the *Prayer of Joseph* in that he does not equate the historical Jacob with the heavenly Israel; for him two distinct persons merely share the same name. While it is not certain that Justin knew this apocryphon, he may have been familiar with a tradition similar to it. The witness of Origen, Eusebius, and possibly Justin, demonstrate that the *Prayer of Joseph* was not unknown among Christians in the second and third centuries. It is possible, therefore, that the *Prayer of Joseph* provided the catalyst for a Jewish-Christian understanding of Christ as the incarnation of an angel.

b) The "Pre-existent" angel of the Magharians Similarly, it is possible that the shadowy Magharians also attest to a pre-Christian Jewish belief in the human incarnation of an exalted angel. According to very late sources,[91] the Magharians flourished at the turn of the eras and taught that the world was made by an angel created by God for that very purpose. In addition, the Magharians apparently held that the Torah was revealed by this angel, that he was the subject of all the anthropomorphic language about God in the OT, that he possessed the Name of God, and that he appeared on earth in the form of a man as the messenger of God.[92] Since none of our sources for the Magharians pre-date the ninth century, we must exercise extreme caution. We simply cannot be sure that our authors are correct about a sect which flourished nine hundred years, or more, before their times, especially in their placing this sect in the first century. A later date would justify identifying the Magharians with Epiphanius' "Ebionites"

---

[91] These include Qirqisani's *Kitab al-Anwar w'al-Marakib* (Book of Lights and Watchtowers) chapt. 7; and Shahrastani's *Kitab al-Milal wa'al-Nihal* (Book of Religious and Philosophical Sects) 1.19. Qirqisani and Shahrastani, both of whom flourished in the tenth century, appear to be dependent upon Da'ud b. Marwan who lived a century earlier. In addition, Qirqisani speaks of a certain Benjamin al-Nahawandi (9th century) who held views similar to the Magharians and may be an independent witness to their views. Cf. Wolfson, "Pre-Existent Angel"; Harkavy "al-Qirqisani"; and Fossum, *Name of God*, 329-332.

[92] Created world: Qirqisani, Nahawandi. Revealed Torah: Nahawandi, Shahrastani. Subject of anthropomorphic language in OT: Qirqisani, Shahrastani. Possessed the Name of God: Shahrastani. Appeared on earth as a man: Shahrastani.

or a similar Jewish Christian sect. On the other hand, if our authors are correct that the Magharians were a pre-Christian Jewish sect, the Magharians may constitute even earlier evidence than the *Prayer of Joseph* that some non-Christian Jews believed that an exalted angel could appear on earth as a man.

4) Summary

All that has been said thus far indicates the variety of forms angel Christology could take in Christian circles in the second and third centuries. Some held that Christ had been created as an archangel and then "promoted" to the rank of Son (*De Centesima*, Epiphanius, *Pan.* xxx.16.4), others that Christ was the spirit or angel which descended on and entered into the man Jesus at his baptism (Epiphanius, *Pan.* xxx.3.6, 18.5-6). Still others saw in Christ a particularly powerful "thwarting" angel in their battle against demons (*Testament of Solomon*), while some Gnostics believed that Christ had an angelic nature and appeared as an angel for the salvation of angels (Tertullian, *Carn.* 14). To be sure, every example of angel Christology mentioned to this point would have been rejected, even in the second and third centuries, by the Great Church as heretical. Finally, in none of the texts cited to this point is Christ identified with the archangel Michael. Indeed, in two texts, the amethyst amulet and the *Testament of Solomon*, Christ and Michael are clearly distinguished. However, it would not have been a large step for the author of *De Centesima* or "Ebionites" known to Epiphanius to have equated Christ with Michael.

b. Christ as Michael

We must now examine one work which demonstrates that in the second and third centuries at least one author did indeed make such an identification of Christ with Michael. I mean Hermas' *Shepherd*. Moreover, other more ambiguous texts, which I offer only as supporting evidence, may indicate that Hermas' Michael-Christ Christology was by no means unique.

1) The Shepherd of Hermas

The early Christian apocalypse, the *Shepherd* of Hermas, provides us with evidence for a Michael-Christ identification in a text which was widely known and which held a certain authority in many areas of the Church from late in the second century until, perhaps, the end of the third.

a) The Glorious Angel Throughout this document reference is made to an angel variously named "the glorious Angel" (ὁ ἔνδοξος ἄγγελος; *Sim.* vii.2; v.4.4), "the Angel of the Lord" (ὁ ἄγγελος τοῦ κυρίου; *Sim.* vii.5), and "the most venerable angel" (τοῦ σεμνοτάτου ἀγγέλου; *Vis.* v.2, *Man.* v.1.7). It is this angel who sent the Shepherd, or angel of repentance, to Hermas (*Vis.* v.2, *Sim.* vii.2); and who is responsible for the justification of believers (*Man.* v.1.7).[93] This glorious Angel, then, appears to be more than an angel of high standing. He justifies sinners and commissions angels in his service. Further, in one passage he is seemingly identified with "the Lord" (*Sim.* v.4.4).[94]

b) The Glorious Angel: Michael In the eighth *Similitude* Hermas sees a great willow tree being pruned by ἄγγελος τοῦ κυρίου ἔνδοξος λίαν ὑψηλός. The judgement of believers is portrayed in terms of this angel giving the branches he prunes to believers and then, after a time, inspecting the branches. Those that have borne fruit or remained green are allowed to enter into the kingdom, those that are dried or cracked are turned over to the Shepherd that he might discipline them and lead them to repentance. This relationship between the glorious angel and the Shepherd indicates beyond doubt that this is the same "glorious" or "most venerable" angel that we encounter throughout Hermas' work. In the interpretation of this "parable" we learn 1) that the willow tree represents the Law of God, which is none other than the Son of God "preached to the ends of the earth", and 2) that the glorious angel who prunes the tree is the archangel Michael (*Sim.* viii.3.2-3). The affinity here between the Son of God, who is the Law of God, and Michael, who gives the Law, is to be noted. Indeed, elsewhere in the *Shepherd* it is the Son of God who gives the Law and governs his people (*Sim.* v.6.2-3, ix.14.5). All this suggests an identity between Michael and the Son of God: First, Michael is the glorious angel who seems to have divine characteristics, in that he justifies sinners and other angels serve him, and second, in two different passages,

---

[93] ἐδικαιώθησαν γὰρ πάντες ὑπὸ τοῦ σεμνοτάτου ἀγγέλου.

[94] σὺ δὲ ἐνδεδυναμωμένος ὑπὸ τοῦ ἐνδόξου ἀγγέλου καὶ εἰληφὼς παρ' αὐτοῦ τοιαύτην ἔντευξιν καὶ μὴ ὢν ἀργός, διατί οὐκ αἰτῇ παρὰ τοῦ κυρίου σύνεσιν καὶ λαμβάνεις παρ' αὐτοῦ;

both Michael and the Son of God are accredited with the giving of the Law and the government of believers. Finally, in *Sim.* viii Michael exercises the divine prerogative of judgement.

c) The Glorious Angel: The Son of God This identification of Michael and the Son of God is confirmed by the ninth *Similitude*, which corresponds in many details with the eighth. In this "parable", Hermas witnesses the building of a tower which represents the Church. Later he watches as the tower is inspected by its "Lord", who is "so tall that he overtopped the tower" (*Sim.* ix.6.1). Further, this "Lord of the Tower" is termed "the glorious man" (ὁ ἀνὴρ ὁ ἔνδοξος; *Sim.* ix.7.1) and is surrounded by the six "glorious men" who were in charge of the tower's construction (*Sim.* ix.3.1-5, 6.2). After inspecting the tower, the Lord turns over those stones which do not measure up to the Shepherd, that he might bring them to repent. In the interpretation of this parable it is disclosed that these six men are six glorious angels and that the glorious man is the Son of God (*Sim.* ix.12.1-8).

As many interpreters have recognized, the many parallels between these two parables demonstrate that Hermas intended Michael to be understood as the Son of God.[95] Some would counter that the Son of God is distinguished from Michael in *Sim.* viii.3.2-3, where the willow tree represents the Son of God and Michael stands by it pruning its branches.[96] Such an objection, however, fails to consider the fluidity of Hermas' use of symbols. In the ninth *Similitude*, for example, the Tower, the door of the Tower and the glorious man are all identified as the Son of God (*Sim.* ix.12.1, 6, 8). Furthermore, in *Vis.* iii.3.3, the Church is represented both by a tower and by an old woman.[97] Furthermore, it should be added that if Michael in *Sim.* viii.3.3 is not understood as the Son of God, then the reader is left with the ridiculous image of the inferior, in this case the archangel Michael, "pruning" the superior, the Son of God![98] Given Hermas' flexibility with symbols, there is no difficulty in recognizing that the Son of God is symbolized by the willow tree, and at the same time identified as Michael.[99]

---

[95] E.g., Brox, *Hermas*, 362-365, 490-492; Kelly, *Doctrines*, 94-95; Daniélou, *Theology*, 123-124; Moxnes, "God and His Angel"; Gieschen, "Angel", 799-802; and very tentatively Lueken, *Michael*, 155.

[96] Pernveden, *Church*, 59.

[97] So also Brox 363, 491-492.

[98] Cf. John 15.1-2.

[99] *Sim.* ix.14.5 may be mentioned as a final piece of supporting evidence. Here it is stated the "name of the Son of God", which appears to be synonymous with the Son of God himself, is "great and incomprehensible, and supports the whole world". The incomprehensibility of the Name and its role in creation both recall *1En.* 69, in which Michael is the angel of the Name. See above pp. 51-53.

d) The Pneumatological Christology of Hermas Some commentators have attempted in various ways to explain away Hermas' Michael-Christ equation. Dibelius, for example, suggested that the presence of the name Michael at *Sim.* viii.3.3 resulted from the author failing to fully christianize an underlying Jewish source.[100] Similarly, Barbel asserted that the Michael-Christ identification is due to Hermas' compositional clumsiness.[101] However, the careful attention which Hermas gives in constructing parallels between *Similitudes* viii and ix make it highly unlikely that he did not intend to equate Michael, in the former, with the Son of God, in the latter.[102] On another track, one could argue that this apparent identification arises from Hermas' muddled thought, rather than from his limited writing ability. It is generally recognized that Hermas was not a skilled theologian and that his Christology seems to lack a systematic unity. Some would suggest the existence of both an angel Christology and an apparently adoptionistic Christology (*Sim.* v.6) in the *Shepherd* demonstrate the degree to which Hermas could accommodate contradictory positions.[103] Nevertheless, while a certain tension between these two Christologies is undeniable, they can be understood to cohere to a considerable degree.

In *Sim.* v.2, the Shepherd tells Hermas a parable about a landowner who, before going on a journey, entrusted the care of his vineyard to one of his servants. Upon returning and discovering the servant had exceeded all his commands and expectations he proposed to elevate this servant to be a joint heir (συγκληρονόμος) with his son, a proposal welcomed by the son and the landowner's friends. In the interpretation, the Shepherd explains that the son, in the parable, is the Holy Spirit, while the servant stands for the Son of God (⟦ὁ δὲ υἱὸς τὸ πνεῦμα τὸ ἅγιόν ἐστιν·⟧ ὁ δὲ δοῦλος ὁ υἱὸς τοῦ θεοῦ ἐστιν· *Sim.* v.5.2).[104] When he is questioned by the puzzled Hermas, the Shepherd explains that the pre-existent Holy Spirit was united

---

[100] Dibelius, *Hermas*, 576.
[101] Barbel, *Christos Angelos*, 232.
[102] So Brox, *Hermas*, 364.
[103] E.g., Brox, *Hermas*, 485-486; Pernveden, *Church*, 70-71.
[104] The Greek words in double brackets are a translation of one Latin version (L^1) which reads: *filius autem spiritus sanctus est*. This sentence is omitted by A L^2 E and, unfortunately, M is lacunose. However, there are good reasons to suppose that this is the original reading. The omission can be explained as an example of haplography, the eye skipping from ΟΔΕ... to ΟΔΕ.... The omission could also have resulted of dogmatic concerns, for it teaches that there are two divine Sons (so Chadwick, "Hermas", 275; Snyder, *Hermas*, 106 and Dibelius, *Hermas*, 569). *Sim.* ix.1.1 shows that Hermas could make such a statement. Cf. Brox (*Hermas*, 315-316) and Whittaker's text, which prints the words in brackets.

with the human Jesus during the incarnation to form "the Son of God". After the incarnation, the humanity of the Son of God is exalted to become a "companion with the Holy Spirit" (*Sim.* v.6.5-7a). Thus, for Hermas, "the Son of God" signifies the union of the pre-existent Holy Spirit with the human Jesus.[105]

Two observations need to be made regarding this adoption motif. First, this identification of the pre-existent Son with the Spirit (or a spirit) is by no means unique in second and third century Christianity. The most striking parallel probably occurs in *2Clem.* 9.5, but similar conceptions can be found in Justin Martyr (*1 Apol.* 33), Tertullian (*Marcion* iii.16; *Praxeas* xxvi), Hippolytus (*Noetus* 4, 16), and Cyprian (*Idols* xi).[106] Second, this pneumatic-adoptionistic Christology is not necessarily inconsistent with Hermas' angel Christology. As we have seen with Epiphanius' account of the Ebionites (*Pan.* xxx.16.2-5), an angel Christology could be harmonized with an adoptionistic Christology. If it could be shown that Hermas identified the pre-existent Holy Spirit with an angel, then it would be likely that he shared with Epiphanius' "Ebionites" an adoptionistic angel Christology. Significantly, in an important passage Hermas seems to suggest that the Holy Spirit is an angel (*Man.* xi.9).[107] In this text, Hermas places the "Holy Spirit" and "the angel of the prophetic spirit" in parallelism and seems to imply their equation.[108]

We must be careful not to attribute too much precision to Hermas' thought. He clearly did not work out all the theological implications of his imagery. Nonetheless, based on what has been said thus far, it is possible that Hermas' pneumatic-adoptionistic Christology and his angel Christology were, in his mind, complementary. The Holy Spirit, who is also an angel, pre-existed. At the incarnation, the Spirit is joined to a human nature resulting in "the Son of God". Since this "Son of God" can also be identified with the archangel Michael, it is not impossible that Hermas identified the pre-existent Christ/Holy Spirit with Michael.[109] This, however, cannot be demonstrated. It must be admitted that Hermas never

---

[105] So e.g., Lake, *Apostolic Fathers*, II.165, n.1; Kelly, *Doctrines*, 144; Brox, *Hermas*, 320-322, 486-488; Dibelius, *Hermas*, 573; Harnack, *Dogma*, I.191, n.1 and I.193, n.1.; Snyder, *Hermas*, 108-109; and Pernveden, *Church*, 42-52.

[106] Cf. Kelly, *Doctrines*, 142-145, 149-151; and Dix, "Epiclesis", 188-190.

[107] The reading ὁ ἄγγελος τοῦ πνεύματος τοῦ προφητικοῦ, found in L² and E, is now confirmed by P.Oxy. 5. Cod. A reads ὁ ἄγγελος τοῦ προφήτου.

[108] So Gieschen, "Angel", 791-792. Cf. Reiling, *Hermas*, 104-109.

[109] Note that in the *AscenIs.* the Holy Spirit is understood as an angel, the "Angel of the Holy Spirit".

explicitly takes this step and allows the two Christologies to stand in his work without any attempt to harmonize them.

e) The Status of the Shepherd in the Early Church Before leaving Hermas, it must be asked how a work with a heretical angel Christology came to be so popular in certain circles of the Great Church. To be sure, it was not universally popular. As with many early Christian works, Hermas' *Shepherd* did not have a uniform reception. It had its enthusiastic champions (Irenaeus,[110] Clement of Alexandria,[111] Origen[112]), its equally enthusiastic detractors (Tertullian[113]), and others whose opinion of the text can only be called ambiguous (author of the Muratorian Canon). More importantly, however, in many provinces of the early Church Hermas' work seems to have been unknown or steadfastly ignored. This is especially true of Syria, Asia Minor, and Greece.[114] It was certainly known in the West and Egypt and, after Origen's removal to Caesarea, in Palestine as well. The witness of Origen is instructive here. He regarded the *Shepherd* highly, at times citing it as Scripture. After his move to Caesarea, however, he becomes more cautious,

> almost always (introducing) a citation with some apologetic formula, protesting his personal belief in its divine inspiration but well aware that he cannot expect its authority to be taken for granted by all his readers (in Palestine).[115]

Indeed, even in *Princ.* iv.2.4, which dates from his Alexandrian period, he must admit that it is "despised by some". In both the West and in Egypt the *Shepherd* appears to have been gradually demoted from a "canonical" work to a document accepted for private reading.[116] It is conceivable,

---

[110] Irenaeus quotes *Man.* i.1 once (*Adv. Haer.* iv.20.2), referring to it as scripture (ἡ γραφή). He also alludes to this verse on a number of other occasions (i.15.5, i.22.1, ii.10.2, ii.30.9, iv.20.1; *Dem.* 4).

[111] *Strom.* ii.1, 9, 12; iv.9; vi.15.

[112] *Princ.* iv.2.4; *CommRom.* x.31; *CommMatt.* xiv.21.

[113] In *Modesty* x, which dates from his Montanist period, Tertullian is extremely negative toward the *Shepherd*. However, in *Prayer* xvi, which is from his catholic period, he is neutral.

[114] See Chadwick, "Hermas", 275-280.

[115] Chadwick, "Hermas", 276. For an example of Origen's Caesarean attitude, see esp. *CommMatt* xiv.21.

[116] For the West, contrast Irenaeus *Adv. Haer.* iv.20.2 with the *Muratorian Canon*; for Egypt, contrast Origen or the early Athanasius (*Incarnation* 3) with the late Athanasius (*Festal Epistle* 367).

although hardly certain, that the work's Christology contributed to its decline in some circles and its being ignored in others. Moreover, some of those who held Hermas in high esteem, especially Clement and Origen, had at their disposal an allegorical method of interpretation which enabled them to avoid the implications of particularly difficult problem passages. Hermas' Michael-Christ identification rests above all on reading two passages (*Sim.* viii.3.3 and ix.12.8) in light of each other, and the connection between these two passages does not seem to have occurred to any ancient exegete.[117]

2) P. Oxy. 1152

The remaining evidence for a Michael-Christ identification in second and third century Christianity is admittedly more speculative than that based on Hermas and, therefore, is offered only tentatively.

Another text, of uncertain date, which seems to have identified Michael with Christ is a magical incantation written on a scrap of papyrus (P.Oxy. 1152), dated by its editors to the fifth or sixth century.[118] It reads: ωρωρ φωρ 'Ελωει 'Αδωναει 'Ιαω Σαβαωθ Μιχαὴλ 'Ιησοῦ (MS: 'Ιεσου) Χριστέ, βοήθει (MS: βοηθι) ἡμῖν καὶ τούτῳ οἴκῳ. ἀμήν. The meaningless words at the beginning of the text indicate that this is a magical text and should be regarded as an incantation rather than a prayer. The singular form of the imperative verb βοηθέω may indicate that the composer of this incantation regarded the seven names as referring to the same individual. Michael would then be another name of Jesus, as are Eloi, Adonai, Iao, and Sabaoth. However, it is not unusual for the verb and subject to disagree in magical texts,[119] so the author of this text may have intended an invocation to three different divine figures: The Jewish God ('Ελωει 'Αδωναει 'Ιαω Σαβαωθ), Jesus Christ, and Michael. It is, consequently, not safe to assume that the author of this incantation was concerned about, or even

---

[117] To my knowledge, only the former is ever commented on. Origen appeals to *Sim.* viii.3.3 in *CommMatt.* xiv.21, but does not connect it with ix.12.8.

[118] So Hunt (*Oxyrhynchus*, VIII.253) and Wessely ("Anciens monuments", 403-404).

[119] Cf. the examples collected in Stuckenbruck, *Angel Veneration*, 192-198. Arnold (*Syncretism*, 242-243) apparently understands every name in this text to refer to a different deity. If this is so, given that four ('Ελωει, 'Αδωναει, 'Ιαω, Σαβαωθ) are traditional designations for the Jewish God, we must conclude that the author's understanding of Judaism and Christianity was limited indeed.

aware of, the theological implications of his composition. The text may be nothing more than the ramblings of a magician inadequately instructed in the teachings of Christianity. Nonetheless, it is just possible that the text reflects a popularization of a Michael-Christ Christology such as we found in Hermas. Possible, but far from certain.

3) The Gospel of the Hebrews

One of the few surviving fragments of the *Gospel of the Hebrews* offers a perplexing picture of Mary, the Mother of Jesus, as the incarnation of Michael:

> It is written in the [Gospel] of the Hebrews that when Christ wished to come upon the earth to men the Good Father called a mighty 'power' in the heavens which was called 'Michael', and committed Christ to the care thereof. And the 'power' came down into the world, and it was called Mary, and Christ was in her womb for seven months.[120]

This passage from the *Gospel of the Hebrews* is quoted in a sermon attributed, probably wrongly, to Cyril of Jerusalem and only survives in a Coptic translation. In other fragments of this gospel the mother of Christ is named "the Holy Spirit", not Mary.[121] This may be an indication that this passage does not belong to the same *Gospel of the Hebrews*. However, it is also possible that we have here further evidence that the Holy Spirit was understood as an angel, in this case as Michael. This is a difficult fragment to evaluate; far too little of its original context has survived.[122] At best it offers supporting evidence for the close relation of Christ and the archangel Michael in certain circles.

4) Epiphanius Pan. xxx.16.2 and the Dualism of Qumran

The description of Christ as "one of the archangels" and "the ruler both of angels and of all creatures of the Almighty" (*Pan.* xxx.16.4) in the

---

[120] Budge, *Misc. Coptic Texts*, 637.
[121] See Vielhauer and Strecker in "Jewish-Christian Gospels", *NTApoc.* I.177-178.
[122] Cf. Barbel, *Christos Angelos*, 225, n.200, who cites it only "als Kuriosität".

"Ebionite" Christology known to Epiphanius recalls Michael's position in Jewish and early Christian apocalyptic. Significantly, in this context Epiphanius also attributes a cosmic dualism to the Ebionites:

> But as I said, they set two divine appointees side by side, one being Christ, but one the devil. And they say that Christ has been allotted the world to come, but that this world has been entrusted to the devil--by the Almighty's decree, if you please, at the request of both (*Pan.* xxx.16.2).

This dualism, which is also found in the *Pseudo-Clementines* (e.g., *Hom.* iii.2, viii.21, xx.2-3 and *Rec.* ii.24, iii.52), is not unlike the dualism of Qumran with its conflict between the "Prince of Light" or Michael, on the one hand, and "the Prince of Darkness" or Belial, on the other.[123] A number of interpreters have suggested the dualism of Epiphanius' "Ebionites" and the *Pseudo-Clementines* originated with the Essenes of Qumran.[124] If this is correct, it could explain the origin of the Michael-Christ identification: Once converted to Christianity or "Ebionitism", the former Essenes kept their dualism and identified Christ with the Angel of Light, that is, with Michael.

5) The Pseudo-Clementines

While the above suggestion is speculative, it receives support from two considerations. First, the True Prophet Christology of the *Pseudo-Clementines* seems to owe something to angel Christology. For example, in *Rec.* i.34 the True Prophet is identified with the angel who appeared to Moses in the bush and as the angel of the Exodus.[125] Second, a passage appearing in both the *Homilies* and the *Recognitions*, and thus probably belonging to the *Grundschrift*, describes Christ as the angel set over the nation of Israel (*Rec.* ii.42.3-5, 8; *Hom.* xviii.4). As we have seen, this is

---

[123] Cf. e.g., 1QS 3.13-4.26 and 1QM 13.10-11, 17.4-9. See above pp. 62-66.

[124] E.g., Daniélou, *Theology*, 144; Schoeps, *Theologie*, 247-255; idem., *Jewish Christianity*, 86, 118-121. Indeed, Epiphanius asserts that the Elchasaites, who influenced the Ebionites, were influenced by the Ossaens ('Οσσαίων; *Pan.* xix.1.1-4, 2.2). This has been taken as a reference to the Essenes. Cf. Schoeps, *Theologie*, 251-252.

[125] Cf. *Hom.* xvi.14, which identifies the "angel" who appeared to Moses in the bush and who wrestled with Jacob as "Emmanuel, ...who is called the Mighty God".

Michael's role in many Jewish apocalypses.[126] To be sure, in neither passage is Christ explicitly identified with Michael, and the simple adoption of roles traditionally belonging to an archangel does not necessarily imply an identification with that archangel. Nonetheless, the presence of a dualism so characteristic of Qumran, and the influence of angel Christology on the True Prophet Christology generally, certainly make a Michael-Christ equation in the *Pseudo-Clementines* a possibility.[127]

6) Gabriel, the angel of the Holy Spirit?

Finally, the Christ-Michael identification may have been paralleled by a Holy Spirit-Gabriel equation. The evidence for this is, to be sure, tentative and very limited. The *Ascension of Isaiah* envisions the Holy Spirit as an angel, for it regularly refers to him as "the angel of the Holy Spirit" (3.16, 7.23, 9.36, 40, 11.4, 33), or "the angel of the Spirit" (4.21, 9.39, 10.4). It is possible that the archangel Gabriel is intended. First, the original text of 3.16 may have read Γαβριὴλ, ὁ ἄγγελος τοῦ πνεύματος τοῦ ἁγίου. The Ethiopic version does not include the name, but 1) the mention of Μιχαὴλ ἄρχων τῶν ἀγγέλων τῶν ἁγίων later in the verse seems to require a name here as well, and 2) the fragmentary Greek manuscript of the *Ascension of Isaiah* has a lacuna here which shows that it included a word before "the angel of the Holy Spirit" which is not found in the Ethiopic, and Γαβριήλ would fit.[128] Second, at 11.4 it is "the angel of the Spirit" who appears to Joseph in a dream to warn him not to put Mary away secretly. This passage is clearly based upon Matt. 1.20, where it is an ἄγγελος κυρίου who appears to Joseph. Gabriel, of course, does not appear in Matthew's account, but it was common in the early Church to harmonize Matthew with Luke's birth narrative and to conclude that Gabriel is referred to in both.[129] So, if the author of the *Ascension* knew the Gospel of Luke, it is possible, but by no means certain, that he

---

[126] See above pp. 33-38.
[127] So also Daniélou, *Theology*, 184-185.
[128] So Charles (*Ascension*, 19-20, 93) following a suggestion of Grenfell and Hunt. However, Norelli ("Resurrezione", 322-323) has questioned this reconstruction and has suggested another just as plausible.
[129] So *ProtJames* 11-14; and Cyprian *Testimonies* ii.7 (*ANF.* V.519). For later works, cf. also Ps.-Gregory Thaumaturgos *Twelve Topics on the Faith* (*ANF* VI.50-51) 4 [fifth cent.]; and *History of Joseph the Carpenter* 6 (*ANF* VIII.389) [fifth cent.].

harmonized Matthew with Luke and identified Gabriel with the Holy Spirit.[130] This conclusion, if accepted, offers a parallel to the Michael-Christ identification.

c. Christ Disguised as an Angel

1) The Annunciation

I turn now to a related phenomenon. Some Christians in the second and third centuries while not identifying Christ with an angel, did conceive of events, especially his descent into the world and the Annunciation, in which Christ disguised himself as an angel. For example, in a complex of texts Christ is portrayed "in the form" of the archangel Gabriel at the annunciation to Mary (*EpApos.* 14; *SibOr.* viii.456-462; *Pistis Sophia* 7-8). The earliest form of this tradition appears in the *Epistula Apostolorum*, whose Coptic version runs as follows:

> [Jesus said,] 'For you know that the angel Gabriel brought the message to Mary.' We answered, 'Yes, O Lord.' Then he answered and said to us, 'Do you not then remember that a little while ago I told you: I became an angel among the angels. I became all things in everything?' We said to him, 'Yes, O Lord.' Then he answered and said to us, 'On that day I took the form of the angel Gabriel, I appeared to Mary and spoke with her. Her heart received me and believed; I formed myself and entered into her womb; I became flesh, for I alone was servant to myself with respect to Mary in an appearance of the form of an angel'.[131]

It must be stressed that no identification of Christ with Gabriel is intended here, for the text explicitly states that Christ came to Mary in the

---

[130] So Daniélou, *Theology*, 127-131; Simonetti, "Cristologia", 190, n.16.

[131] The Ethiopic version is very similar. Müller's (*NTA*, I.257) translation.

I hold this text to be dependent on and a correction of the fragment from the *Gospel according to the Hebrews*, cited above, for the following reasons: It is more probable that Gabriel has replaced Michael than vice versa, for it is more likely for a tradition to be revised towards a Gospel text (Luke 1), than away from one. Second, the difficult phrase "for I alone was servant to myself with respect to Mary in an appearance of the form of an angel" makes sense as a reaction against Christ being "committed to the care" of Michael. In other words, the author of the *Epistula Apostolorum* protests that Christ *in the form of* an angel, but *without the aid of* an angel or archangel, appeared to Mary.

"form" of Gabriel.[132] Indeed, Christ and Gabriel are clearly distinguished in the previous chapter. Christ merely appears in the guise of Gabriel, and in this guise only for the annunciation itself. Thereafter, he assumes human flesh and becomes a man (cf. chapts. 3 and 19). By stressing that it was Christ himself, the author of the *Epistula Apostolorum* identifies Christ with the πνεῦμα ἅγιον and the δύναμις ὑψίστου of the Gospel narrative (Luke 1.35), an exegesis common among Fathers of the second and third centuries.[133] The re-appearance of this tradition in the *Sibylline Oracles* and *Pistis Sophia* shows that it continued to enjoy some popularity in both Orthodox and Gnostic circles.

2) Christ's Descent

Similarly, both the *Epistula Apostolorum* and the *Ascension of Isaiah* knew of a tradition whereby Christ disguised himself as an angel in order to keep secret his descent through the heavens. This is merely alluded to in the *Epistula Apostolorum* (13-14), but it is a major theme of the *Ascension of Isaiah*, especially of the vision which is described in chapters 6-11. The divine commission (10.9-12) to the Beloved, or Christ, to descend through the seven heavens to the earth particularly emphasizes this theme. He is told to make his

> likeness like that of all who (are) in the five heavens, and you shall take care to make your form like that of the angels of the firmament and also (like that) of the angels who (are) in Sheol. And none of the angels of that world shall know that you (are) Lord with me of the seven heavens and of their angels.[134]

In the narration of the descent of the Beloved which follows, the Beloved transforms himself to appear as an angel of each heaven as he enters that heaven. The purpose of each transformation is clearly one of camouflage (cf. also 9.15). No attempt is being made to equate Christ with an angel or to assert that he has taken on an angelic nature. Rather, Christ's real nature is merely hidden as he assumes various angelic guises. The power of this motif comes when Christ, after the resurrection, ascends back through the

---

[132] So Daniélou, *Theology*, 131-132.
[133] Cf. Justin, *1 Apol.* 33; Tertullian, *Praxeas* 26; and Cyprian, *Idols* xi.
[134] Knibb's translation from *OTP* II.173.

seven heavens. This time there is no disguise. The angels of each heaven are dismayed to see their Lord and wonder how he got past them without their knowledge.

In other passages, the author speaks of the Beloved's transformation into a human (8.10, 9.13, 11.17). Indeed, 3.13 alludes to two transformations: the first, angelic, by which Christ passes through the heavens and the second, the transformation into a man. Although the author often attributes the same purpose to these different kinds of transformations, i.e., to hide his true identity (9.13, 11.17), the two seem to be only superficially similar. Whereas the taking of an angelic form is merely cosmetic, some kind of real incarnation is implied for the Beloved's transformation into a human. For he really suffers and dies (3.13, 11.18-21) and, as an infant, he actually suckles the breast (11.17).[135]

The first actual transformation into an angel which the Beloved undergoes (9.30) is described prior to the divine commission to descend through the heavens.[136] It seems oddly out of place in this context and may have been misplaced in an early copy of the *Ascension*, or, more likely, this first transformation serves a completely different purpose. Here the sense seems to be that Christ was transformed so that he could be worshipped by Isaiah. The parallels (9.33 and 9.37-39) appear to confirm this. The Angel of the Holy Spirit is not transformed (9.33),[137] for as an angel the Holy Spirit does not need to be transformed to be worshipped by a human. The Beloved, on the other hand, was transformed into an angel precisely at the moment Isaiah begins to worship him. Similarly, before Isaiah worships the Father "the eyes of (his) spirit" are opened to enable Isaiah to see the Father (9.37-39). Even the angels without this special grace cannot see God (9.37). In other words, a human such as Isaiah needed help, in one

---

[135] Contrast Tobit 12.19; *TAb*. A 4.9-10; Philo, *Abr*. 118; Josephus, *Ant*. i.197; and *GenR* 48.14. These texts, all of which except the first refer to the three "men" who appear to Abraham in Gen. 18, explain that the angels involved did not really eat or drink; it only seemed to be so to the human observers. By contrast, the Christ child in *AscenIs*. truly suckles. He suckles not because he needs the nourishment, but to hide his true identity. Cf. Clement of Alexandria, *Strom*. vi.9. For a fuller statement of the argument of the last two paragraphs, see Hannah, "Docetic Christology".

[136] Although L^2 and S have Isaiah being transformed, rather than the Beloved ("And I was transformed and became like an angel"), the Ethiopic version, "And He (i.e., Christ) was transformed and became like an angel", has now been confirmed by a Coptic manuscript and is to be preferred as the more difficult. So also Knibb, *OTP*, II.171, n.o2.

[137] Charles emends the text here, against all the textual evidence (Eth., L^2, and S), to support his preference of L^2 S at 9.30. Charles believes the original read: "But my glory was not transformed into accordance with their form". But the Eth., L^2, and S versions all agree in reading: "But his glory...".

form or another, to worship either the Beloved or the Father, but this was not necessary with the Holy Spirit who is an angel. Thus, the *Ascension of Isaiah* seemingly speaks of Christ's transformation into the form of an angel for two different purposes: first, he transforms himself so that Isaiah might worship him, and second, he assumes the form of an angel in each of the different heavens that his descent into the world might not be known. Neither implies that Christ actually became an angel, or that he was originally an angel by nature.

d. The Tradition behind the Ascension of Isaiah[138]

Therefore, the *Ascension of Isaiah* does not contain an angel Christology: it does not assert, or even imply, that Christ is an angel. At most it describes him disguising himself as an angel.[139] However, there is reason to believe that the primitive depiction of the Trinity found in 9.27-42 and 11.32-33 depends on both an angel Christology and an angel Pneumatology. First of all, the Holy Spirit continues to be identified with an angel. Second, and more importantly, an exegetical tradition which appears in Origen (*Princ.* i.3.4; iv.3.14; cf. *Cels.* vi.18; *HomIsa.* i.2, iv.1; *Com m Rom.* iii.8) may point back to an earlier source or oral tradition behind the *Ascension of Isaiah*. The clearest passage in Origen for this exegetical tradition is found at *Princ.* i.3.4:

> The Hebrew used to say that the two six-winged seraphim in Isaiah who cry one to another and say, 'Holy, holy, holy, is the Lord Sabaoth', were the only-begotten Son of God and the Holy Spirit. And we ourselves think that the expression in the song of Habakkuk, 'In the midst of the two living creatures thou shalt be known' is spoken of Christ and the Holy Spirit.[140]

Here we find Christ and the Holy Spirit identified with the Seraphim and offering God worship. The parallel with the *Ascension of Isaiah* is all the more striking when it is recognized that both texts, *Princ.* 1.3.4 and *AscenIs.* 6-11, result from reflection upon Isaiah 6. Interestingly, Origen

---

[138] For a more detailed and developed presentation of the argument of this section, see Hannah, "Isaiah's Vision".

[139] So also Simonetti, "Cristologia", 187-193.

[140] Based on Butterworth's (*Principles*, 32) translation of the Greek fragment.

explicitly attributes this interpretation to a Jewish source; either to his "Hebrew master", if the Latin translation of Rufinus is followed, or more simply to "the Hebrew", if the Greek fragment is preferred.[141] The limited state of our knowledge does not allow an identification of this person,[142] but given his distinctively Christian interpretation of Isa. 6 we may perhaps assume that he was either a Jew converted to Christianity, or a Jewish Christian.[143]

A number of scholars have pointed to a similar exegetical tradition in Philo's understanding of the Cherubim (*De Deo* 3-6; *Mos.* 2.97-100; *Cher.* 27-28; *Q.G.* 1.57).[144] The strongest parallel appears in *De Deo* 3-6 where Philo identifies the three men who appeared to Abraham as "the architect of the world (ὁ Κοσμοποιός)" and his two powers, one of which is known as θεός, or the creative (ποιητικῆς) power, and the other as κύριος, or the royal (βασιλικῆς) power (3-4). Philo also finds this identification appropriate for Ex. 25.21 where God speaks to Moses from above the two Cherubim. Here again he identifies the Cherubim as the creative (ποιητικῆς) and royal (βασιλικῆς) powers, with God enthroned between them speaking through His Logos (5). Then in chapt. 6 he connects this with Isaiah's vision of God flanked by the two Seraphim. While the differences between Philo's and Origen's exegesis are not insignificant, one could easily assume some Philonic influence, either directly or indirectly on Origen or his Hebrew master.[145]

Another text parallel to the Trinitarian passages of the *Ascension of Isaiah* occurs in Irenaeus' *Demonstration* 10:

> This God, then, is glorified by His Word, who is His eternal Son, and by the Holy Spirit, who is the Wisdom of the Father of all. And their Power(s), (that of the Word and of Wisdom), who are called Cherubim and Seraphim, with unceasing voice glorify God, and the entire establishment of heaven gives glory to God the Father of all.[146]

---

[141] For the scant possibility that this refers to a Jewish Christian commentary on the Book of Isaiah, see Pritz, *Nazarene*, 22-23.

[142] So De Lange, *Origen*, 23-27.

[143] So Hanson, *Allegory and Event*, 174 and Daniélou, *Theology*, 135-136. De Lange (*Origen*, 43), however, is of the opinion that "the Hebrew" may have been a non-Christian Jew and appeals to similar language in Philo to show that a Jew could speak of "the only-begotten of God" (*Conf.* 146; *Agr.* 51; *Som.* 1.215) and the divine Spirit.

[144] Esp. Kretschmar, *Trinitätstheologie*, 82-91. Cf. Daniélou, *Theology*, 134-140; Barbel, *Christos Angelos*, 270-275.

[145] So Daniélou, *Theology*, 135-136.

[146] Smith's (*Proof*) translation. Irenaeus' *Demonstration* is unfortunately only preserved in an Armenian translation. The single MS reads "Power" rather than "Powers", but all the translations I have consulted accept the emendation of the plural. See Smith,

Two parallels should be noted, possibly three. According to Irenaeus, the Logos and the Holy Spirit join the heavenly host in praising God. Second, in the previous chapter Irenaeus describes the seven heavens and implies that God, His Word and Wisdom are situated in the seventh heaven. Third, Daniélou argues that this text identifies the Logos and the Holy Spirit with the Cherubim and Seraphim. He approvingly cites Lanne's paraphrase that "the Word and Wisdom, which are powers of the Father, *and are also called* Cherubim and Seraphim, give glory to God with their unceasing voice".[147] This last point seems to me to be very unlikely as the text now stands. However, a simple emendation of would produce the same sense. Consider the following:

Rousseau's Text: Τούτων δὲ αἱ δυνάμεις τοῦ τε Λόγου καὶ τῆς Σοφίας, αἵτινες καλοῦνται Χερουβὶμ και Σεραφίμ,...

Suggested emendation: Ταῦτα δὲ αἱ δυνάμεις, ὁ Λόγος καὶ ἡ Σοφία, αἵτινες καλοῦνται Χερουβὶμ και Σεραφίμ,...

If Irenaeus here utilized source material, he could very well have introduced the plural and other changes to avoid the difficulty of identifying the Son and the Spirit with angels. In other words, Irenaeus' text, as it now stands, does not identify the Son and the Spirit with the Cherubim and Seraphim. Nonetheless, this passage is suspiciously close to the portrait of the Trinity as it appears in *AscenIs.* 6-11 and Origen's exegesis of Isaiah 6-- close enough to raise the possibility that Irenaeus has here used a source, but modified it in a more orthodox direction. If this, admittedly speculative, suggestion is accepted, then we have here another witness to the same exegetical tradition found in the *Ascension of Isaiah*.

Finally, the Elchasaite description of the Son of God and the Holy Spirit as gigantic male and female angels is to be remembered. Taken together, these texts, Philo through Origen, point to an interpretive tradition which identified Christ and the Holy Spirit as the two highest angelic beings who stood before or sat on either side of God's throne. While both Irenaeus and Origen are later than the *Ascension of Isaiah*, the possibility of their mutual

---

Proof, 148, n.62. See also Rousseau's translation and commentary, *Démonstration*. Rousseau's reconstructs the original Greek thus: Ὁ μὲν οὖν Θεὸς οὗτος δοξάζεται ὑπὸ τοῦ Λόγου αὐτοῦ, ὅς ἐστιν Υἱὸς αὐτοῦ, διηνεκῶς, καὶ ὑπὸ τοῦ Πνεύματος τοῦ ἁγίου, ὅ ἐστιν Σοφία τοῦ Πατρὸς τῶν ὅλων. Τούτων δὲ αἱ δυνάμεις τοῦ τε Λόγου καὶ τῆς Σοφίας, αἵτινες καλοῦνται Χερουβὶμ και Σεραφίμ, ἀπαύστοις φωναῖς δοξάζουσι τὸν Θεόν.

[147] Daniélou, *Theology*, 138; emphasis added.

mutual dependence on a Philonic tradition suggests an earlier Jewish Christian exegetical tradition which stood behind the *Ascension of Isaiah*, and which the latter seemingly corrects by avoiding any suggestion that the Beloved is an angel, emphasizing that he was merely disguised as one.

e. The "Theophanic" Angel Christology of the Fathers

During the second century a number of Church Fathers, influenced by Platonic ideas of divine transcendence, interpreted the OT מלאך יהוה passages as referring to the Logos, that is, the pre-existent Christ. In doing so, they did not shy away from giving Christ the appellation ἄγγελος.[148] As we shall see, however, this title was more indicative of function than ontology.[149] The same is true of the early Patristic christological exegesis of the phrase ἄγγελος μεγάλης βουλῆς, from Isa. 9.5 in the LXX.

1) Justin Martyr

Justin must be the starting point for any discussion of the second century theophanic angel Christology, for he is the earliest, as well as the most prolific exponent of this type of angel Christology. While Irenaeus's works are more voluminous, his statements of this motif are very brief.

a) The OT Theophanies Justin routinely identifies the subject of OT theophanies with the pre-existent Christ or Logos. Thus it was the Logos who, accompanied by two angels, visited Abraham at Mamre and destroyed Sodom (*Dial.* 56, 60, 126). The Logos also appeared to Jacob in dreams at Bethel (Gen. 28) and Haran (Gen. 31) and wrestled with him at Jabbok (*Dial.* 58). It was the Logos who appeared to Moses in the burning bush

---

[148] Cf. my discussion above of the rabbinic exegesis of these same OT passages, pp. 112-114.

[149] Of course, I do not mean to imply that function and ontology are necessarily mutually exclusive. However, as we shall see, when the Fathers examined in this chapter set out to discuss the christological use of ἄγγελος, they invariably offer only a functional nuance while at the same time affirming that Christ shared in the essence of God. Indeed, Tertullian (*Carn.* xiv) expressly appeals to the functional meaning of ἄγγελος to the exclusion of the ontological.

(*Dial.* 59-60, 126-127; *1 Apol.* 62-63) and whom Joshua encountered outside Jericho (*Dial.* 61-62). In addition, the Logos spoke to the Israelites from the pillar of cloud (*Dial.* 38) and He is to be identified with the Rock from which the children of Israel drank in the wilderness (*Dial.* 113-114). While Justin does not refer to all the OT theophanic passages, he affirms that even those he does not cite should be interpreted christologically (*Dial.* 127.1).

b) The Philonic Logos Justin may have been dependent, directly or indirectly, upon Philo's Logos doctrine for his exegesis of the OT theophanic passages. Regardless of influence, however, his philosophical starting point is certainly the platonic doctrine of the absolute transcendence of God. These two points require further justification. Philo often identified the Logos as the subject of the very theophanies with which Justin is concerned. For example, Philo identified both Jacob's opponent in the nocturnal wrestling match (*Som.* 1.129; *Mut.* 87) and the angel who appeared to him in dreams (*Som.* 1.70; *Mig.* 5-6) as the Logos. While Philo at times interprets Abraham's three visitors as God himself accompanied by his kingly and creative powers (*Abr.* 119-132; *Sac.* 59), he can also identify the central figure with the Logos (*Som.* 1.70; *Mig.* 173-174; cf. *Leg. All.* 3.217-219; *Som.* 1.85). In addition, in both Justin and Philo we find similar lists of names and descriptions of the Logos.[150] Indeed, just as Philo refers to the Logos as ἄγγελος or ἀρχάγγελος (*Conf.* 146), Justin frequently uses the former appellation for Christ (e.g., *Dial.* 61.1; 128.1).

Nevertheless, we should be careful not to press direct philonic influence on Justin's doctrine of the Logos. First of all, many of Justin's interpretations are not found in Philo.[151] Furthermore, if Justin depends on Philo, he does so only in the broadest possible sense and does not follow him closely.[152] Above all, for Justin the Logos remains intrinsically tied to

---

[150] E.g., Cf. *Conf.* 146 with *Dial.* 61.1; 126.1; 128.1. Trakatellis (*Pre-Existence*, 53-92) and Goodenough (*Theology*, 168-175) particularly argue for philonic influence, on the basis of these parallels.

[151] For example, the burning bush and Joshua's *archistrategos* are not found in Philo. For the burning bush, Trakatellis (*Pre-Existence*, 73-80) can only appeal to *Mos.* 1.66 and Pseudo-Ezekiel's *Exagoge*. The latter is not philonic. The former speaks not of the Logos, but rather of an angel which may or may not be identified with the Logos. More importantly, as Skarsaune (*Proof*, 418) points out, Philo parallels Trypho's, not Justin's, interpretation of the text! Regarding Jos. 5.13-6.2, even Trakatellis must admit that nothing in Philo approaches Justin's exegesis of this passage.

[152] See Barnard, *Justin Martyr*, 92-99; Chadwick, "Justin's Defence", 296-297; and esp. Skarsaune's devastating critique of Trakatellis, *Proof*, 409-424.

Christian revelation: The Logos became incarnate in Jesus. There is, of course, no parallel to this in Philo. Nonetheless, for Philo and Justin the subject of at least some of the OT theophanies is a figure who can justly be referred to as both "Logos" and "God". Indeed, while Philo's bold phrase "the second God" (ὁ δεύτερος θεός; *Q.G.* 2.62) is not found in Justin, he can call the Logos "another God and Lord" (θεὸς καὶ κύριος ἕτερος; *Dial.* 56.4). So it is possible that, even if Justin did not know Philo directly, he was familiar with an interpretative tradition similar to Philo's.

c) The Platonic Doctrine of God's Transcendence There is a general agreement among interpreters that Justin was moved to insist that it was the Logos who is described in the OT theophanies because of his adoption of the Platonic view of God's absolute transcendence.[153] First of all, Justin himself informs us that he was a Platonist before he became a Christian (*Dial.* 2-6). Secondly, when Justin undertakes to give his definition of "God" he is dependent upon Platonic conceptions and language (*Dial.* 3.5).[154] Above all, as in Platonism, Justin's doctrine of divine transcendence excludes anthropomorphic conceptions of the Deity, especially any suggestion of spatial movement. In one very significant passage Justin explains to his opponents that since God is present everywhere he cannot be confined to a single location in the world, and thus could not have appeared to Abraham, Jacob, or Moses (*Dial.* 127.1-3; cf. 56.1; 60.2). All this creates a problem for Justin. Who was the "God" described in the OT who appeared to the patriarchs, saved Israel from Egypt, delivered the Law to Moses, etc.? Justin solves this by positing the Logos who shared the same essence with God (*Dial.* 61.2-3; 128.4) and as such could be called "another God and Lord" (*Dial.* 56.4), but was also numerically distinct from the Father of all (*Dial.* 56.11) whom he serves as minister or servant (*Dial.* 61.1). In effect, the Logos is Justin's intermediary between the utterly transcendent God and His creation.

d) The Relation of the Logos to the Father All this leads Justin to a view of the Logos which later theologians would regard as a dangerous example of subordinationism. This subordination is clearly seen in Justin's use of phrases like τῷ τοῦ πατρὸς θελήματι ὑπηρετῶν, to describe the Logos'

---

[153] So e.g., Chadwick, *Classical Tradition*, 15-16; Barbel, *Christos Angelos*, 38-45, 56-57; Trakatellis, *Pre-Existence*, 86-88; and Barnard, *Justin Martyr*, 79-84, 91. Barnard adds the important distinction that Justin was dependent not on classical Platonism, but Middle Platonism. The Aristotelian element of God as the non-spatial Unmoved Mover suggests a system similar to that of the middle platonist Albinus (*Justin Martyr*, 29-37, 82-83).

[154] Cf. *Dial.* 4.1, where Justin cites Plato's description of God.

relation to the Father (*Dial.* 113.4; cf. 127.4), and in his insistence that the Logos acts only in accordance with the Father's will (*Dial.* 56.11) and was begotten by the Father as an act of His will (*Dial.* 61.1). Justin even asserts that the Logos is worshipped in "the second place" after the Father (*1 Apol.* 13.3).[155] Precisely because he is not as transcendent as the Father, the Logos can act as the former's mediator. However, it would be wrong to conclude that the Logos' distinction from and subordination to God led Justin to conclude that the Logos was simply an angel by nature, superior to other angels only in degree. As already stated, Justin held that the Logos shared the same divine essence with God (*Dial.* 61.2-3; 128.3-4). He further asserts that, although the Logos is numerically distinct from the Father, he nevertheless remains united with Him.[156] The Logos is the rational thought of the Father; the Divine Reason who was originally indistinct from the Father but was begotten of Him just prior to the creation of the world (*Dial.* 61.1; cf. *2 Apol.* 6.3).[157] Justin does not seem to have worked out all the difficulties which arise from his understanding of God's transcendence and the role of the Logos, such as how one reconciles his implicit ditheism with his assertion of monotheism. He simply allows a certain tension to stand in his theology.

e) *The Logos as the Angel (Messenger) of God* However, there is another reason why Justin could not have regarded the Logos as essentially an angel as other angels. Although he often uses the term "Angel" for the Logos, especially in his exegesis of the OT theophanic passages, Justin clearly intends the term to be understood functionally. No less than three times in the *Dialogue with Trypho* (56.4, 10; 76.3; cf. 127.4) and once in his first *Apology* (63.5) Justin explicitly states that the Logos is called "Angel" precisely because he is the messenger from God to humanity. That is, he is "Angel" because he announces (ἀγγέλλειν/ἀναγγέλλειν) to men whatever the Father of all wishes. Indeed, in *1 Apol.* 63.5 ἄγγελος is equated with ἀπόστολος. Justin's statement in *Dial.* 56.10 is particularly instructive: The Logos *was* God even before the creation of the world (πρὸ ποιήσεως κόσμου ὄντα θεόν), but is merely *called* angel (ἄγγελος καλεῖται). The clear implication is that when Justin uses the term ἄγγελος for the Logos he uses it functionally in the sense of "messenger".[158]

---

[155] See esp. Barbel, *Christos Angelos*, 52-55. Cf. Trakatellis, *Pre-Existence*, 87-88.
[156] Interestingly, in his first *Apology* (63.3-7) the Logos is both "Angel" (ἄγγελος) and "Apostle" (ἀπόστολος), both of which imply subordination, *and* "the Self-Existent One" ('Ἐγώ εἰμι ὁ ὤν), which, of course, implies unity with the Father.
[157] See esp. Barnard, *Justin Martyr*, 89-91.
[158] So also Barbel, *Christos Angelos*, esp. 52, 56.

To summarize, Justin understood the OT theophanic passages as witnesses to the activity of the Logos in the period prior to his incarnation in Jesus. The Logos could with justice be called the "angel of God", because he was the messenger of God to humanity. But this appears to be a functional use of the term, without any indication that Justin grouped the Logos with the host of angels.[159] Indeed, although Justin was a subordinationist in that he held that the Logos was the servant of God the Father, he also affirmed the essential unity of the Logos with the Father.

2) Theophilus

Sometime before A. D. 180 Theophilus of Antioch addressed his Apologia for the Christian Faith to a certain Autolycus. In it he advocates a Logos Christology very similar to that of Justin in many respects. He does not use the term ἄγγελος for the Logos, but he does assert that the transcendence of God means that He cannot be contained in any space, and thus could not have appeared on earth. When confronted with the difficulty of OT stories of God appearing to the patriarchs, he argues, as did Justin before, that the "God" who is meant is the Logos (*To Autolycus* 2.22). However, unlike Justin, he refers not to a מלאך יהוה passage, but rather to Gen. 3.8-21. He also asserts that the Logos is the Mind or Intelligence of the Father, thus implying a unity of essence. With Justin, he holds that the Logos was generated just prior to the creation of the universe (*To Autolycus* 2.22, cf. 2.10). While no angelic Christology can be found in the writings of Theophilus, his Logos Christology indicates that the foundational assumptions and formulations of Justin were by no means unique in the Church of the second century.

---

[159] *1 Apol.* 6.2 stands out as an exception to the the rest of Justin's thought in this regard. Here Justin places the host of good angels after the Son and before the Spirit and asserts both that Christians "worship and adore" (σεβόμεθα καὶ προσκυνοῦμεν) "the good angels" and that these good angels "follow and are like" (ἑπομένων καὶ ἐξομοιουμένων) the Son! However, other "trinitarian" passages in the same document (13.3, 61.3, 9-13), not to mention his Christology generally, demonstrate the uniqueness of this text in Justin's thought. Needless to say, any reconstruction of Justin's thought must rest, not on the distinctive passages, no matter how interesting, but on his work as a whole. Cf. Barbel, *Christos Angelos*, 50-51.

3) Irenaeus

At the end of the second century Irenaeus continued to interpret the OT theophanic passages christologically (*Adv. Haer.* iii.6.1-2; *Dem.* 43-49). However, unlike Justin he never applies the term ἄγγελος to the Logos, except when he is citing or alluding to the LXX version of Isa. 9.5 and, as we shall see, in one of the two such occasions he clearly understands the term "angel" in the functional sense of "messenger". Indeed, in commenting on Gen. 2.7, Irenaeus asserts that angels did not assist when the Deity formed the first humans, but rather God's own hands, who are ever with Him, i.e., His Word (Logos) and Wisdom (the Spirit), were his agents of creation (*Adv. Haer.* iv.20.1). Moreover, he twice cites Isa. 63.9 to support his assertion that it was God the Word, and not an angel, who effected the salvation of humanity (*Adv. Haer.* iii.20.4; *Dem.* 88). Barbel speculates that Irenaeus avoids the title "Angel" because he is sensitive to its misuse by Gnostics.[160] As we have seen, certain Gnostic christologies did identify Christ with an angel.[161] Such a supposition is, then, at least credible, if not likely. However, Irenaeus may have been uncomfortable with the term for other reasons as well. He differs significantly from Justin's doctrine of divine transcendence and the subordinationist tendencies which followed from it. For Irenaeus, God is invisible precisely because He cannot be measured or circumscribed (e.g., *Adv. Haer.* iv.20.1, 6). However, the divine Invisibility is not absolute, for the Logos makes visible the Invisible God. Indeed, "the Father is the invisible of the Son, but the Son the visible of the Father" (*Adv. Haer.* iv.6.6). In a similar vein, Irenaeus can write: "Well spake he, who said that the unmeasurable Father was Himself subjected to measure in the Son; for the Son is the measure of the Father, since He also comprehends Him" (*Adv. Haer.* iv.4.2). In addition, Irenaeus confesses the eternality of the Son alongside the Father (*Adv. Haer.* ii.30.9; iv.20.3).[162] Thus, Irenaeus' understanding of the divine unity does not allow him to follow Justin's subordinationist tendencies.

In addition, while Justin does not seem to have appreciated any significant difference between the various pre-incarnate appearances of the Logos and the incarnation itself,[163] Irenaeus understood the two to be of entirely different orders. For Irenaeus, the purpose of the pre-incarnate

---

[160] Barbel, *Christos Angelos*, 63, 68.
[161] See above pp. 179-181.
[162] Cf. Minns, *Irenaeus*, 36-53; and Barbel, *Angelos Christos*, 63-68.
[163] *1 Apol.* 63.16; *Dial.* 113.4; 128.1. Cf. Chadwick, "Justin's Defence", 290; Trakatellis, *Pre-Existence*, 89-91; and Barnard, *Justin Martyr*, 119-120.

theophanies was preparatory; the Logos chose such means to prepare both the human race and himself for the eventual incarnation (*Adv. Haer.* iii.17.1; iii.20.2; iv. 12.4; *Dem.* 46). They point beyond themselves toward that event of which they are merely types.[164]

Clearly, then, although Irenaeus followed Justin in interpreting the OT theophanies as appearances of the pre-existent Christ, he parted company with the former's doctrine of absolute transcendence and the subordinationism which necessarily follows from it. He also distanced himself from Justin's tendency to regulate the incarnation to one of many divine appearances throughout sacred history. It is hardly surprising, then, that he also avoids the term ἄγγελος which could easily have been understood to imply a form of subordination, as well as to call in question the uniqueness of the incarnation.

There is one possible occasion, however, in which Irenaeus refers to Christ unambiguously as an angel, but it is of questionable authenticity. The Syriac and Armenian catena fragments from works of Irenaeus contain a parallel passage, which may be from a composition entitled *On the Lord's Resurrection*,[165] and in which we find the following:

> He is all in all: Patriarch among the patriarch; Law in the laws; Chief Priest among priests; Ruler among kings; the Prophet among prophets; the Angel among angels; the Man among men; Son in the Father; God in God; King to all eternity. For it is He who sailed (in the ark) with Noah, and who guided Abraham; who was bound along with Isaac, and was a Wanderer with Jacob; the Shepherd of those who are saved, and the Bridegroom of the Church; the Chief also of the cherubim, the Prince of the angelic powers; God of God; Son of the Father; Jesus Christ; King for ever and ever. Amen.[166]

This creedal-like extract, confesses Christ to be an angel in that he is "the Angel among angels" and "the Prince of the angelic powers". But he is also affirmed to be divine in no uncertain terms. In all this it differs from Irenaeus' work generally only in that it does not shy way from the word

---

[164] Cf. Minns, *Irenaeus*, 41-42, 49.

[165] Frags. 53 & 54 in *ANF* (= frags. 30 & 31 in Harvey, *Sancti Irenaei*). The Syriac MS does not give the title of the work from which the extract comes, but the Armenian attributes it to this otherwise lost document.

[166] The *ANF* translation of the Syriac. The Armenian appears to be an expanded version, but is clearly the same extract. Interestingly, in the latter, Christ is not the "Chief of the cherubim", but the "Charioteer of the cherubim".

"Angel". It certainly portrays the pre-existent Christ as active in the OT period. Nonetheless, it is not certain that we have here an authentic fragment from the Bishop of Lyon. Indeed, parallel fragments attribute this "confession" or "poem", to Melito of Sardis.[167] Undoubtedly, the piece circulated in the early Church under many different names. Nonetheless, regardless of its original author, the extract illustrates very well the attitude toward the christological use of the title ἄγγελος which was current in the Great Church from, at least, the mid-second century: Christ is an angel in that he is *the* messenger of the Father, but he also shares God's divinity and, thus, does not possess an angelic nature.

4) The Angel of Great Counsel

a) The Origin of the Phrase Before concluding, some remarks should be made regarding the popularity of the christological title Μεγάλης βουλῆς ἄγγελος in the early Church. This title is found in the LXX version of Isa. 9.5 (9.6 MT).[168] It replaces the Massoretic text's פלא יועץ אל גבור אבי־עד שר־שלום. It is impossible to be certain whether a different Hebrew text lay behind the LXX or whether the LXX is simply paraphrastic. However, the LXX reading is at least as early as Justin Martyr (*Dial.* 76.3; 126.1) and in all likelihood much earlier, given its widespread attestation in both the textual tradition and among the early Fathers. It is hardly surprising that the title Μεγάλης βουλῆς ἄγγελος was understood christologically by the Fathers as the context in which it is found (Isa. 9.5-6) lends itself to messianic interpretation.

b) The Popularity of the Title The title appears to have had a wide currency. It is found in writings of Fathers from nearly every part of the Empire: Rome, Gaul, North Africa, Egypt, and Asia Minor.[169] In addition, Μεγάλης βουλῆς ἄγγελος found its way into the liturgy (*Apostolic*

---

[167] See the brief discussion in Hall (*Melito*, xxxvii-xxxviii) and the works he cites there.

[168] However, certain manuscripts of the LXX have been influenced, probably through Origen's Hexapla, by the later Greek versions of Aquila, Symmachus and Theodotion, all of which follow the MT much more closely.

[169] Rome: Justin (*Dial.* 76.3) and Hippolytus (*CommDan.* ii.32.6); Gaul: Irenaeus (*Dem.* 56); North Africa: Tertullian (*Carn.* xiv); Egypt: Clement (*Paed.* i.5.24) and Origen (*CommJo.* i.31.218; *Cels.* v.53.22; viii.27.6); Asia Minor: Gregory Thaumaturgos (*Pan.* 4.42).

Tradition 4.4; *Apostolic Constitutions* viii.12.7), from where it would have had a wide influence on all worshippers, not just on the Church's theologians. Finally, its appearance in the *Testament of Solomon* (12.3) shows that it had a certain appeal among Christians with syncretistic tendencies.

c) *Justin, Irenaeus, Hippolytus, and Tertullian* The phrase Μεγάλης βουλῆς ἄγγελος is ambiguous. Βουλῆς can mean either "counsel" or "council".[170] In the case of the latter, it could be taken to imply that Christ was the principal angel of the angelic council. However, the Fathers never concluded on the basis of this title that Christ should be understood as an angel by nature. With the important exception of Origen, they invariably interpret Μεγάλης βουλῆς ἄγγελος functionally. Justin, for example, understands the term as a prophecy of Jesus' teaching ministry (*Dial.* 76.3). Similarly, Irenaeus explains the import of the title as an indication of Jesus' role as the "messenger of the Father, whom he announced to us" (*Dem.* 56).[171] Hippolytus, the student of Irenaeus, writes in the same vein: "Scripture (i.e., Isa. 9.5) also calls him 'angel of God'; for he himself announced to us the mysteries of the Father" (*CommDan.* ii.32.6-7).[172] Indeed, Tertullian explicitly denies that this title implies that Christ is to be understood analogous to a Michael or Gabriel. Rather, it refers to his office of messenger, not to his nature,[173] "for he was to announce to the world the Father's great project, that concerned with the restitution of man" (*Carn.* xiv).[174]

d) *Origen* Origen was not unfamiliar with this functional interpretation of Μεγάλης βουλῆς ἄγγελος. Indeed, at times he affirms it in much the same language as Irenaeus and Hippolytus (*Cels.* v.53.22; *CommJo.* i.38.277-278).[175] However, there can also be found in Origen, in the for-

---

[170] Cf. Werner, *Entstehung*, 328-329 (= *Formation*, 132-133), and Trigg, "Angel", 42.

[171] Irenaeus knew both the LXX and MT forms. He evidently regarded both as authoritative, for in *Dem.* 54-56 he cites and interprets both "Wonderful, Counsellor" and "Angel of Great Counsel".

[172] τοῦτον ἡ γραφὴ καὶ ἄγγελον θεοῦ ὡμολόγησεν· αὐτὸς γὰρ ἦν ὁ ἀναγγείλας ἡμῖν τὰ τοῦ πατρὸς μυστήρια.
So the critical text of Bonwetsch on the basis of the Slavonic version. The most important Greek MS reads τὰ τοῦ πνεύματος μυστήρια.

[173] ...*officii non naturae vocabulo*...

[174] Clement of Alexandria cites Isa. 9.5 LXX once (*Paed.* i.5.24), but does not discuss the significance of μεγάλης βουλῆς ἄγγελος. Rather his interest lies in the word παιδίον. Clement once refers to Christ with the similar phrase μυστικὸς ἐκεῖνος ἄγγελος (*Paed.* i.7.59). His intention appears to be purely functional. On this cf. Trigg, "Angel", 43.

[175] Cf. *Sel. Ps.* 49.2 (*PG* XII.1449) which expresses the same idea, but is of questionable authenticity.

mulation of Joseph Trigg, a "dispensational" use of the phrase.[176] In his *Commentary on John*, Origen cites Isa. 9.5 to support his contention that

> the Saviour accordingly became, in a diviner way than Paul, all things to all, that He might either gain all or perfect them; it is clear that to men He became a man, and to the angels an angel (*CommJo*.i.31.218).

Indeed, Origen leaves open the possibility that just as Christ suffered for humanity he will one day suffer for angels (*Princ.* frag. 30).[177] Trigg is right to insist that this does not imply a "separate angelic incarnation", for Origen assumed that humans and angels shared the same rational nature and were distinguished only by differing levels of perfection (*CommJo.* ii.23.144-148; *Princ.* iv.4.9).[178] Therefore, it is not surprising to find Origen assigning to Christ angelic roles, such as the guarding of Christian souls (*Cels.* viii.26.6; *CommMatt.* xiii.26.607; *CommJo.* i.25.165).[179] Nevertheless, even with this distinctive perspective Origen refuses to equate Christ, ontologically, with angels (*Cels.* v.53.22). For Origen the Logos ontologically shares the divine nature.[180]

e) Heretical Use of the Title However, not all those who made use of the phrase Μεγάλης βουλῆς ἄγγελος avoided the conclusion that Christ was an angel as other angels, superior only in degree. For example, the Valentinian Theodotus once refers to Christ as ὁ τῆς βουλῆς ἄγγελος (Clement Alex. *Ex. Theod.* 43.2). Theodotus elsewhere refers to Christ as the ἄγγελος ἦν τοῦ πληρώματος (*Ex. Theod.* 35.1) and, as I have already argued,[181] his system seems to be advocating some form of angel Christology. To this ontological understanding can be added a passage from the *Testament of Solomon* (12.3), discussed above,[182] in which Christ as the "Angel of Great Counsel" is portrayed as a particularly powerful angel for the "thwarting" of demons.

---

[176] Trigg, "Angel", 37.

[177] A passage absent from Rufinus' translation, but preserved by Justinian (*Ep. ad Mennam*) and Jerome (*Ep. ad Avitum* xii). For text and translation see Koetschau, *De Principiis*, 344-345; and Butterworth, *First Principles*, 310.

[178] Trigg, "Angel", 45. Cf. Barbel (*Christos Angelos*, 284-297).

[179] Cf. Origen's student Gregory Thaumaturgos, *Pan.* 4.42; and Trigg, "Angel", 45-51.

[180] See esp. Crouzel, *Origen*, 186-192. Cf. Trigg, "Angel", 45.

[181] See above pp. 180-181.

[182] See above pp. 181-183.

5) Conclusions

This brief overview of Patristic evidence from the second and early third centuries has shown that the Fathers of this period felt little compunction in alluding to Christ as an angel, either in their interpretations of OT theophanic passages or in their use of the title Μεγάλης βουλῆς ἄγγελος. Nonetheless, it is clear that their assumptions regarding his divinity kept them from concluding that Christ shared an angelic nature. They, with the exception of Origen, invariably use ἄγγελος functionally when they use it with reference to Christ. Origen uses it both functionally and "dispensationally". There is, then, a great difference between Justin or Irenaeus' understanding of Christ as an angel and that of the author of *De Centesima* or Epiphanius' "Ebionites", who describe Christ as one of the first created angels.

3. Conclusions

In this chapter we have seen the diversity which angel, angelomorphic, and angelic Christologies could take in the second and early third centuries. Valentinian Gnostics speculated on Christ as an angel for the salvation of angels (Tertullian *Carn.* xiv). Among circles which practiced magic Christ was viewed as an especially potent angel by which to "thwart" demons (*Testament of Solomon*). In certain Jewish-Christian circles Christ was identified with the highest of the archangels (*De Centesima*, Epiphanius' "Ebionites"). Some even went so far as to identify Christ with the archangel Michael (Hermas). Other Christians, while suggesting that Christ disguised himself as an angel during his descent or at the Annunciation, were careful to avoid the impression that he actually became an angel (*Ascension of Isaiah*, *Epistula Apostolorum*). Finally, many of the theologians of the early Church found the epiphanies of the מלאך יהוה, recorded in the OT, particularly useful in asserting both the deity of Christ and his distinction from the Father.

To some degree this diversity can be explained as arising from the ambiguity of the New Testament documents and some of the Christologies circulating in the first century. Jude described Christ as the Exodus angel, thus preparing the way for Justin and those who followed him. The Revelation of John and Hebrews ascribe to Christ roles which traditionally belong to the archangel Michael, thus possibly explaining Hermas' confusion. Above all, if I am correct in my exegesis of Hebrews 1-2, the author of *De Centesima* and the "Ebionites" opposed by Epiphanius are probably to be identified with the theological descendants of the group or groups opposed by the Epistle to the Hebrews.

Significantly, while sociological factors have contributed to this diversity, a neat cleavage between the theologians and the authors of "popular" literature does not appear to exist. For example, although the theologians, both orthodox (Justin) and gnostic (the Valentinian Theodotus), hold very complex views, it is not the case that all the theologians rejected angel Christologies for more nuanced angelic or angelomorphic Christologies. In other words, a "true" angel Christology can be found both among intellectuals (Theodotus) and writers of popular literature (Hermas). In addition, if my suggestion about the *Ascension of Isaiah*'s use and transformation of an angel Christology is correct, then in a work of a popular nature we have a very carefully thought out and nuanced angelomorphic Christology.

Conclusions: Michael and Christ

It remains to summarize the findings of the previous chapters and to offer some synthesis of those findings. This study has identified three basic forms in which widespread and diverse speculation about principal angels from various movements and social groups within ancient Judaism influenced the development of early Christology: The theophanic angel Christology of the early Fathers; "true" angel Christologies which identify Christ with an angel; and the angelic Christology of some New Testament and later authors. In the second and third of these Michael speculations are not insignificant and, in some cases, decisive.

1. Summary: Three Forms of Angel Christologies

Early Fathers such as Justin, Theophilus, and Irenaeus interpreted the subject of OT theophanic passages as a manifestation of the pre-incarnate Christ. While Theophilus and Irenaeus avoided the term ἄγγελος in this connection, Justin often applies the term to Christ. However, even for Justin the term is functional, indicating Christ's role as God's messenger *par excellence*, and does not imply that Christ had an angelic nature. Jude (vss. 5-6) may be an early example of this category; however, it is also possible that he held a "true" angel Christology. In addition, in both the Great Church and among some heretical movements the Μεγάλης βουλῆς ἄγγελος of Isa. 9.5 LXX was invariably understood as a reference to Christ from, at least, the mid-second century. While some Gnostics may very well have used the term as support for their belief in the angelic nature of Christ, "orthodox" theologians carefully interpret the title functionally and, in the case of Origen, dispensationally.

Other early Christians understood the pre-incarnate Christ, ontologically, as an angel. This "true" angel Christology took many forms and may have appeared as early as the late first century, if indeed this is the view opposed in the early chapters of the Epistle to the Hebrews. The Elchasaites, or at least Christians influenced by them, paired the male Christ with the female Holy Spirit, envisioning both as two gigantic angels. Some Valentinian Gnostics supposed that Christ took on an angelic nature that he might be the Saviour of angels. The author of the *Testament of Solomon* held Christ to be a particularly effective "thwarting" angel in the exorcism of demons. The author of *De Centesima* and Epiphanius' "Ebionites" held Christ to have been the highest and most important of the first created archangels, a view similar in many respects to Hermas' equation of Christ with Michael. Finally, a possible exegetical tradition behind the *Ascension of Isaiah* and attested by Origen's Hebrew master, may witness to yet another angel Christology, as well as an angel Pneumatology.

Finally, angelic Christology seems to have been useful to some of the NT authors, as well as to some Christians in the second century. Some early Christians applied principal angel and Michael traditions to Christ, but in doing so transformed them. Revelation, the Epistle to the Hebrews, and possibly the Gospel of Luke all attribute to Christ roles or functions which traditionally belonged to principal angels. Speculation concerning the OT Angel of the Name appears to have informed the hymn found in Phil. 2.6-11, as well as the Johannine tradition (Rev. 19.11-16; John 17). Finally, some second century works teach that Christ disguised himself as an angel either during his descent or at the annunciation or both (*Ascension of Isaiah*; *Epistula Apostolorum*).

2. Michael and Christ

In these three rather dissimilar approaches, beliefs and traditions about angels are taken up and made to serve Christology. They do so, however, in very different ways. Thus, I have used three terms (theophanic angel Christology, angel Christology, and angelic Christology), rather than one. In two of these three categories beliefs about Michael had a significant influence. In the first Michael traditions may, at best, have been in the background.

a. Theophanic Angel Christology

While there was a tendency in Rabbinic exegesis of OT מלאך יהוה texts to identify this angel with Michael, and the earliest evidence for this tendency is contemporary with the earliest Christian exponent (i.e., Justin Martyr) of a theophanic angel christology, there does not appear to have been any contact between the two. The Rabbinic exegesis of these passages is completely free of the polemic one would expect if an anti-Christian stance was being taken. Nonetheless, Rabbinic and Patristic exegesis of these passages suggests the interest and importance of principal angel speculations to both groups, as well as the usefulness of such speculations for early Christology.

b. Angel Christologies

In those Christologies which actually identified Christ with an angel, Michael traditions play a decisive role. This is, of course, especially true for Hermas who equated Christ with Michael. However, insofar as the author of *De Centesima* and Epiphanius' "Ebionites" identified Christ as the Highest of the archangels, Michael's influence may be presumed here as well. This holds true even if, contrary to one of my more speculative suggestions, there is no connection between the sectarians of Qumran, on the one hand, and Epiphanius' "Ebionites" and the author of the Pseudo-Clementine *Grundschrift*, on the other. To be sure, some of those who understood Christ as possessing an angelic nature clearly distinguished him from Michael (*Testament of Solomon*, the ΙΧΘΥΣ amethyst amulet). However, even here the influence of Michael traditions cannot be completely ruled out, for again Christ is in these texts portrayed as the highest archangel.

c. Angelic Christology: Transformation of Michael Traditions

Michael traditions were also helpful to those who transferred principal angel traditions to Christ while carefully avoiding any implication that Christ shared an angelic nature. The Apocalypse of John (19.11ff), as well as Justin Martyr (*Dial.* 61.1, 62.4-5), portray Christ in Michael's role of heavenly ἀρχιστράτηγος. For the author of the Epistle to the Hebrews,

Christ not Michael serves as the heavenly High Priest. The Apocalypse of John (1.18), the *Questions of Bartholomew* (1.29), and possibly Luke (23.43), all envision Christ as the gate keeper of paradise, a role often attributed to Michael in Jewish sources. These all found Michael traditions useful in elucidating the significance of Christ, while carefully distinguishing Christ from Michael.

Clearly conceptions other than that of "angel" also influenced the early developments in Christology: Logos, Sophia, the Son of Man, Son of God to name just a few. Indeed, these and other motifs are often combined by the same NT authors. However, it seems likely that principal angel motifs were useful precisely because they implied a distinct personality in ways that Logos or Sophia speculation would not. The christological utilization of Logos or Sophia terminology, on the other hand, imply a unity with the Godhead which does not necessarily follow from the use of principal angel traditions. In other words, early Christians availed themselves of varying conceptions to explain different aspects of their experience of Christ. Furthermore, the fact that we find no anti-Michael polemic in the NT or elsewhere in Christian literature seems to suggest that early Christians, with the exception, of course, of individuals and groups such as Hermas, Epiphanius' "Ebionites" and the author of *De Centesmia*, did not *consciously* transfer Michael or principal angel traditions to their Lord. The use of Michael traditions was, by and large, an unconscious process, unlike Logos, Sophia, Son of Man, and Son of God "Christologies".

1) The Usefulness and Fluidity of Michael Traditions

Although traditions about other principal angels (e.g., Yahoel, Metatron) may have been made to serve Christology, Michael traditions were unquestionably more important for Christology than those of any other single principal angel simply because they were the most pervasive and the most multifarious in the Judaism of the Second Temple period.[1] This usefulness of Michael traditions for early Christians in their attempt to understand and express the significance of Christ should not be considered very surprising in view of Philo's Logos doctrine. Philo did not identify

---

[1] Cf. Davis' ("Divine Agents", 502-503) conclusion that of the many Jewish divine mediators of the Second Temple Period only Michael, the Qumran Prince of Light, and Enoch operate in the triple pattern of past, present, and future. As we have seen, Michael and the Prince of Light of the Qumran sect are, most likely, one and the same.

his Logos with Michael; his philosophical presuppositions would not have allowed him to arrive at such a conclusion. Nonetheless, he found Michael traditions useful in describing various offices of the Logos. In the same way, early "orthodox" Christians utilized Michael traditions to illustrate the heavenly significance of Christ, particularly his protection of and intercession for Christians. However, to have identified Christ as the highest archangel would have undermined the very point these Christians were trying to make about Christ.

Similarly, if the "one like a son of Man" in Daniel 7.9-13 was originally intended to be Michael, but was later, as far as we can tell, almost universally understood as the Messiah, first by Jews and then later by Christians, we must conclude that Christians and Philo were not the only Jews who transformed Michael traditions for their own purposes. The messianic interpretation of Dan. 7 appears to have completely eclipsed the angelic one. That a passage which originally referred to Michael could be understood messianically, and that this messianic exegesis developed early on, is a fact of considerable significance. It demonstrates how spontaneous and subtle the whole process of utilizing and transforming principal angel traditions could be.

Interestingly, the attribution to Christ of roles traditionally associated with Michael does not result in a decline in the same roles being applied to Michael in Christian literature. For example, both Christ (Justin, Origen) and Michael (*Epistula Apostolorum*, Hippolytus, Origen, *Questions of Bartholomew*) are termed the heavenly ἀρχιστράτηγος by Christians of the second and third centuries. In addition, both continue to have priestly functions: Christ (*1 Clem.* 36.1, 61.3, 64.1; Ignatius *Phil.* 9.1; Polycarp *Phil.* 12.2; Justin *Dial.* 116.1); Michael (*ApPaul* 43-44; *EpApost.* 13; *3Bar.* 11-16).[2] This can happen because in the vast majority of Christian circles there is no question of a rivalry between Michael and Christ. Michael was only the chief of the angels, while Christ was the divine Logos, the Son of God.

2) Angelomorphic Christology as a Reaction against Angel Christology

The angelomorphic Christology found in a work such as the *Ascension of Isaiah* appears to have been a reaction to and correction of an earlier angel Christology. In this work Christ is portrayed as having merely disguised

---

[2] This last text is, of course, Jewish, but it was preserved by Christians.

himself as an angel. This is significant because the evidence of Origen's Hebrew master, among others, suggest that behind this work was a tradition which identified both Christ and the Holy Spirit as the two Seraphim of Isaiah's vision (Isa. 6). If this is correct, then an angelomorphic Christology was used to correct a Christology which was thought to identify Christ too closely with the angelic order. Two conclusions arise from this. First, given the early dating accepted by most authors for the *Ascension of Isaiah*, "true" angel Christology must reach back to, at least, the end of the first century, a fact supported by the exegesis of Hebrews 1-2 offered above. Second, angelomorphic Christology was seen by some "orthodox" Christians as a safe alternative to a "true" angel Christology. It was not a problem for members of the Great Church to portray Christ in the form of an angel so long as he was not held to have had an angelic nature. This conclusion is, in turn, supported by the theophanic angel Christology of Justin and other early Fathers.

3. A Conjectural Synthesis

Based on the conclusions offered in this study it is possible to construct a conjectural synthesis of the development of these various angelic Christologies and their relation to each other. The second and third categories appear to have been already current in the first century. The opening chapters of the Epistle to the Hebrews testifies that some Christians identified Christ with an angel. Jude's epistle may support this conclusion, but it is impossible to be certain, for it may be merely an early example of a theophanic angel Christology. However, "true" angel Christology does not appear to have been held by most first century Christians. Of the first century documents which have come down to us the identification of Christ with an angel is, in one instance, explicitly rejected (Hebrews), while other NT authors appear to favour angelic Christology to the apparent, but not explicit, exclusion of "true" angel Christologies. In the second and third centuries this ambiguity, as well as the growth of Gnosticism and the gradual separation of Jewish Christianity from the Gentile Church, among other factors, produced a plethora of angelic Christologies. Some, perhaps especially in Jewish Christianity and Gnosticism, followed the lead of the opponents of the author of Hebrews and concluded that Christ was an angel pure and simple. This was opposed by the "orthodox". However, even members of the Great Church, such as Justin, could happily describe Christ as an angel when this was understood to mean "messenger" and did not threaten his divinity. Eventually, this theophanic angel Christology was seen to be suspect, a process already under way in Irenaeus, because of its implicit subordinationism and its tendency to neglect the uniqueness of the incarnation. This synthesis attributes less significance to angelic Christologies in the earliest period than is the case with many previous studies. Explicit evidence for the influence of Michael or principal angel traditions in the NT is too thin to demonstrate that they are the "key" to the origins of Christology. Nonetheless, Michael traditions are present in the NT and other early Christian writings. Their usefulness in the earliest attempts at Christology was real, even if they cannot be said to have been the most important element in emerging Christianity's efforts to understand and elucidate the significance of Jesus Christ.

Bibliography

Primary Literature

Alexander, P. S. (Tr.). "3 Enoch." *The Old Testament Pseudepigrapha*. 2 Vols. J. H. Charlesworth (Ed.). Vol. 1. Garden City, NY: Doubleday, 1983. 223-315.

Andersen, F. I. (Tr.). "2 Enoch." *The Old Testament Pseudepigrapha*. 2 Vols. J. H. Charlesworth (Ed.). Vol. 1. Garden City, NY: Doubleday, 1983. 91-221.

Argyle, A. W. (Tr.). "The Greek Apocalypse of Baruch." *The Apocryphal Old Testament*. H. F. D. Sparks (Ed.). Oxford: Clarendon, 1984. 897-914.

Baillet, M. (Ed.). *Qumrân Grotte 4 III (4Q482-4Q520)*. DJD 7. Oxford: Clarendon, 1982.

Barton, J. M. T. (Tr.). "The Ascension of Isaiah." *The Apocryphal Old Testament*. H. F. D. Sparks (Ed.). Oxford: Clarendon, 1984. 775-812.

Black, M. and A. -M. Denis (Eds.). *Apocalypsis Henochi Graece et Fragmenta Pseudepigraphorum Quae Supersunt Graece*. PVTG 3. Leiden: Brill, 1970.

Blatz, B. (Tr.). "The Coptic Gospel of Thomas." *New Testament Apocrypha*. 2 Vols. Rev. Ed. W. Schneemelcher (Ed.). R. McL. Wilson (Tr.). Vol. 1. Louisville: Westminster/John Knox, 1991. 110-33.

Bonwetsch, G. N. and H. Achelis (Eds.). *Hippolytus Werke: Exegetische und homiletische Schriften*. GCS 1. Leipzig: Hinrichs' Buchhandlung, 1897.

Box, G. H., with J. I. Landsman. *The Apocalypse of Abraham*. TED I.10. London: SPCK, 1918.

Braude, W. G. (Tr.). *The Midrash on the Psalms*. 2 Vols. New Haven, CN: Yale UP, 1959.

---. *Pesikta Rabbati. Discourses for Feasts, Fasts, and Special Sabbaths*. 2 Vols. New Haven, CN: Yale UP, 1968.

Budge, E. A. W. (Ed. &. Tr.). "Discourse on Abbatôn." *Coptic Martyrdoms, etc. in the Dialect of Upper Egypt*. London: Trustees of the British Museum, 1914.

---. "Discourse on Mary Theotokos." *Miscellaneous Coptic Texts in the Dialect of Upper Egypt*. London: Oxford UP, 1915.

Burchard, C. (Tr.). "Joseph and Asenath." *The Old Testament Pseudepigrapha*. 2 Vols. J. H. Charlesworth (Ed.). Vol. 2. Garden City, NY: Doubleday, 1985. 177-247.

Butterworth, G. W. (Tr.). *Origen on First Principles*. London: SPCK, 1936.

Chadwick, H. (Ed.). *Origen: Contra Celsum*. Cambridge: Cambridge UP, 1953.

Charles, R. H. (Ed.). *The Greek Versions of the Testaments of the Twelve Patriarchs*. Oxford: Clarendon, 1908.

Charlesworth, J. H. (Ed.). *The Old Testament Pseudepigrapha*. 2 Vols. Garden City, NY: Doubleday, 1983, 1985.

Cohn, L. and P. Wendland (Eds.). *Philonis Alexandrini Opera Quae Supersunt*. 6 Vols. Berlin: De Gruyter, 1896-1915.

Colson, F. H., and G. H. Whitaker (Trs.). *Philo (Greek Texts with an English Translation)*. 10 Vols. Loeb Classical Library. Cambridge, MA: Harvard UP, 1929-62.

Duling, D. C. (Tr.). "The Testament of Solomon." *The Old Testament Pseudepigrapha*. 2 Vols. J. H. Charlesworth (Ed.). Vol. 1. Garden City, NY: Doubleday, 1983. 944-87.

Eisenman, R. and M. Wise (Eds. & Trs.). *The Dead Sea Scrolls Uncovered*. Shaftesbury, Dorset: Element, 1992.

Elliott, J. K. *The Apocryphal New Testament: A Collection of Apocryphal Christian Literature in an English Translation*. Oxford: Clarendon, 1993.

Epstein, I. (Ed.). *The Hebrew-English Edition of the Babylonian Talmud*. 24 Vols. London: Soncino, 1962-88.

Evans, E. (Ed. &. Tr.). *Q. Septimii Florentis Tertulliani De Carne Christi Liber: Tertullian's Treatise on the Incarnation*. London: SPCK, 1956.

Freedman, H. and M. Simon (Eds.). *Midrash Rabbah. Translated Into English with Notes, Glossary and Indices*. 10 Vols. London: Soncino, 1961.

García Martínez, F. *The Dead Sea Scrolls Translated: The Qumran Texts in English*. W. G. E. Watson (Tr.). Leiden: Brill, 1994.

García Martínez, F., E. J. C. Tigehelaar, and A. S. van der Woude (Eds.). *Qumran Cave 11 II (11Q2-18, 11Q20-31)*. DJD 23. Oxford: Clarendon, 1998.

Gaylord, H. E. (Tr.). "3 Baruch." *The Old Testament Pseudepigrapha.* 2 Vols. J. H. Charlesworth (Ed.). Vol. 1. Garden City, NY: Doubleday, 1983. 653-79.

Goldin, J. (Tr.). *The Fathers According to Rabbi Nathan.* New Haven, CN: Yale UP, 1955.

Grenfell, B. P. and A. S. Hunt (Eds.). *The Oxyrhynchus Papyri.* 60 Vols. London: Egypt Exploration Fund, 1898-1994.

Gruenwald, I. (Ed.). "Re'uyyot Yehezqel." *Temirin: Texts and Studies in Kabbala and Hasidim (Hebr.).* Vol. 1. I. Weinstock (Ed.). Jerusalem: Mossad Harav Kook, 1972.

Harrington, D. J. (Tr.). "Pseudo-Philo." *The Old Testament Pseudepigrapha.* 2 Vols. J. H. Charlesworth (Ed.). Vol. 2. Garden City, NY: Doubleday, 1985. 297-377.

Harvey, W. W. (Ed.). *Sancti Irenaei. Libros quinque adversus Haerese.* 2 Vols. Cambridge: Cambridge UP, 1857.

Hall, S. G. (Ed. & Tr.). *Melito of Sardis:* **On Pascha** *and Fragments.* Oxford: Clarendon Press, 1979.

Holl, K. (Ed.). *Epiphanius Werke. Ancortaus und Panarion Haer. 1-33.* GCS 25. Leipzig: Hinrichs' Buchhandlung, 1915.

Irmscher, J. (Tr.). "The Book of Elchasai." *New Testament Apocrypha.* 2 Vols. Rev. Ed. W. Schneemelcher (Ed.) R. McL. Wilson (Tr.). Vol. 2. Louisville: Westminster/John Knox, 1992. 685-90.

Isaac, E. (Tr.). "1 Enoch." *The Old Testament Pseudepigrapha.* 2 Vols. J. H. Charlesworth (Ed.). Vol. 1. Garden City, NY: Doubleday, 1983. 5-89.

James, M. R. (Ed. & Tr). *The Apocryphal New Testament.* Oxford: Clarendon, 1924.

Jellinek, A. (Ed.). *Bet Ha-Midrasch.* 6 Vols. Jerusalem: Wahrmann Books, 1967.

Kee, H. C. (Tr.). "The Testaments of the Twelve Patriarchs." *The Old Testament Pseudepigrapha.* 2 Vols. J. H. Charlesworth (Ed.). Vol. 1. Garden City: Doubleday, 1983. 775-828.

Knibb, M. A. (Ed. &. Tr.). *The Ethiopic Book of Enoch.* 2 Vols. Oxford: Clarendon, 1978.

Knibb, M. A. (Tr.). "The Ascension of Isaiah." *The Old Testament Pseudepigrapha.* 2 Vols. J. H. Charlesworth (Ed.). Vol. 2. Garden City, NY: Doubleday, 1985. 143-76.

Koetschau, P. (Ed.). *Origenes Werke. De Principiis [ΠΕΡΙ ΑΡΧΩΝ].* GCS 5. Leipzig: Hinrichs' Buchhandlung, 1913.

Kraft, R. A. and A. -E. Purintun (Eds. &. Trs). *Paraleipomena Jeremiou.* T. & T. 1. Missoula, MT: Scholars, 1972.

Lake, K. (Tr.). *Apostolic Fathers.* 2 Vols. LCL. Cambridge, MA: Harvard Univ., 1913.

Lauterbach, J. Z. (Tr.). *Mekilta De-Rabbi Ishmael.* 3 Vols. Philadelphia: Jewish Publication Society of America, 1961.

Lightfoot, J. B., (Tr.). *The Apostolic Fathers.* J. R. Harmer, (Ed.). London: Macmillan & Co., 1891.

Lohse, E. (Ed. &. Tr.). *Die Texte aus Qumran: Hebräisch und Deutsch.* Darmstadt: Wissenschaftliche Buchgesellschaft, 1964.

Marcus, R. *Philo Supplement.* 2 Vols. Loeb Classical Library. Cambridge, MA: Harvard UP, 1953.

McCown, C. C. (Ed.). *The Testament of Solomon.* UNT 9. Leipzig: Hinrichs' Buchhandlung, 1922.

Metzger, B. M. "A Magical Amulet for Curing Fever." *Historical and Literary Studies, Pagan, Jewish, and Christian.* Leiden: Brill, 1968. 104-10.

Müller, C. D. G. (Tr.). "The Ascension of Isaiah." *New Testament Apocrypha.* 2 Vols. Rev. Ed. W. Schneemelcher (Ed.) R. McL. Wilson (Tr.). Vol. 2. Louisville: Westminster/John Knox, 1992. 603-20.

Neusner, J. (Tr.). *Pesiqta DeRab Kahana. An Analytical Translation.* 2 Vols. Brown Judaic Studies 122, 123. Atlanta, GA: Scholars, 1987.

---. *Sifre to Deuteronomy. An Analytical Translation.* 2 Vols. Brown Judaic Studies 98, 101. Atlanta, GA: Scholars, 1987.

---. *The Tosefta.* 6 Vols. Hoboken, NJ: KTAV Publishing House, 1977-81.

Newsom, C. A. (Ed. &. Tr.). *Songs of the Sabbath Sacrifice: A Critical Edition.* HSS. Atlanta: Scholars, 1985.

Norelli, E. et al (Ed. & Tr.). *Ascensio Isaiae. Textus.* CCSA 7. Brepols: Turnhout, 1994.

Odeberg, H. (Ed. &. Tr.). *3 Enoch or the Hebrew Book of Enoch.* Cambridge: Cambridge UP, 1928.

Pennington, A. (Tr.). "The Apocalypse of Abraham." *The Apocryphal Old Testament*. H. F. D. Sparks (Ed.). Oxford: Clarendon, 1984. 363-391.

---. "2 Enoch." *The Apocryphal Old Testament*. H. F. D. Sparks (Ed.). Oxford: Clarendon, 1984. 321-362.

Preuschen, E. (Ed.). *Origenes Werke: Der Johanneskommentar*. GCS 10. Leipzig: Hinrichs' Buchandlung, 1903.

Priest, J. (Tr.). "The Testament of Moses." *The Old Testament Pseudepigrapha*. 2 Vols. J. H. Charlesworth (Ed.). Vol. 1. Garden City, NY: Doubleday, 1983. 919-34.

Rabin, C. (Tr.). "Jubilees." *The Apocryphal Old Testament*. H. F. D. Sparks (Ed.). Oxford: Clarendon, 1984. 1-139.

Reitzenstein, R. "Eine Frühchristliche Schrift von den Dreierlei Früchten des Christlichen Lebens." *ZNW* 15 (1914): 60-90.

Roberts, A. and J. Donaldson (Eds.). *Ante-Nicene Fathers; Writings of the Fathers Down to A.D. 325*. 10 Vols. Rev. Ed. A. C. Coxe (Rev.). Peabody, MA: Hendrickson, 1994 (Orig. pub. 1885).

Robinson, J. M. (Ed.). *The Nag Hammadi Library in English*. 3rd Ed. Leiden: Brill, 1988.

Robinson, S. E. (Tr.). "4 Baruch." *The Old Testament Pseudepigrapha*. 2 Vols. J. H. Charlesworth (Ed.). Garden City, NY: Doubleday, 1985. 413-25.

Rousseau, A. (Ed. & Tr.). *Irénée de Lyon. Démonstration de la Prédication apostolique*. SChr 406. Paris: Les Éditions de Cerf, 1995.

Rubinkiewicz, R. (Tr.). "Apocalypse of Abraham." *The Old Testament Pseudepigrapha*. 2 Vols. J. H. Charlesworth (Ed.). Vol. 1. Garden City, NY: Doubleday, 1983. 681-705.

Sanders, E. P. (Tr.). "The Testament of Abraham." *The Old Testament Pseudepigrapha*. 2 Vols. J. H. Charlesworth (Ed.). Vol. 1. Garden City, NY: Doubleday, 1983. 871-902.

Schäfer, P. (Ed.). *Synopse zur Hekhalot-Literatur*. TSAJ 2. Tübingen: Mohr (Siebeck), 1981.

Schäfer, P. (Tr.). *Übersetzung der Hekhalot-Literatur*. Vol. 2, §§ 81-334. TSAJ 17. Tübingen: Mohr (Siebeck), 1987.

---. *Übersetzung der Hekhalot-Literatur*. Vol. 3, §§ 335-597. TSAJ 22. Tübingen: Mohr (Siebeck), 1989.

---. *Übersetzung der Hekhalot-Literatur.* Vol. 4, §§598-985. TSAJ 29. Tübingen: Mohr (Siebeck), 1991.

Scheidweiler, F. and W. Schneemelcher (Trs.). "The Gospel of Bartholomew." *New Testament Apocrypha.* 2 Vols. Rev. Ed. W. Schneemelcher (Ed.) R. McL. Wilson (Tr.). Vol. 1. Louisville: Westminster/John Knox, 1991. 537-53.

Schneemelcher, W. (Ed.). *New Testament Apocrypha.* 2 Vols. Louisville: Westminster/John Knox, 1991, 1992.

Siegert, F. *Philon von Alexandria: Über die Gottesbezeichnung "wohltätig verzehrendes Feuer" (De Deo).* Tübingen: Mohr (Siebeck), 1988.

Smith, J. P. (Tr.). *St. Irenaeus. Proof of the Apostolic Preaching.* ACW 16. Westminster, ML: Newman, 1952.

Smith, J. Z. (Tr.). "The Prayer of Joseph." *The Old Testament Pseudepigrapha.* 2 Vols. J. H. Charlesworth (Ed.). Vol. 2. Garden City, NY: Doubleday, 1985. 699-714.

Stone, M. E. (Tr.). "Greek Apocalypse of Ezra." *The Old Testament Pseudepigrapha.* 2 Vols. J. H. Charlesworth (Ed.). Vol. 1. Garden City, NY: Doubleday, 1983. 561-79.

Thackeray, H. St. J., et al (Trs.). *Josephus with an English Translation.* 10 Vols. Loeb Classical Library. Cambridge, MA: Harvard UP, 1926-65.

Townsend, J. T. (Tr.). *Midrash Tanhuma: Translated into English.* Hoboken, NY: KTAV Publishing House, 1986.

Tov, E., R. A. Kraft, and P. J. Parsons (Eds.). *The Greek Minor Prophets Scroll from Nahal Hever (8HevXIIgr).* DJD 8. Oxford: Clarendon, 1990.

Turner, N. (Tr.). "The Testament of Abraham." *The Apocryphal Old Testament.* H. F. D. Sparks (Ed.). Oxford: Clarendon, 1984. 393-421.

Ulrich, E., F. M. Cross, S. W. Crawford, et al. (Eds.). *Qumran Cave 4 IX. Deuteronomy, Joshua, Judges, Kings.* DJD 14. Oxford: Clarendon, 1995.

VanderKam, J. C. (Ed. &. Tr.). *The Book of Jubilees.* CSCO 510-511. Louvain: Peeters, 1989.

Vermes, G. (Tr.). *The Complete Dead Sea Scrolls in English.* 5th Ed. London: Penguin, 1997.

Vielhauer, P. and G. Strecker (Trs.). "Jewish-Christian Gospels." *New Testament Apocrypha.* 2 Vols. Rev. Ed. W. Schneemelcher (Ed.) R. McL. Wilson (Tr.). Vol. 1. Louisville: Westminster/John Knox, 1991. 134-78.

Wells, L. S. A. (Tr.). "The Books of Adam and Eve." *The Apocrypha and Pseudepigrapha of the Old Testament*. 2 Vols. R. H. Charles (Ed.). Vol. 2. Oxford: Clarendon, 1913. 123-54.

Wessely, K. "Les Plus Anciens Monuments du Christianisme écrits sur Papyrus." *PO* 18 (1924): 341-511.

Whittaker, M., (Ed.). *Die Apostolischen Väter I: Der Hirt Des Hermas*. GCS. Berlin: Akademie-Verlag, 1956.

Wintermute, O. S. (Tr.). "Jubilees." *The Old Testament Pseudepigrapha*. 2 Vols. J. H. Charlesworth (Ed.). Vol. 2. Garden City: Doubleday, 1985. 35-142.

Zimmerman, F. (Ed. &. Tr.). *The Book of Tobit*. New York: Harper, 1958.

Secondary Literature

Abegg, M. "Who Ascended into Heaven? 4Q491, 4Q427, and the Teacher of Righteousness". *Eschatology, Messianism and the Dead Sea Scrolls*. C. A. Evans and P. W. Flint (Eds.). Grand Rapids, MI: Eerdmans, 1997. 61-73.

Acerbi, A. *L'Ascensione di Isaia. Cristologia e profetismo in Siria nei primi decenni del II secolo*. Milan: Vita e Pensiero, 1989. 277-82.

Alexander, P. S. "The Historical Setting of the Hebrew Book of Enoch." *JJS* 28 (1977) 162-67.

Arnold, C. E. *The Colossian Syncretism: The Interface Between Christianity and Folk Belief at Colossae*. WUNT 77. Tübingen: Mohr (Siebeck), 1995.

---. "Mediator Figures in Asia Minor: Epigraphic Evidence." Paper Presented at the Consultation on Jewish and Christian Mediator Figures in Greco-Roman Antiquity, SBL Meeting 1992. 29pp.

Aschim, A. "Melchizedek the Liberator. An Early Interpretation of Genesis 14?" *Society of Biblical Literature: 1996 Seminar Papers*. Atlanta: Scholars, 1996. 243-258.

Ashton, J. "Bridging Ambiguities." *Studying John*. Oxford: Clarendon, 1994. 71-89.

---. *Understanding the Fourth Gospel*. Oxford: Clarendon, 1991.

Attridge, H. W. *The Epistle to the Hebrews: A Commentary on the Epistle to the Hebrews*. Hermeneia. Philadelphia: Fortress, 1989.

Aus, R. D. "God's Plan and God's Power: Isaiah 66 and the Restraining Factors of 2 Thess 2:6-7." *JBL* 96 (1977) 537-53.

Bakker, A. "Christ an Angel? A Study of Early Christian Docetism." *ZNW* 32 (1933) 255-65.

Bammel, E. "Christian Origins in Jewish Tradition." *Judaica: Kleine Schriften I.* WUNT 37. Tübingen: Mohr (Siebeck), 1988. 220-38.

Barbel, J. *Christos Angelos. Die Anschauung von Christus als Bote und Engel in der gelehrten und volkstümlichen Literatur des christlichen Altertums.* Bonn: Hanstein Verlagsbuchhandlung, 1941.

Barker, M. *The Great Angel: A Study of Israel's Second God.* London: SPCK, 1992.

Barnard, L. W. *Justin Martyr: His Life and Thought.* Cambridge: Cambridge UP, 1967.

Barr, J. "The Question of Religious Influence: The Case of Zoroastrianism, Judaism and Christianity." *JAAR* 53 (1985) 201-35.

Barrett, C. K. *The Acts of the Apostles.* 2 Vols. ICC. Edinburgh: T. & T. Clark, 1994.

---. *The Gospel According to John.* 2nd Ed. London: SPCK, 1978.

Bauckham, R. "The Apocalypse as a Christian War Scroll." *The Climax of Prophecy: Studies in the Book of Revelation.* Edinburgh: T. & T. Clark, 1993. 210-37.

---. "The Conversion of the Nations." *The Climax of Prophecy: Studies in the Book of Revelation.* Edinburgh: T. & T. Clark, 1993. 238-337.

---. "Gospel Traditions in the 'Ascension of Isaiah'" *Unpublished Paper.* 81pp.

---. "Jesus, Worship of." *Anchor Bible Dictionary.* 6 Vols. David Noel Freedman (Ed.). Vol. 3. Garden City, NY: Doubleday, 1992. 813-19.

---. *Jude, 2 Peter.* WBC 50. Waco, TX: Word Books, 1983.

---. *Jude and the Relatives of Jesus in the Early Church.* Edinburgh: T. & T. Clark, 1990.

---. "The Lion, the Lamb and the Dragon." *The Climax of Prophecy: Studies in the Book of Revelation.* Edinburgh: T. & T. Clark, 1993. 174-98.

---. "Structure and Composition." *The Climax of Prophecy: Studies in the Book of Revelation.* Edinburgh: T. & T. Clark, 1993. 1-37.

---. *The Theology of the Book of Revelation.* New Testament Theology. Cambridge: Cambridge UP, 1993.

---. "The Worship of Jesus." *The Climax of Prophecy: Studies in the Book of Revelation.* Edinburgh: T & T Clark, 1993. 118-49.

Beasley-Murray, G. R. "The Interpretation of Daniel 7." *CBQ* 45 (1983) 44-58.

---. *Revelation*. NCB. Grand Rapids, MI: Eerdmans, 1978.

Beatrice, B. F. "De Centesima, Sexagesima, Tricesima." *Encyclopedia of the Early Church*. 2 Vols. A. di Berardino (Ed.). A. Walford (Tr.). Vol. 1. Cambridge: Clarke & Co., 1992. 223.

Beckwith, I. T. *The Apocalypse of John*. London: Macmillan, 1919.

Best, E. *A Commentary on the First and Second Epistles to the Thessalonians*. BNTC. London: A. & C. Black, 1972.

Betz, H. D. *Galatians: A Commentary on Paul's Letter to the Churches in Galatia*. Hermeneia. Philadelphia: Fortress, 1979.

Betz, O. *Der Paraklet*. AGJU 2. Leiden: Brill, 1963.

Bietenhard, H. "ἄγγελος." *The New International Dictionary of New Testament Theology*. C. Brown (Ed.). Exeter: Paternoster, 1975. 101-03.

Bigg, C. *The Epistles of St. Peter and St. Jude*. ICC. Edinburgh: T. & T. Clark, 1902.

Black, M. *The Book of Enoch or 1 Enoch: A New English Edition with Commentary and Textual Notes*. SVTP 7. Leiden: Brill, 1985.

Boccaccini, G. *Beyond the Essene Hypothesis: The Partying of the Ways between Qumran and Enochic Judaism*. Grand Rapids, MI: Eerdmans, 1998.

Bockmuehl, M. N. A. "Recent Discoveries in the Dead Sea Scrolls." *Crux* 28 (1992) 14-21.

---. *Revelation and Mystery in Ancient Judaism and Pauline Christianity*. WUNT 2.36. Tübingen: Mohr (Siebeck), 1990.

---. "A 'Slain Messiah' in 4Q Serekh Milhamah (4Q285)?" *Tyndale Bulletin* 43 (1992) 155-69.

---. *This Jesus: Martyr, Lord, Messiah*. Edinburgh: T & T Clark, 1994.

---. "'The Trumpet Shall Sound': Shofar Symbolism and Its Reception in Early Christianity." *Templum Amicitiae. Essays on the Second Temple Presented to Ernst Bammel*. W. Horbury (Ed.). JSNTSup 48. Sheffield: JSOT, 1991. 199-225.

Borgen, P. "Philo of Alexandria." *Jewish Writings of the Second Temple Period: Apocrypha, Pseudepigrapha, Qumran Sectarian Writings, Philo, Josephus*. M. E. Stone (Ed.). Philadelphia: Fortress, 1984.

---. "Philo, Survey of Research Since World War II." *Aufstieg und Niedergang der römischen Welt II.21.1*. Berlin: De Gruyter, 1984.

Braverman, J. *Jerome's Commentary on Daniel: A Study of Comparative Jewish and Christian Interpretations of the Hebrew Bible*. CBQMS 7. Washington: The Catholic Biblical Association of America, 1978.

Brown, R. E. *The Gospel According to John*. 2 Vols. AB 29-29A. Garden City, NY: Doubleday, 1966, 1970.

---. "The Messianism of Qumran." *CBQ* 19 (1957) 53-82.

---. "The Paraclete in the Fourth Gospel." *NTS* 13 (1966-67) 113-32.

---. "The Teacher of Righteousness and the Messiah(s)." *The Scrolls and Christianity*. M. Black (Ed.). London: SPCK, 1969.

Brox, N. *Der Hirt des Hermas*. Göttingen: Vandenhoeck & Ruprecht, 1991.

Bruce, F. F. *The Book of the Acts*. Rev. Ed. NICNT. Grand Rapids, MI: Eerdmans Publishing, 1988.

---. *The Epistle of Paul to the Galatians*. NIGTC. Exeter: Paternoster, 1982.

---. *The Epistle to the Hebrews*. NICNT. Grand Rapids, MI: Eerdmans, 1964.

Bühner, J.-A. *Der Gesandte und sein Weg im 4.Evangelium. Die kultur- und religionsgeschichtlichen Grundlagen der johanneischen Sendungs-christologie sowie ihre traditionsgeschichtliche Entwicklung*. WUNT 2.2. Tübingen: Mohr (Siebeck), 1977.

Bultmann, R. *The Gospel of John. A Commentary*. G. R. Beasley-Murray, R. W. N. Hoare and J. K. Riches (Trs.). Philadelphia: Westminster, 1971.

Burge, G. M. *The Anointed Community: The Holy Spirit in the Johannine Tradition*. Grand Rapids, MI: Eerdmans, 1987.

Burkitt, F. C. *Jewish and Christian Apocalypses*. London: Oxford UP, 1914.

Burton, E. D. W. *The Epistle to the Galations*. ICC. Edinburgh: T. & T. Clark, 1920.

Caird, G. B. *A Commentary on the Revelation of St. John the Divine*. HNTC. New York: Harper & Row, 1966.

---. "On Deciphering the Book of Revelation, I. Heaven and Earth." *ET* 74 (1962) 13-15.

Callan, T. "The Exegetical Background of Gal. 3:19b." *JBL* 99 (1980) 549-67.

Carr, W. *Angels and Principalities: The Background, Meaning and Development of the Pauline Phrase HAI ARCHAI KAI HAI EXOUSIAI*. SNTSMS 42. Cambridge: Cambridge UP, 1981.

Carrell, P. R. *Jesus and the Angels: Angelology and the Christology of the Apocalypse of John*. SNTSMS 95. Cambridge: Cambridge UP, 1997.

Chadwick, H. *Early Christian Thought and the Classical Tradition*. Oxford: Clarendon, 1966.

---. "Justin Martyr's Defence of Christianity." *BJRL* 47 (1964-65) 275-97.

---. "The New Edition of Hermas." *JTS* n.s. 8 (1957) 274-80.

Charles, R. H. *Ascension of Isaiah*. London: A. & C. Black, 1900.

---. *The Assumption of Moses*. London: A. & C. Black, 1897.

---. *The Book of Enoch or 1 Enoch*. 3rd Ed. Oxford: Clarendon, 1912.

---. *The Book of Jubilees or the Little Genesis*. London: A. & C. Black, 1902.

---. *A Critical and Exegetical Commentary on the Book of Daniel*. Oxford: Clarendon, 1929.

---. *The Revelation of John*. ICC. Edinburgh: T. & T. Clark, 1920.

---. *The Testaments of the Twelve Patriarchs*. London: A. & C. Black, 1908.

Charles, R. H. and W. R. Morfill. *The Book of the Secrets of Enoch*. Oxford: Clarendon, 1896.

Charlesworth, J. H., et al (Eds.). *Graphic Concordance to the Dead Sea Scrolls*. Tübingen: Mohr (Siebeck), 1991.

Chester, A. "Jewish Messianic Expectations and Mediatorial Figures and Pauline Christology." *Paulus und das antike Judentum*. M. Hengel and U. Heckel (Eds.). WUNT 58. Tübingen: Mohr (Siebeck), 1991. 17-89.

Cohen, M. S. *The Shi'ur Qomah: Liturgy and Theurgy in Pre-Kabbalistic Jewish Mysticism*. Washington: UP of America, 1983.

---. *The Shi'ur Qomah: Texts and Recensions*. TSAJ 9. Tübingen: Mohr (Siebeck), 1985.

Collins, J. J. *The Apocalyptic Imagination: An Introduction to the Jewish Matrix of Christianity*. New York: Crossroad, 1984.

---. *The Apocalyptic Vision of the Book of Daniel*. HSM 16. Missoula, MT: Scholars, 1977.

---. *Apocalypticism and the Dead Sea Scrolls*. London: Routledge, 1997.

---. *Daniel*. Hermeneia. Minneapolis: Fortress, 1993.

---. "Introduction: Towards the Morphology of a Genre." *Semeia* 14: *Apocalypse. The Morphology of a Genre* (1979) 1-20.

---. "The Jewish Apocalypses." *Semeia* 14: *Apocalypse. The Morphology of a Genra* (1979) 21-59.

---. "Messianism in the Maccabean Period." *Judaisms and Their Messiahs at the Turn of the Christian Era*. J. Neusner, W. S. Green and E. Frerichs (Eds.). Cambridge: Cambridge UP, 1987.

---. "The Son of Man and the Saints of the Most High in the Book of Daniel." *JBL* 93 (1974) 50-66.

---. "The Son of Man in First-Century Judaism." *NTS* 38 (1992) 448-66.

Collins, J. J. and D. Dimant. "A Thrice-Told Hymn: A Response to Eileen Schuller". *JQR* 85 (1994) 151-155.

Conzelmann, H. *Acts of the Apostles. A Commentary*. A. T. Kraabel, J. Limburg, D. H. Juel. Hermeneia. Philadelphia: Fortress, 1987.

Craigie, P. C. *The Book of Deuteronomy*. NICOT. London: Hodder and Stoughton, 1976.

Cross, F. M. *The Ancient Library of Qumran and Modern Biblical Studies*. 2nd Ed. Grand Rapids, MI: Eerdmans, 1980.

Crouzel, H. *Origen. The Life and Thought of the First Great Theologian*. A. S. Worrall (Tr.). San Francisco: Harper & Row, 1989.

Daniélou, J. *The Origins of Latin Christianity*. Vol. 3. *A History of Early Christian Doctrine*. D. Smith & J. A. Baker (Trs.). London: Darton, Longman & Todd, 1977.

---. *The Theology of Jewish Christianity*. Vol. 1. *A History of Early Christian Doctrine*. D. Smith & J. A. Baker (Trs.). London: Darton, Longman & Todd, 1964.

Daube, D. "On Acts 23: Sadducees and Angels." *JBL* 109 (1990) 493-97.

Davila, J. R. "Melchizedek, Michael, and War in Heaven." *Society of Biblical Literature: 1996 Seminar Papers*. Atlanta: Scholars, 1996. 259-272.

Davidson, M. J. *Angels at Qumran: A Comparative Study of 1 Enoch 1-36, 72-108 and Sectarian Writings from Qumran*. Sheffield: JSOT, 1992.

Davies, P. R. *The Damascus Covenant: An Interpretation of the "Damascus Document"*. Sheffield: JSOT, 1982.

Davis, P. G. "Divine Agents, Mediators, and New Testament Christology." *JTS* n.s. 45 (1994) 478-503.

de Jonge, M. "The Transmission of the Testaments of the Twelve Patriarchs by Christians." *VC* 47 (1993) 1-28.

de Jonge, M. and A. S. van der Woude. "11Q Melchizedek and the New Testament." *NTS* 12 (1965-66) 301-26.

de Lacey, D. R. "'One Lord' in Pauline Christology." *Christ the Lord: Studies in Christology Presented to Donald Guthrie*. H. H. Rowdon (Ed.). Leicester: Inter-Varsity, 1982.

de Lange, N. *Origen and the Jews. Studies in Jewish-Christian Relations in Third-century Palestine*. Cambridge: Cambridge UP, 1976.

Delcor, M. "Melchizedek from Genesis to the Qumran Texts and the Epistle to the Hebrews." *JSJ* 2 (1971) 115-35.

---. *Le Testament d'Abraham*. SVTP 2. Leiden: Brill, 1973.

Dibelius, M. *Der Hirt des Hermas*. Tübingen: Mohr (Siebeck), 1923.

---. *An die Thessalonicher I-II. An die Philipper*. HNT 11. Tübingen: Mohr (Siebeck), 1937.

Dillon, J. "Philo's Doctrine of Angels." *Two Treatises of Philo of Alexandria: A Commentary on De Gigantibus and Quod Deus Sit Immutabilis*. D. Winston and J. Dillon (Eds.). Chico, CA: Scholars, 1983.

Dimant, D. "Qumran Sectarian Literature." *Jewish Writings of the Second Temple Period*. M. E. Stone (ed.). Philadelphia: Fortress, 1984.

Dix, G. "The Origins of the Epiclesis. Part II." *Theology* 28 (1934) 187-202.

Dix, G. H. "The Influence of Babylonian Ideas on Jewish Messianism." *JTS* n.s. 26 (1925) 241-56.

---. "The Seven Archangels and the Seven Spirits: A Study in the Origin, Development, and Messianic Associations of the Two Themes." *JTS* 233-250 (1927).

Dodd, C. H. *The Interpretation of the Fourth Gospel*. Cambridge: Cambridge UP, 1953.

Driver, S. R. *Deuteronomy*. 3rd Ed. ICC. Edinburgh: T. & T. Clark, 1902.

Drummond, J. *Philo Judaeus or the Jewish Alexandrian Philosophy in Its Development and Completion*. London: Williams & Norgate, 1888.

Dunn, J. D. G. *Christology in the Making. A New Testament Inquiry Into the Origins of the Doctrine of the Incarnation.* Philadelphia: Westminster, 1980.

---. *The Epistle to the Galatians.* BNTC. London: A. & C. Black, 1993.

---. *The Partings of the Ways Between Christianity and Judaism and Their Significance for the Character of Christianity.* London: SCM, 1991.

Ego, B. "Der Diener im Palast des himmlischen Königs. Zur Interpretation einer priesterlichen Tradition im rabbinischen Judentum." *Königsherrschaft Gottes und himmlischer Kult in Juden, Urchristentum, und in der hellenistischen Welt.* M. Hengel and A. M. Schwemer (Eds.). Tübingen: Mohr (Siebeck), 1991. 361-84.

Eichrodt, W. *Theology of the Old Testament.* 2 Vols. J. A. Baker (Tr.). London: SCM, 1967.

Elior, R. "Mysticism, Magic, and Angelology. The Perception of Angels in Hekhalot Literature." *JSQ* 1 (1993) 3-53.

Ellis, E. E. "Χριστός in 1 Corinthians 10.4, 9." *From Jesus to John: Essays on Jesus and New Testament Christology in Honour of Marinus de Jonge.* M. C. De Boer (Ed.). JSNTSup 84. Sheffield: JSOT, 1993. 168-73.

Farrer, A. *The Revelation of St. John the Divine.* Oxford: Clarendon, 1964.

Fitzmyer, J. A. "Further Light on Melchizedek from Qumran Cave 11." *JBL* 86 (1967) 25-41.

---. "Implications of the New Enoch Literature from Qumran." *TS* 38 (1977) 332-45.

---. "The Semitic Background of the New Testament *Kyrios*-Title." *A Wandering Aramean: Collected Aramaic Essays.* Missoula, MT: Scholars, 1979. 115-42.

Fletcher-Louis, C. H. T. *Luke-Acts: Angels, Christology and Soteriology.* WUNT 2.94. Tübingen: Mohr (Siebeck), 1997.

Flusser, D. "The Hubris of the Antichrist in a Fragment from Qumran." *Judaism and the Origins of Christianity.* Jerusalem: Magnes, 1988. 207-13.

Fossum, J. "Jewish-Christian Christology and Jewish Mysticism." *VC* 37 (1983) 260-87.

---. "Kyrios Jesus as the Angel of the Lord in Jude 5-7." *NTS* 33 (1987) 226-43.

---. *The Name of God and the Angel of the Lord. Samaritan and Jewish Conceptions of Intermediation and the Origin of Gnosticism.* WUNT 36. Tübingen: Mohr (Siebeck), 1985.

Frame, J. E. *The Epistles of St. Paul to the Thessalonians.* ICC. Edinburgh: T. & T. Clark, 1912.

Francis, F. O. "Humility and Angelic Worship in Col 2:18." *Conflict at Colossae: A Problem in the Interpretation of Early Christianity Illustrated by Selected Modern Studies*. Rev. Ed. F. O. Francis and Wayne A. Meeks (Eds. and Trs.). Missoula, MT: Scholars, 1974.

Freedman, D. N., and B. E. Willoughby. "מַלְאָךְ." *Theologisches Wörterbuch zum Alten Testament*. H. Ringgren, G. J. Botterweck, H.-J. Fabry (Eds.). Vol. 4. Stuttgart, Verlag W. Kohlhammer. 887-904.

Frost, S. B. *Old Testament Apocalyptic: Its Origins and Growth*. London: Epworth, 1952.

García Martínez, F. "The Eschatological Figure of 4Q246." *Qumran and Apocalyptic: Studies on the Aramaic Texts from Qumran*. STDJ 9. Leiden: Brill, 1992. 162-79.

---. "The Origins of the Essene Movement and of the Qumran Sect." *The People of the Dead Sea Scrolls: Their Writings, Beliefs and Practices*. F. García Martínez and J. T. Barrera (Eds.). W. G. E. Watson (Tr). Leiden: Brill, 1995. 77-96.

---. "Qumran Origins and Early History: A Gröningen Hypothesis". *Folia Orientalia* 25 (1988) 113-136.

Gieschen, C. "The Angel of the Prophetic Spirit: Interpreting the Revelatory Experiences of the *Shepherd of Hermas* in Light of *Mandate* XI." *Society of Biblical Literature: 1994 Seminar Papers*. E. H. Lovering (Ed.). Atlanta: Scholars, 1994. 790-803.

---. "The Apostle as God's Angel, Namely Christ Jesus: An Exegesis of Galatians 4.14b." Unpublished Seminar Paper: University of Michigan, 1993. 19pp.

Gilbert, M. "The Wisdom of Solomon." *Jewish Writings of the Second Temple Period: Apocrypha, Pseudepigrapha, Qumran Sectarian Writings, Philo, Josephus*. M. E. Stone (Ed.). Philadelphia: Fortress, 1984.

Ginzberg, L. *The Legends of the Jews*. 7 Vols. H. Szold (Tr.). Philadelphia: Jewish Publication Society, 1909-1938.

Goldin, J. "Not by Means of an Angel and Not by Means of a Messenger." *Religions in Antiquity. Essays in Memory of Erwin Ramsdell Goodenough*. J. Neusner (Ed.). Leiden: Brill, 1968.

Goldingay, J. E. *Daniel*. WBC 30. Milton Keynes, England: Word Books, 1987.

Goodenough, E. R. *By Light, Light: The Mystic Gospel of Hellenistic Judaism*. New Haven: Yale UP, 1935.

---. *The Theology of Justin Martyr*. Jena: Verlag Frommannsche, 1923.

Green, M. *The Second Epistle General of Peter and the General Epistle of Jude.* TNTC. London: Tyndale, 1968.

Grözinger, K. -E. "Die Namen Gottes und der Himmlischen Mächte--Ihre Funktion und Bedeutung in der Hekhalot-Literatur." *Frankfurter Judaistische Beiträge* 13 (1985) 23-41.

Gruenwald, I. *Apocalyptic and Merkavah Mysticism.* AGAJU 14. Leiden: Brill, 1980.

Gundry, R. H. "Angelomorphic Christology in the Book of Revelation." *Society of Biblical Literature 1994 Seminar Papers.* E. H. Lovering (Ed.). Atlanta: Scholars, 1994. 662-78.

Gunkel, H. *Schöpfung und Chaos in Urzeit und Endzeit.* Göttingen: Vandenhoeck und Ruprecht, 1895.

Haenchen, E. *The Acts of the Apostles: A Commentary.* R. McL. Wilson et. al. (Trs.). Philadelphia: Westminster, 1971.

Hall, R. G. "The *Ascension of Isaiah*: Community, Situation, Date, and Place in Early Christianity." *JBL* 109 (1990) 289-306.

---. "Living Creatures in the midst of the Throne: Another Look at Revelation 4.6." *NTS* 36 (1990) 609-13.

Halperin, D. *The Faces of the Chariot. Jewish Responses to Ezekiel's Vision.* TSAJ 16. Tübingen: Mohr (Siebeck), 1988.

Hannah, D. D. "The Angelic Restrainer of 2 Thessalonians 2.6-7." *Calling Time: Religion and Change at the Turn of the Millennium.* M. Percy (Ed.). Sheffield: Sheffield Academic Press, Forthcoming 1999.

---. "The Ascension of Isaiah and Docetic Christology." Forthcoming *VC* April (1999).

---. "Isaiah's Vision in the Ascension of Isaiah and the Early Church." Forthcoming *JTS* April (1999).

Hanson, A. T. *Jesus Christ in the Old Testament.* London: SPCK, 1965.

Hanson, R. P. C. *Allegory and Event: A Study of the Sources and Significance of Origen's Interpretation of Scripture.* London: SCM, 1959.

Harkavy, A. A. "Abu Yusuf Ya'qub al-Qirqisani on the Jewish Sects" *Ya'qub Al-Qirqisani on Jewish-Sects and Christianity.* B. Chiesa and W. Lockwood (Eds. & Trs.). Judentum und Umwelt 10. Frankfurt: Verlag Peter Lang, 1984.

Harlow, D. C. *The Greek Apocalypse of Baruch (3 Baruch) in Hellenistic Judaism and Early Christianity.* SVTP 12. Leiden: Brill, 1996.

Harnack, A. *History of Dogma*. 7 Vols. 2nd Ed. N. Buchanan (Tr.). London: William & Northgate, 1897-99.

Hartman, L. F. and A. A. DiLella. *The Book of Daniel*. AB 23. Garden City, NY: Doubleday, 1978.

Hawthorne, G. F. *Philippians*. WBC 43. Waco, TX: Word Books, 1983.

Heidt, W. *Angelology of the Old Testament: A Study in Biblical Theology*. Washington: Catholic University of America Press, 1949.

Hengel, M. *Judaism and Hellenism. Studies in Their Encounter in Palestine During the Early Hellenistic Period*. J. Bowden (Tr.). Philadelphia: Fortress, 1974.

---. "The Son of God." *The Cross of the Son of God*. J. Bowden (Tr.). London: SCM, 1976. 1-90.

Hirth, V. *Gottes Boten im Alten Testament. Die alttestamentliche Mal'ak-Vorstellung unter besonderer Berücksichtigung des Mal'ak-Jahwe-Problems*. ThA 32. Berlin: Evangelische Verlagsanstalt, 1975.

Holland, G. S. *The Tradition That You Received from Us: 2 Thessalonians in the Pauline Tradition*. HUT 24. Tübingen: Mohr (Siebeck), 1988.

Hollander, H. W. and M. de Jonge. *The Testaments of the Twelve Patriarchs: A Commentary*. SVTP 8. Leiden: Brill, 1975.

Holm-Nielsen, S. *Hodayot: Psalms from Qumran*. ATDan 2. Aarhus: Universitetsforlaget, 1960.

Holtz, T. *Die Christologie der Apocalypse des Johannes*. Berlin: Akademie Verlag, 1962.

Hooker, M. D. *The Son of Man in Mark*. London: SPCK, 1967.

Horbury, W. "The Messianic Associations of 'The Son of Man'" *JTS* 36 (1985) 34-55.

Horton, F. L. *The Melchizedek Tradition: A Critical Examination of the Sources to the Fifth Century A.D. and in the Epistle to the Hebrews*. SNTSMS 30. Cambridge: Cambridge UP, 1976.

Hurtado, L. W. *One God, One Lord. Early Christian Devotion and Ancient Jewish Monotheism*. London: SCM, 1988.

Isaacs, M. E. *Sacred Space. An Approach to the Theology of the Epistle to the Hebrews*. JSNTSup 73. Sheffield: JSOT, 1992.

Jeremias, G. *Der Lehrer der Gerechtigkeit*. Göttingen: Vandenhoeck & Ruprecht, 1963.

Johnston, G. *The Spirit-Paraclete in the Gospel of John.* SNTSMS 12. Cambridge: Cambridge UP, 1970.

Jones, F. S. "The Pseudo-Clementines: A History of Research." *The Second Century* 2 (1982) 1-33, 63-96.

Kasher, R. "Angelology and the Supernal Worlds in the Aramaic Targums to the Prophets." *JSJ* 27 (1996) 168-191.

Kelly, J. N. D. *A Commentary on the Epistles of Peter and Jude.* HNTC. San Francisco: Harper & Row, 1969.

---. *Early Christian Doctrines.* 2nd Ed. New York: Harper & Row, 1960.

Kiddle, M. and M. K. Ross. *The Revelation of St. John.* MNTC. London: Hodder and Stoughton, 1940.

Kim, Seyoon. *The 'Son of Man' as the Son of God.* WUNT 30. Tübingen: Mohr (Siebeck), 1983.

Kittel, G. "δόξα." *Theological Dictionary of the New Testament.* 10 Vols. G. Bromiley (Tr.). G. Kittel (Ed.). Vol. 2. Grand Rapids, MI: Eerdmans, 1964. 232-53.

Klijn, A. F. J., and G. J. Reinink. *Patristic Evidence for Jewish-Christian Sects.* NovTSup 36. Leiden: Brill, 1973.

Knibb, M. A. "The Date of the Parables of Enoch: A Critical Review." *NTS* 25 (1979) 345-59.

---. *The Qumran Community.* Cambridge: Cambridge UP, 1987.

Knight, J. *Disciples of the Beloved One: The Christology, Social Setting and Theological Context of the Ascension of Isaiah.* JSPS 18. Sheffield: Sheffield Academic Press, 1996.

Kobelski, P. J. *Melchizedek and Melchiresa'* CBQMS 10. Washington: The Catholic Biblical Association of America, 1981.

Koch, H. "Die ps.-cyprianische Schrift De Centesima, Sexagesima, Tricesima in ihrer Abhängigkeit von Cyprian." *ZNW* 1932 (1932) 248-72.

Kraft, H. *Die Offenbarung Des Johannes.* HNT 16a. Tübingen: Mohr (Siebeck), 1974.

Kretschmar, G. *Studien zur Frühchristlichen Trinitätstheologie.* BHT 21. Tübingen: Mohr (Siebeck), 1956.

Kuhn, H. B. "The Angelology of the Non-Canonical Jewish Apocalypses." *JBL* 67 (1947) 217-32.

Lacocque, A. *The Book of Daniel*. D. Pellauer (Trs.). Atlanta: John Knox, 1979.

Lake, K., and H. J. Cadbury. *The Acts of the Apostles: Translation and Commentary*. Vol. 4 of *The Beginnings of Christianity. Part I: The Acts of the Apostles*. F. J. F. Jackson and K. Lake (Eds.). 5 Vols. London: Macmillan, 1933.

Lane, W. L. *Hebrews*. 2 Vols. WBC 47. Dallas: Word Books, 1991.

Lanne, E. "Cherubim et Seraphim. Essai d'interprétation du chapitre 10 de la Démonstration de saint Irénée." *RSR* 43 (1955) 524-35.

Larson, E. "4Q470 and the Angelic Rehabilitation of King Zedekiah." *DSD* 1 (1994) 210-28.

Laubscher, F. du Toit. "God's Angel of Truth and Melchizedek: A Note on 11QMelch 13b." *JSJ* 3 (1972) 46-51.

Leaney, A. R. C. *The Rule of Qumran and Its Meaning: Introduction, Translation and Meaning*. NTL. London: SCM, 1966.

Leclerq, H. "Anges." *Dictionnaire D'Archéologie Chrétienne et de Liturgie*. 15 Vols. R. P. F. Cabrol, et al (Eds.). Vol. I.2. Paris: Letouzey et Ané, 1907-53. 2080-2161.

Lieberman, S. "Metatron, the Meaning of His Name and His Functions." I. Gruenwald. *Apocalyptic and Merkavah Mysticism*. AGAJU 14. Leiden: Brill, 1980. 235-41.

Lightfoot, J. B. *Saint Paul's Epistles to the Colossians and to Philemon*. 3rd Ed. London: Macmillan, 1879.

---. *Saint Paul's Epistle to the Philippians*. London: Macmillan, 1879.

Lindars, B. *The Theology of the Letter to the Hebrews*. New Testament Theology. Cambridge: Cambridge UP, 1991.

Loewenstamm, S. E. "The Death of Moses." *Studies on the Testament of Abraham*. G. W. E. Nickelsburg (Ed.). Missoula, MT: Scholars, 1976. 185-217.

Lohmeyer, E. *Die Offenbarung des Johannes*. HNT 16. Tübingen: Mohr (Siebeck), 1953.

Lohse, E. *Colossians and Philemon*. Hermeneia. Philadelphia: Fortress, 1971.

Longenecker, R. N. *The Christology of Early Jewish Christianity*. London: SCM, 1970.

---. "The Melchizedek Argument of Hebrews: A Study in the Development and Circumstantial Expression of New Testament Thought." *Unity and Diversity in New Testament Theology: Essays in Honor of George E. Ladd*. R. A. Guelich (Ed.). Grand Rapids, MI: Eerdmans, 1978.

---. "Some Distinctive Early Christological Motifs." *NTS* 14 (1967-68) 526-45.

Lueken, W. *Michael. Eine Darstellung und Vergleichung der jüdischen und der morgenländisch-christlichen Tradition vom Erzengel Michael*. Göttingen: Vandenhoeck & Ruprecht, 1898.

Lust, J. "Daniel 7,13 and the Septuagint." *ETL* 54 (1978) 62-69.

Luttikhuizen, G. P. *The Revelation of Elchasai*. TSAJ 8. Tübingen: Mohr (Siebeck), 1985.

Mach, M. *Entwicklungsstadien des jüdischen Engelglaubens in vorrabbinischer Zeit*. TSAJ 34. Tübingen: Mohr (Siebeck), 1992.

Manson, W. *The Epistle to the Hebrews. An Historical and Theological Reconsideration*. Baird Lectures. London: Hodder & Stoughton, 1951.

Marshall, I. H. *The Acts of the Apostles*. TNTC. Leicester: Inter-Varsity, 1980.

Martin, R. P. *Carmen Christi: Philippians ii.5-11 in Recent Interpretation and in the Setting of Early Christian Worship*. 2nd Ed. Cambridge: Cambridge UP, 1983.

---. *Philippians*. NCB. Grand Rapids, MI: Eerdmans, 1976.

Menken, M. J. J. *2 Thessalonians*. New Testament Readings. London: Routledge, 1994.

Metzger, B. M. *A Textual Commentary on the Greek New Testament*. Stuttgart: United Bible Societies, 1971.

Meyers, C. L. and E. M. Meyers. *Haggai, Zechariah 1-8*. AB 25B. Garden City, NY: Doubleday, 1987.

Michaelis, W. *Zur Engelchristologie im Urchristentum: Abbau der Konstruktion Martin Werners*. Basel: Heinrich Majer, 1942.

Michel, O. *Der Brief an die Hebräer*. MeyerK. Göttingen: Vandenhoeck & Ruprecht, 1966.

Milik, J. T. "4Q Visions de 'Amram et une citation d'Origène." *RB* 79 (1972) 77-97.

---. *The Books of Enoch: Aramaic Fragments of Qumrân Cave 4*. Oxford: Clarendon, 1976.

---. "Milkî-sedeq et Milkî-reša' dans les anciens écrits juifs et chrétiens." *JJS* 23 (1974) 95-144.

---. *Ten Years of Discovery in the Wilderness of Judaea*. J. Strugnell (Tr.). London: SCM, 1959.

Miller, W. T. *Mysterious Encounters at Mamre and Jabbok*. Brown Judaic Studies 50. Chico, CA: Scholars, 1984.

Minns, D. *Irenaeus*. Outstanding Christian Thinkers Series. London: Geoffrey Chapman, 1994.

Mitchell, H. G., J. M. P. Smith and J. A. Bewer. *Haggai, Zechariah, Malachi and Jonah*. ICC. Edinburgh: T. & T. Clark, 1912.

Montefiore, H. *The Epistle to the Hebrews*. HNTC. San Francisco: Harper & Row, 1964.

Montgomery, J. A. *The Book of Daniel*. ICC. Edinburgh: T. & T. Clark, 1927.

Morenz, L. D. "Der Seraph in der hebräischen Bibel und in Altägypten." *Or* 66 (1997) 365-386.

Morray-Jones, C. R. A. "Transformational Mysticism in the Apocalyptic-Merkabah Tradition." *JJS* 43 (1992) 1-31.

Moule, C. F. D. *An Idiom-Book of New Testament Greek*. Cambridge: Cambridge UP, 1959.

Mounce, R. H. *The Book of Revelation*. NICNT. Grand Rapids, MI: Eerdmans, 1977.

Mowinckel, S. *He That Cometh*. Nashville: Abingdon, 1954.

Moxnes, H. "God and His Angel in the Shepherd of Hermas." *ST* 28 (1974) 49-56.

Müller, P. *Anfänge der Paulusschule. Dargestellt am zweiten Thessalonicherbrief und am Kolosserbrief*. ATANT. Zürich: Theologischer Verlag, 1988.

Murphy-O'Conner, J. "An Essene Missionary Document? CD II, 14-VI,1." *RB* 77 (1970) 210-229.

---. "A Literary Analysis of Damascus Document VI,2-VIII,3." *RB* 78 (1971) 210-232.

---. "The Original Text of CD 7:9-8:2 = 19:5-14." *HTR* 64 (1971) 376-386.

---. "The Translation of Damascus Document VI,11-14." *RQ* 7 (1971) 553-556.

---. "The Critique of the Princes of Judah (CD VIII,3-19)." *RB* 79 (1972) 200-216.

---. "The Essenes and Their History." *RB* 81 (1974) 215-244.

---. "The Damascus Document Re-visited." *RB* 92 (1985) 223-46.

Neusner, J. *Aphrahat and Judaism: The Christian-Jewish Argument in Fourth Century Iran*. SPB 19. Leiden: Brill, 1971.

Newman, C. C. *Paul's Glory-Christology: Tradition and Rhetoric*. NTSupp 69. Leiden: Brill, 1992.

Newsom, C. A. "Angels: Old Testament." *Anchor Bible Dictionary*. 6 Vols. D. N. Freedman (Ed.). Vol. 1. New York: Doubleday, 1994. 248-53.

Neyrey, J. H. *2 Peter, Jude*. AB 37C. New York: Doubleday, 1993.

Nickelsburg, G. W. E. *Jewish Literature Between the Bible and Mishnah: A Historical and Literary Introduction*. London: SCM, 1981.

Nikiprowetzky, V. *Le Commentaire de l'Écriture chez Philon d'Alexandrie*. ALGHJ 11. Leiden: Brill, 1977.

---. "Note sur l'interprétation littérale de la loi et sur l'angelologie chez Philon d'Alexandrie." *Mélanges André Neher*. E. A. Levy-Valensi. Paris: Librairie d'Amérique et d'Orient, 1975.

Norelli, E. "La resurrezione di Gesù nell'Ascensione di Isaia." *CrSr* 1 (1980) 315-366.

Osburn, C. D. "The Text of Jude 5." *Biblica* 62 (1981) 107-15.

Paulsen, H. *Der Zweite Petrusbrief und der Judasbrief*. MeyerK. Göttingen: Vandenhoeck & Ruprecht, 1992.

Pétrement, S. *A Separate God: The Origins and Teachings of Gnosticism*. C. Harrison (Tr.). San Fransisco: Harper Collins, 1990.

Pernveden, L. *The Concept of the Church in the Shepherd of Hermas*. I. and N. Reeves (Trs.). Studia Theologica Lundensia 27. Lund: Gleerup, 1966.

Pesce, M. "Presupposti per l'utilizzazione storica dell'*Ascensione di Isaia*. Formazione e tradizione del testo; genere letterario; cosmologia angelica." *Isaia, il Diletto e la Chiesa. Visione ed esegesi profetica cristiano-primitiva nell'Ascensione di Isaia*. M. Pesce (Ed.). Brescia: Paideia Editirice, 1983. 13-76.

Petersen, D. L. *Haggai & Zechariah 1-8: A Commentary*. OTL. London: SCM, 1985.

Philonenko, M. *Joseph et Aseneth: Introduction, Texte Critique, Traduction et Notes*. Leiden: Brill, 1968.

Pokorny, P. *Colossians: A Commentary*. S. S. Schatzmann (Tr.). Peabody, MA: Hendrickson, 1991.

Polhill, J. B. *Acts*. NAC 26. Nashville: Broadman, 1992.

Porteous, N. *Daniel*. OTL. London: SCM, 1965.

Preisendanz, K. "Ein Wiener Papyrusfragment zum Testamentum Salomonis." *Eos: Commentarii Societatis Philologae (Polonorum)* 48 (1956) 161-67.

A Preliminary Concordance to the Hebrew and Aramaic Fragments from Caves II to X. Göttingen: Distributed by H. Stegemann, 1988.

Pritz, R. A. *Nazarene Jewish Christianity: From the End of the New Testament Period Until Its Disappearance in the Fourth Century*. SPB 37. Leiden: Brill, 1988.

Puech, E. "11QPsAp^a: Un Rituel D'Exorcismes. Essai de Reconstruction." *RevQ* 14 (1990) 377-408.

Quasten, J. *Patrology*. 4 Vols. Westminster, MD: Christian Classics, 1993-4.

Rainbow, P. "Jewish Monotheism as the Matrix for New Testament Christology: A Review Article." *NovT* 33 (1991) 78-91.

Reiling, J. *Hermas and Christian Prophecy: A Study of the Eleventh Mandate*. NovTSup 37. Leiden: Brill, 1973.

Ringgren, H. *The Faith of Qumran: Theology of the Dead Sea Scrolls*. Philadelphia: Fortress, 1963.

Rohland, J. P. *Der Erzengel Michael: Arzt und Feldherr. Zwei Aspekte des vor- und frühbyzantinischen Michaelskultes*. BZRGG 19. Leiden: Brill, 1977.

Roloff, J. *The Book of Revelation*. J. A. Alsup (Tr.). A Continental Commentary. Minneapolis, MN: Fortress, 1993.

Röttger, H. *Mal'ak Jahwe - Bote von Gott. Die Vorstellung von Gottes Boten im hebräischen Alten Testament*. RST 13. Frankfurt: Verlag Peter Lang, 1978.

Rose, M. "Names of God in the OT." *Anchor Bible Dictionary*. 6 Vols. D. N. Freedman (Ed.). Vol. 4. New York: Doubleday, 1994. 1001-11.

Rowland, C. "Apocalyptic Visions and the Exaltation of Christ in the Letter to the Colossians." *JSNT* 19 (1983) 73-83.

---. "John 1.51, Jewish Apocalyptic and Targumic Tradition." *NTS* 30 (1984) 498-507.

---. "A Man Clothed in Linen: Daniel 10.6ff and Jewish Angelology." *JSNT* 24 (1985) 99-110.

---. *The Open Heaven. A Study of Apocalyptic in Judaism and Early Christianity*. London: SPCK, 1982.

---. "The Vision of the Risen Christ in Rev. I.13ff.: The Debt of an Early Christology to an Aspect of Jewish Angelology." *JTS* 31 (1980) 1-11.

---. "The Visions of God in Apocalyptic Literature." *JSJ* 10 (1979) 137-54.

Rowley, H. H. *The Relevance of Apocalyptic: A Study of Jewish and Christian Apocalypses from Daniel to the Revelation.* 2nd Ed. London: Lutterworth, 1944.

Rubinstein, A. "Observations on the Slavonic Book of Enoch." *JJS* 13 (1962) 1-21.

Rudolph, K. *Gnosis: The Nature and History of Gnosticism.* P. W. Coxon, and K. H. Kuhn (Trs.). San Francisco: Harper & Row, 1987.

Runia, D. T. *Philo of Alexandria and the Timaeus of Plato.* Philosophia Antiqua 64. Leiden: Brill, 1986.

Russell, D. S. *The Method and Message of Jewish Apocalyptic 200 BC - AD 100.* OTL. Philadelphia: Westminster, 1964.

Safrai, S. (Ed.). *The Literature of the Sages. First Part: Oral Tora, Halakha, Mishna, Tosfeta, Talmud, External Tractates.* CRINT 3.1. Philadelphia: Fortress, 1987.

Sanders, E. P. *Judaism: Practice and Belief, 63 BCE - 66 CE.* London: SCM, 1992.

Sandmel, S. *Philo of Alexandria: An Introduction.* Oxford: Oxford UP, 1979.

Schäfer, P. "The Aims and Purpose of Early Jewish Mysticism." *Hekhalot-Studien.* TSAJ 19. Tübingen: Mohr (Siebeck), 1988. 277-95.

---. "Engel und Mensch in der Hekhalot-Literatur." *Hekhalot-Studien.* TSAJ 19. Tübingen: Mohr (Siebeck), 1988. 250-76.

---. *The Hidden and Manifest God: Some Major Themes in Early Jewish Mysticism.* A. Pomerance (Tr.). Albany, NY: State U of New York P, 1992.

---. "New Testament and Hekhalot Literature. The Journey Into Heaven in Paul and in Merkavah Mysticism." *Hekhalot-Studien.* TSAJ 19. Tübingen: Mohr (Siebeck), 1988. 234-49.

---. *Rivalität zwischen Engeln und Menschen. Untersuchungen zur Rabbinischen Engelvorstellung.* Berlin: de Gruyter, 1975.

Schiffman, L. H. "Messianic Figures and Ideas in the Qumran Scrolls." *The Messiah: Developments in Earliest Judaism and Christianity.* J. H. Charlesworth et al (Eds.). Minneapolis: Fortress, 1992.

Schmidt, C. *Gespräche Jesu mit seinen Jüngern nach der Auferstehung. Ein katholisch-apostolisches Sendschreiben des 2. Jahrhunderts.* TU 43. Leipzig: J. C. Hinrichs' Buchhandlung, 1919.

Schmidt, W. H. "דָּבָר." *Theological Dictionary of the Old Testament*. 6 Vols. G. T. Botterweck and H. Ringgren (Eds.). J.T. Willis and G. W. Bromiley (Trs.). Vol. 3. Grand Rapids, MI: Eerdmans, 1978. 111-25.

Schnackenburg, R. *The Gospel According to John*. 3 Vols. K. Smyth et al (Trs.). London: Burns & Oats, 1968, 1980, 1982.

Schoeps, H. -J. *Jewish Christianity. Factional Disputes in the Early Church*. D. R. A. Hare (Tr.). Philadelphia: Fortress, 1969.

---. *Theologie und Geschichte des Judenchristentums*. Tübingen: Mohr (Siebeck), 1949.

Scholem, G. *Jewish Gnosticism, Merkabah Mysticism, and Talmudic Tradition*. 2nd Ed. New York: Jewish Theological Seminary of America, 1965.

---. *Major Trends in Jewish Mysticism*. 3rd Ed. New York: Schocken, 1954.

Schuller, E. "The Cave 4 Hodayot Manuscripts: A Preliminary Description." *JQR* 85 (1994) 137-150.

Schürer, E. *The History of the Jewish People in the Age of Jesus Christ*. 4 Vols. Rev. Ed. F. Millar, M. Goodman, G. Vermes, M. Black (Eds.). Edinburgh: T. & T. Clark, 1973-87.

Schweizer, E. *The Letter to the Colossians*. A. Chester (Tr.). London: SPCK, 1982.

Segal, A. F. "The Risen Christ and the Angelic Mediator Figures in Light of Qumran." *Jesus and the Dead Sea Scrolls*. New York: Doubleday, 1992. 302-28.

---. "Ruler of This World: Attitudes About Mediator Figures and the Importance of Sociology for Self-Definition." *Jewish and Christian Self-Definition: Aspects of Judaism in the Greco-Roman Period*. Volume 2. A. I. Baumgarten, E. P. Sanders, and A. Mendelson (Eds.). London: SCM, 1981. 245-68.

---. *Two Powers in Heaven. Early Rabbinic Reports About Christianity and Gnosticism*. SJLA 25. Leiden: Brill, 1977.

Shaked, S. "Qumran and Iran: Further Considerations." *IOS* 2 (1972) 433-46.

Silberman, L. H. "Prophets/Angels: LXX and Qumran Psalm 151 and the Epistle to the Hebrews." *Standing Before God: Studies on Prayer in Scriptures and in Tradition with Essays in Honour of John M. Oesterreicher*. A. Finkel and L. Frizzell, (Eds.). New York: KTAV Publishing House, 1981. 91-101.

Simon, M. *Verus Israel. A Study of the Relations Between Christians and Jews in the Roman Empire (AD 135-425)*. H. McKeating (Tr.). Oxford: Oxford UP, 1986.

Simonetti, M. "Note sulla cristologia dell'*Ascensione di Isaia*." *Isaia, Il Diletto e la Chiesa: Visione ed esegesi profetica cristiano-primitiva nell'Ascenione di Isaia*. M. Pesce (Ed.). Brescia: Paideia Editirice, 1983.

Skarsaune, O. *The Proof from Prophecy. A Study in Justin Martyr's Proof Text Tradition: Text-Type, Provenance, Theological Profile*. NovTSup 56. Leiden: Brill, 1987.

Skehan, P. W. "A Fragment of the 'Song of Moses' (Deut. 32) from Qumran." *BASOR* 136 (1954) 12-15.

Skinner, J. *Genesis*. 2nd. Ed. ICC. Edinburgh: T. & T. Clark, 1930.

Slater, T. B. "One Like a Son of Man in First-Century CE Judaism." *NTS* 41 (1995) 183-98.

Smith, M. "Ascent to the Heavens and Deification in 4QM^a." *Archaeology and History in the Dead Sea Scrolls*. L. H. Schiffman (Ed.). JSPSup 8. Sheffield: JSOT Press, 1990. 181-188.

---. "Two Ascended to Heaven--Jesus and the Author of 4Q491." *Jesus and the Dead Sea Scrolls*. J. H. Charlesworth (Ed.). New York: Doubleday, 1992. 290-301.

Smith, J. Z. "The Prayer of Joseph." *Religions in Antiquity: Essays in Memory of Erwin Ramsdell Goodenough*. J. Neusner (Ed.). Leiden: Brill, 1968. 253-94.

Snaith, J. G. "Aphrahat and the Jews." *Interpreting the Hebrew Bible: Essays in Honour of E. I. J. Rosenthal*. J. A. Emerton and S. C. Reif, (Eds.). Cambridge: Cambridge UP, 1981. 235-50.

Snyder, G. F. *The Shepherd of Hermas. The Apostolic Fathers: A New Translation and Commentary*. R. M. Grant (Ed.). London: Nelson & Sons, 1968.

Speiser, E. A. *Genesis*. AB. Garden City, NY: Doubleday, 1964.

Stegemann, H. *Die Entstehung der Qumrangemeinde*. Bonn: Privately Published, 1971.

Stone, M. E. *A Commentary on the Fourth Ezra*. Hermeneia. Minneapolis: Fortress, 1990.

---. *A History of the Literature of Adam and Eve*. SBLEJL 3. Atlanta: Scholars, 1992.

Strack, H. L. and G. Stemberger. *Introduction to the Talmud and Midrash*. M. Bockmuehl (Tr.). Edinburgh: T & T Clark, 1991.

Strecker, G. "Elkesai." *Reallexikon für Antike und Christentum*. 16 Vols. F. J. Dölger et al (Eds.). Vol. 4. Stuttgart: Anton Hiersemann, 1959. 1171-86.

---. *Das Judenchristentum in den Pseudoklementinen*. TU 70.2. Berlin: Akademie-Verlag, 1981.

Strousma, G. G. "Form(s) of God: Some Notes on Metatron and Christ." *HTR* 1983 (1983) 269-88.

Stuckenbruck, L. "An Angelic Refusal of Worship: The Tradition and Its Function in the Apocalypse of John." *Society of Biblical Literature 1994 Seminar Papers*. E. H. Lovering (Ed.). Atlanta: Scholars, 1994. 679-96.

---. *Angel Veneration and Christology. A Study in Early Judaism and in the Christology of the Apocalypse of John*. WUNT 2.70. Tübingen: Mohr (Siebeck), 1995.

Sweet, J. *Revelation*. TPINTC. London: SCM, 1979.

Swete, H. B. *The Apocalypse of Revelation*. London: Macmillan, 1911.

Talmon, S. "Waiting for the Messiah: The Spiritual Universe of the Qumran Covenanters." *Judaisms and Their Messiahs at the Turn of the Christian Era*. J. Neusner, W. S. Green and E. Frerichs (Eds.). Cambridge: Cambridge UP, 1987.

Taylor, V. *The Gospel According to St. Mark*. London: Macmillan & Co., 1963.

Tiller, P. A. *A Commentary on the Animal Apocalypse of 1 Enoch*. SBLEJL 4. Atlanta: Scholars, 1993.

Tobin, T. "Logos." *Anchor Bible Dictionary*. 6 Vols. D. N. Freedman. Vol. 4. New York: Doubleday, 1992. 348-56.

Torrey, C. C. "Alexander Jannaeus and the Archangel Michael." *VT* 4 (1954) 208-11.

Trakatellis, D. C. *The Pre-Existence of Christ in Justin Martyr: An Exegetical Study with Reference to the Humiliation and Exaltation Christology*. HDR 6. Missoula, MT: Scholars, 1976.

Treves, M. "The Two Spirits of the Rule of the Community." *RevQ* 3 (1961) 449-52.

Trigg, J. W. "The Angel of Great Counsel: Christ and the Angelic Hierarchy in Origen's Theology." *JTS* n.s. 42 (1991) 35-51.

Tromp, J. *The Assumption of Moses: A Critical Edition with Commentary*. SVTP 10. Leiden: Brill, 1993.

---. "Taxo, The Messenger of the Lord." *JSJ* 21 (1990) 200-09.

Urbach, E. E. *The Sages. Their Concepts and Beliefs*. I. Abrahams (Tr.). Cambridge, MA: Havard UP, 1979.

van der Ploeg, J. *Le Rouleau de la Guerre*. STDJ 2. Leiden: Brill, 1959.

van der Woude, A. S. "Melchisedek als himmlische Erlösergestalt in den neugefundenen eschatologischen Midraschim aus Qumran Höhle XI." *OTS* 14 (1965) 354-73.

VanderKam, J. C. *Textual and Historical Studies in the Book of Jubilees*. Missoula, MT: Scholars, 1977.

Vanhoye, A. "Un Médiateur des anges en Ga 3,19-20." *Biblica* 53 (1978) 403-11.

Vermes, G. *The Dead Sea Scrolls: Qumran in Perspective*. London: Collins, 1977.

---. "The Use of בר נשא/בר נש in Jewish Aramaic." M. Black. *An Aramaic Approach to the Gospels and Acts*. 3rd Ed. Oxford: Clarendon, 1967. 310-330.

Vermes, G. (with additional contributions by T. H. Lim and R. P. Gordon). "The Oxford Forum for Qumran Research Seminar on the Rule of War from Cave 4 (4Q285)." *JJS* 43 (1992) 85-94.

Viviano, B. T. and J. Taylor. "Sadducees, Angels, and Resurrection." *JBL* 111 (1992) 496-98.

von der Osten-Sacken, P. *Gott und Belial: Traditionsgeschichtliche Untersuchungen zum Dualismus in den Texten aus Qumran*. SUNT 6. Göttingen: Vandenhoeck & Ruprecht, 1969.

von Rad, G. "Deuteronomy's Name Theology and the Priestly Document's 'Kabod' Theology." *Studies in Deuteronomy*. (Tr.). SBT 9. Chicago: Henry Regnery, 1953. 37-44.

---. *Deuteronomy*. OTL. London: SCM, 1966.

---. *Genesis: A Commentary*. Rev. Ed. J. H. Marks (Tr.). OTL. London: SCM, 1972.

---. *Old Testament Theology*. 2 Vols. D. M. G. Stalker (Tr.). Edinburgh: Oliver and Boyd, 1962.

---. "ἄγγελος, ἀρχάγγελος, ἰσάγγελος." *The Theological Dictionary of the New Testament*. 10 Vols. G. Kittel (Ed.), and G. Bromiley (Tr.). Vol. 1. Grand Rapids, MI: Eerdmans, 1964. 76-80.

Weinfeld, M. "כָּבוֹד." *Theologisches Wörterbuch zum Alten Testament*. 7 Vols. H. Ringgren and H. -J. Fabry (Eds.). G. J. Botterweck. Vol. 4. Stuttgart: Verlag W. Kohlhammer, 1984. 23-40.

Wenham, G. J. *Genesis 1-15*. WBC. Waco, TX: Word Books, 1987.

Wernberg-Møller, P. *The Manual of Discipline*. STDJ 1. Leiden: Brill, 1957.

---. "A Reconsideration of the Two Spirits in the Rule of the Community (1 Q Serek III,13-IV,26)." *RevQ* 3 (1961) 413-41.

Werner, M. *Die Entstehung des Christlichen Dogmas.* 2nd Ed. Tübingen: Katzmann Verlag, 1954.

---. *The Formation of Christian Dogma: An Historical Study of Its Problem.* S. G. F. Brandon (Tr.). London: A. & C. Black, 1957.

Westcott, B. F. *The Epistle to the Hebrews.* London: Macmillian, 1889.

Westermann, C. *Genesis: A Commentary.* 3 Vols. J. J. Scullion (Tr.). London: SPCK, 1985.

Williams, A. L. "The Cult of the Angels at Colossae." *JTS* o.s. 10 (1909) 413-38.

Williamson, R. *Jews in the Hellenistic World: Philo.* Cambridge: Cambridge UP, 1989.

Wilson, I. *Divine Presence in Deuteronomy.* Unpublished Dissertation: Cambridge University, 1992.

Winston, D. *Logos and Mystical Theology in Philo of Alexandria.* Cincinnati: Hebrew Union College, 1985.

---. *The Wisdom of Solomon.* AB 43. Garden City, NY: Doubleday, 1979.

Wohlenberg, G. "Eine pseudocyprianische Schrift über dreifach ver-schiedenen Lohn." *Theologisches Literaturblatt* 35 (1914) 169-75, 193-98, 217-20.

Wolfson, H. A. *Philo: Foundations of Religious Philosophy in Judaism, Christianity, and Islam.* 2 Vols. Cambridge, MA: Harvard UP, 1948.

---. "The Pre-Existent Angel of the Magharians and Al-Nahawandi." *JQR* 51 (1960-61) 89-106.

Wright, N. T. *The New Testament and the People of God.* London: SPCK, 1993.

Yadin, Y. "The Dead Sea Scrolls and the Epistle to the Hebrews." *Aspects of the Dead Sea Scrolls.* C. Rabin and Y. Yadin (Eds.). Scripta Hierosolymitana 4. Jerusalem: Magnes, 1965. 36-55.

---. *The Scroll of the War of the Sons of Light Against of the Sons of Darkness.* Oxford: Oxford UP, 1962.

Yarbro Collins, A. *The Combat Myth in the Book of Revelation.* HDR 9. Missoula, MT: Scholars, 1976.

---. "The 'Son of Man' Tradition and the Book of Revelation." *The Messiah: Developments in Earliest Judaism and Christianity.* J. H. Charlesworth, et al (Eds.). Minneapolis: Fortress, 1992.

Index of Modern Authors

Abegg, M. 69
Acerbi, A. 164
Alexander, L. 181
Alexander, P. S. 115, 117, 118, 119, 120
Andersen, F. I. 39
Argyle, A. W. 39
Arnold, C. E. 106, 107, 108, 109, 192
Aschim, A. 74
Ashton, J. 7, 10, 145, 160
Attridge, H. W. 125, 138, 139, 150
Aus, R. D. 133

Baillet, M. 69
Bakker, A. 3
Bammel, E. 94
Barbel, J. 5, 10, 173, 180, 184, 189, 193, 200, 204, 205, 206, 207, 211
Barker, M. 11, 78, 145
Barnard, L. W. 113, 204, 205, 207
Barr, J. 63
Barrett, C. K. 125, 146, 160
Barton, J. M. T. 164
Bauckham, R. 41-42, 128, 129, 130, 131, 140, 153, 154, 155, 160, 164
Beasley-Murray, G. R. 34, 127, 128, 144, 155
Beatrice B. F. 171
Beckwith I. T. 154
Beer, G. 52
Best, E. 133
Betz, H. D. 134
Betz, O. 135-136
Billerbeck, P. 124
Bietenhard, H. 16, 17
Bigg, C. 131
Black, M. 29, 30, 33, 36, 37, 43, 48, 51-52, 157

Blatz, B. 183
Boccaccini, G. 43, 57, 65
Bockmuehl, M. N. A. 66, 94, 133, 168
Bonwetsch, G. N. 210
Borgen, P. 77
Bousset, W. 2, 11, 12
Box, G. H. 53
Braverman, J. 98
Brown, R. E. 58, 136, 145, 146, 160
Brox, N. 165, 188, 189, 190
Bruce, F. F. 125, 134, 137
Budge, E. A. W. 42, 193
Bühner, J.-A. 7, 10
Bultmann, R. 146
Burchard, C. 40
Burge, G. M. 136
Burton, E. D. W. 134, 156
Butterworth, G. W. 199, 211

Cadbury, H. J. 125
Caird, G. B. 128, 129, 130, 144
Callan, T. 134
Carr, W. 36, 76, 107
Carrell, P. R. 10, 11, 12, 148, 155, 156
Chadwick, H. 108, 189, 191, 204, 207
Charles, R. H. 29, 30, 31, 32, 34, 36, 37, 38, 39, 41, 44, 49, 52, 127, 130, 135, 148, 154, 164, 195, 198
Charlesworth, J. H. 64, 67
Chester, A. 10, 12, 58, 66, 76
Cohen, M. S. 178
Collins, J. J. 26-28, 34, 35, 38, 40, 47, 58, 65, 69, 148, 156
Colson, F. H. 78, 85
Conzelmann, H. 125
Craigie, P. C. 18
Cross, F. M. 56
Crouzel, H. 211

Daniélou, J. 6, 10, 171, 173, 188, 194, 195, 196, 197, 200, 201, 220
Daube, D. 125
Davidson, M. J. 30, 36, 37, 39, 59, 60, 61, 62, 63, 65, 68, 71
Davies, P. R. 57, 63
Davis, P. G. 9, 12, 217
Davila, J. R. 74
Davka Judaic Classical Library 97
De Jonge, M. 38, 43, 44, 70, 184
De Lacey, D. R. 143
De Lange, N. 200
Delcor, M. 40, 46, 70
Denis, A.-M. 133
Dibelius, M. 133, 165, 189, 190
DiLella, A. A. 34
Dillman, A. 52
Dillon, J. 84
Dimant, D. 39, 57, 58, 63, 69
Dix, G. 190
Dix, G. H. 3, 33, 76
Dodd, C. H. 81, 146
Driver, S. R. 18
Drummond, J. 86
Duling, D. C. 181, 182
Dunn, J. D. G. 5, 82, 134, 143, 152, 154, 156

Ego, B. 45, 101
Eichrodt, W. 16, 17, 18, 20, 21, 22
Eisenmann, R. 51, 66
Elior, R. 116, 117, 118
Elliott, J. K. 164
Ellis, E. E. 140
Epstein, I. 100, 104
Evans, E. 179

Farrer, A. 145, 154
Fitzmyer, J. A. 30, 70, 143
Fletcher-Louis, C. H. T. 10, 11
Flusser, D. 73
Fossum, J. 8, 10, 12, 52, 88, 120, 140, 141, 143, 178, 185
Frame, J. E. 133
Francis, F. O. 107
Freedman, D. N. 17
Freedman, H. 98
Frost, S. B. 20

García Martínez, F. 57, 59, 64, 66, 70, 73
Gaylord, H. E. 39, 45
Gieschen, C. 155, 188, 190
Gilbert, M. 81, 91
Ginzberg, L. 96, 97, 112
Goldin, J. 95
Goldingay, J. E. 33, 35, 38, 47
Goodenough, E. R. 76, 81, 113, 203
Green, M. 131
Grenfell, B. P. 195
Gruenwald, I. 120
Grözinger, K.-E. 117, 118
Gundry, R. H. 10, 11, 153, 154
Gunkel, H. 125

Haenchen, E. 125
Hall, R. G. 154, 164
Hall, S. G. 209
Halperin, D. 119
Hannah, D. D. 96, 132, 147, 198, 199, 220
Hanson, A. T. 140, 146
Hanson, R. P. C. 200
Harkavy, A. A. 185
Harlow, D. C. 39, 45
Harnack, A. 190
Harrington, D. J. 53
Hartman, L. F. 34
Harvey, W. W. 208
Hawthorne, G. F. 143
Heidt, W. 17
Hengel, M. 6-7, 12, 37, 65, 80, 150
Hirth, V. 17, 20
Holl, K. 173
Holland, G. S. 133
Hollander, H. W. 38, 43, 44
Holm-Nielsen, S. 59
Holtz, T. 145, 152
Hooker, M. D. 34
Horbury, W. 35, 103, 156
Horton, F. L. 70, 71, 72
Hunt, A. S. 192, 195
Hurtado, L. W. 8-9, 12, 34, 38, 40, 44, 53, 76, 82, 88, 104, 106, 107, 108, 111, 143, 160

Irmscher, J. 177, 178

Isaac, E. 30, 52
Isaacs, M. E. 138, 150

Jastrow, M. 104
Jeremias, G. 56
Johnston, G. 135-136
Jones, F. S. 175

Kasher, R. 99
Kee, H. C. 38, 44
Kelly, J. N. D. 131, 140, 141, 188, 190
Kiddle, M. 144
Kim, S. 158
Kittel, G. 23
Klijn, A. F. J. 174, 175, 177
Knibb, M. A. 30, 34, 52, 56, 60, 63, 65, 164, 197, 198
Knight, J. 164
Kobelski, P. J. 63, 70, 72
Koch, H. 171
Koetschau, P. 211
Kraft, H. 130
Kraft, R. A. 22, 47
Kretschmar, G. 6, 10, 200, 220
Kuhn, H. B. 28

Lacocque, A. 34, 38, 47
Lake, K. 125, 165, 166, 190
Landsman, J. I. 53
Lane, W. L. 139
Lanne, E. 201
Larson, E. 66-67
Laubscher, F. du Troit 70
Leaney, A. R. C. 59, 63, 65
Leclerq, H. 173
Leonardi, C. 167
Lieberman, S. 121
Lightfoot, J. B. 106, 143, 165, 183
Lindars, B. 138, 139, 150
Loewenstamm, S. E. 46
Lohmeyer, E. 130
Lohse, E. 39, 56, 64, 73, 106, 107
Longenecker, R. 6, 11, 108, 150, 155
Lueken, W. 2-3, 11, 12, 37, 40, 72, 76, 96, 101, 106, 137, 188
Lust, J. 157
Luttikhuizen, G. P. 175, 177, 178, 179

Mach, M. 10, 17, 28, 106, 109

Manson, W. 139
Marcus, R. 78
Marshall, I. H. 125
Martin, R. P. 143
McCown, C. C. 181, 182
Menken, M. J. J. 133
Metzger, B. M. 140, 183
Meyers, C. L. 22
Meyers, E. M. 22
Michaelis, W. 4-5
Michel, O. 137
Milik, J. T. 29, 30, 33, 37, 56, 66, 67, 70, 72, 73
Miller, W. T. 112
Minns, D. 207
Mitchell, H. G. 22
Montefiore, H. 125, 137-138
Montgomery, J. A. 34, 38
Morenz, L. D. 17
Morfill, W. R. 39
Morray-Jones, C. R. A. 115, 121
Moule, C. F. D. 131
Mounce, R. H. 144, 148
Mowinckel, S. 34
Moxnes, H. 188
Müller, P. 133
Müller, C. D. G. 164, 196
Murphy-O'Conner, J. 57

Neusner, J. 40, 104
Newman, C. C. 23
Newsom, C. A. 16, 17, 20, 28, 61, 62, 73, 75
Neyrey, J. H. 41
Nickelsburg, G. W. E. 39, 81, 91
Nikiprowetzky, V. 76, 77
Norelli, E. 167, 195

Osburn, C. D. 140, 141

Parsons, P. J. 22
Paulsen, H. 131
Pennington, A. 53
Pétrement, S. 169
Pernveden, L. 188, 189, 190
Pesce, M. 164
Petersen, D. L. 22
Philonenko, M. 40

Pokorny, P. 106
Polhill, J. B. 125
Porteous, N. 34, 38, 47
Preisendanz, K. 181
Priest, J. 38
Pritz, R. A. 200
Puech, E. 67
Purintun, A.-E. 47

Quasten, J. 165

Rabin, C. 49, 64
Rainbow, P. 9
Reiling, J. 190
Reinink, G. J. 174, 175, 177, 180
Reitzenstein, R. 171
Ringgren, H. 59, 63, 65
Robinson, S. E. 47
Rohland, J. P. 40, 41, 164
Roloff, J. 128, 130
Röttger, H. 20
Rousseau, A. 201
Rose, M. 21
Rowland, C. 8, 10, 11, 23, 26-28, 29, 34, 47, 107, 137, 147, 151-152, 153, 157, 160, 161
Rowley, H. H. 26, 37
Rubinkiewicz, R. 53
Rubinstein, A. 39
Rudolph, K. 169, 174
Runia, D. T. 77, 78, 79, 82, 83, 84
Russell, D. S. 15, 18, 26, 27, 33, 36

Safrai, S. 94
Sanders, E. P. 27, 39, 56, 58
Sandmel, S. 77, 79, 82
Schäfer, P. 95-96, 105, 106, 115, 116, 117, 118
Scheidweiler, F. 164, 166
Schiffman, L. H. 58
Schmidt, C. 164, 170
Schmidt, W. H. 80
Schnackenburg, R. 146
Schoeps, H.-J. 174, 175, 177, 179, 194
Scholem, G. 98, 115, 119, 120
Schuller, E. 69
Schürer, E. 3
Schweizer, E. 106, 107

Segal, A. F. 7, 9, 52, 78, 86, 88, 94, 95, 98, 103, 105, 110, 110, 120
Shaked, S. 63
Siegert, F. 86
Silberman, L. H. 124
Simon, M. 98, 175, 176
Simonetti, M. 196, 199
Skarsaune, O. 203
Skehan, P. W. 18
Skinner, J. 19
Slater, T. B. 35
Smith, J. P. 200
Smith, M. 69
Smith, J. Z. 89, 90, 184-185
Snaith, J. G. 40
Snyder, G. F. 189
Speiser, E. A. 19
Stegemann, H. 56, 67
Stemberger, G. 94, 101, 102
Stone, M. E. 24, 25, 39
Strack, H. L. 94, 101, 102, 124
Strecker, G. 175, 176, 177, 178, 193
Strousma, G. G. 121
Stuckenbruck, L. 9-10, 11, 104, 106, 107, 109, 138, 139, 144, 151, 153, 155, 157, 192
Sweet, J. 128, 130, 145, 155
Swete, H. B. 129, 130, 144, 154

Talmon, S. 58
Taylor, J. 125
Taylor, V. 125
Thackeray, H. St. J. 87
Tigchelaar, E. J. C. 70
Tiller, P. A. 29, 37, 43
Tobin, T. 80, 81
Torrey, C. C. 37
Tov, E. 22
Trakatellis, D. C. 203, 204, 205, 207
Treves, M. 63
Trigg, J. W. 210, 211
Tromp, J. 38, 41, 130
Turner, N. 40

Urbach, E. E. 23, 52, 88, 94, 99, 102, 106, 111
Ulrich, E. 18

van der Ploeg, J. 64
van der Woude, A. S. 70
VanderKam, J. C. 31, 43, 49, 50
Vanhoye, A. 134
Vermes, G. 3, 35, 39, 55, 56, 57, 59, 61, 65, 66, 72
Vielhauer, P. 176, 193
Viviano, B. T. 125
von der Osten-Sacken, P. 65
von Rad, G. 16, 17, 18, 20, 21

Weinfeld, M. 23
Wells, L. S. A. 42
Wenham, G. J. 19
Wernberg-Møller, P. 59, 63, 65
Werner, M. 3-7, 11, 142, 156-157, 179, 210
Wessely, K. 192
Westcott, B. F. 139
Westermann, C. 19, 20

Whitaker, G. H. 78, 86
Whittaker, M. 189
Wikgren, A. 140
Williams, A. L. 108, 109
Williamson, R. 77, 78, 79, 80, 82, 84, 86
Willoughby, B. E. 17, 20
Wilson, I. 21
Winston, D. 77, 79, 80, 81, 82, 91
Wintermute, O. 49
Wise, M. 51, 66, 69
Wohlenberg, G. 171
Wolfson, H. A. 76, 77, 78, 79, 80, 81, 82, 83, 84, 86, 88, 89, 185
Wright, N. T. 27, 34

Yadin, Y. 39, 60, 64, 65, 66, 73, 150
Yarbro Collins, A. 127, 157-158

Zimmerman, F. 34

Index of References

Old Testament

Genesis
1	80
2.7	207
3.8-21	206
6.2	16
6.4	16
14	74
16.7-16	19
17.17	146
18	112, 113, 146, 198
18-19	112, 114
18.1	113
18.1-2	113
18.2ff	113
18.33	19
19.1	16
19.15	16
19.24	111
21.8-19	19
22.9-18	19
28	202
28.12	16, 17, 160-161
31	202
31.10-13	19
32	114
32.2	16
32.22-32	19
32.24-30	112
32.24-31	89
48.15-16	19-20

Exodus
3	114
3.1-15	19
3.1-6	21
3.2	112, 113
3.14	86
4.22	90
12.23	91-92
13.21-22	21
14.19-20	21, 23, 50
14.19	21
14.24	21
15.3	149
23.20-21	8, 21, 23, 51, 52, 85, 88, 111, 114, 140, 142, 144, 146
23.20-33	21, 60
23.20-28	145
23.21	110-111, 143
23.23	21
24.1	110-111
25.9	32
25.21	200
25.40	32
28.36	87
28.41	37
29.9	37
32.34	21
32.31-33.6	144
33.1-3	21
33.2f	21
33.2	21, 60, 145
33.15	110-111
34.28	80
39.30	87

Leviticus
21.10	37

Numbers
2.2	97
8.4	32
13.13	33

16.41-50	141	18.15	18
16.46	141	22.19	17
20.16	21	22.19ff	16
22.21-35	21	22.19-22	17, 84
22.31	17		
24.17-19	66	2 Kings	
		6.15-17	17, 60
Deuteronomy		6.17	18
4.19	16, 19	19.35	18, 22, 60, 99
5.5	82	21.4	21
6.4-9	143	21.7	21
7.1-2	149		
7.17-24	149	1 Chronicles	
10.4	80	5.13f	33
12.5	21	6.40	33
12.11	21	7.3	33
12.21	21	8.16	33
14.23f	21	12.20	33
16.2	21	21.1	18
16.6	21	21.16	178
16.11	21	21.14-16	18
23.14	60	27.18	33
26.2	21		
32.8	18-19	2 Chronicles	
33.2	18	2.3-4	101
		21	22
Joshua		21.2	33
5.13-15	21, 74, 165	32.21	22, 60
5.14-15	16, 18		
5.13-6.2	203	Ezra	
		8.8	33
Judges			
2.1-5	21	Esther	
5.20	16	4	18
6.11-24	21		
13.1-23	21	Job	
		1-2	18
1 Samuel		1.6-12	16, 17
4.4	18	2.1-7	17
24	22	5.1	18
		15.8	16, 17
2 Samuel		16.19	18
5.22-25	17, 60	16.21	34
24.15-17	18	21.22	17
		28	80
1 Kings		33.23-28	18
11.36	21	42.7-17	18
14.21	21		

Psalms

2.9	128, 144, 149
8.4	34
18.6-19	149
29.1	16, 17
29.1-2	18
58	19
68.1-35	149
68.18	18
78.25	17
78.49	18
80.18	34
82	16, 17-18, 19
82.1	74, 84
89.5-7	84
89.6-9	16, 17
89.6	17
89.8	17
103.21	17
106	161
107	161
107.20	80
110	72, 74, 156
121	161
147.15	80
148.2	17, 18

Proverbs

3.19	80
8.22-31	80

Isaiah

6	123, 147, 172, 199, 201, 219
6.1-4	18
6.1-5	147
6.1-8	17
6.3	18
6.5	18
6.10	147
9.6	209
11.4	149
10.32	99
24.21	16
24.21-23	149
27.1	149
27.13	168
37.36	18
40.7-8	80
40.26	16
45.21-23	143
52.7	71
55.10-11	80
63	149
63.1-3	149
63.9	49, 140, 207

Jeremiah

23.18	16, 17

Ezekiel

1	151
1.1	99
1.14	96
1.26-28	8, 23
2.1	34
3.23	23
8.2-4	8, 23
9.2	101
9.3	23
10.1-5	23
10.18-19	23
11.22-24	23
28.13	152
43.1-9	23
44.4	23

Daniel

	15, 22, 25, 27, 33, 34, 38, 39, 40, 68, 123, 133, 134, 148
3.25	99
7	35, 36, 157-158, 218
7.9	152
7.9-10	96, 123
7.9-13	218
7.13	3, 35, 48, 156
7.13-14	34, 41, 156
7.16-18	31
7.18	35
7.17	35
7.27	35
8	35
8.10-11	35
8.11	40

8.15ff	47	**Ancient Translations**	
8.15-16	31		
8.15	35	*Aquila*	
8.16	98	Isaiah	
8.17	34	9.5	209
9.21	35		
10	152, 157		
10-12	35, 47, 134	*Septuagint*	
10.5-12.3	3	Genesis	
10.5-6	151-152	39.20	133
10.5-9	8		
10.5	35	Exodus	
10.13	31, 38, 48, 65, 133	4.24-26	19
		12.23	91, 92
10.13-21	130		
10.20-21	38	Numbers	
10.21	31, 34, 40, 65, 98	14	140
		16	140
11.36	35	20.16	140
11.36-37	133		
11.36-12.3	133	Joshua	
11.40-12.4	65	5.13-15	40
12.1	31, 34, 35, 37, 38, 40-41, 65, 98, 102, 133, 148	1 Kings	
		7.26ff	45
12.1-3	127	Psalms	
12.2-3	126	2.9	128
12.3	35	23.9-10	84
12.5-7	34	32.6	80
12.7	35	102.20-21	84
		147.7	80
Joel		148.2	84
2.1	168	148.8	80
3.11	127		
		Isaiah	
Zephaniah		2.1	80
1.14-16	168	9.5	202, 207, 209, 210, 214
Zechariah		9.5-6	209
1-8	22, 24		
1.12-13	18	Jeremiah	
1.14	180	1.2	80
3	18		
3.1-5	22	Ezekiel	
3.2	42	3.16	80
14.5	127		

Daniel	
7.9	158
7.10	158
7.13	157-158
7.14	158

Habakkuk	
3.2	199

Symmachus
Isaiah	
9.5	209

Theodotion
Isaiah	
9.5	209
Daniel	
10.21	133

Deuterocanonicals

Tobit	
	7, 68
8.3	133
12.15	29, 84, 123
12.19	96, 198

Wisdom of Solomon	
	78, 91-92
7.21	91
7.22-30	80
7.23	91
8.4	91
9.1	80, 81, 91
9.4	91
9.10	91
9.17	91
18.13-16	91-92
18.14-16	80
18.20-25	87, 141

Sirach	
1.10	80
17.17	31
24.1-34	80

Baruch	
3.29	80

1 Maccabees	
2.42	56
4.30-35	37
7.41	60

2 Maccabees	
10.29	60
11.6	60
11.6-12	37
15.22	60
15.23	60

Old Testament Pseudepigrapha

Apocalypse of Abraham
	25, 52, 88, 143, 144, 145
10	151
10.3	51, 53, 145
10.6	53
10.8	51, 53
10.8-17	145
10.16b-17	53
10.17	51
13.1-4	182
15-18	31
17	107
17.13	53
20.1-7	182
23.11	182
31.5	182

Testament of Abraham
	40, 46, 48
Rec. A	
	39, 49
2.4-5	39
4.9-10	198
6.4-6	98
7	49
7.2-7	152
7.11	84, 123
10-15	31
14.5-6	43
14.12ff	43

Index of References

19-20	32	*2 Baruch*	
20.10-12	46, 168	4.1-6	32
		12.4	133
Rec. B		21.6	28
4.5	49	51.1-12	126
6.10-13	98	59.11	28, 29
8-12	31		
14.6	39	*3 Baruch*	
14.7	32, 168		25, 40, 44-45, 47
The Adam Literature	9, 25, 27	1.8 (Grk.)	1.8
Greek *Apocalypse of Moses*		2.1 (Slav.)	2.1
	25	4.7 (Slav.)	29
Preface	67, 124, 134, 165	11-16	31, 32, 100, 120, 125, 150, 218
22.1-3	169	11.2	47, 150, 168
29.4	53	11.4-6	49
29.16	32	11.4	45
33.4-5	32	11.4 (Grk.)	39
33.5	53	11.6 (Grk.)	39
37	32, 46	11.7	(Grk.) 39, 49
37.4-5	150	11.8	(Grk.) 39
37.4-6	168	11.9	45
39.2-3	42	13.3 (Slav.)	39
40.2	24, 29	14.2	45
43.2-3	48		
Latin *Vita Adae et Evae*		*4 Baruch*	
	25	9.5	47, 150, 168
9.3	32		
12-16	42, 166	*1 Enoch*	
15.1	159		25, 55, 68
16.1	159	*Book of Watchers* (1-36)	
22.2	48		9, 33, 48, 49, 141
47	46	8.1	182
47.2-3	168	9	42
48.3	48	9-10	24, 29, 30, 36, 37, 123, 127, 132
51.2	48		
Slavonic *Vita Adae et Evae*		9.2-3	32
	25	9.6	182
Armenian *Penitence of Adam*		10	141
	25	10.4	133
12-16	42	10.4-8	182
Georgian *Book of Adam*		10.11-12	133
	25	13.1ff	182
12-16	42	14	123
		14.8-25	96

14.20	152	*Astronomical Book* (72-82)	
14.23	84	72.1ff	65
15.2	32	74.2	51
15.4	28	75.3	51
15.6	28	79.6	51
15.6-7	96	81.5	30
17-36	31, 69	*Dream Visions* (83-90)	
18.12-19.2	133		25
19.3-21.9	34	*Animal Apocalypse* (85-90)	
20	29, 30, 33, 123, 132		29, 30, 36, 43, 49, 68
20 (Grk)	24	87-89.1	36
20.2	34	87.2	30
20.5	34, 37, 38	88.1-2	36
20.7	47	88.3	36, 37
21-37	47	89-90	31
21.1-6	133	89.1	36, 126
21.5	48	89.9	126
24-25	46, 47	89.36	126
24.6	48	89.61	36
Similitudes (37-71)		89.68-76	36
	29, 30, 52, 141, 156	89.70-77	41, 150
		90.14	37, 39
39.12-40.10	123	90.14-22	36
40	29, 49, 97, 123	90.17	37, 41, 150
40.9	49, 97	90.20-27	127
42	80	90.21-22	30, 37
46.1	152	90.22	36
51.4	126	90.22-25	37
54.4-6	133	90.24-25	37
54.5	182	*Epistle of Enoch* (91-108)	
55.4	182	99.3	32
60.4-5	49	100.5	32, 125
60.11-24	96	104.4	126
60.16-21	29	104.6	126
61.10	29, 157		
62.5	157	*2 Enoch*	
68	49		40
68.2-5	43	Long Rec.	
69	53, 141, 188	1.4	178
69.2	182	1.3-10	31
69.13-25	51-52, 88, 119, 143, 144, 145	14.3	29
		19.1-3	159
69.13	51-52	19.3	29
69.14-15	52	19.3-4	96
71	4, 48, 49, 150, 156	19.4-5	29
		20-22	123
		22	150
		22.1	152

Index of References

22.6	39	*Jubilees*	
29.1-3	95, 172		25, 27, 43, 49,
29.3	28		61, 68, 134-135
33.10	39, 44	1.20	
39.5	152	1.27-2.1	49, 124, 165
71-72	46-47, 150	1.27-2.2	134
71.28-29	47	1.29	31, 49
		1.29-2.2	67
Short Rec.		2.2ff	29
22.6	39	2.2	28, 29, 49, 96
71-72	47, 74	2.17-19	61
		6.17-18	61
4 Ezra		6.31-35	61
	24, 31, 47	10.1-14	50
2.43	178	10.8	63
3.14	146	11.5	63
4.36	24	11.11	63
6.23	168	15.31-32	31
8.21	96	15.33	64
11-12	152	17.16	63
13	156	19.28	63
		31.13-14	61
Greek Apocalypse of Ezra		31.14	32
1.4	39	31.14-20	58
4.6-43	48	35.17	31, 125
4.25	133	36.7	52
6.1-2	29	48	50
		48.1-19	31
Testament of Isaac		48.2	63
2.1ff	168	48.13	50
6.24-28	168	48.15	133
		49.2	91-92
Testament of Jacob			
1.5-6	168	*4 Maccabees*	
		5.7	107
Testament of Job		7.11	141
	46		
52	32	*Assumption of Moses*	
		10.2	37-38, 45
Joseph and Aseneth		11.7-8	46
14	151	Lost Ending	32, 41-42, 46,
14.1-10	8		102, 130-131
14.8	40		
		Pseudo-Philo (LAB)	
Prayer of Joseph		11.12	31
	6, 7, 24, 51, 85,	15.5	31, 125
	89-90, 184-185	19.16	46
		26.12	53
		59.4	31

263

Lives of the Prophets
4.6	64
4.20	64
17.2	64

History of the Rechabites
14-16	32

Apocalypse of Sedrach
5	42

Sibylline Oracles (III-V)
III.63	64
III.73	64

Testaments of the Twelve Patriarchs
27, 43, 58, 64, 68

Testament of Reuben
5.7	178
6.8	58
6.11	58

Testament of Simeon
7.1	58

Testament of Levi
27
2-5	43, 45, 48
3	45
3.4-6	61
3.4-7	150
3.5-6	32, 125
3.5-7	43
3.5	51
5	45
5.1-6	38
5.5	43
5.6	100
5.7	44
8.10	37
18.1-9	58
18.12	133

Testament of Judah
24.1-6	58

Testament of Issachar
5.7-8	58

Testament of Dan
183-184
6	45
6.1-8	184
6.2-7	38
6.2	43, 44

Testament of Naphtali
27
5.1-5	58
8.2	58

Testament of Joseph
19.11	58

Apocalypse of Zephaniah
6.11-17	51

Qumran Texts

The Blessings (1QSb)
55
4.24b-26	61
4.25-26	107
5.20-29	65
5.27-28	58

Catenae (4Q177)
63
4.12-16	65, 71

The Community Rule (1QS, 4QS)
55, 71, 136

1QS
1.10	63
2.12	71
3.13-4.26	58, 62, 63, 72, 194
3.20	63, 71
3.21	63
3.22	63
3.24-25	75
3.24	63, 65, 71
3.25	63
4.15-16	62
4.18-19	64
4.23-25	62
4.23-26	64
5.20ff	68
6.13ff	68

Index of References

8.1ff	68	2.13	71
8.13-14	57	2.16	71
9.11	58	2.24	72
9.16-17	68	2.24-25	71-72
11.6-8	60		
11.7-8	59	*The Messianic Rule* (1QSa)	
			55
The Damascus Document (CD, 4QD)		2.3ff	60, 107
	55		
CD		*Songs of the Sabbath Sacrifice*	
1.10b-12	57		55, 60, 75
2.3-13	63	4Q400	
2.7-11	62	1 i,14b-16	61
2.19	178	2 i,6-7	61, 107
5.17b-19	50, 63, 72	4Q401	
7.18-21 (A)	58	11 3	74
12.23	58	22	74
14.19	58	4Q403	
15.15-17	60	1 i 1-9	74
19.10-11 (B)	58	1 ii 1-29	74
20.1 (B)	58		
		Testament of Amram (4QAmram)	
4QD^a (4Q266)			42, 55, 70, 72,
	60		150
		1.9-15	72
Book of Enoch		2.3	73
4QEn^{astr}	65	2.4-5	72
		2.5	73
Book of Noah (1Q19)		2.6	72, 73
2 1.4	67	3.2	72
Florilegium (4Q174)		*The Thanksgiving Hymns* (1QH)	
1.4f	60		55, 69
1.8-9	63	5.8	63
		7.13-20	63
Habakkuk Pesher (1QpHab)		9.9ff	63
2.8-10	58	11.20ff	60
7.1-5	58	11.20-22	107
		11.20-23	59
The Melchizedek Document (11Q13)		11.29-36	59
	55, 70, 71, 72,	12.31	63
	73, 75, 150	12.31ff	62
2.5	70	14.13-14	59, 60
2.6	71	15.28ff	64, 159
2.6b	71	18.8ff	64
2.6b-7	71	19.10-14	59, 60
2.8	70, 71		
2.10	70, 74		

The War Scroll (1QM, 4QM)		4Q186	
	39, 40, 55, 65, 67, 68, 69, 71, 73, 75, 136		62
		4Q246	
1QM			73
1.5	71		
1.9b-10	59	4Q285	
1.13b-15	60		55, 66, 67, 68
1.14f	64		
4.2f	71		
5.1-2	66	4Q427	
7.3b-7	60	7	70
9	123		
9.14-16	29, 60, 62	4Q470	
9.14-17	97		55, 66-67, 72, 135, 165
9.15-16	55, 65, 66-67, 68		
		4Q471b	
9.15	97		69
10.8b-11a	59-60		
11.1ff	58	4Q491	
11.1-6	60	11	69-70
11.4-7	66		
12.4ff	59	4Q529	
12.6-8	60		51, 55, 67, 69
13.5	71		
13.9-12	63	11Q11 (11QapPs^a)	
13.10	63, 71, 73, 75		67
13.10-11	194		
13.11-12	64	11Q14	
13.13f	64		66
13.13-14	159		
13.13-16	58		
15.1	71	**Hellenistic Jewish Literature**	
15.14b-16.1	59		
16-17	75	Aristobulus	
17	65, 123		81
17.4-9	194		
17.7	71	Ezekiel's *Exagoge*	
17.5b-8	65		203
17.6-7	55, 67	159	91
17.7b	71		
17.7-8	74, 75	Josephus	
17.6-8a	60, 64	*Antiquities of the Jews*	
17.6-8	40	i.197	198
19.2-8	58	iii.178	87
		x.267-277	27
4Q180		xii.253	107
	57	xiii.171-2	56
		xvi.115	107

xviii.18-22	56
xviii.63-64	3

The Jewish War

i.78-80	56
ii.113-161	56
ii.142	68
ii.198	107
ii.567	56
iii.11	56
iv.438	74
v.235	87

Life

x-xi	56

Philo

De Abrahamo

115	85
118	198
119-132	203

De Agricultura

51	81, 87, 88, 200

Apologia pro Iudaeis

	56

De Cherubim

27-28	84, 86, 200
28	84
29	84
125-127	81

De Confusione Linguarum

63	81
146	54, 76, 81, 85, 88, 89, 90, 143, 200, 203
146-147	85
168-175	84, 85
171	85

De Decalogo

65	78

De Deo

3	86
3-4	200
3-6	200
5	200
6	200

Quod Deterius Potiori insidiari soleat

54	81
118	81
160	78, 86

Quod Deus sit Immutabilis

182	81, 85

De Fuga et Inventione

50-51	81
66	85
94-96	84
96-100	84, 86
106-112	87
109	81
110	86
111	86
112	79, 86

De Gigantibus

6	84, 123
6-18	84
12	84
16	84, 85
52	87

Quis rerum divinarum heres sit

188	79
191	81
205	76, 81, 85, 88
205-206	82, 85, 86, 87

Legum Allegoriarum

1.65	81
2.1	78
3.79-82	74
3.175	81
3.177	81, 85
3.207-208	88
3.217-219	203

De Migratione Abrahami

5-6	203
6	81

102-103	87	1.239-240	81, 85
173-174	203	2.227-230	78, 81
174	88	2.228-230	78
		2.242-245	81

De Vita Mosis
1.66	203
1.166	86
2.97-100	200
2.114-115	87
2.132	87
2.133	79
2.291	46

De Specialibus Legibus
1.45-48	84
1.66	85, 87
1.97	87

De Mutatione Nominum
87	81, 85, 203

Quaestiones et Solutiones in Genesin
1.57	81, 200
2.62	78, 81, 204

De Opificio Mundi
16-25	79
24-25	79, 81

Quaestiones et Solutiones in Exodum
2.13	88
2.68	84, 86

De Plantatione
9	79
14	84

New Testament

Matthew
1.20	195
11.10	122
13.41	127, 149, 185-159
13.41-42	156
16.27	158-159
18.10	125, 126
22.30	96, 126
24.30	149, 158-159
24.30-31	127, 159, 168
25.31	158, 159
28.2-7	124
28.18	159

De Posteritate Caini
91	85
91-92	89

Quod omnis probus liber
75-91	56

De Sacrificiis Abelis et Caini
5	126
59	203

De Somniis
1.62	78, 84
1.70	203
1.85	203
1.129	203
1.137-143	84
1.141	84, 123
1.141f	85
1.142	85
1.147	85
1.157	86, 88
1.215	87, 200
1.230	81

Mark
1.2	122
1.13	156
2.7	111
8.38	156
12.25	96, 126
13	27
13.24-27	156
13.26	149, 158, 159
13.26f	127
13.26-27	156, 159
13.32	155
14.62	156

Index of References

16.5-7	124	Acts	
		2.32-36	4, 156
Luke		7	142
	215	7.30-34	142
1.19	84, 123	7.31-32	142
1.26	124	7.35	142
1.26-38	169	7.38	124, 134
1.35	197	7.42	108
2.13-14	124	7.53	124, 134, 165
7.24	122	8.10	177
10.18	130	10.3	124
16.22	32	12.15	125, 126
20.35-36	96, 126	12.6-10	124
21.27	127, 149, 158-159	13.2	160
		23.8	126
22.43	156		
23.43	149, 168, 217	Romans	
24.4-7	124	8.26-27	151
		8.34	150
John		8.38	84, 122
1.1-18	160	8.38-39	124, 138
1.18	147	10.9-13	161
1.51	160-161, 162		
5.23	160	1 Corinthians	
5.37	147	4.9	122
6.46	147	6.2-3	124
8.56	112, 146-147	6.3	122
8.58	146	8.6	143
10.30	146	10.4	140, 147
12.31-32	130	10.9	140
12.40	147	10.10	141
12.41	147	10.14-17	161
14.9	147	11.10	60, 122
14.17	136	12.1-3	161
15.1-2	188	13.11	122
15.26	136	15.23-28	159
17	215	15.52	127, 168
17.4	145	16.22	161
17.6	145		
17.11b	145	2 Corinthians	
17.11-12	111, 144, 145-146, 147	6.15	64
		6.15 *vl*	64
17.11b-12	145	11.14	122
17.22	145	12.8	161
17.26	145	13.13	161
20.11-13	124		

Galatians		1 Timothy	
1.8	122	2.5	44, 184
3.19	122, 124, 134-135, 156, 165	3.16	122
		5.21	122
3.19a	135		
3.19b	134	2 Timothy	
4.14	6, 122, 155-156	4.18	161
Ephesians		Hebrews	
1.20-22	143-144, 158, 159		125, 137-139, 212, 215, 216-217, 220
1.21	84, 138		
5.19	160	1	138
		1.1-4	158, 159
Philippians		1.4	144
2.6-11	143, 144, 146, 159, 160, 215	1.5-14	159, 160
		1.5	159
2.9	111, 143-144, 147	1.6	159, 161
		1.6-7	139
2.9-10	138	1.7-8	159, 162
2.10	161	1.7-9	139
2.10-11	159	1.8-9	159
2.11	143	1.11-12	159
		1.13	159, 162
Colossians		1.14	124
1.15-18	138	1-2	3, 6, 138, 212, 219
1.15-20	159, 160		
1.16	160	2.1-4	138
1.16-17	162	2.2	124, 135, 165
1.17	160	2.2-3	139
2.18	6, 106-108, 122, 125	2.9	138
		7	74, 125, 138
		7.2	74
1 Thessalonians		7.3	150, 151
3.11-13	161	7.25	150
4.16	127, 156, 168	8.1-6	150
		9.24	150
2 Thessalonians			
	133	James	
1.7	122, 127, 149, 158		122
		1.7	4
2	134	2.25	122
2.3-12	132		
2.5	134	1 Peter	
2.6-7	132-134, 136	1.12	124
2.7	132	3.22	84, 138, 158, 159
2.16-17	161		
3.5	161	5.8	152

Index of References

2 Peter		4.3	152
	131, 132	4.11	153
2.11	131	4-5	123, 159
3.18	161	5.5	129, 152
		5.8	45, 125
1 John		5.8-13	161
2.1	150	5.8-14	153, 160
		5.11-13	155
Jude		5.13	161
	137, 151, 212, 219	6	154
		6.9	129
4	140	6.12	154
5	139, 141	7	154
5b	141	7.2	154
5-6	139-142, 147, 161, 214	7.2-3	153
		7.9	154
7	141	7.9-10	154
9	41, 46, 102, 122, 123, 130-132, 134, 136, 140	7.14	129
		7.17	153, 154, 160
		8	154
		8.1	154
14	140	8.1-5	127
14-15	127, 132, 141	8.3	45, 135, 155
17	140	8.3-5	125
21	140	9.11	127
25	140	10.1	151, 152-154, 155
Revelation		12	127, 128, 136, 144
	125, 136, 148, 149, 212, 216	12.1	152
1	153, 157	12.4	127
1.1	153, 154	12.4b-5	129
1.5b-6	161	12.5	128
1.8	153	12.7	39, 42, 122, 123, 127-130, 134, 136, 148, 159
1.12-18	8, 10, 151-154		
1.12-20	144, 158		
1.14	144		
1.16	153, 155	12.7-9	129-130
1.18	149, 168, 217	12.7-12	128
1.20	125, 126, 155	12.10	130, 136
2-3	125, 126	12.10-12	128-129, 130
2.7	129	12.11	129
2.11	129	12.12	128
2.17	129	14.1	145
2.26-27	128	14.6	154
3.5	129	14.8	154
3.12	129, 145	14.9	154
3.21	129, 153, 160	14.14	10
		14.14-15	154-155

14.15	154	**Rabbinic Literature**	
14.16	154-155		
14.17	154	The *Mishnah*	
14.18	154	*mMeg*	
14.19-20	155	4.10	27
14.20	155		
15.2	129	*mHag*	
15.6	125	2.1	27
17.14	129		
18.1	154	*mAZ*	
18.1-3	153	3.3	105
18.21	153		
19.10	10, 153, 159, 160	*mAbot* 3.14	96
19.11ff	128-129, 130, 216	*mHul*	
19.11-16	10, 127, 144-145, 148, 153, 215	2.8	104
		The *Tosefta*	97
19.11-17	128		
19.11-20.3	148, 149	*tSot*	
19.11-20.10	128	6.5	96
19.12	144, 153		
19.12c	144	*tHul*	
19.13	149	2.18	97, 104, 105, 106, 114
19.13-15	149		
19.14-15	129		
19.15	128, 144, 149, 153, 155	The *Palestinian Talmud*	98
19.20	155		
20.1-3	127, 128, 153	*pBer*	
20.2	133, 135	iv.5.8c	100
21.6	153	ix.1.13a	97-98
21.7	129	ix.12.13a	109-110
22.3	153, 160		
22.3-4	145	*pYoma*	
22.8-9	10, 153, 159, 160	vii.2.44b	100
22.13	153	*pRH*	
22.16	153, 154	1.2.54d	33
22.20	161	i.2.56d	98
		The *Babylonian Talmud*	94, 97
		bBer	
		4b	98
		17a	126

bShab			94a	98
55a	99, 127		94b	99
63b	87		95b	99
89a	127			
			bAZ	
bErub			42b	105, 114
54b	98			
			bZeb	
bYoma			62a	100, 150
37a	98, 112, 113, 146		*bMen*	
67b	182		110a	100, 101, 150
77a	100, 150			
			bHul	
bTaan			40a	104, 114
5a	100		60a	98, 119
			91b	96
bHag				
12b	100, 120, 150		*Abot de Rabbi Nathan* A	
13b-14a	96			97
14a	172		12	102
15a	106, 118			
16a	96		*Abot de Rabbi Nathan* B	
			1	95
bYeb			24	96, 172
16b	98		25	102
			27	96
bKet			44	96
104b	32			
			Mekilta de Rabbai Ishmael	
bSot			Pisha 7	95
10b	99		Bahodesh 5	106
12b	99		Bahodesh 6	105
13b	99		Bahodesh 10	104
33a	110		Shabbeta 1	95
bBM			*Sifre Deuteronomy*	
86b	98, 99, 112, 113, 146		42	95
			305	102
			306.21	96
bBB			325	95
75a	103		330	52
bSanh			*Genesis Rabbah*	
26ab	99		1.3	95, 97
38b	96, 106, 110-111, 114, 119, 143		3.8	95, 97
			14.3	96
			44.22	146
			44.13	99

48.9	33	3.11	97
48.10	98, 112, 113, 146	*Lamentations Rabbah*	
48.11	96	Proem 24	100
48.14	198	2.1	99, 101
50.2	98, 99, 112, 113, 146	*Midrash on Psalms*	
51.2	111	4.3	110
65.21	96	19.7	110
77.2-3	112	24.4	95
78	125	91.6	96
78.1	96, 97, 112	104.24	98
97.3	40, 165	104.7	96, 172
Exodus Rabbah		*Midrash on Proverbs*	
	102, 112	14.34	119
2.5	102, 112, 113, 142	*Midrash Abkir*	
15.6	172		112
18.5	99, 100, 102, 150	*Pesiqta Rabbati*	
32.2-3	40, 165	14.9	96
32.4	95	16.2	95
32.9	102	46.3	97
47.5	95, 96	*Pirqe de Rabbi Eliezer*	
Numbers Rabbah		4	87, 97
2.10	97	26	99
11.3	97	27	98, 100, 119
12.8	97	36	99
12.12	101	37	43, 112
19.3	96	38	99
21.16	95	50	99
Deuteronomy Rabbah		*Yalqut*	
2.34	105	Had.	
5.12	97	114/5.3.19	72
10	46	Wa-Yishlah	
11.10	100	132	101
Ruth Rabbah		*Tanhuma*	
Proem 1	100, 150	Wa-Yera 18	96
		Kedoshim 6	96
Song of Songs Rabbah			
1.2	124	*Tanhuma* Buber Ed.	
1.12	99	1.1	95, 97
3.6	112	1.12	95, 97
3.7	97	1.17	119
		8.7	112

9.15	99	76	53
9.17	99	100	117
Saw 1	101	147-151	117
Balak 16	101	148	117, 121
Wa-Ethannen 6	119	170-171	117
		174-178	117

Signs of the Messiah
(Jellinek *BHM* II.58-62)

8-9	102, 169	185-186	117
		207ff	117
		224ff	117
		234-236	117

Zohar
Had.

22.4	72	241ff	117
41.3	72	241-242	118
		277-279	118
		287-292	117
		295	117, 118

Targum *Ps.-Jonathan*
Gen.

		302-304	116
6.4	182	310	118
32.25	43, 112	356	117
38.25-26	99	363	117
		372	117
		407ff	117

Exod.

		413ff	117
20.22-23	104	421	117
		425-426	117

Deut.

		557	118
34.3	102	562	117
34.6	46	565	117
		582	117
		588	118

Hekhalot Texts

		590	117
		590-593	117

According to Schäfer's *Synopse* numbers
(§§)

		623	116
1-80	117	655	118
4	119	678	118
5-15	144	688	117
5	182	691-692	117
8	182		
12	178	*Hekhalot Rabbati*	
13	118		115
14	118	*Hekhalot Zutarti*	
15	118, 143, 145		115
17	118		
20	118	*Ma'aseh Merkavah*	
21	121		115
58	172		
71	118	*Merkavah Rabbah*	
73	178		115

3 Enoch (§§1-80)

	6, 115, 116, 118, 119, 145
3.1 (§4)	119
4-12 (§5-15)	144
4.5 (§5)	182
5.9 (§8)	182
9.2 (§12)	178
10 (§13)	118
11 (§14)	118
12 (§15)	118, 143, 145
14 (§17)	118
16 (§20)	118
17 (§21)	121
40.4 (§58)	172
48B (§71)	118
48C.5 (§73)	178
48D.1 (§76)	53

Visions of Ezekiel (ראויות יחזקאל)

	119-120

Qaraite Text

Ya'qub al-Qirqisani
Kitab al-Anwar w'al-Marakib

7	185

Greco-Roman Writings

Aristotle
De Anima

iii.4.429a	80

Metaphysics

xii.7.1072b	80
xii.9.1075a	80

Chariton
De Chaerea et Callirhoe

vii.6.6	107

Plato
Timaeus

28A-29B	79
30C-31A	79
39E-40D	84

Symposium

202E	84, 85

Pliny
Natural History

v.17.4 (§73)	56

Early Christian Literature

Discourse on Abbatôn

pp. 483-484	42

Acts of Pilate

16.6	111

Aphrahat
Demonstrations

3.14	40

Apocalypse of John the Theologian

9	169

Apocalypse of Peter

4	168
6	168
12	168

Apocalypse of Paul

14	164, 165
22	168
25-27	168
43	167
43-44	164, 218
48	164, 165
49	168

Apostolic Constitutions

viii.12.7	210

Aristides
Apology

14	107-108

Ascension of Isaiah

	10, 64, 167, 190, 195, 197, 198, 199, 200, 201, 212, 215, 218
1.8-9	64
3.13	198
3.14-16	165
3.16	164, 195
3.16-17	170
4.14	148
4.21	195
6-11	197, 199, 201
7.13-9.33	107
7.23	195
8.10	198
9.13	198
9.15	197
9.23 (L^2S)	167
9.27-42	199
9.29 (L^2S)	167
9.30	198, 199
9.33	198
9.36	195
9.37-39	198
9.39	195
9.40	195
9.42 (L^2S)	167
10.4	195
10.9-12	197
11.4	195
11.17	198
11.18-21	198
11.32-33	199
11.33	195

Assumption of the Virgin (Lat. B)

9.2	168
17.1	168

Athanasius
On the Incarnation

3	191

Festal Letters

367	191

Augustine
On Christian Doctrine

ii.29.45	182

Cave of Treasures

pp. 52-56	42

1 Clement

36.1	218
61.3	218
64.1	218

2 Clement

9.5	190

Clement of Alexandria
The Instructor

i.5.24	209, 210
i.7	112
i.7.59	210

Stromata

ii.1	191
ii.9	191
ii.12	191
iv.9	191
vi.5.41	108
vi.9	198
vi.15	191

Excerpts from Theodotus

12.2	172
21.1-3	180
22.5	180
35.1	180, 211
35.1-4	180
43.2	211

Cyprian of Carthage
Testimonies

ii.7	195

That Idols are Not Gods

xi	190, 197

Didache

10.6	161

Epiphanius
Panarion

	177
ix.4.13	46

xix.1.1-4	194
xix.2.2	177, 194
xix.4.3	178, 179
xxx.2.2	174, 176
xxx.3.1	176
xxx.3.1-6	173
xxx.3.2	176
xxx.3.3	176, 179
xxx.3.4	173, 176
xxx.3.5	176, 179
xxx.3.5-6	174
xxx.3.6	174, 176, 186
xxx.3.7	175
xxx.13.7-8	174, 176
xxx.14.4	176
xxx.15.1-4	175
xxx.16.2	176, 193-194
xxx.16.2-5	176, 190
xxx.16.3	176
xxx.16.4	173, 176, 186, 193
xxx.16.6	175
xxx.16.7	175
xxx.17.4-8	176
xxx.17.7	177
xxx.18.5-6	174, 186
xxx.34.6	174, 176, 179
liii.1.8	179
lxiv.69.6	46

Epistle to Diognetus
7.2	184

Eusebius
Ecclesiastical History
iii.27	174
vi.24.4	167
vi.36.1-3	164
vi.36.2	167

Preparation for the Gospel
vi.11.64	90, 184
viii.6-7	56
xiii.12.10-13	81

Epistula Apostolorum
	163, 196, 212, 215, 218
3	197
13	164, 167, 170, 218
13 (Copt)	148, 166
13-14	197
14	196-197
19	197

5 Ezra (= 4 Ezra 1-2)
2.43	178

Gelasius Cyzicenus
Ecclesiastical History
ii.21.7	41

Gospel of the Ebionites
	174, 176

Gospel of Nicodemus
15-16	183
25.1	168
26.1	168

Gospel of Peter
10 (40)	178

Gregory Thaumaturgos
Panegyric to Origen
4.42	209, 211

The *Shepherd* of Hermas
	3, 163, 170, 178, 187, 212, 215, 216, 217
Visions	
iii.3.3	188
iii.4.1-2	172
v.2	187
Mandates	
i.1	190
v.1.7	187
ix.9	190-191
Similitudes	
v.2	189
v.4.4	187
v.5.2	189

v.5.3	172	*History of Joseph the Carpenter*	
v.6	189	6	195
v.6.2-3	187	22-23	168
v.6.5-7a	190		
vii.2	187	Ignatius of Antioch	
vii.5	187	*Epistle to the Philippians*	
viii	187, 188, 189	9.1	218
viii.1.2	178		
viii.2.5	167	Irenaeus	
viii.3.2	166	*Against Heresies*	
viii.3.2-3	187		174
viii.3.3	67, 134, 165, 178, 188, 192	i.2.6	180
		i.4.5	180
viii.3.3-6	164, 165	i.7.1	180
viii.3.5-8	166	i.7.2	174
ix	188, 189	i.13.2	182
ix.1.1	190	i.15.5	191
ix.3.1-5	188	i.22.1	191
ix.6.1	188	i.25.1	174
ix.6.1-2	178	i.26.1	174
ix.6.2	188	i.26.2	174
ix.7.1	188	ii.10.2	191
ix.12.1	188	ii.30.9	191, 207
ix.12.1-8	188	iii.6.1-2	207
ix.12.6	188	iii.16.1	174
ix.12.8	172, 173, 178, 188, 192	iii.17.1	208
		iii.20.2	208
ix.14.5	187, 188	iii.20.4	207
		iv.4.2	207
Hippolytus		iv.6.6	207
Apostolic Tradition		iv.10.1	112
4.4	209	iv.12.4	208
Comm. on Daniel		iv.20.1	191, 207
ii.32.6	209	iv.20.2	191
ii.32.6-7	210	iv.20.3	207
iv.36-40	165	iv.20.6	207
Homily on the Heresy of Noetus		iv.20.11	145
4	190	*Demonstration*	
16	190		200
Refutation of all Heresies		4	191
	174, 177	10	200
vii.34	174	43-49	207
ix.13.1	177	44	112
ix.13.2-3	177	46	112, 208
ix.14.1	179	54-56	210
x.29	172, 184	56	209, 210
		88	207
		On the Lord's Resurrection	
		Frags. 30-31	208

Jerome		61.2-3	204
Comm. on Daniel		61-62	203
ii	98	62.4-5	148, 149, 216
ii.8.16	99, 167	63.5	205
Epistles		75.1-2	140, 185
xii	211	76.3	205, 209
cxii.13.1-2	174	113.4	205, 207
cxxi.10	107-108	113-114	203
		116.1	218
John Chrysostom		126	112, 202
Against the Jews		126.1	203, 209
viii.5	182	126.3	112
		126-127	203
Justin Marytr		127.1	203
1 Apology		127.1-3	204
6.2	206	127.4	205
13.3	205, 206	128.1	203, 207
33	190, 197	128.3-4	205
61.3	206	128.4	96, 204
61.9-13	206		
62-63	203	Justinian	
63	112	*Epistle to Mennas*	
63.3-7	205		211
63.5	205		
63.16	207	*Kerygma of Peter*	
2 Apology			107-108, 109
6.3	205		
Dialogue with Trypho		Melito of Sardis	
2-6	204		209
3.5	204		
4.1	204	*Muratorian Canon*	
34.2	148		191
38	203		
56	112, 202	*Narrative of Pseudo-Melito*	
56.1	146, 204	9.2	168
56.4	204, 205	17.1	168
56.5	113		
56.10	205	*Obsequies of the Holy Virgin*	
56.11	204	1	168
57.2	146		
58	202	Origen	
58.10	112	*Contra Celsum*	
59-60	112, 203		167
60	202	i.21-24	108
60.1	113, 142	i.25	167
60.2	204	i.26	108-109
61.1	1, 148, 149, 203, 204, 205, 216	ii.44	184
		ii.70	184
		v.6	108-109

v.52-55	184	*Sel. on Joshua*	
v.53.22	209, 210, 211	PG 12.821	40, 148, 165, 166
v.61	173-174		
vi.18	199	*Sel. on Psalms*	
vi.24-38	169	PG 12.1449	210
viii.13	170		
viii.26.6	211	*Passion of Perpetua*	
viii.27.6	209	1.3	168
viii.60-61	182	10	178
Comm. on John			
i.25.165	211	Polycarp of Smyrna	
i.31.218	180, 209, 211	*Epistle to the Philippians*	
i.38.277-278	210	12.2	219
ii.23.144-148	211		
ii.31	28, 90, 184	*Protevangelium of James*	
xiii.17	108	11-14	195
Comm. on Matthew			
xiii.26.607	211	Pseudo-Clementies	
xiv	165		175, 216
xiv.21	164, 191, 192	*Homilies*	
Comm. on Romans		iii.2	194
iii.18	199	iii.17-28	176, 179
x.31	191	iii.33.2	172
Hom. on Ezekiel		viii.21	194
i	119	xvi.14	194
i.7	165	xviii.4	176, 194
Hom. on Isaiah		xx.2-3	194
i.2	199	*Recognitions*	
iv.1	199	i.33-71	175
Hom. on Joshua		i.34	194
vi.2	165	ii.24	194
xv.6	184	ii.42.3-8	176
Hom. on Judges		ii.42.3-5	194
ix.1	165	ii.42.8	194
On First Principles		iii.52	194
	167		
i.3.4	199	Ps.- Cyprian	
i.8.1	99, 100	*De Centesima, Sexagesmia,*	
i.8.1-3	166	*Tricesima*	171, 173, 176, 186, 212, 215, 216, 217
iii.2.1	41		
iv.2.4	191		
iv.3.14	199	50-54	172
iv.4.9	211	216-220	172
Frag. 30	211		
Philocalia		Ps.- Cyril of Jerusalem	
xxiii.15	90		193-194
xxiii.19	90		

Ps.- Gregory Thaumaturgos
   Twelve Topics on the Faith
   4   195

Questions of Bartholomew
                                 219
   1.9   166, 170
   1.23-26   166
   1.29   149, 168, 217
   4.12   133, 168, 170
   4.25   64
   4.28-29   164, 166
   4.29 *vl*   166
   4.52-55   42, 166
   4.54   172

The Revelations of Elchasai
                               177-179

Sibylline Oracles (I-II, VI-VIII)
   II.167   64
   II.214ff   24, 29
   VIII.456-462   196

Syncellus
   Chronographia
   49.6-15   50

Tertullian
   Against Marcion
   iii.9   172
   iii.16   190
   Against Praxeas
   xiv   112
   xvi   112
   xxvi   190, 197
   On the Flesh of Christ
   vi   181
   x-xiii   180
   xiv   170, 173, 179-
                     181, 186, 202,
                     209, 210, 212
   xiv.1   179
   xiv.1-4   180
   xiv.2-10   180
   xiv.5   179
   xiv.10   179
   xiv.19   180
   xiv.25   180
   xiv.27   179
   xiv.32   179
   xiv.32-33   180
   xiv.32ff   179
   xiv.32-39   180
   xv-xvii   180
   On Modesty
   x   191
   On Prayer
   xvi   191

Theodoret of Cyrus
   Against Heresies
   ii.3   174
   Comm. on the Epistles of Paul
   Col. 2.18   106

Theophilus of Antioch
   To Autolycus
   2.10   206
   2.22   206

Gnostic Texts

Apocryphon of John (NHC II.1)
   17.30   169

Gospel of the Egyptians
(NHC III.2)
   52.23   169
   53.6   169
   57.7   169
   64.1-4   174
   64.26   169

Gospel of Thomas (NHC II.2)
                           183
   13   143, 183

Gospel of Truth (NHC I.3)
   38.6-41.14   143

Melchizedek (NHC IX.1)
                           74, 150
   18.5-6   148

Trimorphic Protennoia
(NHC XIII.1)
   50.12-13   174

Zostrianos (NHC VIII.1)
   57.9   169
   58.22   169

Pistis Sophia
                  169
   7   169
   7-8   196
   64-67   169

Magical Texts

Testament of Solomon
                  171, 181-183,
                  186, 212, 215,
                  216
   1.6-7   181
   2.4   181
   4.11   182
   5.9   181
   6.8   182
   7.7   182
   11.6   182
   12.3   182, 210, 211
   13.6   181
   15.10-12   182
   17.4   182
   18.5   181
   18.6   181
   18.7   181
   18.8   181
   22.20   182

PGM
   4.2770   134
   36.168-178   183

P. Oxy. 1152
                  192-193

"IXΘTC" Amethyst
                  173, 176, 183,
                  186, 216

Islamic Texts

The Qur'an
   7.11-22   42
   15.26-44   42
   38.71-85   42

'Abd al-Karim ash-Shahrastani
Kitab al-Milal wa'al-Nihal
   1.19   185

Index of Subjects

Abba Hilfi b. Samkai (pA2) 111
Abraham 51, 98, 112, 198, 200-201, 202, 203, 208
Adam 42, 51
Adam and Eve 42
Aher 118
Alexandria 77
Alexandrian Judaism 77-78, 80-81
Allegorical Interpretations 192
Amoraim 93
'Anafi'el 118
Ancient Near East 15-16, 17
Angel of Great Counsel 182, 202, 210-212
Angel of the Name 8, 21, 51-54, 88, 110-111, 118, 143-146, 147, 188, 215
Angel of the Presence 31, 49-51, 117, 134-135
Angelology
    of Apocalyptic literature 18, 22, 95, 100, 110, 126, 127
    of Early Christianity 122-127, 163-170
    of Hekhalot Literature 115, 116-121
    of New Testament 122-127
    of Old Testament 15-23, 28
    of Philo 76, 84-85
    of Qumran Sect 59-64, 64-70, 95, 100, 110, 126
    of the Rabbis 95-97, 97-103, 117, 126
    of Second Temple Judaism 26, 28-32, 58, 123, 124, 125, 137, 147, 163, 217
Angels 17-18, 22, 50, 28-32
    armies of, hosts of 16, 17, 18, 22-23, 128
    as a heavenly council 18
    as agents of creation 85, 95
    as agents of revelation 30-31, 85, 117, 123, 124
    as interpreters 18, 22, 31, 124, 154, 159, 167
    as intercessors 22-23, 32, 43-44, 85, 86, 179
    as priests 32, 45-46, 60-61, 85, 87, 100
    as psychopomps 32, 46
    classes of 29-30, 49, 84
    hierarchy of 29-30
    fallen angels/Watchers 36-37
    guardian
        of churches 125
        of individuals 31-32, 125-126
        of nations 18, 31, 36-37
    heavenly cult performed by 18, 32, 60-61, 100, 110, 124-125, 150-151
    immense size of 177-178
    immortality of 96
    over natural phenomena 28-29
    punishers of evil 85
    worship of 106-111
Antichrist 132-134
Antiochus Epiphanes 35, 133
Apelles 181
Apocalyptic literature 15, 18, 26-28
Apocalyptic
    and early Christianity 3, 25, 163, 194
    and eschatology 26-27
    and Qumran 25, 57-58
    and Rabbinic Judaism 25
    determinism 57-58
    in the New Testament 25, 129-130
Apollyon 123, 127

Archangels 24, 29-30
Aristobulus 81
Aristotle 77, 80, 204-205
Azael/Azâzêl 133, 173, 181, 183

Belial 50, 64-66, 73, 194
Beliar 64, 166

Carpocrates 174
Cerinthus 174
Cherubim and Seraphim 17, 18, 76, 200-202, 208, 219
Christ
  as an angel 137-147, 163, 171-195, 213, 216
  as agent of creation 160
  as ἀρχιστράτηγος 128, 148-149, 151, 161, 217
  as divine 153-154, 159-162
  as heavenly high priest 125, 138, 150-151, 161, 217
  as object of worship 153, 160-161
  disguised as a angel 163, 196-202, 212
  exaltation of, 159
  intercession of, 151
  parousia of, 133, 158-159
  Pre-existence of, 4, 112-114, 139-142, 146-147, 162, 202-209
  superior to angels 159-162, 170
Christology
  adoptionistic 174-176, 179, 186, 189, 190
  angel 3-6, 8, 11, 12-13, 137-138, 142, 151, 159, 162, 163, 171-193, 199-200, 211, 214, 216, 219, 220
  angelic 2-3, 11, 12, 137, 143-151, 162, 171-214, 219, 216-217
  angelomorhic 2, 6-11, 12-13, 163, 218-219
  Gnostic 171, 179-181, 186, 214, 215
  Docetic 181, 198-199
  Logos 202-209, 218
  New Testament 122
  Subordinationist 6, 204-205, 208
  theophanic angel 13, 163, 202-209, 214, 216, 219, 220

Cultic devotion 9, 104, 153-154, 161

Daemons/Demons 84, 181-183, 186, 211, 212

Ebion 174, 179-180
Ebionites 171, 173-177, 179, 180, 190, 194, 212, 215, 216, 217
El and El Elyon 11, 16
Elchasaites 171, 173, 176-179, 201, 215
Elijah-Phineas 101
Emmanuel 182-183
Encratism 171-172
Enoch 9, 30, 36, 48, 217
Eremiel 51
Eschatology 26-27, 57-58, 60, 102, 127
Essenes 56-57
Exalted Patriarchs 8
Exodus Angel 8, 21, 23-24, 49-50, 88, 140-142, 142-146, 147, 151-152, 212

Gabriel 29-30, 36, 37, 42, 47, 48, 51, 62, 66, 67, 68, 69, 76, 93, 95, 97, 98, 99, 100, 101, 102, 109, 112, 114, 117-118, 123, 146, 157, 164, 166, 169, 173, 181, 195-197
Gematria 52
Gnosticism 8, 169, 179-181, 215, 219
God
  as Great Glory
  Heavenly Throne/Chariot of, 46, 48, 91, 123, 129, 154, 160-161
  immanence of, 79, 95
  Name of, 8, 21, 23, 51-54, 88, 110-111, 118, 142-146, 146-147, 161
  transcendence of, 3, 79, 95, 202, 203, 204-205, 206, 208

Haggadah 94-95
Halakhah 94-95
Hasidim 56-57
Haverim 95
Heavens
  Ascents to 43, 47, 48, 69
  Number 43
  Heavenly cultus/temple 18, 32, 43, 45, 60-61, 100, 110, 119-120, 150-151

Hekhalot Literature 12, 15, 51, 88, 93, 115-121
Hellenism 77, 123
Hellenistic Judaism 77-78, 81, 91
Hexapla of Origen 209
Holy Spirit 135-136, 151, 170, 189-191, 193, 195-196, 199-202, 206, 207, 215, 219
Hypostasis 80, 81-83, 117-118, 121, 157

Iaoel see "Yahoel"
Israel
   nation of 16, 20, 33-38, 48, 50, 78, 134, 149
   archangel 7, 51, 85, 89-90, 184-185

Jacob 89-90, 112, 160-161, 184-185, 202-203, 208
Jahel see "Yahoel"
Jaol see "Yahoel"
Jesus of Nazareth 4, 121
Jewish Christianity 6, 7, 111, 173-179, 184-186, 212, 219
Johannine Christianity 7-8
Jonathan Maccabeus 56
Joshua
   High Priest 22
   Successor of Moses 165, 203, 204
Judas Maccabeus 29, 39

Kabod/Glory 23, 161
Kerygma 138

Laodicea, council of 106, 182
Logos
   as hypostasis 81-83
   in Early Christianity 202-209, 218
   in Revelation of John 128
   Philonic 76, 78-83, 85-90, 121, 143, 203-204, 217-218
   Platonic 79-80, 81
   Stoic 80

Maccabean Revolt 36
Magharians 185-186
Magic 116-117, 171, 181-183, 212
Mary 174, 193, 195-197
Mastema 50, 63, 91-92

Melchizedek 6, 45, 46, 101, 125, 138-139, 150, 151
Melchiresa 72-73
Merkavah mysticism 115-116
Messiahs and Messianism 4, 58, 65-66, 157-158, 218
Metatron 6, 51, 53-54, 88, 90, 97, 98, 101, 110-111, 114, 115, 117-118, 118, 119-121, 143, 145, 146, 217
Michael
   and Paradise 47, 54, 150, 167-168, 170, 217
   appeared to Abraham 98, 112, 147
   as advocate of the righteous 40-42, 99-100, 130-132, 136, 137
   as agent of creation 95
   as agent of the eschaton 47, 102, 132-134, 136, 167-169
   as archangel 2, 29-30, 36, 37, 62, 85, 86, 96-97, 123, 132, 164, 169, 173, 181, 213
   as angel of the Name 51-52, 85, 88, 143, 144, 145, 188
   as *angelus interpres* 47-48
   as ἀρχιστράτηγος 2, 38-40, 54, 85, 86, 91, 98-99, 128-130, 136-137, 148, 149, 164, 165-166, 170, 217
   as Christ 152, 162, 163, 170, 171, 186-196, 212, 215, 216
   as Danielic Son of Man 34-36, 49, 157-158, 219
   as guardian of Israel 31, 33, 48, 54, 75, 89, 91, 98-99, 100, 126, 165, 166, 170, 195
   as guardian of the Church 165-166, 170
   as heavenly high priest 2, 34, 37-38, 45-46, 51, 54, 75, 85, 87, 100-102, 120, 150-151, 166-167, 170, 216
   as heavenly intercessor 2, 42-44, 86, 109-110, 166-167, 170
   as highest archangel 48-51, 54, 64-70, 75, 86, 87, 97-98, 106, 127-132, 164, 170
   as mediator of the Law 66-67, 134-135, 165
   as Metatron 111, 114, 115, 119-121

as Melchizedek 6, 45, 55, 70-74, 150
as object of worship 103, 104-110
as opponent of Satan 40-42, 100, 128-130, 130-132, 136, 165-166, 170, 181
as psychopomp 46-47, 51, 54, 102, 132, 136, 167-168, 170
as Prince of Light 50, 64-70, 75, 136, 194-195, 217
as מלאך יהוה 3, 49-50, 51-52, 112-114
at Qumran 12, 36, 43, 45, 50, 54, 55, 59, 60, 64-70, 70-75, 97, 103
in early Christianity 12, 122, 163-170, 181-183
in Jewish apocalyptic 9, 12, 25, 33-54, 97, 102, 103
in Hekhalot literature 12, 117-118
in the New Testament 12, 123, 127-137
in Philo 76, 85-90
in Rabbinic literature 12, 51, 54, 97-103
traditions 12, 26, 33-54, 64-70, 76, 90, 91, 92, 93, 103, 122, 143, 161, 163, 169, 215, 217
Monotheism 9, 95, 205
Moses 51, 78, 101, 132, 134-135, 200, 202
Muratorian Canon 191, 192

Ophites 169

Paraclete 135-136
Paradise 47, 48, 150
"Parting of the ways", the 45
Paul, the Apostle 4, 44, 122-123
Personified divine attributes 8
Phanuel 29, 47, 97
Philo 12, 15, 76-90, 121, 123, 143, 200-201, 203-204, 217-218
Plato and Platonism 77, 79-80, 81, 84-85, 90, 202, 203, 204-205
Pleroma 180
Pneumatology 199-200
Popular literature 27-28, 94-95
Pythagoreanism 77

Qumran Community 36, 43, 45, 50, 54, 55-75, 217
and the Essenes 56-57
angelology of, 58, 59-64, 64-70, 95, 100, 110, 126
belief in a heavenly cult 60-61, 100, 110
communion with angels 59-60
cultic purity of, 60
determinism of, 57-58, 62
dualism of, 58, 62-64
eschatology of, 57-58, 60
Messianism of, 58, 65-66, 157
Prince/Angel of Light 9, 50, 62, 63, 64-70, 73, 136, 194-195, 217
Prince/Angel of Darkness 62, 63, 64-65, 73, 194
rejection of the Temple
ruins of, 56
sectarian Calendar 61
sectarian literature from, 6, 15, 55, 68
Teacher of Righteousness 56-58

Rab (Abba Arikha; bA1) 96, 99, 100, 101, 110, 126
Rabbinic Judaism 7, 93-95
Rabbinic Literature 15, 51, 54, 93-95
R. Abba 110
R. Abaye (bA4) 104
R. Aha b. Hanina (pA3) 99
R. Aibo (pA4) 97
R. Aqiba (T2) 96, 146
R. Ashi (bA6) 100
R. Berekhyah (pA5) 112
R. Eleazer b. Abina 98
R. Eleazer b. Pedat (pA3) 99, 100
R. Eleazer b. Shammua (T3) 111
R. Eliezer b. Yose (T3) 87, 99
R. Gamaliel (T2) 105
R. Giddal (bA2) 100
R. Haggai (pA4) 95
R. Hama bar Hanina (pA2) 112, 125
R. Hanina (pA1) 112
R. Helbo (pA4) 96, 97, 112
R. Hiyya bar Abba (T5) 100
R. Hiyya (pA3) 98
R. Isaac (pA3) 95, 97, 99, 111
R. Ishmael (T2) 104

R. Idith (A4?) 100-111, 114
R. Jeremiah b. Abba (bA2) 99
R. Levi (pA3) 97
R. Lulyani b. Tabri (T2/3) 95
R. Mosheh ha-Darshan 42
R. Meir (T3) 96
R. Nahman 110
R. Nehemyah (T3) 99
R. Phinhas (T4 or pA5) 110
R. Resh Laqish (pA2) 33, 99, 100
R. Samuel b. Nahmani (pA3) 103, 172
R. Simeon b. Gamaliel (T3) 96
R. Simeon b. Yohai (T3) 97, 99
R. Simeon 96
R. Simon (pA3) 101
R. Yehoshua b. Qarha (T3) 99
R. Yehudah ha-Nasi (T4) 100, 102
R. Yehudah b. Ilai (T3) 96
R. Yehudah (pA2) 96, 111
R. Yohanan (pA2) 97, 98, 99, 100, 101, 110, 112, 124, 172
R. Yohanan b. Zakkai (T1) 146
R. Yose 100
R. Yudan (pA4) 95, 97, 109-110
R. Yudan (pA5) 97
Raguel 29, 47
Raphael 7, 29-30, 36, 37, 42, 47, 62, 66, 67-68, 97, 98, 99, 112, 117-118, 123, 133, 141, 146, 164, 166, 169, 173, 181, 183
Remiel 24, 29
Renel 173

Sabaoth 18, 172, 200
Sammael 100, 102
Sandalphon 118
Sariel 29-30, 36, 37, 42, 62, 66, 67, 97
Satan 18, 22-23, 40-42, 64, 100, 127, 128-130, 130-132, 133, 137, 164, 166
Semjâzâ 133
Seraphim and Cherubim 17, 18, 76, 200-202, 209, 220
School of Ishmael (T2-T3) 182
Shekinah 23
Simon Maccabeus 56
Solomon 181

Son of Man
    in Daniel 3, 7, 34-36, 48, 103, 156-159, 218
    in early Christianity 4, 7, 153, 155-159, 159-161, 217
    in the Gospels 7, 156-158, 159-160
    in the Revelation of John 153, 155-156, 158-159
    in the Sim.Enoch 3, 7, 48, 141, 156-158
Sophia/Wisdom 80-81, 91-92
Spinoza 77
Stoics and Stoicism 77, 80, 90
Suriel 29, 169, 183
Syzygy 180

Tannaim 93
Taxo 38
Temple, Jerusalem 32
Tetragrammaton 87, 143-145
Theodotus 181
Trinity, the 112, 199-202, 206
Trypho 113-114, 203

Uriel 3, 24, 29-30, 34, 36, 42, 47, 51, 65, 89, 97, 98, 117-118, 164, 167, 168, 173, 181

Valentinianism 171, 179, 180-181, 211, 212, 215

Watchers 36-37, 42-43
Worship see "Cultic Devotion"

Yahoel 8, 51, 53-54, 88, 90, 143, 144, 145, 146, 217
Yahweh 11, 16, 17, 18, 149
Yored Merkavah 116-117

Zagzagel 102
Zedekiah 67
Zoroastrianism 63

בליעל 64
דבר יהוה 80
מלאך
    meaning of, 17

Index of Subjects

מלאך יהוה 3, 13, 15, 19-24, 94, 103, 111-114, 137, 142, 146, 147, 151, 162, 202, 206, 212, 216
מאלך אלהים 16
צבאות 18
שליח 7
שטן 64

ἄγγελος
  meaning of, 17
  frequency in NT 122
ἄγγελος μεγάλης βουλῆς 202, 210-212, 214
ἀρχιστράτηγος 38-40, 128-129, 148-149, 204, 216, 218
ἀρχαὶ, ἐξουσίαι, δυνάμεις 122, 134
κατέχειν/κατέχων 132-134
ΙΧΘΥΣ 173

www.ingramcontent.com/pod-product-compliance
Lightning Source LLC
Chambersburg PA
CBHW071933240426
43668CB00038B/1458